History from
South Africa

A *Radical History Review* book
in the series
Critical Perspectives on the Past

History from South Africa

Alternative Visions and Practices

edited by
JOSHUA BROWN, PATRICK MANNING,
KARIN SHAPIRO, JON WIENER
for *Radical History Review*

BELINDA BOZZOLI, PETER DELIUS
for the History Workshop

TEMPLE UNIVERSITY PRESS
Philadelphia

Temple University Press, Philadelphia 19122

Published 1991

The paper used in this publication meets the minimum requirements of
American National Standard for Information Sciences—Permanence of Paper
for Printed Library Materials, ANSI Z39.48-1984

Library of Congress Cataloging-in-Publication Data

History from South Africa : alternative visions and practices / edited by
    Joshua Brown . . . [et al.].
        p.   cm. — (Critical perspectives on the past)
    "A Radical History Review book"—Ser. t.p.
    Includes bibliographical references.
    ISBN 0-87722-848-5 (cloth)
    ISBN 0-87722-849-3 (pbk.)
        1. South Africa—History.   I. Brown, Joshua, 1949– .
II. Series
DT1787.H57   1991
                                        968—dc20   91-8995

Contents

Preface   *viii*
Joshua Brown, Patrick Manning, Karin Shapiro,
and Jon Wiener

1   **Radical History and South African Society**   3
Belinda Bozzoli and Peter Delius

Part I   **Radical Historians and South Africa's Past**

2   **Suicide or Genocide? Xhosa Perceptions of the Nongqawuse Catastrophe**   29
J. B. Peires

3   **Highways, Byways, and Culs-de-Sac: The Transition to Agrarian Capitalism in Revisionist South African History**   39
Helen Bradford

4   **The Politics of Black Squatter Movements on the Rand, 1944–1952**   59
Philip Bonner

5   **An Image of Its Own Past? Towards a Comparison of American and South African Historiography**   82
Colin Bundy

6   **Literature and History in South Africa**   105
Stephen Clingman

7   **Charters from the Past: The African National Congress and Its Historiographical Traditions**   119
Tom Lodge

8 The Unity Movement Tradition: Its Legacy
   in Historical Consciousness   144
   Bill Nasson

9 South African Labor History: A
   Historiographical Assessment   165
   Jon Lewis

10 Popular Struggle: Black South African
   Opposition in Transformation   183
   C.R.D. Halisi

11 Buthelezi, Inkatha, and the Problem of
   Ethnic Nationalism in South Africa   194
   Chris Lowe

12 Intellectuals, Audiences and Histories:
   South African Experiences, 1978–88   209
   Belinda Bozzoli

Part II **Photo Essays**

13 Labor Tenancy in Bloemhof   235
   Santu Mofokeng

14 Promised Land   245
   Gideon Mendel

Part III **Popular History and Popular Culture**

15 Popular History in the Eighties   257
   Luli Callinicos

16 History and History Teaching in Apartheid
   South Africa   268
   Melanie Walker

17 South African People's History   277
   David Anthony

18 A Positional Gambit: Shaka Zulu and the
   Conflict in South Africa   287
   C. A. Hamilton

19 Musical Form and Social History: Research
   Perspectives on Black South African
   Music   309
   Deborah James

20 *Performing History off the Stage: Notes on Working-Class Theater* 319
Bhekizizwe Peterson

21 *"Bearing Witness": Ten Years Towards an Opposition Film Movement in South Africa* 328
Harriet Gavshon

22 *Oral History and South African Historians* 342
Paul la Hausse

23 Staffrider *Magazine and Popular History: The Opportunities and Challenges of Personal Testimony* 351
A. W. Oliphant

24 *Developments in Popular History in the Western Cape in the 1980s* 361
Andre Odendaal

25 *The Write Your Own History Project* 368
Leslie Witz

26 *Every Picture Tells a Story, Don't It?* 379
Joshua Brown

Chronology: South Africa, 1800–1990 391

Notes 397

Contributors 467

Preface

Radical interpretations of South Africa's past have blossomed over the past two decades. Influenced by New Left currents from Europe and America in the 1960s and reinforced by social conflict at home, this group of scholars has creatively remolded the contours of South African historiography. In the early 1970s, radical historians began to challenge a central tenet of traditional South African historiography—that capitalist development and the discriminatory racial order were historically incompatible. As their research has evolved, they have paid particular attention to the ways in which African societies and ordinary working people influenced the construction of their societies. Significantly, radical history in South Africa has extended beyond the academy. This scholarship has both responded and contributed to a broad popular interest in recovering a past that South Africa's rulers either suppressed or distorted. Academic historians, community groups, trade unions, alternative newspapers, and alternative education projects have transmitted the findings of the new scholarship to a wide range of constituencies, experimenting with film, theater, music, and other art and communications media to address popular audiences. Popular involvement has not simply meant a widened audience for historians; it has also brought them fresh sources of criticism and new stores of information, as lay participants have contributed both their perspectives on and their memories of the past. The following collection presents the evolving visions of radical South African historians, inside and outside of academia, and explores the relationships among their work, activism, and social change.

This literature defies reduction to a single focus, methodology, or interpretation. While some scholars have found inspirations in Althusserian structuralist analyses, others have drawn on the socialist-humanist approaches of historians such as E. P. Thompson and Eugene Genovese, and others still have taken their cue from Africanist resistance models and underdevelopment theories. Such vastly different modes of inquiry have been shaped in part by the diverse problems these scholars have explored, ranging from global economic relationships to community politics and biographies of the famous and "unknown." The subjects these scholars have tackled include: the connection between racist state policies and capitalist growth; the place of land segregation in subsidizing cheap industrial labor; the relationship between state construction and class formation in racially privileged groups; the world that mine owners constructed in the aftermath of late nineteenth century mineral discoveries; the emergence and decline of a South African peasantry; the conquest and transformation of African societies after 1879; the ways in which urban and rural communities shaped an emerging industrial society; and the significance of individual experience in a continually shifting social order. Most recently, these scholars have begun to re-examine their intellectual antecedents and the assumptions of their scholarship. No single volume, then, can present the new radical history in an exhaustive fashion. We have sought to include articles that reflect the range of research, analysis, and modes of presentation that has emerged in the new radical historiography.

The volume is based on a special double issue of the *Radical History Review* (46–47), which appeared in February, 1990. The double issue emerged from several years of international collaboration. In 1977, a group of South African scholars at the University of Witwatersrand formed a History Workshop, modelled on the collective of the same name in England. The Workshop quickly became a forum for radical scholars from all parts of the country. History Workshop also reached beyond the academy to engage labor, political, and other grassroots community organizations.

In 1983, during a Social Science Research Council conference in New York, members of the Workshop came into contact with the City University of New York's American Social History Project. Exchanging ideas about the use of media to present alternative histories to a wide audience, representatives from both groups began to discuss the possibility of collaborative work. In 1986, three members of the ASHP staff visited South Africa; their work involved a pilot program on South African working-class history and audio-visual skills workshops for trade unionists, educators, and community groups. One of the visitors, Joshua Brown (a *Radical History Review* editor), returned to South Africa on a 1987 follow-up visit, and came home with a proposal for the journal issue.

Brown's proposal struck a chord with the *RHR* collective, which had become increasingly interested in expanding the journal's focus beyond the United States and Europe. The contemporary urgency of South African issues made such a project especially compelling, as did the Workshop's commitment to merging radical historiography with popular history.

The *RHR* collective designated four of its members—Brown, Pat Manning, Karin Shapiro, and Jon Wiener—to collaborate with History Workshop's Belinda Bozzoli and Peter Delius in producing the special issue, "History from South Africa." In 1988 the Workshop editors convened a conference in Johannesburg, where authors presented several of the essays we offer below. After discussing the ways in which the issue could best convey work in popular history and the breadth of the new historiography to an American audience, both groups of editors commissioned and collected additional articles, photo essays, and illustrations. The *RHR* editors then sent all of the contributions to inside and outside reviewers, mostly in the United States, and edited the revised articles. Although all of the American editors shared the task of shaping a broad range of material into a cohesive volume, specific roles also developed. Drawing on a knowledge of South Africa and American history, Karin Shapiro often served as a cultural interpreter, suggesting how South African writers could make their arguments more accessible to an American audience and clarifying the nuances of South African conceptual categories for the other editors. Working with Bozzoli and Delius, Josh Brown supervised the collection and production of graphics. Pat Manning oversaw the transformation of a journal issue into a more streamlined book manuscript.

This complex project involved extensive and, at times, vigorous dialogue among editors, authors, and outside readers; we think the resulting chapters are better for it. As in any large endeavor, we have incurred numerous debts. We would like to thank the members of the *RHR* editorial collective and the host of dedicated outside readers who evaluated the many articles. In addition, we express our appreciation to Edward Balleisen, William Beinart, Steve Brier, David Conrad, Janet Francendese, Dan Letwin, Joanna Roberts, and Pat van Heerden for their advice and hard work in the making of this volume.

JOSH BROWN
PAT MANNING
KARIN SHAPIRO
JON WIENER

*History from
South Africa*

Chapter 1

Radical History and South African History

Belinda Bozzoli and Peter Delius

Jonathan Shapiro

The subject of this book is the emergence of a new, radical, South African historiography over the past twenty years. Our aim is to chart its precursors, origins and development, and to introduce the many debates it has generated. This writing is neither simply the intellectual hand-maiden of the wider struggles which have characterized South African society in this century, nor a mere echo of metropolitan thought. While radical South African historiography has been tugged by the ebb and flow of popular struggles, and by a wide range of currents in international left-wing thought, it has a momentum of its own; there has been a hon-ing of categories and explanations to make them more effective in ex-ploring the particular nature of South African society.

Specific problems of analysis have confronted left-wing intellectuals: the nature of the South African political economy and of its peculiarly African version of capitalism; the role played by Africans in the formation of that system; the complex interlocking of racial and class structures, and the powerful and authoritarian nature of the state. We explore the roots of a radicalism which attempts to make sense of these features in both local and international settings.[1]

The various intellectual strands identified and discussed here do not form a single, cumulative, or coherent body of work. There have been sharp discontinuities between the approaches of different periods and groupings. Bitter disputes have left ugly scars which have often proved to be barriers to constructive intellectual exchanges. Part of our aim in edit-ing this book is to attempt to retrieve for all who have been part of recent debates a sense of a whole greater than the warring parts; and to suggest that further advances can be achieved if polemic and destructive criticism give ground to attempts at critical engagement and synthesis.[2]

Roots of Radicalism

Four early patterns of radical thought, three of them associated with social movements, and one more clearly located within universities, preceded the revival of radicalism in the 1970s. While they did not necessarily feed into one another, evidence of the influences of each can be found in modern thinking. The first of these is the pioneering work done by black writers from the last decades of the nineteenth century. Such writers, mainly drawn from the Christian and educated elite of the time, explored precolonial and African history and sought to recover the oral traditions of their communities. Sol. T. Plaatje and S. Modiri Molema, for example, provided rich portraits of Tswana history, while John Henderson Soga published a survey of the history of the Xhosa-speaking people.[3] Plaatje also wrote a classic work of contemporary history focussed on the upheavals caused by the 1913 Natives Land Act, and from the 1920s onward there was a proliferation of local histories written in African languages which have only in recent years started to receive the attention they merit.[4] The more radical of these works form part of what became the more substantial body of polemical and historical work associated with the growth of African nationalism during the remainder of this century.[5] Crafted mainly outside of university history departments, these studies grappled with the experiences of African dispossession and resistance, and questions of race and nationalism and their variable and complex relationships to those of class and capitalism.

The second strand of radical thinking, that associated with the South African Communist Party, had substantial roots in the Eastern European socialism which many Jewish immigrants brought to South Africa from the early twentieth century onward.[6] By the early 1950s, Communist party strategy had begun to consolidate around the theory that South Africa was characterized by "colonialism of a special type," and in subsequent decades this vision gained a considerably wider influence, not least among intellectuals associated with the ANC. The central premise of "colonialism of a special type"—that South Africa is an example of "internal colonialism," combining the characteristics of both an imperialist state and a colony within a single, indivisible, geographical, political, and economic entity[7]—has played an important part in underpinning a political strategy of national democratic struggle. But it was not used widely as a starting point for historical research until the 1970s.

A third strand of thinking was the remorselessly materialist and combative historical tradition created from the 1940s by the mainly middle-class intellectuals of the Non-European Unity Movement.[8] Largely restricted to the "Coloured" communities of the Cape (but involving the work of white left intellectuals as well), the NEUM was the early seedbed of South African Trotskyism, a tradition which denied any salience to race, was contemptuous of liberalism and nationalism, and defined itself in opposition to historical study based in universities.

The principal university-based strand of early radical thought was that associated with W. M. MacMillan and his leading protege C. W. de Kiewiet in the 1920s and 1930s.[9] Both of these are widely regarded as the founding fathers of liberal historiography: they argued that contemporary forms of racism were rooted in a preindustrial world, and imperialism was a benign force.[10] Moreover, they neither explored the history of African societies in any detail, nor did they use class as a principal analytical tool.

But, Macmillan and de Kiewiet's work represented a form of social democratic thought which had radical implications. Concerned as they were to debunk the then dominant version of South African history as the story of the triumph of white settlers over barbarous blacks and meddlesome missionaries, they rejected the segregationist perspectives which dominated intellectual and political life—including that of contemporary liberals—in the interwar period; they argued that economic interaction and interdependence between black and white were the central themes of South Africa's past and present. Influenced by Fabianism and British social historians, they saw industrialization, and social and economic history, as vitally important, showing sensitivity to processes of proletarianization and socioeconomic divisions. They argued that history should also tell of the "everyday life of the people"; MacMillan travelled widely, collected oral testimony, and took his work outside the environs of the university, playing an active role in education programs for white and black workers. Both historians left South Africa in the 1930s, partly because of the hostility which their radical views engendered within university circles. A narrowly defined, political history filled the gap left by MacMillan and de Kiewiet. For many in this new tradition, African societies slipped out of historical focus and became the domain of anthropologists. Thus, it was ironic that when a radical critique of this conservative liberal historiography was developed in the 1970s, both MacMillan and de Kiewiet were subjected to harsh criticism and not distinguished from those who had replaced them. In reality, their work provided foundations on which later scholarship could build.[11]

In spite of the presence of black thinkers in three of these traditions, the fact remains that in these early years as in later decades, black historians and social scientists have been few in number. The miserly and ideologically loaded provisions of black education are largely to blame. In the 1950s, the government even closed down or restricted missionary educational institutions which had provided space for the intellectual development of an earlier generation of black thinkers. "Bantu education" was created and government restrictions excluded black students from "open universities" and channeled them into the "tribal colleges." Here, students who had previously suffered through school history that celebrated white power and black subjugation, found themselves confronted by history departments often dominated by Afrikaner historians of an extremely conservative bent. This stultifying context helped ensure that the genres of autobiography, fiction, journalism, photography, and historical fiction have been the most common means through which the black intelligentsia has found its voice.[12]

Black intellectuals have also been forbidden entrance into some of the basic institutions required to practice history, such as archives and public libraries. They have never found easy outlets for publication of their works, and many have been driven into exile. This situation has, in recent years, begun to change. While schools remain bastions of grim convention—at least as far as formal syllabi are concerned—most universities are now formally open to students of all races. In some (the Universities of the Witwatersrand, Natal, Rhodes, Cape Town, and the Western Cape, for example), classes are, to varying degrees, racially heterogeneous, and syllabi have undergone significant revision since the late 1970s. These changes are also reflected at a post-graduate level; increasing numbers of black students are proceeding overseas to continue their studies. Within the next decade, it seems certain that the racial composition of South African historians will undergo a marked change.

The 1960s: Repression and Innovation

The mass mobilization and political ferment of the 1950s, which stimulated the creation and dissemination of the early oppositional versions of South Africa's past did not last.[13] In the aftermath of the shootings at Sharpeville, and the banning of the African National Congress and Pan Africanist Congress, the state used considerably expanded repressive power in the 1960s to attempt to extinguish political resistance and to effect the most extreme expression of apartheid. Black politics and cultural expression were forced underground or into exile. The center of gravity of white politics swung steadily to the right, and the South African economy boomed. The combination of repression and economic growth broke the back of organized black resistance.

Liberals facing the apparent hopelessness of constitutional protest confronted the choice of either endorsing the new military strategy of the ANC, or of putting their faith in an assumed incompatibility between racism and capitalism. The decision of most to opt for the latter was encouraged by the pervasiveness of modernization theory in intellectual circles at the time, and flew in the face of the fact that apartheid received its fullest elaboration in a decade of accelerated capitalist expansion. This was a climate which had bleak consequences for intellectual life in general. The pulse of university life slowed; the state enforced segregation on the English-speaking campuses and there was a steady exodus of left and liberal intellectuals, weakening the ties between older generations of radicals and the younger students of the time.

This situation was in marked contrast to what was happening in the rest of the continent where a decade of decolonization provided the context for the emergence of an Africanist scholarship which disputed colonial denial of a meaningful precolonial African history and stressed the centrality of African initiative in shaping the past and present of the continent.[14] These years also saw a rapid expansion of African studies in Europe and America.[15] By the early 1970s a leading historian of Africa, Richard Gray, commented that "to an extraordinary degree, South African historical research has fallen behind that of other African countries, let alone that of other modern industrial countries."[16]

Still, a continuation of radical thought, albeit in a much weakened form, was to provide sustenance to many, including scholars and students who were later to become leading figures in the revival of radicalism in the 1970s. Oral tradition and personal testimony, which proved much more difficult to police and stifle than the written word, kept a popular history of opposition alive, while a small corpus of banned texts were read and circulated surreptitiously.[17] Even in legal forums, radical perspectives surfaced. The National Union of South African Students (NUSAS) was one crucial arena; there students debated the appropriate relationship between themselves and exiled political movements. The youth wings of both the Liberal and Progressive Parties also saw wide-ranging discussion, while Jewish youth organizations provided a forum in which socialism remained a vibrant tradition. Some radical academics such as the eminent Communist party historian H. J. Simons, managed to continue teaching at universities.[18]

As the decade progressed the Africanist perspectives which had made such an impact elsewhere started to seep into scholarship on South Africa. In times of intellectual exile, it is not surprising that the initial influence was on historians who travelled, studied, or even settled abroad. Initially the leading figure was Leonard Thompson who was exposed to an Africanist paradigm from the late 1950s during travels in Africa and America. In the early 1960s he emigrated to the United States.[19] At the same time two University of Cape Town graduates, Shula Marks and Anthony Atmore, went to England to study at the main center of African history, the School of Oriental and African Studies, London University. Grounded in the work of MacMillan and de Kiewiet and influenced by a more radical strand within Africanist writing, they embarked on studies of African resistance to colonial rule.[20]

This exile connection continued; in the late 1960s metropolitan universities also started to attract a flow of doctoral students interested in South African precolonial history, particularly the emergence of African states and the early history of interaction between settlers and African societies.[21] Considerable stress was laid on the use of oral traditions but, while existing collections were quarried, a limited amount of new material was gathered.[22] Aside from a shift of research focus, the epistemology of this group showed considerable continuity with the liberal empiricism in which most had been trained. By the late 1960s these intellectual currents were belatedly felt more strongly in South African universities, which began to appoint Africanists, including some of those trained in England, and to develop courses in, and centers of, African Studies.[23]

However, just as an Africanist paradigm started to make itself felt in South African universities it came under strain in the heartlands of its development. Decolonization did not bring the anticipated political progress and economic prosperity to newly independent African nations. As economies stagnated and political crises and military coups rocked country after country, the original Africanist framework appeared increasingly inadequate to meet the intellectual challenges thrown up by contemporary realities. The concern to demonstrate African initiative increasingly gave way to a search for the constraints on, and determinants of Africa's thorny path of economic and political development. These concerns led students of Africa to seek new theoretical tools. Scholars initially turned to underdevelopment theory and subsequently to Marxism as instruments with which the essentials of the continent's predicament could be laid bare. No sooner had an Africanist perspective established its relevance to South African studies than its credentials were challenged north of the border. But equally alarming was the growing materialist assault on orthodox liberal history. These developments threatened to leave a concern with the precolonial as a quaint sideshow.

The Emergence of Historical Materialism
1) The Rise of Revisionism

The climate of repression, the move into exile of scholars with experiences of various attenuated left traditions at home, and the rise of the new left in the West combined to create a paradigm shift in South African left scholarship in the late 1960s. A variety of left-wing academics, teachers, and students came together in London, Oxford, and Sussex where a recasting of entire periods and explanations took place—all in terms of the strident and confident neo-Marxism of the time. These young scholars invented a new language, one which did not speak of "Bantu, Boer and Briton" (MacMillan's phrase), but of "inhabitants of precapitalist societies forced into wage labor by the processes of primitive accumulation"; "agriculturalists incorporated by the influences of mercantile imperialism"; or "middle and upper class owners of the means of production." Though economistic, these linguistic shifts were perhaps necessary and certainly aided the process of rethinking categories.

Among the "revisionists" was a Canadian Marxist, F. A. Johnstone, who sought to demonstrate the basic compatibility between the requirements of capital in general, and the mining industry in particular, for "ultra-cheap" labor power and the policies of racial segregation and discrimination.[24] The emigre Stanley Trapido argued that the emergence of South African capitalism over the preceding century was racist only in form, while in content, it was explicable as a case of labor-repressive capitalism.[25] Exiled Martin Legassick wrote a series of papers which effectively remapped the outlines of South African history since the sixteenth century from a materialist perspective, and set out to explore critically the social and intellectual history of the liberalism within which he himself had been trained.[26] Africanist-trained Shula Marks in London was drawn into the new paradigm, and she and Trapido both ran seminars which deeply influenced the growing exile culture of the time.[27] Trapido in Durham and Oxford, Marks in London, and Legassick in Brighton and subsequently also Oxford and Warwick, supervised a number of students who were to become the next "cohort" of radicalized scholars, each of whom had, in turn, come to the moment of paradigmatic overthrow with his or her own particular experiences of sixties South Africa.[28]

The new interpretations captured the imagination of many. Numerous seminal essays were published at the time, and reached a wide audience, both in Britain and at home. They began to suggest reasons for the obvious success the South African state had controlling the contradictions over which it presided: for they saw violence and forced labor as having been essential to capital accumulation, rather than archaic leftovers from preindustrial times. Their insights grew primarily from an attempt to re-think the nature of the birth and subsequent evolution, through specific periods, of a South Africa perceived as thoroughly, if complexly, capitalist. The insights of mid-twentieth-century Marxism allowed for such an explanation to place "race" at the level of an "effect" of capitalist relations, rather than a cause (although nobody went as far as the NEUM's virtual denial of its historical presence).[29] This concern with holism made the detailed and often culturally-specific concerns of the existing Africanists somewhat marginal to the whole enterprise.

The nationalism which had concerned both liberals and Africanists was treated as being of peripheral importance in these years, as indeed it appeared to be at the time. The apparent demise of black nationalism could be explained, it was thought, by the fact that capitalism prevailed, rendering class a more important criterion for mobilization than race. But the absence of nationalism as an object of study was more a result of neglect than of any conscious attempt to exclude it.[30] The British-based historical materialists were not as "workerist"[31] as some of their counterparts within South Africa would later become. Classes were to some extent conceived as cultural as well as economic constructions, and the matters of consciousness and ideology were given consideration.[32] Clearly, the school attempted to establish the credentials of Marxism in a society which at first sight appears to be constructed racially, and to set itself against the prevailing assumptions of evolutionism and integration.

Epistemologically, the school adopted what might be called a "realist" stance, which distinguished it from the empiricism of earlier times.[33] Empirical evidence was highly respected, but was engaged with theoretical and conceptual categories, often in a dialectical manner. Theory building took place through the construction of new categories from combinations and adaptations of existing ones, or through the extension of the logic of existing frameworks into the specifically South (or southern) African case.

The work of exile Harold Wolpe, an ANC and Communist party intellectual and sociologist at Essex University, stands somewhat at a distance from that of the other revisionists of this time: his major contribution to the concerns of the seventies drew from a structuralist heritage.[34]

He argued that "segregation," as a political construction, was designed to ensure the cheapness of black labor power by transferring the responsibility for its reproduction to the "reserve" economies, and allowing capital to get away with low wages. "Apartheid" was the political response to the collapse of the reserve economies' capacity to fulfil this role.[35] The fundamental insight of Wolpe's work lay in its posing of a relationship—albeit functionally conceived—between rural precapitalist and urban capitalist modes of production, an issue which the revisionists had tended to downplay. It is probably true that Wolpe had been led to address such concerns by his Communist party involvement. The concept of the "articulation of modes of production" offered more Marxist content to the official analysis of "colonialism of a special type." Wolpe's structuralism was not easily compatible with the more historical revisionism—for he portrayed the evolution of this relationship as a series of set pieces, within each of which the economic necessity for cheap labor found expression in a political program. But whatever these differences, Wolpe's insights commanded wide attention.

2) *The Re-emergence of an Indigenous Left*

The new perspectives generated in England in these years were consumed with great eagerness in South Africa. Dog-eared copies of papers given at Oxford, Sussex, or London soon circulated (surreptitiously in most cases) in Johannesburg and Durban. This "photocopying culture" emerged, we suggest, in tandem with a series of major political and intellectual developments in South Africa toward the end of the repressive decade of the 1960s.

In the late 1960s the emergence of the Black Consciousness movement, mainly among youth and students, emphasized black leadership and denounced alliances with white liberals, and led to a black breakaway from the previously non-racial National Union of South African Students.[36] This rejection by black intellectuals caused a general confusion among the white left over what role they could or should play. This crisis coincided broadly with the rise of the new left in Europe and America, which offered a Marxism held to be free of the taint of Stalinism. In the late 1960s universities in South Africa also became beneficiaries of the accumulated economic boom and started to expand. A number of South Africans, and others, who had studied in Europe and were familiar with the new left were able to secure posts at South African universities.[37]

Probably the most influential of these returnees was Richard Turner, who completed a doctorate on Sartre in Paris, and returned to South Africa in the late 1960s to teach at Natal University. Rising above the suffocating political climate of the time, he outlined a Marxism that emphasized the capacity of people to change the world in which they lived, stressing the importance of participatory democracy. But most important of all, in his teaching and his writing he laid a central emphasis on the position and latent power of black workers.[38]

For a growing number of white students and intellectuals in these years, Marxism, stripped of its Stalinist accretions and with its emphasis on class, offered a coherent alternative to liberalism on the one hand, black nationalism on the other. After 1971, this intellectual position was increasingly translated into practice as left intellectuals such as Turner, as well as student groups, made contact with black workers. When in January of 1973 thousands of workers went on strike in Natal, they dented the complacency of much of white South Africa and provided what appeared to be powerful confirmation for activists that Marxism and class analysis were now the appropriate tools for South African society. Whites in Cape Town, Durban, and Johannesburg were to play an important and often courageous role—to give one extreme example Turner was banned in 1973 and assassinated in 1978—in the difficult birth of an independent trade union movement in the remainder of the 1970s.

In the early phases of this engagement, many of these white intellectuals, like a number of the revisionists in England, had a strong sense that they were involved in a decisive rupture with the past. Many believed that the ANC, PAC, and the South African Congress of Trade Unions (SACTU) had been defeated in the early 1960s, and that the exclusivism of Black Consciousness and the sorry record of independent Africa—not least in the treatment of workers—made for a sometimes strident hostility to nationalism and a stark privileging of class over race. The first explorations in labor history produced by intellectuals involved with the labor movement—prompted by the need for material for fledgling worker education programs—were strongly influenced by these perceptions.[39] This conceptualization was easily reconciled with, and was often reinforced by, the functionalist and reductionist tendencies in the revisionist literature being produced in England at the time.

Some of those who stopped to listen to what workers had to say about the past, found that oral tradition had much to tell about continuities between past nationalism and present class consciousness,[40] but most chose to ignore these uncomfortable realities. Furthermore, the state's remorseless attacks on SACTU activists and others ruptured the contacts which did take place, and decisively limited the influence among the leadership of a tradition of unionism more sensitive to nationalism.

Thus the new unions of the 1970s emerged in a climate of extreme repression. Unionists believed that a low political profile and a distancing from SACTU and the ANC were essential to their survival. They emphasized the building up of factory-based, democratic unions capable of establishing a bridgehead within industry and surviving attacks from the state. These concerns also stamped their mark on the work of a group of labor historians that emerged in the 1970s, closely linked to the union movement; they helped to explain this group's central concern with issues of organization, worker control, the labor process, and the machinery of industrial relations.

3) Structuralism

While the revisionists advanced their work, and while an internal radical tradition was reborn, a group of researchers came together at Sussex University, and began to develop a body of work that fitted unambiguously within the tradition of French structuralist Marxism. These writers formed a remarkably cohesive, if diverse, group.[41] They asked why the South African state had managed to accumulate and retain such an extraordinary degree of power; how it was able to oversee the process of capitalist accumulation with such success. Disillusionment with the "neo-colonial" order elsewhere in Africa drew many into a concern with analyzing and understanding the weaknesses which characterized Third World states in general. South Africa stood as an example of a peripheral state with a considerable set of capacities, both for repression and for apparently successful accumulation. Using the ideas of Poulantzas in particular, this grouping set out to demonstrate that the capacities of the state were the cumulative result of a series of periodic shifts in the "power bloc" that controlled it. South African capitalism, they suggested, had not evolved so much as proceeded by a series of leaps from one conjuncture to the next, the boundary between each leap being conceived of as the moment at which a "change in hegemony" in the "power bloc" took place. Each of the several "power blocs" was constructed from a series of alliances between classes and "fractions" of classes, and each was lent a particular strength as a result of the forces which underlay it.[42]

Bold and innovative as these analyses proved to be, the structuralists found themselves to be under fire almost as soon as they had completed their work.[43] Althusserianism in general, and Poulantzas's early work in particular, were subjected to searching criticism by both socialist-humanists, epitomized by *The Poverty of Theory*; and by British-based Marxists of a different ilk—central among whom was a University of Warwick sociologist Simon Clarke.[44] The mechanistic rigidities, the implicit Stalinism, the reification of rigid theoretical categories, the inherent functionalism and economism, and the ignoring of the role played by subordinate classes in the construction of capitalism, were all identified as serious flaws in the structuralist perspective. Not all of these criticisms could justifiably be applied to the South African school: who did at least conceive of transitions from one conjuncture to the next as a result of the contradictory relations between 'classes', and the commitment of most, like that of Poulantzas himself, was to a democratic rather than a Stalinist politics.[45] But Clarke and others did demonstrate that the Poulantzians conception of power as a kind of zero-sum result of the forging of alliances—and their consequent failure to take full account of the impact of the subordinate classes, not simply upon state capacity, but also upon the state form itself—was seriously flawed.[46]

Ironically, the area in which Althusserian structuralism is at its weakest—its tendency to adopt an idealist approach toward "theoretical categories" and thus to value empirical work primarily as a means of validating existing theory—has been one of the enduring legacies of this work. Furthermore, adherents to this epistemology regarded some of the questions which were to concern later Marxists as secondary: particularly questions of consciousness and ideology, both of which were handled by this school on the basis of a somewhat simplified base-superstructure model.

4) The Resurgence of African Studies

In Britain there was a further group involved in the creation of a materialist approach during the seventies: those rooted in the existing, but rapidly changing, Africanist paradigm. In the early part of the decade, Marks and Atmore had developed a critique of the liberal *Oxford History of South Africa* which stressed its failure to provide a dynamic account of African societies. Then they embarked on a seminal re-evaluation of the Imperial factor in the nineteenth century which—in contrast to de Kiewiet and Thompson—argued that British intervention in South Africa could not be fruitfully assessed in terms of its contribution to the maintenance of liberal values; far more telling was the role it had played in securing the conditions for capitalist development and in safeguarding Imperial economic interests.[47]

Underdevelopment theory continued to prove seductive for some Africanists seeking to recast their subject matter in more materialist forms. But for others, its emphasis on external structural constraints was not easily reconciled with a concern with the internal dynamics of African societies and African initiative.[48] A rich, growing, comparative literature on peasantries provided important perspectives, but the concept of a peasantry also seemed to offer limited analytical leverage.[49] Most immediately appealing was the work of French anthropologists who attempted to demonstrate the relevance of Marxist categories to the study of (mainly West) African communities. Their elaboration of concepts of mode of production, articulation, and social formation and their attempts to identify class cleavages even in uncentralized societies seemed to offer the opportunity to participate in a wider materialist transformation of South African studies.[50]

Initially, the incorporation of these perspectives produced some rather clumsy transplants to southern African communities of models which were rooted in the different realities of other parts of the continent and which were often highly functionalist, reductionist, or—in the case of the work of Hindess and Hirst which held brief sway—idealist.[51] But although it became clear that these concepts were not a panacea they helped to provide historians with a quiver-full of new questions which helped to transform historical understanding—most importantly about the economy and the nature of power, divisions and struggles within African societies. These concerns also resulted, in some instances, in wider explorations in contemporary anthropological literature which provided important insights into kinship systems and political processes.[52]

But the focus was not only on the internal dynamics of African societies. The stress laid on the emergence and impact of capitalism in the wider radical literature on South Africa, and the issues thrown up by a concern to understand the leaden phrase "the articulation of modes of production" in terms of a historical process rather than a mechanical metaphor, led this group of historians to focus in a less functionalist fashion on the interaction between the societies they were studying and the processes involved in the prolonged and painful birth of an industrial economy. The conquest of African states was firmly placed in the context of the development of capitalism. Interest grew in the origins of migrant labor which was to become a central feature in the twentieth century political economy of the region.[53] This body of work demonstrated that the functionalist model proposed by Wolpe and others failed to take into account the extent to which migrancy had been molded by the internal dynamics of African societies and by the struggles of migrants. Bundy's path-breaking work on the rise and fall of the peasantry was also considerably modified by accounts which asked questions about the economic and political relations and struggles within rural communities. Historians also began to draw on these new insights to provide an account of the development of capitalist agriculture which went beyond notions of "a transition from feudalism" and of a "Prussian path" to root its particular course in "a complex and conflict ridden process of articulation or interaction" between specific forms of African and settler society in the context of the creation of an industrial economy.[54]

The Creation of a New Milieu

If the 1973 strikes sent tremors through apartheid South Africa, the 1976 student revolt, which started in Soweto and then seared its way through township after township, shook the edifice of white power to its foundations. Brutal repression finally snuffed out the rising and the organizations which had helped shape it, but few believed that South Africa would ever be the same again. The elaboration of ever more refined policies of ethnic division and racial segregation which had preceded 1976 gave way to gropings toward "reform"—firstly through some accommodation of black trade unions and then in attempts to incorporate politically the "Coloured" and Indian communities. But these strategies for a managed transformation of society did not stay on the routes that government planners had charted. As the economy zig-zagged into decline, trade unions thwarted attempts to corral and coopt them and started to grow apace, and there was a proliferation of youth and community organizations by the early 1980s. Limited constitutional change was overshadowed by mass mobilization from 1983 onward under the broad banner of the United Democratic Front. A steady public reassertion of the presence of the ANC, and later the Communist Party, took place. It became increasingly clear to all but the most blinkered observers that the "national question" could not be ignored. The formation of the Congress of South African Trade Unions in 1985 brought a merging of "workerist" and more nationalist traditions of unionism in a powerful if sometimes uneasy federation.[55]

In the aftermath of the savage suppression of the 1976 revolt, many black intellectuals found in prose, drama, and poetry, a means of expressing and evaluating their experiences and raising their voices in protest. This literature was often strongly influenced by Black Consciousness, and contributed to the major revival of black writing which took place in the 1970s.[56] Formal history found little place in this writing but a particular vision of the past was a recurring motif: precolonial African societies were held to have been egalitarian and characterized by an organic collaborative culture. This version of history sustained a view which downplayed class analysis in the present, and stressed the essential unity of black experience.[57] However this was not an approach which facilitated intellectual exchange with mainly white historians intent on pursuing class cleavages in both precolonial and modern times.

The worlds of radical scholarship and local activism were profoundly affected by the events of the mid-1970s. Some left-wing academics judged that South African society was on the move and returned hoping to join local thinkers and activists in making a constructive contribution. The stultifying atmosphere of the 1960s had, by the late 1970s, been replaced with an exhilarating sense of possibility and creativity. University life was transformed by the return of former exiles, by the vitality and commitment of students, and by the growing sense of many that academics could and should continue to make connections with the social movements which had arisen. This was a context which intensified a melding of localist and revisionist approaches. An initial forum for this process was a Labour History conference held in Johannesburg in 1976, and it was consolidated by the formation of the University of the Witwatersrand History Workshop in 1977. These and other initiatives facilitated many intellectual developments on the left, providing mechanisms whereby academics could attempt to reconcile their intellectual and political commitments.[58]

These and a wide range of other intellectuals embarked upon exercises in popularization;[59] and this in turn fed from and fed into a series of important intellectual innovations. Writing for and teaching worker and popular audiences soon brought it home to academics that the abstract categories of analysis largely developed in England needed to be translated into the living categories of experience if they were to make headway.[60] There was a great difference between "class" and actual classes; or between, say, Legassick's broad sweep of analysis or Johnstone's analytical precision on the one hand, and the immediacy of "what to do now" on the other. And there was a contradiction between the theoretical analyses which proclaimed the death of "race" on the one hand, and on the other, the social movements of 1976 onward—movements which were based in communities as well as at workplaces, which erupted in townships as well as through trade unions, many of which were black, youthful, and implicitly or explicitly nationalist in orientation.

Popularizers set out to create and develop a series of alternative or oppositional cultural forms, locking into the widespread cultural and educational renaissance which the society at large was undergoing at the time.[61] The receptiveness of audiences to popularizing initiatives, as well as the obviousness of the extent to which popular consciousness was deeply nationalist in form, had profound effects upon intellectuals, leading them into a reconsideration of some of their more inflexible notions of "class."

At first, there was an elaboration, rather than a challenging, of the concept; an attempt to incorporate notions of culture and consciousness into that of "class." So powerful had the "workerist" perspective become by the late 1970s, and so compelling were the perceived arguments of the revisionists, that the emerging local tradition committed itself almost entirely to the effort of demonstrating that class analysis was applicable and illuminating for almost every situation.[62] The resulting work bore considerable fruit.

Charles van Onselen's work on the early history of Johannesburg—which was already under way when the Soweto revolt occurred, but was given an added immediacy by these events—helped stimulate and shape a new urban historiography, alerting a wider audience to the work of British and American Marxist historians. Van Onselen moved beyond the compounds which had been a central focus of his earlier work to explore the experiences and struggles of groups of ordinary people in the wider urban "world the mineowners made." He charted how the ruling classes on the Rand gradually asserted their control over and molded Johannesburg's transition from mining camp to metropolis.[63] Building upon this work, developments in metropolitan scholarship, and the ferment in the townships, local writers and researchers began to expand their vision. Historians analyzed townships such as Alexandra or Sophiatown as conglomerates of classes,[64] and explored the cultural features displayed by such communities, almost invariably attaching "culture" rather mechanically to "class."[65] Other classes, communities, and cultures came under scrutiny; while a number of local oral historians began to build upon the notion of "history from below," and to collect urban testimonies, memories of black cultural history, and biographies.[66]

But the context of diverse forms of struggle and the engagement with oral history and the "view from below" (with indigenous social movements, popular education, public audiences, and the popularization of history) helped make it impossible for old paradigms to continue unchanged. Not all forms of consciousness were explicable in purely class terms. In particular, researchers, writers, teachers, and popularizers found themselves confronted by living expressions of ordinary consciousness for which none of their previous theoretical conceptions had prepared them. The pervasive popular "workerism" of the post-1973 period, which many had taken to be a confirmation of the basic accuracy of the reductionist class position, proved increasingly to represent merely one strand among many in popular ideology rather than the outcome of the inexorable development of class consciousness. Avoiding the easy way out of this—resorting to ideas of "false" consciousness, mediation, or cultural lag—analysts saw this as a reason to re-think the very premises on which notions of "class" had been constructed. A new wave of contemporary work emerged out of these perceptions, with a more complex agenda.

The Beginnings of Synthesis

Radical historians confronted the fact that industrial society had been deeply marked by the particularities of its birth in Africa, particularities not previously well understood by many of the revisionists, structuralists, workerists, or localists. It was "Africanist" research that helped point to the extent to which pre-existing settler and African societies in all their economic, political, and cultural complexity had also played a part in shaping the character of class formation, ideologies, and capitalist development. This was not a capitalism built mainly upon the basis of existing class cleavages (as was the case in the examples of, say, capitalisms emerging out of feudal or slave societies). It may have had elements within settler society on which to build, but it also had to forge classes and ideologies of legitimation from reluctant African social orders where hierarchies and notions of property, deference, and loyalty took diverse and conflicting forms. Thus analysts began to question the idea that a predetermined capitalism which was bound to produce a predetermined "working class" with an ideal-typical consciousness. Rather, the *processes* of capitalization and industrial revolution on land and in cities were seen as having made what they could of the society at their disposal, against ever-resurgent resistance. The resulting analyses, blending Africanism, revisionism, and localism, began to look at how state forms, identities, consciousnesses, and structures took many different forms, only coalescing into larger entities (such as "races") at particular moments, and rendering earlier attempts at correlating class, culture, and consciousness simplistic.

Researchers found their work increasingly distanced from that of structuralists; not only was the idealist methodology which characterized much of the work of structuralists rejected, but it became clear that structuralism was incapable of transcending a vision which froze the social order at particular points in time, and sought to map the relationship between one structured "mode of production" and another. This led structuralists, for example, into arcane arguments about the precise moment at which the one mode of production was destroyed and the other dominant.[67] The realization that preindustrial societies did not lend themselves to such static and derived conceptualizations had already led some authors to reject feudalism or semi-feudalism as an adequate entry point for the analysis of preindustrial realities, and the questioning of reductionist notions of class in the twentieth century.[68] It became clear that the production of class could not be understood without reference to the divisions produced, not only by factors such as the timing of proletarianization,[69] but also by the inherited and imported cleavages of race,[70] religion and other cultural forms,[71] chiefly authority,[72] region,[73] ethnicity,[74] age,[75] community form,[76] and gender,[77] which were in turn refashioned by multiple popular struggles and processes of change.[78] A full understanding of the nature of this dialectic was at first obscured by a division between urban and rural studies, but scholars then started to pursue more fully processes which have spanned town and countryside. As a result, a sense began to emerge of the continual and complex interaction of rural and urban social forms and struggles which had been central to the making of class and community in both contexts; this allowed us to gain a better understanding of the diverse forms of urban and rural protest during the 1980s, as township wars, the clashing of factions, the creation of ethnicities, and the expression of cleavages of gender and generation became more prevalent.

"Human agency" and its relationship to other determinants came to occupy a more central analytical position in these new analyses. It was suggested that it was in the nitty gritty of everyday conflict—on the level of the small conflicts between classes and groups—that the precise and uniquely South African patterns of class, culture, and ideology were and are determined. If migrants as well as capitalists contributed to the development of the system of labor migration (albeit from positions of vastly different strengths),[79] sharecroppers and labor tenants, as well as capitalizing farmers, contributed to the creation of a specific series of patterns taken by the transition to capitalism in the countryside.[80] And urban dwellers, as well as industrialists and planners, gave shape to the configurations of family and community which emerged in the cities.[81] Insights such as these were derived in part from the work of oral historians, who saw their work as more than just an attempt to "fill in" with colorful detail the interpretive frameworks derived by structuralism. Rather it came to be viewed as an attempt to derive categories of explanation which catered both for human agency and for structured reality, affecting our understanding of what happens at the "top" as well.[82] If urban and rural social forms were created out of struggles between groups, then the form taken by the state must be affected by this, as must the complex configurations which we think of as "race" relationships, and the path taken by capital accumulation itself.

The nature of consciousness also emerged as a major subject of analysis in both urban and rural settings.[83] Analysts began to ask not just about the variety of forms of social cleavage but also about the range of world views which existed. A Gramscian influence has been present in some of this work, which has argued that consciousness cannot be deduced from class position, but is a matter for a more complex set of explanations involving an examination of experience, community, the various historical forces impinging on a situation, the nature of the ruling class, the operation of spatial and other kinds of factors, and the processes whereby ideas are transformed from the scattered wisdoms of "common sense" (in many cases drawn from preindustrial world views) into the more formulated discourses of "ideology."[84] Again, the insights into consciousness have been based upon innovative use of source material.

A growing concern to understand nationalism fed upon and into these new insights into the nature of consciousness.[85] Contemporary writers have tended to abandon the false dichotomy of race and class which prevailed in the early seventies.[86] Instead they are looking into the relationship between these forces and nationalisms, both white or black, studying them as ideological creations as well as semi-autonomous discourses, and emphasizing their intricate connections with class and community. Research on the state has also taken a new course. The 1970s and 1980s revealed the apparently monolithic state as a site of conflict and division, and the old questions were replaced by new ones: Of what did these fault lines consist? What contributions had the struggles of working and other subordinate groups made to their formation? What possible scenarios could be envisaged as their outcome? The ideas of the early Poulantzas were not suited to asking or answering such questions, but authors using the work of the later Poulantzas,[87] of Gramsci,[88] or from a more eclectic standpoint began to explore the state from the basis of a set of "axiomatic uncertainties" rather than a more instrumentalist perspective. This shift in perspective led to questions about internal cleavages, the role of African resistance or the impact of capitalist interests upon state form.[89] Thus while the Poulantzians largely failed to reproduce themselves,[90] a large sub-literature on the state has emerged since the mid-seventies, much of which has tended to move away from the larger statements and the functionalism of the earlier times.[91]

There has also been cross-fertilization in the field of labor studies. As nationalist concerns have entered the trade unions, so have more broadly-based analyses become more widely acceptable. Workers are perceived to be complete beings, with a life at home and at work and a complex array of consciousnesses, rather than as producers alone.[92] This transformation has taken place within the context of an ongoing connection between "labor studies" and a trade unionism seeking analyses which assist its understanding of class relations in the workplace. But a focus on the labor process, on workplace issues, and on union struggles has not been abandoned, not least of all because of a context in which the securing of basic union and worker rights remains a matter for bitter struggle.

An apparent weakness in the new radicalism is in the field of gender studies. However, while there is admittedly no school of "women's studies" of any significance, the question of gender has been regarded as an important one by a number of writers over the past ten years, although it has not been accorded the "separate" status which might make it recognizable to American readers. Generally, two approaches may be identified. Those concerned with realist humanism and influenced by Africanism have taken gender into account because gender cleavages are of inescapable importance in understanding the internal mode of operation, the lines of cleavage, and the forms taken by the dissolution of African societies. Thus there are studies of the way in which gender crucially affects the internal operation of preindustrial rural African societies,[93] of the nature of proletarianization,[94] of the reconstitution of urban classes with a clear gender dimension,[95] and of the form taken by women's resistance in these contexts.[96] The second strand has been less directly influenced by Africanism than by the more general feminist literature and its applicability to South African circumstances. While the relative weakness of studies of gender may not directly be attributed to the fact of the absence of a strong women's movement, certainly this must have had an effect. White and African cultures are both powerfully male-dominated; African nationalism is notorious for its tendency to place women's issues low on the agenda, to be solved "after" the revolution; the structure of intellectual life itself is archaic; and finally, many socialists show a concern not to separate gender from other issues. But if we are involved in a re-theorizing of South Africa, based partly on the importance of gender cleavages in preindustrial societies, then our concentration on the relationship between structure and agency in this field must be developed.

Conclusion

Each of the four original strands of thinking that came to constitute South African historical materialism underwent changes under the impact of the crisis of the mid-1970s and subsequent developments. Most markedly, the original functionalism of so many of the first forays into historical materialism was rejected in favor of more dialectical and nuanced approaches. When the sturdy simplicities of the old revisionism proved inadequate to the task, researchers combined revisionist, localist and Africanist concerns, to develop a more "decolonized" scholarship, which questioned imported categories and metropolitan paradigms.

The detailed, often local, nature of some of the work which has provided the basis for these advances is a long way from the short, seminal articles of the early seventies, where whole new paradigms were introduced in a single sweep; and there has been a reorientation away from the dominant classes toward the subordinate ones. But the adoption of the "view from below" has not meant a move toward a simple-minded populism; it entailed an intellectual shift toward ways of explaining how colonized peoples have been drawn into a capitalist society and have resisted their incorporation, leaving their mark on the form taken by the "big" categories of class, race, and state. Further advances must be grounded in empirical research, comparative study and conceptual innovation, and should not be confined to small and local units of study. We suggest that there is room for analyses of the national and the local, the dominant and the subordinate classes, the cultural and the economic—and it will be a rare scholar who can maintain an equally firm grip on all the relevant variables. What is important is that synthesis and intellectual exchange are constants.

Some perhaps long nostalgically for the days when truths were simpler and more easily acquired. Others believe that reductionism equals rigor. By contrast, present day radical scholarship requires an apprenticeship in contemporary and classical Marxism, anthropology, and African history for even a basic understanding to be established. Many of its advances are small and modestly proclaimed. There has been a "realist" pursuit of theories whereby we may understand the South African social order, accompanied by a humanist desire to reconcile structure and agency. The intellectual work being done in these areas, we suggest, constitutes "domain construction" rather than "theory construction." We have not yet reached the stage of making statements on a larger scale. But it would be unfortunate if this process of domain construction were to be halted in its tracks on the incorrect grounds that it constitutes "empiricism." Instead, surely the way forward is to continue domain-definition and strive toward creative theory-building as our work matures.

While the more nuanced, culturally sensitive work that is being produced is more easily translatable into popular discourses, the slow and fragmentary nature of its development runs counter to the politicized demands of the society for instant solutions to "what is to be done." In the context of the damaging state attacks on popular organization between 1986 and 1990 this approach was also criticized for its "populism" and a cry went up in some quarters for priority to be given to the development and application of "revolutionary theory." Those with an eye to the future are also seeking to establish policies which will guide a post-apartheid society in its handling of urban, rural, gender, and development issues. We suggest that action or policy-oriented theories must be doubly certain of the specific context in which they guide strategy, tactics, and planning. No blueprints or perfect theories exist, ready to be "applied." In the context of ever-shortening and intensifying cycles of reform and repression, intellectuals and activists in South Africa will battle to keep their balance, and will need to base their plans for the future on theory and research that are complex and locally-forged, rather than oversimplified and grounded in local realities. The unthinking application by, say, policymakers of unreconstructed theories to the future South African order could have grave consequences.

Part I / Radical Historians and South Africa's Past

History Workshop

Chapter 2 / ## Suicide or Genocide?

Xhosa Perceptions of the Nongqawuse Catastrophe

/ *J. B. Peires*

History Workshop

Nongqawuse (right).

On a certain day in April 1856, two young Xhosa girls went down to their family gardens near the mouth of the Great Kei river to scare the birds away from the standing corn.[1] According to Nongqawuse, the elder of the two, they were approached there by two strangers who entrusted them with the following singular message:

> Give our greetings to your homes. Tell them we are So-and-so . . . and they told their names, those of people who had died long ago. Tell them that the whole nation will rise from the dead if all the living cattle are slaughtered because these have been reared with defiled hands, since there are people about who have been practising witchcraft.
>
> There should be no cultivation. Great new corn pits must be dug and new houses built. Lay out great big cattle folds, cut out new milk-sacks, and weave doors from *buka* roots, many of them. So say the chiefs, Napakade (the eternal), the son of Sifuba-sibanzi (the Broad Chested).

This extraordinary prophecy took a strong hold on the imagination of the Xhosa people, devastated by their sufferings in the long drawn-out Eighth Frontier War (1850–53) against the white Cape Colony. The Xhosa were the southernmost of the Bantu speaking peoples, and the first to encounter the white colonial advance. Fighting along the eastern frontier of Britain's Cape Colony had been almost continuous since the first clashes in 1779, but the bravery and determination of the Xhosa were no match in the long run for the effectively infinite resources of the British Empire. By 1853, the Xhosa were a politically divided nation. Those to the East of the Great Kei river retained their independence under the leadership of the Xhosa king, Sarhili. Those to the West lived under the yoke of the Crown Colony of British Kaffraria.

Hundreds of enquiring Xhosa flocked to the scene of the prophecies, where Nongqawuse satisfied their curiosity by staging a little charade in which she spoke to inaudible "new people," and showed the enquirers dim black shapes rising and falling in the misty sea. Sarhili, the Xhosa king, became a firm believer and ordered his people to kill their cattle.

They did so in increasing numbers. Every disappointment was blamed on the dwindling band of *amagogotya*, or "stingy ones," who refused to slaughter. Starving believers pressed their ears to the ground, where they heard the lowing of great herds of beautiful new cattle ready to rise as soon as the last tainted earthly beast had been finally killed. Since the believers had also destroyed their stores of corn, they lived on roots and mimosa tree bark until even these resources gave out. By the time it was all over (June 1857), an estimated 40,000 people had died of starvation and 400,000 cattle had perished. The survivors set off for the white towns, emaciated and covered with sores, the smell of mimosa coming out of every pore.

British governor, Sir George Grey was ready to receive them. "Instead of nothing but dangers resulting from the . . . excitement," he wrote, "we can draw very great permanent advantages from the circumstance, which may be made a stepping stone for the future settlement of the country."[2] Grey had stockpiled food to meet the anticipated starvation, but he only distributed it to those who signed contracts for farm labor in the Cape Colony. Nearly 30,000 of those who survived were removed from the areas in this way. Charitable whites who attempted to set up a Relief Committee were told that "private benevolence is not requisite," and their modest soup kitchen was brusquely shut down. Altogether, the Xhosa population of British Kaffraria dropped from 105,000 in January 1857 to 25,916 in December 1858.

But this was not enough for Governor Grey. He brought charges of treason and cattle theft against more of the Xhosa chiefs, and imprisoned them on Robben Island. He sent an armed force into independent Xhosaland, and drove its starving people into exile. The fertile lands of British Kaffraria were surveyed into farms and given away to white settlers. The remaining Xhosa, mostly unbelievers, were herded into villages under close colonial supervision. The military power of the Xhosa nation, which had held the line against the white advance for over eighty years, was broken forever.

The official documents of the period shed little light on the inner history of the cattle-killing. Governor Grey decided to cover up his own atrocities by pretending that the movement was a plot by the Xhosa chiefs to provoke a war against the colonial government, and he doctored the evidence accordingly—not stopping short of obtaining fraudulent confessions under duress.[3] But if one seeks enlightenment from

Xhosa oral traditions, one is confronted by a mirror image of Grey's distortions. Time and again, I have tactfully broached the subject of Nongqawuse with knowledgeable old Xhosa men, and time and again, the knowledgeable old man has looked at me shrewdly, thought about it for a while, and finally ejaculated the words, "It was Grey! Governor Sir George Grey!"

But it was not Grey. The governor, as I have made clear, was a sinister and ruthless figure who callously exploited Nongqawuse's prophecies in order to impose white domination on the Xhosa. Not only did he fail to help them in the hour of their need, but he went out of his way to kick them when they were down. That Grey destroyed the Xhosa nation through manipulating the situation created by Nong-qawuse is clear enough, but the accusations of the Xhosa go much further than that. They insist that he was responsible not only for the ramifications of the prophecies but for the prophecies themselves.

And that is simply not true. We have at our disposal in the Cape Archives a complete set of the unofficial correspondence between Governor Grey and Colonel John Maclean, his chief subordinate in British Kaffraria.[4] These letters, the equivalent of today's private telephone calls, are completely reliable and above suspicion. They prove beyond any reasonable doubt that, far from masterminding the whole operation, Grey and Maclean spent most of their time trying to guess what was going on and what would happen next. "All we can do at present," wrote Grey, on first hearing the news of the cattle-killing, "is to be in every possible manner upon our guard, so as to be prepared for anything which may turn up. I still however hope that we shall not be in any manner hurried into a war." Even if these private letters did not exist, it is surely self-evident that no distant Victorian governor could ever have conceived so far-fetched a scheme, let alone blackened his face and hid in the reeds himself. But no matter how much contrary evidence is put before them, the Xhosa cling tenaciously to their belief that Grey was the initiator and originator of the whole calamity.

The belief is a very old one. In 1936, an eighty-year old Xhosa man told the amateur historian, A. W. Burton, that "his father and grandfather often said that certain Europeans were behind the Nongqawuse movement." S.E.K. Mqhayi, generally regarded as the greatest ever Xhosa-language historian, wrote bluntly in 1931 that "we say it was a plan of the whites to break the neck of the amaXhosa because we had not been broken by all the wars." And the venerable chief Ndumiso Bhotomane, born in 1892 and the son of King Sarhili's personal messenger to Nong-qawuse, told me unequivocally that "it was a plan of the white people, because they were continually fighting with the Xhosa. They wanted the Xhosa to become thin, so that they could defeat them the next time they fought."[5]

Even today, the belief in Grey's responsibility is almost universal among all Xhosa, young and old, urban and rural. Nongqawuse's motivations are, however, still open to speculation. The older generation tends to feel that she was tricked or misled. Expressions such as "she was only a young girl, she had never seen a white man before" recur frequently. The nature of the deception varies according to who is telling the story. Some think that Grey blackened his face and impersonated an ancestor in person. Others argue that Grey could not speak Xhosa, and that the supposed ancestors were his black agents. Most well-informed Xhosa know about the voices in the bushes and the shapes in the sea, and a variety of European devices are invoked to explain these, ranging from concealed mirrors and radios, to submarines and airplanes. The following fairly typical tradition will have to suffice for all the rest:

> The daughter of Mhlakaza went to get water at the reedy place, and there she met these "ancestors." . . . They pulled out brown sugar and gave it to her to give to her father, saying that if they slaughtered all the sorghum would taste like this in the future. Everybody who tasted that sugar know that there had never been sorghum so wonderful.
>
> Therefore they truly believed that Nongqawuse was speaking the truth.[6]

The view of Nongqawuse as a foolish young girl who was incited into suicidal actions is most congenial to contemporary black establishment politicians and collaborators under pressure from youth and other progressive organizations. George Matanzima, prime minister of the Transkei "homeland" in 1980, "likened the recent incidence of school unrest with the Nongqawuse cattle-killing episode of 1857." And Gatsha Buthelezi, the leading black opponent of sanctions, recently urged his supporters to "beware of false prophets who urged them to destroy the country's assets. . . . This was what the Xhosa prophetess Nongqawuse had done in the last century, leading to the deaths of tens of thousands from starvation."[7]

Progressive movements, on the other hand, have tended to discount Nongqawuse's youth as a motivating factor, and see her rather as a willing instrument in Grey's hands. The view of Nongqawuse as bribed rather than fooled is a minority opinion, but one of equal antiquity. During a 1988 Soweto Day (June 16) memorial service, Reverend Mcebisi Xundu of Port Elizabeth, one of the leading progressives in the Eastern Cape, referred to "those who can never be forgiven," starting with Judas Iscariot and ending with Nongqawuse and other paid black agents of "the system." The name of the prophetess was greeted with a prolonged hiss from the largely Xhosa audience. A similar sentiment is echoed in a Black Consciousness song of the early 1970s:

> Sir George Grey took our country
> He entered in through Nongqawuse
> The cattle died, the sheep died
> The power of the black people was finished off

A third interpretation of Nongqawuse's motivations emphasizes the role not only of Grey but of the white missionaries. This view probably goes back to *The Role of the Missionaries in Conquest* by "Nosipho Majeke," which was first published in 1952. "Majeke" was in fact the pseudonym of the white Trotskyist, Dora Taylor, but most Xhosa who know the book assume it was written by a fellow-Xhosa. "Majeke" distanced herself from the idea that the mysterious ancestors were directly sent by whites, but continued:

> Confronted with the military force of an unknown civilization, the Xhosa would seize upon those elements in the Christian gospel which seemed most likely to offer him protection: the belief in miracles, the resurrection of the dead, the promise of peace and plenty after tribulations and sorrow. It is in this sense that we say the Nongqawuse Cattle-Killing was missionary-inspired. It was the first fruits of the subjugation of the minds of the people.[9]

This is fair enough, but other writers have not been so circumspect. The Islamic Missionary Society of Johannesburg recently produced a pamphlet in which the part of the ancestors was played by three Christian missionaries who "spoke the Xhosa language fluently and they knew, in detail, all about the Xhosa religion and its ceremonies." It was they who devised the "satanic plot." All whites who pretend to be friendly to blacks are, in fact, suspect. The Grahamstown branch of AZAPO (the pro-Black Consciousness, Azanian People's Organisation) put out a pamphlet for Biko Day (September) 1987, in which they attacked the non-racial United Democratic Front for its links with progressive white organizations. This too referred to the Nongqawuse incident as the classic case of blacks following white advice leading to their doom.[10]

How are we to explain the insistence of most Xhosa on the guilt of Grey and the missionaries? Part of the answer is clearly shame and embarrassment. This is obvious to any outsider who asks questions about the incident. Xhosa frequently deny any knowledge of Nongqawuse, even to other blacks. Alistair Brown, who circulated a questionnaire on

Nongqawuse at the largely Xhosa University of Fort Hare, encountered a "nervous, hostile and uncooperative" attitude. On one occasion, the questionnaire was distributed in a class which contained a fair number of students from the Transvaal who had never heard of Nongqawuse. When the Xhosa students tried to explain the episode to them they burst into roars of laughter and the deeply mortified Xhosa students refused to continue.[11]

But is shame and embarrassment a sufficient explanation? Brown thinks so, and he quotes Robin Winks's concept of "vital lies," "opinions so deeply ingrained that they will be adhered to no matter the weight of opposing evidence." Yet, once one has broken through the initial reserve, one finds that Xhosa people talk eagerly of Nongqawuse and frankly admit the shortcomings of their forefathers. "The Xhosa are a superstitious people," one old man said to me. "They died by Nongqawuse on account of their superstition." And then he proceeded to tell me how Sir George Grey tricked Nongqawuse with the help of a mirror.[12] Grey's intervention does not in any way absolve the Xhosa of responsibility in the matter. Yet it is Grey's role which is crucial.

The key to the problem lies in the structure of Xhosa historical knowledge. Putting aside the question of Nongqawuse for the time being, we need to ask what the Xhosa know about other aspects of their history, how it is transmitted, and what form it takes. If we can understand how other historical episodes have been transformed in the oral tradition, we can perhaps understand the Nongqawuse tradition much better.

The old Xhosa kingdom was highly decentralized, with many chiefs but few specialized officials.[13] The chief's counsellors served him on a voluntary basis, and each chief delegated tasks as he saw fit. There were no official historians as such, though individuals interested in history might accumulate a vast store of knowledge. With the absorption of the chiefs into South Africa's Bantu Authorities system, the written word of the government ethnologist replaced the spoken word of the counsellor as the chief's guide to political practice. Chief Ndumiso Bhotomane, the last of the great oral historians, died in 1978 and left no successors.

Yet historical traditions still survive among the Xhosa. Every well-informed man has learnt eight or ten stories as part of his general upbringing, stories not deliberately inculcated but casually transmitted at the cattle-posts or around the evening fire. There is the story of Tshawe, which explains the creation of chieftainship and defines certain norms of chiefly behavior. There is the story of Ntsikana which relates the conversion of the first Xhosa Christian *before* the coming of the missionaries.

There are a couple of stories concerning the Mfengu refugees who settled among the Xhosa in the 1820s but deserted them in favor of an alliance with the British. Then there is the story of Nongqawuse which explains the defeat of the Xhosa at colonial hands, not openly and fairly through military means but deviously through a hideous trick.

Oral traditions, like living organisms, undergo a process of natural selection. Those which possess relevance, drama, and narrative simplicity survive; the others go to the wall. This process of adaptation can be called "telescoping." In telescoping, the deeds of an entire generation are attributed to a single person; complex sequences of events are reduced to a single dramatic scene; inconvenient facts are brushed aside and loose ends are chopped off; a moral is added to underline the contemporary relevance of the story.

The oral tradition which eventually emerges from this process should not therefore be taken literally as a factual narrative. Its truths are not the kind which can be supported or controverted by footnoted evidence. Its truths are of a different order of reality. The small city of Grahamstown (population 60,000) in which I live is dominated by a huge Anglican cathedral which stands plumb in the heart of the city. Grahamstown's Xhosa population believes that the head of an old Xhosa chief lies buried beneath it. Literally speaking, this is not the case. There are no skulls in the foundations of the Cathedral of St. Michael and St. George. But as a symbolic statement of the historical triumph of settlerdom, the historical image could hardly be bettered.

And therein lies the power of the story of Nongqawuse and Sir George Grey. It is not true that Sir George Grey hid in the reeds pretending to be a Xhosa ancestor. Nor is it true that his agents handed brown sugar around pretending it was a new sorghum. But it is true that the Xhosa themselves must bear a large share of the responsibility. It is true, but it doesn't matter. Because it is also true that the Xhosa were never defeated on the battlefield. And that a young girl under indirect Christian influence told them that the dead would arise if they killed their cattle. Above all, it is true that a foolish mistake was converted into a national catastrophe through the ruthless and implacable policies of Sir George Grey. These latter are the important truths, and all else is detail. The Xhosa don't need white academics to give them a usable past. They already have one.

I spent five years of my life researching the great cattle-killing, and in the course of these five years I discovered the answers to many problems which had puzzled previous historians. Why did the Xhosa adopt so obviously self-destructive a millennarian ideology as the killing of their cattle? Because shortly before Nongqawuse's prophecies, a great epidemic of lungsickness broke out among the Xhosa herds, destroying 95 percent or more of their cattle. Most of the cattle which they slaughtered were doomed to die anyway. Where did the idea of general resurrection of the dead come from? It turned out that Nongqawuse's guardian, Mhlakaza, was no heathen witchdoctor but a frustrated Christian convert whose visions had been derided by his racist white ecclesiastical employer.[14] And so on.

At the time when I was discovering all these things, it seemed to me that the root of the Xhosa problem was a lack of credible information. I rushed to share my discoveries with Xhosa friends whom I knew to be interested in history, but, to my disappointment, I found that as soon as I wandered too far from the all-absorbing question of Sir George Grey's role, their interest waned precipitately. I particularly remember a conversation I has with a leading South African National Students Council (SANSCO) activist. SANSCO, a national organization representing mainly black students, was affiliated to the United Democratic Front (UDF); both are now banned by the South African authorities. My friend listened to me attentively and accepted everything that I said. "But you know," he told me gently, "we still cannot understand Nongqawuse except in the context of the colonial experience."

I can see that now. The Xhosa already have a usable past, and they don't need an accumulation of detail to understand it better. Too much detail might in fact distract attention from the major issues. And having participated in a minor way in the political struggles of the last three years, I have been struck and saddened by how little relevance our academic kind of history has for the broad masses.

It is not that they are uninterested in history. On the contrary, the SANSCO executive took a decision in 1986 to write a history of SANSCO. Organizations such as the Grahamstown Rural Committee and the Transvaal Rural Action Committee have been able to draw on historical skills to contribute to the fight against forced removals. In retrospect, I feel that we academics have made a mistake in determining our research priorities.

We have tended to set our own agendas, to write our own kind of history (perhaps in accordance with overseas trends), and then to present it to the people in a simplified form. But writing people's history is not so much a matter of simplification as a matter of relevance. It is not that there is no value in writing the most detailed history possible of Nongqawuse. Nor should we allow our interpretation of historical events to be influenced by fluctuating political circumstances. But we do, perhaps, need to define our priorities more in terms of needs of the moment. South Africa in the 1990s cannot afford the luxury of an irrelevant history.

Chapter 3 / **Highways, Byways, and Culs-de-Sac:**

The Transition to Agrarian
Capitalism in Revisionist
South African History

Helen Bradford

Sharecropper, 1916.

Think for a moment: what was the "most striking difference" between South African agriculture of the 1960s and the *platteland* of a century before? Tractors? Agribusiness? Proletarians? None of the above, according to the 1971 *Oxford History of South Africa*. It was, "as in many other countries, the breakdown of isolation." White farmers who had previously hauled ox-wagons over hills "were now linked with one another, with the urban areas, and with the wider world by all-weather roads, over which they travelled in large cars." Blacks, too, had their "scale of interaction" enlarged. Even those who could not afford bicycles had greater opportunities: "Seldom would a farmer go to town without at least one of his labourers accompanying him."[1]

"Cooperation" between white and black, and "interaction with the wider world" were characteristic foci of the academic liberal tradition of the 1950s and 1960s, which reached a high water mark in the *Oxford History*. Since then, a "dynamic, innovative and expansive Marxist tradition" has attained hegemony in South African studies, and revisionists have posed very different questions about the agrarian past.[2] Yet if radical historians have agreed that the development of capitalism was more important than Chevrolets, they have diverged dramatically in analyzing transition to this new mode of production. They have disagreed about what preceded capitalism; they have located its emergence anywhere between 1700 and the 1890s; they have pinpointed its consolidation in the 1860s—or the 1970s.

To differ over the timing of the transition to capitalism is common amongst Marxist scholars, but to diverge by a couple of centuries perhaps requires explanation. For one thing, there are enormous empirical lacunae over which those who would analyze capitalism must vault. "In contrast with the situation abroad," lamented a scholar in 1979, "the study of agrarian history in South Africa is still in its infancy."[3] This assessment still stands a decade later: despite the precocious growth of radical rural scholarship, it cannot yet answer "which capitalists emerged when, where and with what crops?" More significantly, there is no consensus on the very meaning of capitalism, let alone on what research would help answer when or how it emerged.

As the conflict with liberal intellectuals demonstrated, theoretical disagreements are not trivial matters. There are steep intellectual and political costs attached to terming the countryside "feudal" or "capitalist" in vastly different periods. They are paid by rural scholars in general— insofar as conceptualizations of one period of history affect analyses of preceding and succeeding eras. If we fail to examine what is meant by capitalism, Mike Morris argued in a recent contribution to the South African agrarian debate, "we have no idea of when the transition to it occurred, what stages it went through and when the forces of capitalism became dominant in the countryside."[4] Moreover, in a society that is itself in painful transition, repercussions arise for all who hold that a better understanding of capitalist development in the past is a prerequisite for analyzing—and changing—the present.

Yet historical materialists, over time, have given different answers to the question: "What is meant by transition to capitalism?" Marx's preliminary statements were endorsed, yet altered, by Lenin. The discourse was further refined by the international exchange stimulated by Dobb and his critics. The most persuasive argument of recent years was that of Robert Brenner. A Marxist analysis of transition, he contended, involved tracing the origin of the class system "of free wage labour—the historical process by which labour power and the means of production became commodities."[5] Despite the acceptance this view has won, it has been challenged by those who ask: is reinvestment of profits necessary as well? Consequently, if we are to understand why South Africanists, too, have provided competing accounts and chafed against existing conceptualizations, we must situate them in their own time and place. Real historical reasons often help explain the emergence of divergent accounts and different contributions to the "transition debate."

The Prussian Road: Feudalism to Capitalism

The [corvée system] consists in the landlord's land being cultivated with the implements of the neighbouring peasants. . . . The capitalist farming system consists of the hire of workers . . . who till the land with the owner's implements.

(V.I. Lenin, *The Development of Capitalism in Russia*, 196–97)

There can no longer be any doubt about the capitalist nature of "commercial agriculture" in South Africa by at least the second decade of the twentieth century.

(M. Morris, "The Development of Capitalism in South African Agriculture," *Economy and Society* 5:3, 307)

Between the mid-1960s and the mid-1970s, Perry Anderson argued, Western Marxism was transformed. The impact of working-class, peasant, and student struggles—together with the advent of international recession and the attractions of Maoism—strongly challenged a tradition in which "questions of theoretical form" had for decades "displaced issues of political substance." In place of Althusserianism, which had effectively excised both the concrete and subjects, an appetite for evidence emerged, often reinforced by a reunion of theory with practice. Classical historical materialism also reappeared, in a form which frequently privileged Lenin-the-revolutionary over Marx-the-economist, and insisted on the centrality of class struggle.[6]

These sea changes within Marxism—and the generalized ferment among radicals attracted to underdevelopment or dependency theory—profoundly influenced the handful of revisionist historians exploring the South African *platteland* in the early 1970s. Peasants were increasingly forcing themselves on the attention of intellectuals as well as imperialists, and Colin Bundy was reinserting black farm tenants into history. Painting on the broad canvas of South Africa at large—and partially transcending the association in underdevelopment theory of feudalism with subsistence and capitalism with commodities—he situated tenants marketing crops in a "quasi-feudal" past. This all too rapidly became a capitalist present: after the commercialization of agriculture associated with the discovery of the world's largest goldfields in 1886, there was a brutal offensive from above to eradicate these "quasi-feudal relations permitting a peasant existence outside the labour market."[7]

Bundy's black tenants were rooted far more deeply in productive structures by Stanley Trapido, who prudently refused to sink all non-capitalist relations in a feudal sea. Between 1840 and the turn of the century, he contended, "two successive modes of production—first slavery and then a system akin to serfdom—dominated agrarian society in the Transvaal." Not that Trapido rejected the feudal analogy: in a pioneering article, he was the first to stress the striking similarities between agrarian South Africa and feudal Prussia. Working on rural Natal, Henry Slater was among the few who eschewed feudal formulations—presciently, he focused instead on the development of merchant, financial, speculative and rentier capital—but his explanation of the transition to capitalism was otherwise thoroughly orthodox. First, the vastly expanded market generated by mining activity had "its corollary of capitalistic farming." Second, this inexorable economic logic was reinforced politically: a "change in the composition of state power" enabled the victory of commercial farmers over both rentier capital and African peasants.[8]

These insights were further developed by Mike Morris. Profoundly influenced by Poulantzas—perhaps the most significant theorist in post-Althusserian Marxism—he was also inspired by contemporary political concerns. After a decade during which the apartheid regime both routed its black opposition and fostered luxuriant economic growth, Morris questioned the extraordinarily high level of economic development of this peripheral country, and asked why it retained a "racially exclusive bourgeois democratic State." The explanation, he decided, lay partly in the countryside, since the development of capitalist agriculture had "radically set South Africa apart from almost all other peripheral social formations."[9]

His main thesis overlapped substantially with the works of Bundy, Trapido, and Slater. After the discovery of gold, Morris argued, the "semi-feudal" countryside of the late nineteenth century was harshly and swiftly transformed from above, along the "Prussian path," into capitalist agriculture. But Morris also broke sharply with the early revisionists by pressing Marxist analytical categories more insistently. His "Prussian path" drew upon Leninist theory rather than German history: it referred to the vanguard role of landlords and the state in transforming feudal agriculture into a bourgeois order which retained feudal features. Yet Lenin's "Prussian path" (but a "concept *in embryo*" according to Anthony Winson) probably led Morris on a detour. His far greater contribution toward remapping the past lay in establishing the distinguishing features of different modes of production.[10]

To periodize the phases involved in transition, Morris rigorously defined feudal and capitalist modes of production in terms of a property relation (referring to ownership of the means of production by the non-worker), and a relation of real appropriation (concerning producers' control over the labor process). Significantly, this theoretical framework blurred relations of ownership or possession between non-workers and producers, but it did stress the centrality of divorcing producers from the means of labor. Once tenants were severed from tools, argued Morris (with Lenin), "labour service under these conditions is clearly capitalist in nature."[11]

Unfortunately, Morris also followed Lenin on Russia more closely than Trapido on the Transvaal when dealing with the specificities of the "semi-feudal" period in South Africa. Unpaid labor tenants, he asserted with no evidence at all, worked two days a week for the landlord using their own implements. They were "completely bound in a serf-like manner to the soil," and production was not oriented to exchange. Bundy's and Slater's conclusions were mirrored more accurately: once the internal markets associated with the discovery of gold had emerged, there was no question but that rural capitalism would develop. For Morris, "the essence of the agrarian question" was rather whether landlords or peasants headed the process of transformation. In South Africa, due to massive intervention by the state (itself predicated on conflict and compromise between landlords and mining capital), and due to the weakness of the black working class and peasantry, the Prussian path dominated. By the 1920s, South African agriculture had allegedly become capitalist. Farmers supposedly owned all the implements; they also bought the labor-power of tenants who could not reproduce themselves from the land.[12]

Although the shaky empirical foundations of this early section of Morris's argument have justifiably attracted criticism, he was primarily concerned with the relationship between the apartheid state and the further development of agrarian capitalism. After deftly dissecting structural contradictions (due to the uneven development of capitalism nationally and internationally), and exposing how these were intensified by class struggle (especially by the desertion of youths), he detailed the solutions of the most capitalized farmers to the labor crisis that threatened them. They clamored for brutal measures to increase the black farm labor supply, decrease its mobility, and dispossess labor tenants—and were thoroughly gratified by the actions of the apartheid regime elected in 1948. Hence,

> It is totally misleading to see Apartheid . . . as a return of a "feudal system" of extra-economic coercion in the countryside. On the contrary, as the outcome of a determinate class struggle, it signalled the victory of capitalist farmers over the direct producers (labour tenants); as the end of a phase of transition, it ushered in a new stage in the development of capitalist agriculture.[13]

This was a seminal intervention in the "transition debate." Morris reclaimed for historical materialism an entire economic sector; his 1976 article was reprinted four times in three different languages and has shaped much of the discussion ever since. Undoubtedly, its empirical inaccuracies have riled many historians—not least because Morris believed, in a profoundly idealist fashion, that "one cannot establish a conceptual error of mine by reference to historical details." Yet most would concur with Tim Keegan that "Morris's work has proved invaluable to [an] understanding of the capitalisation of South African agriculture in the twentieth century . . . there can be no doubt that his preliminary groundwork will remain the starting point for subsequent investigations of the subject."[14]

Prolonging the Journey: *The* Bittereinder *Challenge*

The transformation of money . . . into capital occurs only when a worker's labour-power has been converted into a commodity for him.
(K. Marx, *Capital* I, 950)

There is ample evidence . . . that a capitalist mode of production began to predominate in South African agriculture only in the late 1960's.
(D. Moodie, "Class Struggle in the Development of Agrarian Capitalism," paper presented at History Workshop, 1981, 2)

Morris's findings were, however, soon disputed. One attack came from a disparate group of *bittereinders*: like Boers who refused to believe that the British had won the South African War, these scholars declined to concede that capitalism was victorious by the 1920s. They focused primarily on whether workers were "free," asking questions which Morris's theoretical framework had precluded. Some probed whether labor tenants were free to sell their own labor-power for a limited period of time for wages; others explored when blacks were completely free of the means of production; yet others focused on the political restrictions on free labor markets. Since these scholars were influenced by different intellectual traditions, most shared only the belief that the transition to rural capitalism extended well into the twentieth century. It lasted, as Stanley Greenberg expressed it, "even into the contemporary period."[15]

In the process of reaching this conclusion, many made important conceptual or empirical points. Greenberg drew on the German analogy in tracing why farmers held on "to their 'feudal baggage' in a modern world." Robert Miles focused attention on the centrality of a precondition of capitalism identified by Marx—the generalized transformation of labor-power into a commodity for workers themselves. He convincingly demonstrated the implications of the absence of this crucial capitalist relation of production for resistance, the economy, the state, and racist ideologies. His main contention was recently partially reaffirmed by Keegan: it is only "when labour itself becomes a commodity, that the extraction of relative surplus value becomes possible," and continuous technological innovation occurs.[16]

But when did labor-power become a commodity? Only for the Cape does a partial answer exist, due largely to a sensitive study by Susan Newton-King. By 1800, most Khoisan had lost access to land within colonial boundaries; they strongly resisted the forced labor legally imposed after the abolition of the slave trade in 1807; in a time of acute rural labor shortage, they loafed, stole, destroyed property, and deserted. In 1828, the British colonial state sanctimoniously recognized that unruly and unfree workers who had been dispossessed should have the "liberty to bring their labour to the best market." Settler protests were overridden. Forced labor among the Khoisan was legally abolished, and capitalist contractual law was introduced to govern the conditions under which both Africans and Khoisan sold their labor-power to farmers.[17]

As in so many other aspects of rural capitalist development, the Cape may well have had a century's headstart on the rest of South Africa. Yet as Newton-King stressed, it is difficult to establish this "until more is known about the actual relations of exploitation." When, for example, did labor-power become a commodity for African workers *themselves*? When did most black patriarchs cease making contracts binding on all subordinates? When did they cease appropriating most of the remuneration as well? When and where were young African tenants victorious in their long and bitter struggle against the sale of their labor-power by elders? Not, apparently, in South Africa at large by the 1920s. Did this breakthrough occur only when patriarchs had lost complete access to pastures, and hence were unable to control youths through the provision of bridewealth?[18]

These questions have not yet been posed by many *bittereinders*, and an answer here is necessarily tentative. But tantalizing evidence exists that many African youths decisively broke the power of farm elders in the 1930s and 1940s, when their flight to the towns coincided with rapid industrial expansion. When the state's ruthless efforts to shanghai this influx to forced farm labor were also defeated, many youths were apparently increasingly free to sell their own labor-power (albeit only to agriculturalists.) Was this correlated with the "revolutionary changes" that officialdom perceived in the countryside after the Second World War? Was it linked to the uneven but systematic development of productive forces ably detailed by Tessa Marcus for the second half of the twentieth century? Arguably, yes: struggles of youths against the sale of their labor-power by elders helped usher in this new phase, this "specifically capitalist mode of production in its developed form."[19]

This extremely broad assertion remains, however, to be proven and given regional specificity. Moreover, it is still vital to ask that most basic of questions: "Who buys whose labour-power and under what conditions?" Thus, in the Transvaal in the late 1980s, black tenants seemed unaware that academics had declared the countryside capitalist. They steadily accumulated cattle, prized land occupied for generations, and used the urban wages of homestead members to pay other black youths to work for white farmers.[20] Small wonder that in a countryside where the buying of labor-power is partly the responsibility of African tenants, the *bittereinders* have doubted the extent of capitalist development.

Yet if transition cast its shadow far into the twentieth century, some criticisms of the *bittereinders* retain considerable force. For one thing, scholars who have dragged out this process for decades (if not centuries) have not always been sensitive to regional differentiation. For another, there are problems in insisting on complete dispossession of tenants, or in giving priority to politico-legal measures preventing a "free" labor market among blacks. Donald Denoon—while perhaps underestimating the controls of black elders over juniors—has trenchantly argued that by the mid-nineteenth century, "labour had become a commodity in exactly the same sense as any other commodity—which is to concede that employers could manipulate the labour market, but a market existed none the less."[21] Indeed, since agriculture was an extremely backward sector in a peripheral country, Martin Murray and Charles Post have contended that nascent capitalist farmers were forced "to demand to the unhindered circulation of labor-power . . . the so-called 'labor-repressive policies' were the sine qua non of capitalist production proper."[22]

In sum: tracing the route whereby and the extent to which women and men become obliged to sell their own labor-power, is crucial to understanding their struggles, the state, and the broader economy. But the delicate relationship between the development of labor-power as a commodity, and the phases in the transition to capitalism in a laggard sector of a late-developing country, has yet to be adequately calibrated. Ironically, perhaps, there are important insights in the work of historians impatient with endless theoretical discussions about the transformation of labor-power into a commodity.

Mapping the Route and Remaking the Roads

Setting [Marx's categories] to work has not involved only "testing" them or "verifying" them, it has also entailed revising and replacing them.

(E. P. Thompson, *The Poverty of Theory*, 258)

It may seem anomalous to describe the slave-owners as capitalists, though by any criterion other than the form of labour organisation they clearly were . . . from at least 1700 on.

> (R. Ross, "The First Two Centuries of
> Colonial Agriculture in the Cape,"
> *Social Dynamics*, 44–45)

Among radical South African scholars, a current hostile to "structuralism" began to flow in the late 1970s, under the gravitational pull of both domestic and external events. Struggle and consciousness were placed firmly on the academic agenda by the youth revolt of 1976, the intensification of popular resistance over the next decade, and the spectacular resurgence of the African National Congress. Simultaneously, numerous South Africanists in Britain were affected by intellectual battles waged while labor retreated and Thatcherism advanced. These were inauspicious times for the post-Althusserian Marxism that had been so influential. For some, E. P. Thompson's blistering attack on Althusser and his alleged acolytes such as Poulantzas underscored the limitations of studies written in this tradition. In addition, many scholars had found developments in non-materialist scholarship illuminating: Africanist influences were particularly important for many historians of preindustrial South Africa. Forged by these eclectic intellectual traditions, buttressed by dissatisfaction with earlier analyses, and sustained by the upsurge of resistance, social history thus emerged as a loosely defined school that straddled paradigms.[23]

How did these intellectual modulations affect agrarian scholarship? Significantly, interest in the *platteland* burgeoned (as did interest in other topics "hidden from history" by the earlier focus on urban workers, apartheid and men.) In 1978, Trapido assembled at Oxford a cluster of scholars working on rural transformations. Among them were William Beinart and Peter Delius, historians whose previous work on black polities was "perhaps more sensitive to African history than to the imperatives of capitalist accumulation, but was nonetheless concerned with a materialist interpretation of the past."[24] Together with Keegan, members of this research project were soon pioneering important new paths. In the 1980s, they were joined by a new generation of scholars, drawn to the agrarian sphere partly by the growing support it was receiving in both academic and civil society. From 1979, the Oral History Project at the University of the Witwatersrand was interviewing rural Africans and training black scholars; emerging trade unions and extra-parliamentary bodies were increasingly interested in organizing farm workers or defending their rights.

Within agrarian scholarship, the creation of a new tradition involved the consignment of "theoreticism" if not to the dustbin then at least to the backyard of history. Revisionists were no longer part of one radical school, wrote Keegan in 1981; there was little common ground between historians ("who work in the empirical mode") and others ("for whom 'theory' must be explicit, self-enclosed and pre-existent"). He perhaps overstated the case in claiming that a central characteristic of the "new history" was its "generally microscopic focus," but there were undoubtedly shifts in methodology, content, and discourse.[25] Oral evidence was creatively used to capture particularist experiences. Capital, the state, and the nation often formed merely the backdrop to localized struggles by ordinary people. And studies of "the development of agrarian capitalism in South Africa" were largely replaced by histories of "power and profit in the eastern Transvaal," or "pastures and pastoralism in the northern Cape frontier zone" or "the life story of Nkgono Mma-Pooe."

By the mid-1980s, this "'new school' of scholarship" had "gained hegemony in the field of rural relations." Its adherents insisted on the need to remap the past to allow for the "messy detours, confusing by-passes or older dirt tracks that social historians habitually stumble along"—and the backroads contained important revelations. The development of capitalist agriculture was a far less uniform process than previously postulated. There were regions, argued Beinart, where Africans recommunalized private property; there were times, noted Bundy, when hectic booms yielded to severe slumps. Transition also had a far longer history. On the one hand, scholars claimed that in the mid- or late nineteenth century, rural capitalists were thriving in certain districts of Natal, the Orange Free State, the Transvaal, and the Cape. On the other hand, contended Charles van Onselen, the 1940s was a particularly prosperous decade for black sharecroppers in the south-western Transvaal. Indeed, noted Malete Nkadimeng and Georgina Relly, the sharecropper Kas Maine had his most successful year immediately after the election of the apartheid regime.[26]

Undoubtedly, many scholars were not primarily analyzing phases in the transition to capitalism. (For Beinart and Delius this was a distinct advantage: they advocated instead the use of "the concept of capitalist relations as a heuristic device in attempting to illuminate a process of transformation.") Nonetheless, these histories often vastly increased knowledge of the extraordinarily tangled processes which led to the emergence of capitalist relations of production, at a differential speed, in a regionally specific fashion. In addition, many scholars were implicitly reaffirming what Brenner termed the key to transition: the reaffirmation or destruction of old property relations through "protracted struggle on a piecemeal village-by-village basis." If this was in broad agreement with Morris's "class struggle as the motor of history," it was also considerably more sensitive to culture, subjectivity and local economies.[27]

But the practitioners of the new social history did far more than write rich studies which could be accommodated—with more or less difficulty—by earlier frameworks. Sensitivity to historical specificity also called into question the categories through which transition had previously been opaquely perceived. Since "large" statements were for the most part abjured by social historians, these reformulations were often allusive, and the thrust of an immanent argument emerges only from a close reading of detailed regional studies. A good example is the cumulative challenge to the widely held notion of "feudalism," and the retention of feudal relics in the lumber-room of agrarian relations.

Consider, for instance, the historiographical realignments in work on the nineteenth-century Transvaal. In the course of a decade, "feudalism" was written out of the drama, while either capital or capitalism strode much earlier onto the stage. In 1976, in a key article on transition, van Onselen noted that the Transvaal of the mid-nineteenth century had a "quasi-feudal mode of production." Between the 1870s and 1880s, however, a powerful rural bourgeoisie allegedly emerged. In 1979, Shula Marks and Stanley Trapido extended this argument by abandoning "feudalism" and introducing capitalism: individual Boers were in transition from an "earlier agrarian mode of production" toward an "individualistic form of capitalism." In 1983, Denoon went much further in discarding precapitalist notions: "The transitions which did occur were not from feudalism to capitalism, but from frontier capitalism to more settled and intensive production." Finally, in 1986, Beinart and Delius consolidated the trend with a sustained critique. Semi-feudalism was inappropriate as a characterization of the preindustrial farmlands of the interior, they argued; in South Africa at large, the trend toward capitalist production "was not one which could convincingly be described as a transition from feudalism."[28]

Why not? Beinart and Delius concentrated mainly on undermining Morris's arguments, and on contesting the connotations which "feudalism" had acquired from underdevelopment theory. To exorcise the feudalist ghost—and to put flesh on ill-defined frontier capitalism—they might have invoked more preindustrial history, drawing not least on their own work. For one thing, in the Cape, in Natal, and in the Free State, nineteenth-century British colonial states made far-reaching attempts to make "South Africa safe for British settlement and capital investment." For another, for centuries, Cape rulers, merchants, and money-lenders played key roles in the long history of primitive accumulation. By transforming land into a commodity, and by facilitating concentration of this vital means of production in ever fewer hands, they were establishing a crucial precondition for capitalist agrarian production, a potent solvent of precapitalist relations, and a key contra-indication of "feudalism."[29]

If "quasi-feudalism" could accommodate a land market, its elasticity was stretched to breaking point by the nature of the societies established outside the Cape during the nineteenth century. Scholars increasingly revealed that these were regions which, in an era subsequent to the emergence of capitalism in Europe, were colonized by white pastoralist conquistadors, wracked by repeated clashes between white and black polities, ruled intermittently by Britain, and reshaped by merchant capital. How was surplus labor appropriated from peasants by noncapitalists under these conditions? With great difficulty, scholars suggest. In the mid-nineteenth-century Transvaal, for example, Delius argued that there was no "notion of property to which all the parties subscribed," and tenants were often extremely recalcitrant. In the late nineteenth century, Trapido noted that the labor loads of young African males were light (they averaged perhaps fifteen days a year before 1900), and that farmers constantly complained: "These natives are not under supervision and do exactly as they like!" As long as black polities had not been defeated and dispossessed, and as long as vast tracts of land were held by rentier and speculative capital, brute force could not defeat tenants' "wanderlust." Understandably, arable production left primarily in the hands of black tenants was always of minor or negligible importance to the mass of pastoralist Boers.[30]

What of the ruling classes in the Boer republics? They "arose on the back of merchant capital," but pursued interests "which were not reducible to the merchant capital that had spawned them," argued Keegan. His claim that land speculation, trade, and looting were far more important than the appropriation of surplus labor from servants was reinforced by Delius's study of a Transvaal notable. Abel Erasmus clawed his way to the realms of wealth by raiding, trading, and hunting, by speculating in land and servicing productive capital, by the coercion and corruption that greased the careers of so many salaried state officials—not primarily by exploiting tenants on his farms. No dominant class of feudal landlords could arise through the extraction of surplus labor from black peasants—who dwelt on private property from which they could move. Nor did any nineteenth-century state give priority to the interests of those who would turn tenants into "an appendage of the soil, exactly like draught cattle."[31]

If feudalism did not exist in the past, its relics could not be transmitted to the future. Why, then, have so many scholars perceived racist Boers lugging their feudal baggage into the twentieth century? Because, suggests the work of social historians, such observers have a unilinear and often liberal view of history. In fact, seemingly medieval relations of exploitation, and racist relations of oppression, were created and institutionalized in the same struggles that culminated in the conquest of capitalism.

Thus in the mid-nineteenth century, argued Keegan, "the Boers' 'baasskap' over their servants was very localized and limited."

> The most isolated of the Boers, those in the eastern or northern Transvaal, for all their slaving and raiding activities, continued to be a far less intrusive, disruptive presence in the social environment than were the capitalist accumulators (whether Boer or British) of the Cape Colony and the Orange Free State. . . .[32]

Moreover, the *metayage* that some have perceived in a later period emerged alongside the investment of capital in land and the entrenchment of private property. It was created as merchants clamored for arable produce, and as Africans resisted dispossession. In the *highveld*, this relatively free tenantry reached its high water mark in the decade after the turn of the century. "Far from being a 'quasi-feudal' relationship associated with the precapitalist past," sharecropping was a product of capital penetration and an industrial revolution. Far from systematic racial domination being forged in this crucible, argued van Onselen, relations between "badly under-capitalised white landlords and marginally better-off black farmers" helped generate "social equality . . . in everything but name."[33]

Yet as the sharecropper Kas Maine laconically observed, when whites "were poor we got on well," but "rich whites tried to pull you down." Indeed—and "rich whites" were deeply implicated in the creation of "black serfs." First, merchants and money-lenders were not only central in transforming land into a commodity; by forcing many farmers to pay dearly for access to this crucial means of production, they also indirectly shaped relations of exploitation. In the nineteenth-century Cape, land purchases was often upon "capital borrowed at the rate of six, or perhaps eight per cent interest; which presses as a dead weight upon the new possessor, probably for half his lifetime."[34]

But it was largely black labourers, not white landlords, who were crushed by this dead weight of nonproductive capital. In the *highveld* around the turn of the century, argued Keegan, black tenants shouldered the burden of white landlords vulnerable to land loss, in a period "when more and more private capital was seeking lucrative investment in the land against mortgage bonds, when mercantile credit was easily obtainable." Similarly, if labor tenants of the 1920s were commonly subjected to relationships which "violated almost every norm of capitalist exploitation," most farmers were "manacled hand and foot by the chains of debt" to money-lenders and merchants, and struggling to survive an international agricultural depression. Far from being transmitted from the past, "cruder serf forms of exploitation" often emerged as traders and usurers tightened their stranglehold over an extremely backward sector that was being incorporated into a world economy.[35]

Rich capitalist accumulators penetrated and transformed as well as encircled and stifled agriculture. Whether in the Cape of the late eighteenth century, or the frontier districts of the mid- or late nineteenth century, or the *highveld* region of the early twentieth century, or South Africa at large in the 1920s, a highly significant pattern is now visible. The leading rural capitalists, as Keegan most forcibly argued, derived from "men who made their money in mining or mercantile enterprise or in speculation." As regions were colonized, suggested Beinart, Ross, and Tony Kirk, traders in goods and land were particularly prominent among white farmers. By the early twentieth century, however, regular prize-winners at agricultural shows "included such representatives of finance capital as Sir George Farrar, De Beers Consolidated Mines, the Smartt Syndicate, as well as big merchant firms."[36]

Undoubtedly, some of these "check-book" agriculturalists were primarily concerned with conspicuous consumption. Clearly, as Trapido has shown in an illuminating study, corporate capital could extract profits from sharecroppers. But, suggested Beinart and Robert Morrell, farmers who derived from or were linked to more advanced capitalist sectors often experienced older relations of exploitation as fetters on further accumulation. Particularly in periods of economic boom or acute labor shortage, these "progressive" farmers headed the drive to recruit migrants, evict tenants, hew black and white peasants into labor tenants, and grind labor tenants into workers.[37]

All too frequently, they were confronted by resistance, thwarted by incomplete primitive accumulation, and frustrated by competition from other capitalists. Hence they tried to shackle with extra-economic chains their putative laborers who either clung to the land or fled to the towns. Bundy, Ross and Maureen Swan have shown how, in the nineteenth-century Cape and Natal, white, African, Khoisan, and Indian farm laborers were bound by long indentures, subject to criminal penalties for breach of contract, and harshly restricted in their mobility. In the first half of the twentieth century, the noose was drawn so tight around the necks of African tenants that some prayed for "freedom as under the old Boer Republic." Their preference for the past was understandable. In the 1910s, "farmers with substantial capital" evicted sharecroppers under the notorious 1913 Land Act. In the 1920s, "progressive" English-speaking landlords demanded that black children under sixteen "be compelled to work at any time they were wanted by their masters." In the 1930s and 1940s, Lithuanians who were "as much businessmen as agriculturalists" transformed Bethal into one of the most infamous and advanced capitalist districts in South Africa. In short, wealthy, English-speaking capitalists— not struggling Boers rooted in a feudal past—were still in the vanguard of those creating black serfs".[38]

What, then, has the cumulative work of scholars influenced by social history suggested about the development of capitalism? First, it appears more productive to explore the emergence of (still vaguely defined) frontier capitalism than to trace the dissolution of feudal orders. Second, traders, usurers, and ruling classes played a fundamental role in the transition. Third, rural capitalists emerged much earlier than previous accounts allowed. Fourth—as Murray and Post had contended, and as Morris had argued for a later period—"quasi-feudal" relations of exploitation, and racist relations of oppression, were created in the very course of capitalist penetration. Fifth, regionally specific struggles lay at the very heart of transition.

If these are major contributions to understanding the development of capitalism, this body of work has not escaped critical scrutiny. Much has been made of its particularist and anti-theoretical stance. Its materialist credentials have also been questioned—not least by the doyen of Afrikaner nationalist historians, who welcomed the retreat from *dogmatiese Marxisme* to *moderne sociale* scholarship. More accurately: social history became hegemonic at precisely the time its practitioners were jettisoning structuralist categories, opposing theoreticist quibbles, and encouraging the reworking of categories in the light of evidence. Consequently, while many materialist precepts and concepts have been incorporated, these "abstractions" have, in Keegan's words, "become much more fluid and sometimes dissolve[d] completely."[39]

While the liquidation of feudal formulations was welcome, the dissolution of materialist concepts relating to capitalist development has yet to prove its utility. Consider, for example, the influential writings of Robert Ross, who offered the most significant challenge to prevailing periodizations of the development of agrarian capitalism. In his view, the Cape was occupied in 1652 by the Dutch East India Company, "the premier capitalist organisation of the time." Since agrarian capitalism meant "the production of cash crops on a fairly extensive scale under the immediate control of the landowner or his representative," slave-owning wine and wheat farmers were capitalists from "at least 1700 on." The emancipation of slaves, and the abolition of forced labor among the Khoisan, "were non-events": rural class relations remained "more or less constant." Much more momentous was the fate of nomadic white pastoralists: during the eighteenth century they were "drawn, willingly, into the orbit of commercial capitalism." Moreover, by the 1860s, the majority of farm laborers in most of the Cape were alienated from "the means of production. In other words, they were proletarianized." Finally, since most whites lived in the Cape, "the majority of those parts of the rural areas dominated by settlers were unmistakably capitalist in character" before the mineral discoveries.[40]

For Marxists, this account of transition will not do. There is, as Jeremy Krikler tartly noted, "utter confusion of commercialization with capitalism."[41] But more seriously for scholars of transition, Ross's theoretical insouciance—the frequent reduction of labor relations to insignificant details, the privileging of relations of exchange over relations of production, the belief that "commercial capitalism" has meaning, the disregard for the distinction between dispossession and proletarianization—has deeply impoverished his history. Undoubtedly, his work contains fascinating information about merchants in the eighteenth- and nineteenth-century Cape, who were investing in land, establishing huge estates, entangling farmers in debt, dominating wool farming, and transforming ever more use-values into commodities. Yet for those who agree with Ross that the roots of capitalism stretched far back into the past, there are enormously frustrating silences in accounts which find few significant differences between slaves and proletarians, slaveholders and capitalists, the mercantilist Dutch East India Company and the British colonial state. For those who would trace why the form in which surplus labor was appropriated changed, there are few gleanings in studies centered around proving that slaveowners and pastoralists were commercially minded.

If Ross excelled in giving new and unhelpful meaning to terms that Marxists have thus far found useful in analyzing transition, he was far from alone. Idiosyncratic or allusive usages of such key categories as "profit" and "bourgeoisie" abound. Consequently, it is often extremely difficult to perceive when rural capitalists emerged. In addition, scholars all too often used "capital" in the timeless neoclassical rather than historically specific Marxist sense. Thus Keegan—like so many others—embraced all means of production under the term; he claimed that "ownership of a wagon and oxen was as important as a gun and ammunition in the accumulation of capital amongst Boers"; he argued that peasants accumulated "capital, which took the form largely of cattle owner-ship." How tenable are histories of capitalist development that decline to distinguish capital from a cow? For Marx, at least, writings which committed the elementary "folly of identifying a specific *social relationship of production*" with material resources were "superficial rubbish." They obfuscate the distinction between different historical epochs; they imply that capital existed in the Dark Ages and will, like the poor, be with us forever.[42]

Small wonder that some have cried out in frustration when surveying the work of scholars influenced by the hegemony of social history. According to Krikler, the work of many rural historians of the 1980s "is vitiated by a conceptual confusion and evasion which prevents its reader from achieving any clear sense of the development of capitalism in rural South Africa." Or as Morris roundly declared, "We have witnessed a headlong flight, under the banner of social history, into empiricism and away from Marxist concepts, categories and explanation." The central theoretical issues relating to the development of rural capitalism, he contended, "cannot be resolved unless one moves beyond the empirically rich but conceptually poverty-stricken work of the new agrarian social historians."[43]

If Morris's judgement was overharsh, he was far from alone in expressing unease about the prevalent abuse of materialist tenets and categories. Newton-King has sounded "an urgent note of caution" against misuse by some scholars of "primitive accumulation." Keegan has recently acknowledged that "the conceptual inadequacies of past work (my own included) must be the starting point" from which new beginnings are made. And van Onselen "would draw a very radical distinction between Marxist social historians and non-Marxist social historians." For "a lot of people," he maintained, social history had become uncoupled from "relations of production, instruments and tools of production, and the way that they are appropriated by certain groups, the way that they struggled about them." Clearly, those who would defend the role of Marxist theory in history have allies as well as enemies on the other side of intellectual barricades.[44]

Conclusion

What, then, has been established about the development of rural capitalism? A great deal, in my opinion. First, it is impossible to cram the transition to capitalism into forty odd years after the mineral discoveries, and unhelpful to postulate that it emerged from feudalism. If there was any "road" to rural capitalism, it was the "merchant road"; if there are any Marxist writings that provide insights, they are those on the penetration of agriculture by capital from "the outside." Commerce, finance, and mining ruled agriculture internally and externally—and it was this, rather than the "Prussian path," that made for a reactionary, conservative route to capitalism which for decades "simply worsen[ed] the conditions of the direct producers."[45]

Second, the transition to capitalism was not the corollary of the establishment of internal markets as so many scholars once assumed. Labor-power still had to become a commodity, and this involved bitter conflicts which may well have taken an uneven cyclical form. If local outcomes were unpredictable, the overall trend is clear. Far from the dissolution of feudalism giving rise to capitalism, the penetration of capital spawned "feudal" relations of exploitation and oppression.

Third, these were regionally specific struggles critically influenced by the nature of the state. There are many indications that capitalism rapidly became relatively well entrenched in the wine and wheat sectors of the south-western Cape after slavery was abolished from above. There are numerous pointers to the increasingly capitalist nature of wool and sugar production in the nineteenth century. But there are few signs that capitalism had been consolidated—especially in the crucial maize sector—in the rest of the country by the 1920s. If the state of this period favored industry and struggling landlords over rural capitalists; if the vast majority of farmers kept almost no records and were utterly unable to calculate profit rates; if many did not control all the implements and oxen needed for plowing and sowing; if promises of land were the single most important factor that allowed a black nationalist movement to storm the countryside—then the long march to capitalism was not yet over in the heartland of rural South Africa.[46]

Nor is its analysis yet near completion. Key areas, such as the nature of Boers' "earlier agrarian mode of production," have been relatively neglected. Although there are fascinating insights in Keegan's work, there is no systematic account of which instruments of labor were acquired when, let alone a history that accords contradictions between relations and forces of production a central place. There are also frustratingly few analyses of whether, and when, farmers sought subsistence, or conspicuous consumption, or profits (although Trapido's work is an outstanding exception). In addition, many agrarian studies cry out for a gender-sensitive reinterpretation. If control over the productive and reproductive powers of females was crucial in precapitalist African polities, how did the struggles of women help undermine patriarchs? If the largest single category of slaves in the 1830s was "inferior domestics," how many of the laborers bloodily acquired thereafter were directed into household production rather than the male domain of agriculture?

The tasks are many—and the laborers are few. Moreover, some may retreat from a field so infused with polemics and passion. "Anyone entering the study of South African agrarian history," commented an apprehensive British student newly arrived in the country, "needs at least a thick skin and preferably armour plating."[47] She also needs the knowledge that much larger contemporary struggles are finding faint echo on journal pages.

It is not simply a question of "structuralists versus social historians." This obfuscates fundamental divisions among social historians; it also obscures urgent political issues underpinning the clash. Historical details are not unimportant—at a time when activists are reshaping dogma in the light of evidence. Theory is not an abstract concept—when hundreds have paid with their lives for attempting to overthrow the state through populist politics. And Marxism is not an academic issue—when major sectors of the labour movement are battling to assert "the hegemony of the working class" in the struggle for a democratic future. It does not detract from the agrarian debate to suggest that it reflects broader political conflicts—over tactics, strategies, and the social lineaments of post-apartheid South Africa.

Chapter 4 / The Politics of Black Squatter Movements on the Rand, 1944–1952

Philip Bonner

History Workshop

Sofasonke Village.

Belinda Bozzoli, *Town and Countryside in the Transvaal* (Johannesburg: Ravan, 1983)

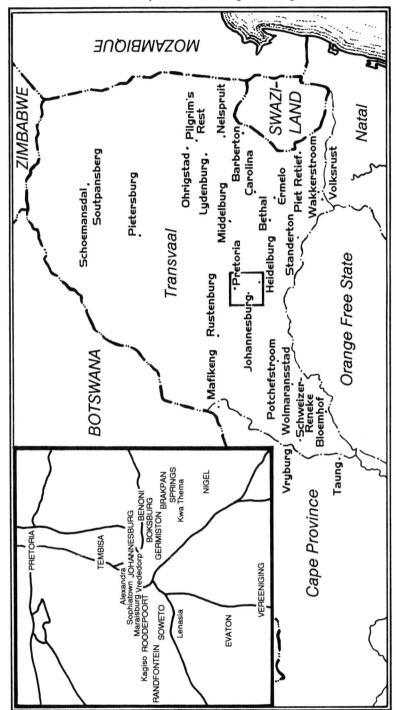

Studies of black urbanization in South Africa have tended to focus on the larger forces impelling African families off the land, on the evolution of state policies of regulation and control, and on the politics and culture of more permanent black communities. Much less well-known and re-searched are the politics of migrant workers in the cities, and of those communities in the process of becoming urban, particularly squatter so-cieties on the fringes of towns. Even where the importance of the latter has been recognized, there has still been a tendency to equate black ur-ban squatting with organized squatter movements and communities like the Orlando squatters outside Johannesburg in 1944 and 1946, the Cato Manor settlement outside Durban in the mid 1940s, and the Crossroads squatter camp outside Cape Town in the 1970s and early 1980s, so that once these have been removed or suppressed, the issue of squatting is deemed to have disappeared.[1] Yet such organized squatter camps have merely been the high points, the most visible concerted expressions of what has been an almost continuous phenomenon of massive propor-tions from the beginning of the century to the present.

Between the 1890s and the 1910s, unregulated squatter shanties sprang up on mining land all along the Rand. Toward the end of the first decade of the 1900s these were broken up and reconstituted into urban locations. The so-called problem seemed briefly to have been brought under control but it soon re-emerged. In 1919, the post-World War I government instituted a new form of land tenure, in the shape of small-holdings around the main towns of the Rand, to provide a kind of pen-sion for ex-miners and other members of the white working class and to help defuse white working class militancy. Instead of breeding a con-tented white citizenry and providing dairy products for the towns, this land quickly became one of the major sites of black urban residence. Tens of thousands of black workers, and eventually hundreds of thousands, found homes in these areas, living in small clusters of shacks on innumerable plots.[2]

In the 1950s, government efforts succeeded in clearing most of these peri-urban squatting communities. But, contrary to the image of the apartheid state as brutally efficient, its success in keeping these areas clear was short-lived. In the 1960s, the freeze on the provision of black housing and the surge of industrial production meant that squatter shanties again made their appearance by the end of the decade.[3] Over the past twenty years they have grown in solidity and size, so that the latest estimate of the combined populations is in excess of four million.

These peri-urban squatter communities, which have been such a substantial and enduring feature of black urban life, have left their own lasting imprint on black urban society. The politics of certain areas of Soweto—Naledi, Phiri, Mapetla—for example, still display their own distinct characteristics in response to this bequest. Likewise, even now, the peri-urban settlements around Cape Town, Pietermaritzburg, and Durban seem to reproduce much of the characteristic cluster of political practices and core components of political culture that other squatter communities have generated in the past.[4] A close examination of the past may thus serve at least partially to illuminate the present. The slice selected for this study is the squatter movement that sprang up on the Rand in the mid and late 1940s and foreshadowed the birth of today's massive African townships on the Rand.

The Second Great Trek

The squatter movements on the Rand trace their origins to the structural changes taking place during the 1920s in the white farming areas of the Orange Free State and Transvaal. The black labor tenantry which lived in these areas was exploited more harshly and ruthlessly by capitalizing and increasingly sub-divided struggling white farmers. The brief explosion of resistance from rural farm workers led by the Industrial and Commercial Workers' Union (ICU) was one expression of this pressure. Emigration to the towns and the city fringes was another. As early as 1927, G. Ballenden, the Non-European Affairs Manager for Johannesburg, complained of six hundred black families streaming into Johannesburg each year, and it is highly probable that the great bulk of these were fleeing from the farms. Certainly, the greater proportion of immigrants arriving in Brakpan at the time were coming from Transvaal farms. Under the impact of a devastating drought which gripped the whole of

South Africa in 1932–23, this exodus gathered force, augmented by increasing numbers from the African reserves whose economies were also cracking in this period of stress.[5]

Every town in South Africa recorded a massive increase in its black population in this period, a growing proportion of which comprised women and juveniles. Between 1926 and 1936 Johannesburg's black population increased by 40 percent. The percentage increase of black women on the Witwatersrand towns in the 1920s ranged from 58.6 percent in Brakpan to 158.6 percent in Germiston. This sudden influx into the towns placed a great strain on available resources, particularly housing and stretched the assimilative capacities of urban culture to its limits.[6]

The stagnant employment market in the towns acted as a limited disincentive to emigration in the 1920s and early 1930s, and helped put a brake on the flow. However, as Martin Legassick and Harold Wolpe have suggested, an increasingly large latent surplus population was being dammed up in the rural areas of South Africa awaiting the opportunity to break out. Its chance came with the sustained expansion of the South African economy following South Africa's departure from the gold standard in 1933. The new revenues accruing to the gold mining industry and government promoted a dramatic surge forward in manufacturing and the creation of countless new jobs. The outbreak of the Second World War accelerated the trend. The numbers of factories in South Africa grew from 6,543 in 1933 to 9,999 in 1946. The black urban population of Johannesburg rose from 229,122 in 1936 to 384,628 in 1948.[7]

The flood of immigrants to the towns changed the face of black urban life. The municipalities initially reacted by attempting to impose a tighter system of permits on women and lodgers. In response, new types of black political organizations began to be formed in the shape of Vigilance Associations and Tenants' Leagues, often loosely linked to the Communist Party of South Africa (CPSA). Little is known about their activities or the political culture to which they gave expression. All that is clear is that under their aegis the mass meeting became an increasingly popular form of political expression.[8] The surge of immigration to the towns also brought new frictions to black urban society. Since virtually no new housing was built for blacks in this period a large proportion of new arrivals found accommodation as sub-tenants in the houses or back yards of the established black urban dwellers. With so many people crammed into such a small space, interpersonal and familial tensions became acute, and with space at such a premium, rack-renting and cavalier treatment of tenants by landlords also became common. The earlier communal spirit consequently began to break down and to be replaced by class animosities between the long established city folk and the new arrivals in the towns.

The alternative to seeking sub-tenancies in the towns was to squat on white small-holdings in the peri-urban areas. This took place on a vast scale until the land surrounding the main urban areas, both on the Reef and around South Africa's other main towns, became like one huge residential sponge. In Brakpan alone, on the far east end of the Rand, a population of between 9,000 and 12,000 Africans lived on the small-holdings, a figure which swelled to 23,000 by the late 1950s. Even greater numbers lived on the fringes of Johannesburg and Benoni and it is probable that a population of close to 100,000 people, who had only a limited exposure to black urban culture, lived on the urban outskirts by the latter stages of the war.[9]

In these congested and increasingly unhygienic black dwelling areas, frustrations and tensions progressively built up. They finally erupted toward the end of the war in a succession of squatter movements that spread across the length and breadth of the Rand. These were organized by grassroots community leaders who, having mobilized a following, organized invasions of what was usually municipally-owned land. Here they established rudimentary administrations for the newly formed squatter settlements, which in most cases were subsequently taken over or removed to municipally controlled "emergency" or squatter camps. The most important of these were set up around Johannesburg and Benoni, beginning with the squatter movements of James "Sofasonke" Mpanza in Johannesburg and Harry Mabuya in Benoni, in April 1944 and December 1945 respectively. These were followed by further squatter movements led by Edward Khumalo and Abel Ntoi near Johannesburg's black township of Orlando in 1946, and then by a spate of lesser movements in Johannesburg and Alexandra led by Oriel Monongoaha, Samuel Kgoma, and Schreiner Baduza, until by the end of the year, 63,000 people were living in Johannesburg's squatter camps alone. At this point the squatter movement paused for a while until it gave its last convulsive shudder in the huge squatter movement to Apex near Benoni in July 1950.[10]

These squatter movements are important for a number of reasons. They signal both the birth of South Africa's modern urban townships and the industrial proletariat they house. They also spawned a distinctive political culture and set of political practices—for the first time since the very beginnings of the Rand, people characterized by a very transitional migrant culture were concentrated together and not immediately assimilable to the urban culture which the older townships had helped form. The political culture of squatter movements persisted in one form or another to the 1970s and even beyond. It also lives on, in grotesquely parodied form, in many of the squatter shanties which have developed in various parts of South Africa in recent years. For this reason alone its origins seem worthy of attention. The squatter communities which sprang up in the mid to late 1940s varied widely depending on the place and time in which they were established, their occupational and ethnic composition, and the origins of their leadership groups. The politics of these settlements did, nevertheless, share a number of common features which developed from the common problems they all faced. The most obvious of these was the creation and protection of pockets of illegal space on which shack communities could be built. However, the squatter communities were also beset by a number of other deep-seated social problems which the squatter leaders could only ignore at their political cost. Foremost among these were crime, uncontrolled youth, family instability, and social disorder, which the squatter leaderships all addressed in comparatively similar ways. The common denominator of each of these social malaises was material deprivation, and this again the squatter leaders made various efforts to allay. One means was the collective provision of basic resources. Another was to permit or promote the activities of petty entrepreneurs who were thus temporarily free of official regulation and control. Each of these activities imparted its own particular dynamics to squatter politics.

The squatter communities of the late 1940s were comprised of groups of highly heterogeneous composition. The records for the Tent Town squatter camp in Benoni, for example, reveal that inhabitants originated from all over South Africa and had seldom been born on the Witwatersrand or spent much time in the town. The same was true of all of the squatter camps established at this time. Their inhabitants also came from the poorest sections of the urban population having spent at least the last few years of the their lives in a ceaseless quest for security and shelter. When the Alberton squatter camp was established in 1944, for example, it immediately attracted residents from Nigel, Benoni, Evaton, Meyerton and the peri-urban areas of Johannesburg. When the Apex camp was founded in 1950, it drew a flood of workers from New Kleinfontein and neighboring mines.[11]

The dominant picture that emerges is one of people ceaselessly on the move in the hope of finding some urban niche or marginally improving their economic position. This fostered a variety of social discords and strains, the most pervasive of which was marital instability. Although the

Johannesburg city council had been apprehensively noting the movement of whole families to the city, from the late 1920s, and particularly
after 1941, the majority of male migrants still came to town by themselves. As the opportunities for employment in industry multiplied,
many stayed for longer and longer periods in the towns, neglecting or
even abandoning their wives on the farms and reserves. Many women
responded by migrating to the towns, either in search of their husbands
or to carve out a life for themselves. The new unions which men and
women formed in these circumstances were often transient and unstable.
In 1946, a not entirely unprejudiced chief social worker for Orlando
location complained of the camps:

> Men jilt their wives to go to the squatter camps. Children run away to
> it. Family life is disrupted in every way. Skokiaan queens and section
> 29s all find refuge among them.[12]

The controlled squatter camps produced different kinds of rifts. To
secure a place in a municipally controlled squatter camp a man or women
had to be living "in married circumstances" to use the official parlance of
the time. As Brigadier Palmer, of Johannesburg's South African Police,
observed, this encouraged "many male natives [to] pick up any odd
woman" in order to successfully squat, and the same observation was
made by most other Rand municipalities.[13] For women this incredibly
fluid environment presented both opportunities and costs. The presence
of large numbers of single male workers allowed them the opportunity to
change partners and offered more independence than most had previously enjoyed. Conversely, it also left them vulnerable to desertion by
established husbands and spouses of convenience. And, without a man,
a woman was particularly unprotected. As the sociologist Laura Longmore noted at the time, "a home without a husband is defenseless in the
townships."[14]

Poverty, migrancy, and the quest for security thus wrought havoc
with family life, and generated not only a deep-seated insecurity but unprecedented scope for social and familial conflict. The search for patrons
and protectors often led women to the doorsteps of the squatter leaders
and their lieutenants in the camps. The squatter leadership thus willy
nilly found thrust upon them a social regulatory role, which required
adjudicating domestic and neighborhood disputes, and ultimately establishing their own courts. This dual role of providing houses and a measure of security and protection ensured the squatter leaders of intensely
powerful support from women. Squatter leaders were hailed as saviors
and cast in the mold of Old Testament prophets. The response of the

women leaders at the Tent Town squatter camp in Benoni to its founder Harry Mabuya, can be taken as typical: "He was our Moses," said Ma-Ntlokwane, "He was like a priest."[15] The social adjudicatory role of squatter leaders was not confined simply to marital disputes. The diverse and impoverished character of the camps meant that problems of crime and social order were always a potential menace. Johanna Mahwaya, who moved from Orlando squatter camp (called Masakeng, or place of sacks—the materials used to build the shacks) to Pimville location and thence to Newlook squatter camp before being finally allocated a site to build a shack by the municipality in Chiawelo (a Soweto suburb), re-called the constant problem of theft among the shack dwellers of Pimville location: "You could not leave your room and go to the toilet without locking it." Squatter shacks made of sacks, corrugated iron and card-board" were likewise easy targets for thieves.[16]

Juvenile delinquents and youth gangs were one of the principal agents of crime. The shortage of schools (there were places for only 3,661 out of a school age population of 15,088 in Moroka East in 1951), the absence of employment opportunities for youth, and the general instabil-ity of family life encouraged juvenile delinquency and crime. Through the mid to late 1940s, a mounting chorus of complaint made itself heard in all the Rand townships about this growing social menace, culminating in a combined protest by the Joint Advisory Boards of the Orlando/Jabuva/Moroka (i.e. Soweto) locations about the "reign of terror, whether in the house [or] in the street, in the train or the bus, or whether in day time or by night time."[17]

To cope with these problems, squatter leaders undertook some rudi-mentary policing: Mpanza, for example, employed twenty police by 1944, set up his own courts and meted out punishments. Municipal officials stigmatized these efforts as intimidation, extortion, and coercion but evidence suggests that these brief periods of self-rule in the camps were more free of crime than any period before or since. Mr. Sek-hukhune recalls of Mpanza's Shantytown "You know . . . when we came home from work sometimes our shacks were destroyed by the wind, but your pot and blankets were still there."[18]

Social policing was required in other areas as well. Even the most elementary of resources could become centers of conflict when they were scarce. In September 1946, Abel Ntoi, leader of the Pimville squat-ter movement, complained of "the constant squabbles in the drawing of water by women" and the "frequent violences at the tap." Lack of food, shelter, and other resources could likewise spark off squatter feuds.[19] Some squatter leaders regulated these scarce resources while others went further and attempted to supply basic services, normally the responsibility of local authorities. During the Second World War, food, fuel, building materials, and many other basic necessities were in desperately short supply. Black markets flourished and the poor, in their vulnerable positions, often had to pay the highest prices of all. The CPSA briefly addressed this problem by attempting to monitor black-marketeering and to set up food committees. Mpanza attacked the problem in a more ambitious fashion, drawing on a model of economic and political action that the black middle class and some other sections of the black population had long clutched to its bosom—the cooperative. At the founding of Sofazonke township, Mpanza established a cooperative comprised of Sofazonke members which bought key commodities like maize, coal, sugar, and meat in bulk and sold them through a network of depots at something like cost price. The cooperatives also sold sacking and wooden poles for the shanties. Benoni's Tent Town leader, Harry Mabuya, operated on similar lines, supplying in this case not only tents but also bricks and other building supplies to build slightly more substantial homes.[20]

Those squatter camps which were able to survive for longer periods free of municipal control, established more sophisticated structures. Edward Khumalo's squatter committee in the peri-urban area of Albertynsville supplied water, pit latrines, and a school for over six hundred children at which twelve teachers taught. As a municipal officer's report admitted in May 1950, the neat and orderly rows of houses in this squatter camp belied any notion that it could unproblematically be labelled "uncontrolled."[21]

Undertaking facilities, an additional service offered by camp leaderships remind us of the persistent proximity of poverty and disease. Sickness and death were constant companions at the camps. Sacks and cardboard offered little protection against the elements and exposed the camps' inhabitants to hazards and ill-health. Fires could easily engulf whole sections of the camps, while any freak climatic change could place them at serious risk. Even fairly unexceptional weather conditions could bring misery to the camps. Mrs. Moteka of Mapetla recalls of Mpanza's Shantytown:

> When it was raining we all got wet. I remember one night it rained very heavily and when we woke up my child was almost covered in water.[22]

As this testimony suggests, children were particularly vulnerable to the primitive conditions in the camps. Infant mortality rose sharply during the Second World War as conditions worsened with overcrowding; one of the striking features about many oral testimonies of people living through these times are the number of children in the informants' families who failed to survive.

The capricious visitations of death and disease led many inhabitants of the camps to seek some kind of insurance. Again, it was up to the squatter leader to fill this gap in social services. According to a member of Mpanza's shantytown committee, "when a person died we gave the family £1 and a coffin" (made by the camp's commissioned carpenter). In Tobruk "all the people who died had had decent coffins and good funerals" provided by Kgoma's camp committee. Both Mabuya and Madingoane, in Benoni's Tent Town and Apex camps respectively, ran undertaker businesses. Other forms of insurance and protection were also sought from faith-healing sects and the practitioners of traditional medicine, who assumed an influential role in the life of the camps.[23]

The last service that the squatter leaders provided was in a sense the obverse of the others so far discussed: holding official policing at bay. In municipal locations, a host of regulations either limited or prohibited a range of formal or informal trading activities. Prospective entrepreneurs had to show evidence of substantial capital and subservience to the authorities before he or she was allowed to lease premises for a business or a shop; as a result, the numbers of licensed traders in the locations were always small.[24] The informal trading and hawking in which many economically marginal women sought to engage was likewise tightly restricted, and the selling of home-brewed beer or indeed any other liquor was completely prohibited and the target of repeated police raids. The squatter camps thus became a haven for scores of frustrated entrepreneurs and hundreds of women who relied on hawking or brewing in order to survive. In Mpanza's shantytown, traders could buy licenses for sums of up to £25 and thereafter remain free to do as they liked. Moreover, no restriction was placed on the number of traders so long as they paid their camp dues. An estimated one hundred traders thus operated in Tobruk, a further 40 in Khumalo's Albertynsville camp, and 26 in Mabuya's Tent Town (and the same was almost certainly true of the other shorter-lived camps).[25] Illicit brewing was likewise rampant in most other squatter settlements although both Mpanza and Edward Khumalo made efforts to limit the scale of this trade.

The possibility for self-employment and capital accumulation was one of the principal attractions of the camps. It was also at the root of the authorities' alarm: while they framed their objections to the squatter settlements principally in terms of health considerations, the ultimate source of their disquiet was the existence of hundreds of people, many of them members of the formal or informal camp leaderships, who were living outside of the discipline of wage employment and council control.

Squatter settlements helped create a spirit of independence and insubordination which the authorities subsequently found difficult to suppress. Vindication of the council's fears came in August 1947 when the coincidence of an apparently discriminatory allocation of trading licenses, and a wave of police raids for beer brewing in the municipally-controlled camp of Moroka triggered a major riot in which local inhabitants looted licensed shops and attacked the police, three of whom were killed. This incident did not put an end to illegal trading. As Johannesburg's Town Clerk Porter complained to the Minister of Native Affairs in 1948, the problem continued to be exacerbated by the arrival of large numbers of ex-squatters in the municipally-controlled camps. Their activities, the town clerk reported, "encourages a general defiance of other persons." Three years later the same battle was still raging as faction leader, Jackson Mtenjane, orchestrated public protests of women against the suppression of the hawking of green mealies and other small goods.[26]

The squatter leaders defended their perimeters in a variety of ways. To begin with, the tightly-packed, unnumbered, and haphazardly located shanties and tents made the camps extremely difficult to penetrate or police. Even the inhabitants sometimes had difficulty identifying their own homes, as Mrs. Moteka's description of Mpanza's shantytown camp reveals:

> People were working, and they came out of that shack in the morning and went back into it at night. Before the Government put numbers on them it was a difficult situation. The houses were alike and at night you could hear the men shouting for their wives because they did not know which one was the right place. And the women would shout back. That was sad but very funny.[27]

Equally important in permitting the establishment and survival of these pockets of illegal space were the legal services and protection they were able to command. One of the most striking features of all the squatter movements at this time was their reliance on the law. Mpanza himself was well versed in legal matters (to some extent the result of several long sojourns in jail), and exploited a 1926 test case against the Johannesburg city council in which the court ruled that people employed in the city could not be removed if they had no alternative housing. Eighteen months later, Harry Mabuya, the Tent Town squatter leader in Benoni, invoked the same principle to protect his fledgling squatter camp. He further added to the council's confusion by establishing his camp on a wedge of land which fell under the neighboring magistracy of Brakpan thereby placing the council's *locus standi* in doubt. In his legal arguments, Mabuya drew on expert legal advice furnished by the CPSA lawyer,

Lewis Baker. One of the surviving squatter leaders tells how Baker explained that the area "did not belong to Benoni but Brakpan. Meaning Brakpan would arrest Benoni and not Mabuya."[28] It was Baker and another lawyer, Slomowitz, who suggested the site of the next squatter settlement in Benoni—a slice of land proclaimed for Benoni's new industrial township. Benoni was then placed in what for these lawyers must have been an exquisite dilemma: no further industrial expansion was possible until the 19,000 Apex squatters had been furnished with suitable housing. Within five years the massive new housing scheme of Daveyton, the township adjacent to Benoni, was underway.[29]

Even the smallest of squatter movements like those involving the Meyer's Farm and Rietpan Farm tenants at Alberton and Benoni respectively, retained their own special lawyers; on to the bigger squatter movements lawyers battened in their dozens. In Tobruk squatter camp, Oriel Monongoaha engaged two firms of attorneys and four counsel, while each of the opposition factions in the camp employed their own particular firms. For all but one or two of the squatter movements, these tactics stalled the council for sufficiently long to secure the *de facto* acknowledgment of the squat, and the ultimate provision of "controlled" squatter camps. Small wonder that Mpanza could proclaim expansively to a squatter gathering in 1946, "I love the law."[30] It was a sentiment in which all of his squatter colleagues would have concurred.

Since these various activities cost money, especially the basic administrative services, another typical feature of the squatter camps was the regular collection of dues. Mpanza collected 2 shillings per family per week along with a host of other irregular levies; Kgoma's compounded dues were between 2 and 4 shillings six-pence a week, while Edward Khumalo charged 10 shillings a month.[31] Such disparate bodies as the Johannesburg city council, the police, and the Communist Party were wont to depict this as extortion and corruption, and there was indeed a tendency toward abuse. However, the reasons for this process of degeneration which shows up in the careers of all the squatter leaders was not simply individual avarice and opportunism and should be sought in some of the fundamental properties of squatter politics as a whole.

The Roots of Squatter Politics

Squatter politics exhibited a number of common traits, developing in the most part out of the common material circumstances of their constituents and the common problems they faced. Nevertheless, from most other perspectives the squatter populations were bewilderingly diverse, encompassing a wide range of cultures, experiences, and political traditions. The precise manner in which squatter politics functioned and the forms in which political authority was expressed were thus subject to considerable variation, depending on the character of the leadership and the cultural materials with which they had to work. At this distance in time these distinctions are not always easy to discern let alone to explain. Nevertheless, if we are to understand black politics at this time and the following three decades, an attempt has to be made. What follows is an uneven and sometimes speculative account, which is to some extent a prospectus for future research. It is with Mpanza and his Sofazonke party that it begins.

Descriptions of James Sofazonke Mpanza, both contemporary and current, are peculiarly culture-bound. The Johannesburg city council at the time wrote him off as a dictator and gangster; twenty years later Mary Benson, who reflected one current of opinion in the ANC likewise dismissed him as a "demagogic township eccentric." More recently, social scientists Kevin French and Alf Stadler presented him as a flamboyant volatile character who, dressed in leopard skins, riding breeches, a helmet, and scarlet plumes, rode around on a horse and portrayed himself as a Moses sent to lead his people to the Promised Land.[32] However sympathetic the overall tenor of their accounts, the portrait nevertheless emerges of a figure who is trifle bizarre. Despite the magnetic effect that Mpanza obviously had on large numbers of his supporters, the cultural logic of his actions and presentation has never been explored.

Such considerations highlight the similarities between such squatter leaders and the charismatic prophet-type leaders of Zionist churches. It is uncertain whether Mpanza, and other squatter leaders of his ilk like Harry Mabuya in Benoni, consciously modelled themselves on Zionist patterns, or whether each drew on a common stock of cultural materials to construct similar bricolages.[33] What is evident, however, is that both squatter and Zionist leaders—though on a dramatically different scale—produced similar solutions to meet analogous needs. Zionist movements, most recent studies agree, cater to two basic needs—the healing of physical affliction and the reestablishment of psychological equilibrium. Anthropologists Bent Sundkler and Martin West both point out the centrality of faith healing and the casting out of spirits in Zionist practice and preaching.[34] Fellow anthropologist Jean Comaroff agrees and extends her analysis in a way which is particularly suggestive for the present discussion:

> Anthropologists have long insisted that physical disorder indexes social disruption, and that healing is a simultaneously individual and collec-

tive process. Indeed the body may be manipulated, *pars proto toto*, in the attempt to reform the immediate world. Thus the symptoms of the Zion followers, symptoms regarded by contemporary observers as "hysterical" and "hypochondriacal" may be seen as somatised signs of a wider social malaise. This was a cult of affliction, but the ills it addressed spoke of more than physical dislocation. They expressed the desire to reconstitute, through the ritualized reconstruction of the body personal, the encompassing orders of power and production that it signified.[35]

Martin West and Philip Mayer make related observations. West speaks of Zionist congregations as "caring communities . . . where strangers are accepted and make friends," while both West and Mayer identify a central function of these churches as social control. Most impose a wide range of prohibitions on potentially socially disruptive practices. Drinking, smoking, dancing, fighting and gossiping are banned. Monogamy is demanded, and those co-habiting outside of marriage are presented with the alternatives of marrying or being expelled. Finally, all sources agree on the preponderance of women in these congregations and their importance in the life of the church, at least partly through the activities of separate, uniformed "manyano" groups (women's prayer groups).[36]

Squatter leaders in the Mpanza mold performed many of the same roles. While in prison, Mpanza himself underwent a profound religious conversion and discovered a hitherto hidden capacity for faith healing. Once head of the Shantytown movement, he depicted himself as a prophet-like figure. According to numerous reports he was wont "to liken himself to Moses, Joseph and Joshua." In February 1945, he told a meeting that he was "sent by God to take the Bantu people to Shantytown." Two months earlier, he was even claiming that "the position of chief was given to me like Jesus. People thought Jesus died but he did not. They thought I was deported but I returned."[37]

In pursuit of social regulation and control, each of the Zulu-speaking squatter leaders attempted, albeit unsuccessfully, to ban the brewing of beer as well as making efforts to regulate marital and family disputes. However, Mpanza seems to have had a broader vision of social harmony and social order than any other of the leading squatter figures. Much more than other leaders, particularly his Sotho-speaking counterparts, he preached an inclusive non-tribal message. Aside from the occasional lapse, Mpanza was at pains to welcome all comers to his camps, irrespective of ethnic origin.[38] He repeatedly proclaimed that "as far as his party was concerned there were no Zulus, Xhosas, Shanganes, Basutos or anything else. They are all one black race." Mpanza conceived of the camp as an organic unity and promoted a communalist vision. Much of the food, coal, and other supplies were provided through a chain of cooperative outlets. Everything in the township, Mpanza asserted, had to be done on a communal basis. When the government's Director of Native Labour, and Johannesburg's Manager of Non-European Affairs visited Shantytown on 11th May 1944, they were greeted by hundreds of uniformed women singing "specially selected songs" and led by two girls carrying a banner inscribed "Everything done in the presence and on behalf of the community. No private interviews. Strictly public. By Order."[39]

The role played by women in the camps highlights further similarities with the Zionist churches. It was in Mabuya's Tent Town outside of Benoni that women occupied the most prominent positions. There, two women sat on the five member executive committee and women organized the daily running and security of the camp. However, in both Mpanza's Masakeng and Monongoaha's Tobruk, a women's committee was established parallel to that of men. The prominence of women on camp committees may to some degree be ascribed to the fact that they were present daily while men left the camp to work, but it is likely that there was more behind it than that. Sundkler reveals that Zionist churches accord women far more important leadership roles than any other African organization in South Africa, while Martin West, Mia Brandel-Syrier and others emphasize the enormously influential role of separate "manyano" women's groups not only in Zionist but in all African churches. These groups, Brandel-Syrier writes, were generally led by the wife of the church minister, wore uniforms, played an important role in regulating social behavior, and were the principal fundraising institutions of the church. The parallel with Masakeng's women's committee is striking. This was led by Mpanza's wife Julia, was uniformed, and received regular subscriptions from those enrolled in its ranks.[40]

Such prescriptions and practices, however, were not uncontested and faced the competition of other traditions and alternative cultural forces. For example, when Mpanza tried to enforce his monopoly on the provision of supplies in the face of an intrusive municipal soup kitchen, he elicited a wave of opposition which led angry residents to destroy his office, loot his coal dump, and beat his coal guard to death. In the aftermath, a number of petty traders were allowed to begin operations while the ban on beer brewing was quietly dropped. Both Mabuya and Edward Khumalo (in Albertynsville) encountered similar opposition and were likewise forced to relax their proscriptions on the brewing of beer.[41]

On the basis of present evidence it is unclear whether Mpanza, Mabuya, and others elicited the enthusiastic response they did because their practices corresponded to Zionist influences to which these communities had already been exposed, or because both they and the Zionists were independently drawing on a common store of symbols and ideas. All that can be said at this juncture is that both types of movement began to blossom in the same sections of these new urban communities at roughly the same time and that it would be surprising if they did not in some way intersect. For example, the number of African independent churches swelled from 600 in 1939 to 1,286 in 1955 and the numbers of their adherents doubled from I to 2 million during approximately the same time—with Zionist congregations constituting most of the increase.[42] The influence of Zionism on the politics of Soweto squatter movements thus seems more probable than not.

In the other squatter communities that grew up at this time, different cultural constellations and political traditions left their own distinct imprints. There, other forms of migrant organization often provided the decisive shaping force. The Apex squatter camp, established near Benoni in 1950, displays this legacy in perhaps its starkest form. To a greater extent than appears to have been the case in the Soweto squatter movements, an exceptionally high proportion of residents had previously lived on small-holdings or on the mines and had only limited exposure to urban life. At the time, a number of mines in the Benoni area were in the process of closing and migrants were finding themselves either returning to the reserves or faced with the need to find urban accommodation and jobs.

Mr. F. Mahungela, who was working at New Kleinfontein mine, recalled the influx of miners into the vacant industrial land which became the Apex squatter camp:

> There were people from Rietpan [small-holdings] who came to New Kleinfontein at night. . .having parcels in boxes and so on. I was actually woken up. These people wanted some water and I gave them. [They came] in hundreds. There were men, women and their children. I asked them where they were going to and they told me they had come to build their shacks. Early in the morning there were shacks erected all over the place. I asked if I could put up my shack and they said, "with pleasure."[43]

There followed a general exodus from the mines, and ex-miners soon constituted the majority of the population.

The political organization of the squatters soon came to reflect the composition of the camp. To begin with, says one resident, "Motswaneng was the Sibonda. So the Sotho and the Kgatla wanted their own leaders." When groups from the mines and from a predecessor squatter camp called Tent Town near Benoni arrived, they made a similar demand. "We [from the small holdings] were threatened and a fight nearly began. We dropped our badges and we went back home."[44] The main leader put forward by these new arrivals was Madingoane, a Pedi, who like other faction leaders arriving in the camp, had retained his own lawyer, the CPSA member, Lewis Baker. Madingoane's principal qualification, all informants agree, was his familiarity with traditional morality: "Madingoane's leadership was not like today when one follows a voting procedure. He knew his tradition."[45]

Other leaders appear to have acquired their authority on a similar basis and because of their prior position in migrant networks on the mines. Shangane ex-miners called on Mahungela, who worked in the mine dispensary, to represent their interests; the Xhosa summoned a clerk at the new Kleinfontein mine, and the South Sotho and Zulu called on Pokane, Buthelezi, and Khumalo respectively to carry out similar functions for them. More research needs to be conducted on the migrant associations and the political cultures out of which such organizations sprang. One group about which a little more can be said are the Southern Sotho. Here, leadership was based on the structures of the notorious migrant ethnic gang known as the "Russians" who at this time numbered some thousands across the Rand. In Apex, Pukane was the leader of the locally dominant Molapo faction of the Russians while the leader in Moroka, Ntoi, was closely associated with the rival Matsieng faction. Russian practices consequently imprinted themselves strongly on these sections of the camps. Ntoi, for example, repeatedly resorted to violence and extortion in which the Russians were often alleged to engage.[46] A powerful male chauvinist impulse also seems to have marked their handling of marital and family disputes particularly when triggered by women. A central impulse in the original formation of the Russian gangs appears to have been the wish to control the increasingly independent behavior of Basotho women, as well as the need to gain access to uncontrolled urban space.[47] This more violent, chauvinist, and ethnic orientation that characterized Basotho-dominated squatter camps most likely impaired rather than improved the quality of squatter life.

Despite these shortcomings, the leadership of Apex and most of the other squatter camps was genuinely popular. In the Apex Advisory Board election of September 1951, 1,711 men voted out of a potential electorate of 3,923. The following year, the number voting had increased to 5,270, which represented almost two-thirds of those entitled to vote, and this rate of participation continued until the closure of the camp. High turnouts likewise marked elections to the other Advisory Boards.[48]

This popularity was perhaps facilitated by the constant presence of the leaders in the camps. Virtually all of the leaders in Apex chose occupations which gave them a great deal of freedom and independence. Sinaba sold coal, while in the second rank of leadership Mkhoma was a coal dealer and a minister of the Apostolic Faith church and Mtshali was a herbalist and an Apostolic Faith Church elder. Not every leader tried to establish himself in an equally independent position. Pokane, for example, worked until his retirement at the nearby Amato Textiles factory. Nevertheless, the advantages of self employment to squatter leaders was obvious as it allowed them to be constantly present and central to the camp. The limited information that exists suggests this pattern was characteristic of squatter settlements across the entire Rand.[49]

The Limits of Squatter Politics

The various aspects of squatter politics that have so far been traced attest to its genuinely popular roots. However, each of the strengths of squatter politics was matched by a corresponding weakness. A preoccupation with the daily problems of social order and survival, for example, lent them an introverted character, which narrowed their political horizons and made them peculiarly impermeable to national political organizations. In Apex, and its successor township, Daveyton, squatter residents gave negligible support to the women's national anti-pass campaign, and an ANC-inspired resistance to ethnic zoning proved a total flop. The attitude of the squatter leaders in Orlando to national politics is best captured in the words of Mpanza when he announced that he was "not interested in Communism, Democracy or any other party. He was only interested in his own party."[50] With the exception of Schreiner Baduza's squatter movement in Alexandra, none of the squatter communities proved responsive to the broader national appeal of the ANC, and the ANC seemed incapable of devising an approach to local issues which could either incorporate squatter leaders or supersede their influence.

Squatter politics were not only parochial and introverted, they were also in many instances deeply sectional and divisive. Feuds rent virtually all of the squatter camps, often following a Nguni/Sotho divide. Early in 1946, a second wave of squatting movements broke out in Orlando, the first led by Edward Khumalo and the second by Abel Ntoi. Both were quickly housed in the newly established Moroka squatter camp, where hostility was soon whipped up between what were described as Ntoi's Basotho, who were closely associated with the Russians, and Khumalo's Zulu. Conflict between Ntoi and Khumalo was averted by the departure of the latter to join the leadership of the newly formed Albertynsville squatter camp. However, fresh gang and ethnic conflicts erupted a couple of years later. In January 1951, a gang of fifty Russians stormed through Moroka, stealing from residents, breaking their way into houses, and demanding protection money from those inside. The following month, a group from Ntoi's section in Moroka East "pounced on" Moroka West killing one person. During the subsequent murder trial involving Ntoi, the principal crown witness, Khumalo, was killed. Other groups defended themselves against such depredation. This triggered a set of Sotho-Zulu faction fights which rumbled through the rest of the decade.[51]

Such conflicts were not just the product of primordial ethnic sentiments. When questioned about ethnic frictions in the Tobruk camp at a meeting designed to resolve some of its internal divisions a local resident, Llewellyn Ncwana, replied that "this was engendered by certain leaders. Except for this there would be no such friction."[52] Though Ncwana, an educated man, was concerned to counter the image of backward-looking ethnic divisions, it is likely that there was a substantial element of truth in what he said. People from diverse origins did generally live in peace until problems in the camps—whether the abuses of the leaders or the depredations of gangs—could be projected by rival leaderships in ethnic terms.

A key problem for the camps was the basic structure of squatter politics and the political cultures on which they drew. Common to all varieties of squatter politics was the highly personalized undemocratic character of their leadership. Central leadership figures like Mpanza, Mabuya, Ntoi, and Kgoma may have initially been elected or chosen, but thereafter only rarely or intermittently subjected themselves to any kind of democratic control. Once elected, Mpanza, Mabuya, and the Russian leaders chose key lieutenants, and relied on personal charisma, daring, and largesse to maintain their control.[53] Thus Mpanza boldly obstructed deportation, while Ntoi directly challenged the authority of the Johannesburg city council by hijacking buses bringing passengers to the perimeter of the camp, and forcing them to deliver their cargo to the camp center. Mpanza in particular, and to a lesser extent the other squatter leaders, dispensed money to the needy with extreme liberality. At least partly for these purposes, Mpanza carried huge sums of money around with him, and when he and his wife were arrested on a charge of public violence in June 1946, he was found to have nearly £60 on his person and his wife, about £45.[54] According to one of his committee members, "when a person died we gave the family £1 and a coffin. Mpanza gave the needy £1 sometimes £2." It was on the basis of the popularity gained by such acts that Mpanza and the other squatter leaders ruled. The only check on their authority—until subjected to Advisory Board elections—was the mass meeting from which a challenge could not easily be launched.[55]

The direct, unmediated populist relationship between leaders and followers lent itself readily to abuse. The roles of dispenser of justice and distributor of largesse presented powerful temptations when not tempered by any kind of democratic scrutiny or check. Most of the squatter leaders to some degree or another succumbed. Mpanza, for example, somehow lost £500 of Sofazonke money at the time of his arrest in 1946. In Tobruk, Kgoma failed to account on different occasions for sums of £200 and £362, and while the treasurer of the camp, Reverend Solomon Sithole, likewise distinguished himself by collecting £28 in the camp square one November day, putting it in a suitcase in his home for safety overnight and then finding only £18 there when he opened it in front of the committee next morning. Behavior of this kind inevitably encouraged opposition, mobilized largely along ethnic lines. When challenged by rival factions, Kgomo imported two lorry loads of Zulu residents from Edward Khumalo's Albertynsville camp to overwhelm the opposition, and Tobruk also increasingly divided along Nguni/Sotho lines.[56] Monongoaha's camp was already predominantly Sotho in composition, and Mrs. Methula remembers Kgoma entrenching this division:

> If you were a Sotho he would send you to Maseru [Monongoaha's section]. But when you refused he would not force you to go. But he would warn you not to do what the MaRashea [Russians] are doing.

There nevertheless remained a substantial minority of Basotho in the camp and these increasingly arrayed themselves under the leadership of Michael Mogatle in opposition to Kgoma.[57] Ultimately, only the removal of the camp to Moroka seems to have averted serious collisions.

The above examples suggest the rich pickings to be had at the camps, and the absence of any structures by which squatter leaders could be held accountable by their constituents could easily lead to coercion, intimidation, and violence. The Reverend Michael Scott who lived briefly in the Tobruk squatter camp, bluntly labelled Kgomo's lieutenants as gangsters, and the same description was applied to others.[58] Those endeavoring to resist such excesses, or trying to muscle in on the fields of capital accumulation represented by the camps, tended to mobilize support along ethnic lines. Thus while one should acknowledge the force of Ncwana's argument about the way the leadership element manipulated ethnic categories, it seems likely that in this climate of volatility and insecurity, ethnic identities may have briefly sharpened, before being worn down in the course of the next two decades.

The Legacy of Squatter Politics

As the authorities gradually disestablished the "uncontrolled" squatter settlements and moved their inhabitants into tightly regulated serviced camps, squatter leaders found both their authority and their financial base progressively whittled down. Each responded to these straightened circumstances in his own particular way but some longer-term patterns can be discerned. Figures like Edward Khumalo and Samuel Kgoma sought to regain their former status by organizing new squatter movements, but as the housing shortage was eased and legal loopholes were closed, these became increasingly difficult to get underway. Mpanza continued to pursue his dream of acquiring a farm from the government in the northern Transvaal, assuming almost certainly without foundation, that a large number of his adherents would follow. Abel Ntoi organized a rent boycott in Moroka against the 15 shillings a month charged simply for serviced sites. This secured a wide measure of support in this particular area but was unable to broaden itself out to the rest of the Johannesburg townships or the Rand, which shared similar problems, partly, if not largely, because of the intensely sectional nature of squatter leadership and squatter politics. As a result the rent boycott ultimately folded.[59]

In the medium–term, squatter leaders or leaders in the squatter tradition moved in two contradictory directions which some managed to keep harnessed for a surprisingly long time. The one was toward explicit gangster and criminal activity. Edward Khumalo, who was arrested for housebreaking in Standerton in 1952, and Abel Ntoi whose "Russian" connections have been previously discussed are representative of this trend. The second tendency was to consolidate authority by collaborating more closely with the municipality and the police in policing the communities. On closer examination the relationship between these two tendencies is clear: as social disorder, particularly the depredations of criminal gangs, grew in the 1950s, squatter leaders were ensured of a social adjudicatory and social policing role which the municipal authorities could or would not fulfill. For the 1950s and 1960s, this role was carried out by Advisory Board members and Urban Bantu councillors. In the early to mid 1950s, squatter leaders and/or Advisory Board members established civilian guards to curb the problem of crime. Oral testimonies suggest that these officially discountenanced groups were genuinely popular bodies, as indeed for a time were Advisory Boards. According to a local resident, when Chiawelo was established on the site of the old Albertynsville camp, for example, "crime was rife. Then we held a meeting from which the civil guard was formed. These patrolled the township day and night so that anyone who tried to commit crimes was chased, and if caught sometimes killed. We were all united in one body, Shanganes, Vendas and Nyasas." Every male who was not a youth was expected to take part. Mqanduli, an "induna" (Advisory Board member), played the leading role in both Advisory Board and civil guard. Malefactors were, as old-time residents remember, "sent to Mqanduli. Then he would decide whether to punish them himself or send them to the police." Mqanduli is also reported to have settled social quarrels "between husbands and wives, as well as disputes which involved neighbors."[60]

The 1960s and 1970s saw a variation on the theme of the civilian guard, when the adherents of both the Mpanza group and the Russians set up separate kgotla movements (parents' courts) to discipline delinquent youth.[61] In the late 1970s and 1980s, Community Councils, the lineal successors of the old Advisory Boards, became comprehensively discredited, for reasons which are reasonably well-known, but the need to perform some of their functions persists. Where street committees have been most popular in recent years has been where they have carried out a democratized version of the same role. Elsewhere the authoritarian version lingers on—in the squatter camps of Crossroads/KCT, Pietermaritzburg, Durban and elsewhere.[62] However vicious and reactionary these squatter communities have become, both history and recent events bid us not to ignore their social materiality or popular historical roots.

Chapter 5 / **An Image of Its Own Past?**

Towards a Comparison of
American and South African
Historiography

Colin Bundy

"On Board an Emigrant Ship—Land ho!" Engraving from a nineteenth-century
South African illustrated newspaper.

(i) To compare Great things with small . . .

(Milton, *Paradise Lost*)

A recent *New Statesman* competition required a history of the world—in a single limerick.[1] Such economy is enviable, but not easily emulated. So let us permit a more expansive project: the U.S. past on a postcard, please. An entry might read as follows:

Five hundred years ago Iberian absolutism sought a sea-route to India and "discovered" a land then peopled by precapitalist societies. Colonization followed in the seventeenth century, but by an ascendant Protestant and not a declining Catholic power. Settlement along the coast involved the military dispossession of indigenous chiefdoms. After about 1660, imported black slaves became central to the production of agricultural commodities. In the eighteenth century, colonial society developed economically within, and increasingly fretted against, mercantilist practices. By the 1770s, territorial expansion saw frontiersmen cross natural boundaries to encounter unconquered nations or "confederacies," societies with greater military capacity than the coastal indigines. Over the next century wars were fought, boundaries established, treaties signed—and the final acts of dispossession came in the 1870s, in an intensified spate of fighting.

After about 1830, large areas of the interior were settled, as the "moving frontier" fanned out from the seaboard. Immigrants from Europe settled, mostly in growing cities; new industrial activities transformed the economy, and in the late nineteenth century, monopoly capitalism was personified in *nouveau riche* entrepreneurs. A civil war fought over ostensibly political issues was also a conflict between the demands of capitalist development and a region unable to meet these. Superior numbers and ruthless tactics saw industrial capitalism overcome the generalship and guerrilla tactics of the agrarian adversary; a period of Reconstruction sought to establish a socioeconomic order on the victor's terms—which soon involved political concessions to the loser.

While industrialization intensified, organized working-class opposition was weakened by ethnic and cultural fragmentation. The country took part in both world wars; the economy survived the depression of the 1930s and then entered a period of sustained accumulation that lasted until the early 1970s. After 1945 there was a period of domestic conservatism and anti-communism; a campaign of civil disobedience by disenfranchised blacks; mounting internal tensions (associated with a "youth revolt" and massive political disaffection) and by the mid-1970s a deep-seated malaise was evident. In the 1980s a right-wing president embraced monetarism, militarism, and a bellicose foreign policy.

That abbreviated outline is even more thrifty than it might appear. Without addition or subtraction, it serves too as a thumbnail sketch of the history of South Africa.

There are, of course, important differences between the two histories which are obscured by the selectivity and artifice of the summary. Among others are the obvious disparity in scale (of area, population, wealth and power); the duration of colonial rule (and hence the terms on which each society was inserted in the capitalist world economy); the dissimilar demographic balance between indigenes and immigrants; and the divergence between the democratic promise of marketplace liberalism, on the one hand, and an exclusive and oligarchic illiberalism on the other.

Yet even when these substantial differences have been recognized, the dual applicability of the summary suggests intriguing parallels and congruencies. Until the late eighteenth century the two chronologies correspond quite closely. The voyages of Columbus and Diaz, the settlements in Virginia and the Cape, land loss and cultural disintegration by Khoikhoi and coastal Indians, the importation of chattel slaves, and the simultaneous breaching of the Appalachians and entry into the Zuurveld are closely keyed variations on a basic theme: primitive accumulation in the age of European merchant capitalist pressure on the wider world. Even the American Revolution is faintly echoed in the burgher rebellions on the Eastern Cape at the end of the eighteenth century.

After 1776, the domestic histories become more divergent, but continue to be simultaneously affected by global developments. At war with France, Britain intervened militarily at the Cape and in the United States. The ginning of upland cotton and the adoption of the Merino sheep were respectively American and South African responses to the appetite of mills in Lancashire and Yorkshire. Covered wagons creaked across untracked land before mineral rushes were fed by rail lines; farmers united politically in opposition to the costs of transport and credit; segregation was codified and extended at the turn of the century—but there is no need to belabor the point. Strong corroboratory evidence exists in the shape of five recent studies of high caliber which undertake comparative analysis of the frontier, segregation and racism, emancipation, and capitalist development in South Africa and the United States.[2] Comparable issues have generated comparative history.

This comparability of the two histories prompts a different enquiry: can one usefully compare the two historiographies? How similar have been shifts in the content, interpretation and methodology in the two areas of scholarship? How and why have they differed? If "the country which is more developed industrially only shows, to the less developed, the image of its own future," might South African historians discern an image of their own past in the more developed U.S. historiography?[3] To what extent have both U.S. and South African historiography reflected global trends within the discipline? This article ventures some highly preliminary answers to these questions.

Two comparative issues are posed. First, sections (ii) and (iii) examine the changing character of South African history through a U.S. lens. They take the familiar sequence of interpretative frameworks that have shaped study of the national past in the United States, and ask whether a periodization of South African historiography might be devised on similar lines. Secondly, sections (iv) and (v) concentrate upon more recent historiographical developments in both cases, examining the notion of a discipline in crisis.

A *caveat* is essential. Comparing and contrasting one historiography with another is complicated in this instance by the sheer differences in scale. Academic history in the United States had been established for over half a century when the first chairs in the subject were created in South Africa. The flood of scholarship from the world's largest university system makes the South African output seem a negligible trickle. In the 1950s, about 300 Americans completed their doctoral programs each year; in South Africa, an average of three per year. In 1972, the peak year, there were almost 1200 history doctorates in the United States, of which nearly 500 were in U.S. history. In the entire decade of the 1970s, South African universities awarded only sixty-five history Ph.D. degrees. That figure would be doubled if one added doctorates gained by South Africans studying overseas—but the substantive point stands.

This basic discrepancy has important implications for the content of both historiographies. Viewed from one angle, it must be the relative callowness of South African scholarship that strikes the eye, the flimsier platform of existing work upon which monographs are constructed, and the lacunae and omissions that are the inevitable result. From a different perspective, however, it may well be that contemporary South African scholars enjoy the "privileges of historic backwardness"—a privilege that "permits, or rather compels, the adoption of whatever is ready . . . skipping over whole series of intermediate stages."[4]

(ii) In them is plainest taught, and easiest learnt,
What makes a nation happy, and keeps it so . . .

(Milton, *Paradise Regained*)

The study of U.S. historiography has generated work of immense subtlety and learning, and the summary attempted here stands somewhere between impertinence and smash and grab raid. It is not intended as historiographical comment in its own right; it is rather and *aide memoire* to Americanists, and introduction to South Africanists, and point of departure for a survey of changes in the writing of South African history.

When historical study in U.S. universities became professionalized in the late nineteenth century, historians "reflected the values of conservatism, continuity and comity." They were self-consciously nationalist, concerned to bind up the wounds of the Civil War; their "overwhelmingly affirmative stance toward the American experience" produced a "convergent, celebratory historiography."[5] It was a second generation of historians—trained in the United States rather than in Europe—that crucially modified the scope, methods, and purpose of U.S. history. Turner, Beard, Becker, Parrington, and Robinson completed their education and commenced their careers as the depression of the 1890s was succeeded by the hectic economic growth of the early twentieth century. Demands for reform by Populists and Progressives, the broader intellectual ferment of "modernism," and the robust nationalism of the era all contributed to a New History.

Impatient with the institutional focus, Rankean positivism, and political conservatism of their teachers, the Progressive historians championed an approach that was socioeconomic, relativist, and reformist. They sought to probe beneath political events so as to reveal the "real" social and economic sources of change. Historical interpretation, they insisted, must always reflect the concerns and perspectives of its period— and they strove self-consciously to create a version of the past consonant with and serviceable to an age of reform. And, as domestic and international crises of the 1930s made political neutrality seem less desirable than commitment, "there was a marked increase in the extent to which explicit and avowed political purposes" appeared in their work.[6]

Their collective project did not create a single, new, convergent vision of the past, but between the wars, U.S. historical understanding was decisively shaped by a coherent, forceful explanatory framework provided by the Progressive historians. "Within the intellectual community at large in these years," comments Novick, "Beard was *the* American historian." Their intellectual influence was not restricted to the discipline of history, but molded interwar thought more generally. "If pragmatism . . . provided U.S. liberalism with it philosophical nerve, Progressive historiography gave it memory and myth, and naturalized it within the whole framework of American historical experience."[7] U.S. history, in its Progressive version, had the dual attraction of epic saga and morality play. Its narrative unfolded as a series of confrontations, struggles and turning points, but at the end of each episode, virtue (or "the people") triumphed and a series of villains (or "special interests") was vanquished. "The pivotal idea of the Progressive historians," suggested Hofstadter, "was economic and political conflict," and the resolution of such conflict was typically "a staightforward victory of enlightened reason over inertia."[8]

The entire Progressive framework—its left-of-center politics, its focus on discontinuity and conflict, its relativism—collapsed in the 1940s. It fell, in part, to a concerted assault by a generation of "counter-Progressive" historians, whose emergence was a component of a broader ideological and political shift—the mobilization of a conservative liberalism for service in the Cold War. Perry Anderson has pointed out that the successful restabilization of global capitalism after 1945 (plus the Stalinization of Marxist thought) endowed major sectors of bourgeois thought with a new confice and vitality.[9]

The counter-Progressive historians defined themselves largely in opposition to the Progressive schema. They attacked its assumptions, faulted its details for defective scholarship, and rejected its explanations. In place of conflict as the source of change in the past, they stressed consensual values as the historic guarantee of continuity. Instead of the sturdy dualism and explanatory simplicity of Progressive history, they (in the words of perhaps their most gifted member) offered "the rediscovery of complexity in American history."[10] Irony, ambiguity, paradox, and skepticism were basic to the vocabulary of Hofstadter, Potter, Morgan, Bailyn and others. Repudiation of Marxism as an intellectual system welled over into a generalized antipathy toward "economic" causality and toward "class" as an analytical category of relevance to the American past.

The adoption of techniques and theories from other social sciences stamped a seal of "scientific" authority on the artifacts of conservative revisionism. The Civil War became a malfunctioning of crisis management; truculent democrats were expectant capitalists and Populist agitators only prejudiced misfits; class-conscious labor leaders were reclassified as would-be entrepreneurs. The Bell tolled for the end of ideology and an enduring moderate pragmatism was celebrated instead. Counter-Progressive history in the Eisenhower years overlapped with the functionalist sociology of Merton and Parsons, the pluralist political science of Lipset and Dahl, and the developmental theories of Rostow and Eisenstadt. The "new realists" like Hofstadter, argued Noble, "became implicit allies of the modernization theorists."[11]

While counter-Progressive history left little of the Progressive interpretation intact, its own more conservative design of the past did not provide a synthesis of comparable persuasiveness or durability. Higham fired the first round in 1959 in a critique of the "cult of consensus." Sniping intensified in the early 1960s and by mid-decade had become an irresistible fusillade. The consensus model, above all, was blown apart by events of the sixties. Blacks, women, and the young were mobilized on terms that mocked consensus. Violence flared in the South, in northern ghettoes, and on campuses. War in Southeast Asia took its toll on domestic politics, the dollar, and also on notions of exceptionalism, abundance, and invincibility. In the early and middle 1960s, the political center of gravity in the United States shifted leftward. Simultaneously, left-orientated historians achieved a new prominence within the historical profession: in 1968 *Toward a New Past* was part manifesto, part agenda for new left historians. Their impact is assessed in section (vi) below.

(iii) . . . all the schools
Of academics old and new

(Milton, *Paradise Regained*)

What applicability has all this for South African historiography? Are there similar interpretive shifts, and have they any correspondence to the periods and categories outlined for the U.S. case? A complication arises. There is a fundamental bifurcation in South African historiography, without parallel in the U.S. case. This is the division between English-speaking and Afrikaans-speaking historians. This is no mere linguistic divide, but bears also upon methodology, subject matter and ideology. Historiographical writing in South Africa has tended to look either at English or at Afrikaans scholarship. Although the sketch that follows is still overwhelmingly weighted toward work written in English, it tries to indicate the potential of a more "bilingual" historiography.

Without underestimating the imprint made upon later work by the early amateur "settler historians," the discipline was placed upon a professional footing in South Africa in the early years of this century. It was between about 1918 and 1945—the years of Progressive pre-eminence in U.S. history—that two major historical tendencies or schools defined themselves in South Africa: "liberal" and "Afikaner nationalist." Liberal history was effectively created by two scholars: William Macmillan and Cornelius de Kiewiet, and they influenced the work of contemporaries like J. S. "Etienne" Marais, Hector Monteith Robertson, and Sheila van der Horst. Gustav Preller's polemical works aimed at a popular readership have been properly recognized for their contribution to a nascent Afrikaner historiography. More scholarly nationalist histories emerged in the 1930s and 1940s by C. J. Uys, C.F.J. Muller, and H. B. Thom.

Several commentators have recently pointed out that Macmillan and de Kiewiet paid far more attention than later liberal historians to social and economic history. They may properly be seen as South African representatives of a countercurrent within Western historiography generally, one challenging the primacy of political history in favor of socioeconomic themes. Tawney (who influenced Macmillan) the Hammonds and Childe, Berr and the *annalistes*, Pokrovsky and the Soviet historians of the 1920s, and of course the Progressives were contemporaries.

In a number of respects, there are generic similarities between Macmillan, de Kiewiet and the U.S. Progressive historians. They were equally conscious of writing "new history": Macmillan said his findings established the need "for a radically new interpretation of new and generally undisputed facts." Macmillan had revealed, wrote de Kiewiet, the shaky foundations of the work by George M. Theal and George Cory "so that I began to see that really there was no South African history. It had to be rewritten, round a fresh architecture."[12] They, too, emphasized socioeconomic themes. Macmillan said that a "really significant" South African history would tell of "the everyday life of the people, how they lived, what they thought and what they worked at, when they did think and work, what they produced and what and where they marketed, and the whole of their social organization." De Kiewiet agreed: "for in social and economic history the infinitesimal events of the daily round . . . become significant happenings, and the total life of a community is seen to depend upon numberless men and women who lived obscure lives."[13]

Quite as much as the Progressives, the interwar liberal historians in South Africa sought an immediately useful past: Macmillan was appalled by the racial policies of his day; he cited Croce in criticizing scholarship "of too great aloofness from common life"; and there are a number of expressly didactic passages in his works. De Kiewiet's second book opened by declaring: "most of these pages speak of South Africa in the 'seventies and 'eighties of the last century; and yet they are also about to-day."[14] And, finally, Macmillan and de Kiewiet strongly resemble the Progressive historians in the organization and structure of their arguments, in their frequent recourse to notions of recurrent conflicts and deep-seated economic forces.

A dualism strongly reminiscent of the Progressives pervades Macmillan's work. The South African past hinges around the clash between enlightenment and obscurantism, between the "road of freedom" and the "road of repression" that he associated respectively with the Cape Colony and the Boer Republics. The central concept that underpins much of De Kiewiet's work is less starkly dualist. Yet it echoes both Turner and Beard in its suggestion that environmental and economic realities underlie political developments. For de Kiewiet, an irreversible economic and social integration in South African history cuts across and confutes political segregation. Thus, "the most distinctive feature of the history of whites and blacks is not race or colour, but a close economic association." The frontiers were lines of "absorption and fusion." The "outstanding social and economic fact . . . is not gold nor diamond mining, nor even agriculture, but the universal dependence on black labour."[15]

While the historical project of the interwar liberals substantially resembled that of the Progressives, it also diverged from them. Macmillan and de Kiewiet did not share with Turner, Beard, or Parrington their nationalism or their optimism. Hostile to nationalism in its South African forms, their vision of history was essentially a pessimistic one. Unlike Turner, when de Kiewiet announced the "victory of the frontier" in South African politics, he was mourning and not celebrating. Yet at the same time, precisely these "missing" elements of the Progressive discourse *were* echoed in South African history, but in the accents of "republican" or Afrikaner nationalist history.

Their methodology and subject matter was quite different to that of the Progressives. If anything, it reminds one of the "stark conservatism" of U.S. nationalist historians writing in the late nineteenth century.[16] The first generation of Afrikaner academic historians was largely trained in Dutch and German universities, and strove to write "scientific" history based upon critical study of available archival material. Their focus was primarily upon political history and its content virtually self-defining. Political history meant the history of the Afrikaner nation: its tribulations at the hands of imperial officials, savage tribes and English armies, and its survival and ultimate unification. Biographies of military and political leaders were a particularly favored genre. Although some scholarly attention was paid to the Dutch colonial period, Afrikaner nationalist historiography was predominantly concerned with the nineteenth century, especially the years 1836 to 1902. This, notes the premier Afrikaner historiographer,

> was a dynamic period and a peculiarly romantic one; it was the period of great epic achievements by the Afrikaner people. . . . A chain of causality linked the Great Trek—the axis of Afrikaans history—with the war of 1899–1902. The Trek divided them and the war united them; in both cases the imperial factor was the determinant. The period . . . gave South Africa its present shape. . . . At the root of the memory of a people was the historical image: fundamentally the Great Trek and the Concentration Camps.[17]

From these central concerns, Afrikaner nationalist history in the 1930s and 1940s drew both its subject matter and its organizing principle. Its introspection and narrowness contrast with the Progressives' expansive faith in human nature and democracy—yet it also offered a saga of nation-building in which an embattled past laid the foundations for a desired present and future. The methods and the concerns of the Progressive historians were replicated in South Africa in this somewhat schizophrenic mode.

One Afrikaner historian of the 1930s and 1940s, however, occupies a position distinctively dissimilar to that of his peers. P. J. van der Merwe's trilogy of studies of Dutch frontier pastoralists is not concerned with the heroic/mythic nineteenth century and only rather perfunctorily with politics or leaders. Instead, it grapples with the social identity and economic activities of the trekboers: their dwellings, furniture, food and dress, and how these changed over time. Other passages trace the pattern of droughts and speculate on longer-term climatic change, and discuss the ecological damage caused by locusts and goats. Thirty years ago, a tribute to van der Merwe suggested that, whether he realized it or not, his work "fits very well into the Turner scheme."[18] Equally, one might suggest that this singular historian was South Africa's first *annaliste.*

Turning to English-language liberal history in the two decades after 1945, comparison with the counter-Progressives seems strikingly apposite. South African historians retreated from socioeconomic concerns, and virtually expunged economic factors from their discussions of causality. Class, as an analytical category, is almost entirely absent. When a U.S.-based sociologist announced in the mid-sixties that "social classes in the Marxian sense of relationship to the means of production . . . are not meaningful social realities in South Africa," he was not challenging, but confirming, the assumptions of local social scientists and historians.[19]

Liberal historians in the 1950s and 1960s produced mainly narrative political histories. Studies of the Afrikaner Bond, imperial policy, the Jameson Raid, the onset of the South African war, and constitution-making after the war, are representative. This corpus of work also reflected a preoccupation with individual actors and personal responsibility. The conflict of 1899–1902 was simplified into "Sir Alfred Milner's war." The aims of imperial policy in the 1870s "were idiosyncratic expressions of the personalities of those in power." A chapter on "The origin of the principal features of the South African constitution: begins with "the personal factor."[20] South African postwar liberals exemplified the preferences outlined by David Potter:

> Political history . . . tends to minimize the deterministic component in history, because it all deals with policy, and the study of policy always assumes that man can modify his circumstances, control his environment, shape his ends, and perhaps even become the captain of his own fate. Liberals . . . have therefore had a natural affinity for political history.[21]

In part, this pattern can be explained as a response by liberal scholars to the result of the 1948 election and their antipathy toward Malan's government. They therefore "devoted most of their energy to analyzing why liberalism in South Africa had failed and Afrikaner nationalism triumphed." It was also partly a reaction to the great surge in popular protest among black South Africans between 1943 and 1955. "The appearance of mobilized masses . . . brought visions of uncontrolled social and political change, always a bugbear for liberals," explain Jeffrey Butler and Deryck Schreuder.[22]

More broadly, their methodological conservatism derived (like that of the counter-Progressives) from the ideological assumptions and concepts of the early cold war period. Writing during the longest internationally coordinated capitalist boom in history, South African liberals operated with an implicit (and in some cases explicit) model of a modernizing capitalism in which economic advance, political democracy and societal equilibrium developed *in pari passu*. Contemporary inequities and injustices stemmed from "archaic" and "irrational" political prejudices which flouted or retarded the socially beneficial operations of the market. Apartheid was castigated as a system "in defiance of economics"; left to itself, capitalist industrialization would transform "gradually, like yeast, the sour dough of South Africa's racial polity into a proper twentieth century loaf of bread."[23] Even after liberal history had been substantially reoriented toward Africanist themes and concerns, such premises remained largely intact. The *Oxford History of South Africa* (its two volumes appeared in 1969 and 1971) "was really the high point of applied modernization theory."[24]

Finally, what of the central counter-Progressive notion of a "consensual" past? Surely, it might be objected, the conflict-ridden chronicles of South Africa simply left no room for a vision of history shaped by compromise and consensus? At one level, this is true enough. Much of the political history written in the 1950s and 1960s deals precisely with the origins and dynamics of conflict between republican Afrikaners and imperial British (or jingoistic English-speaking white South Africans). Yet, despite the conceptual hurdle posed by the sheer level of social and political conflict, the liberal historians of the 1950s and 1960s proffered a variant of consensus history. They invented, in effect, a wistful "if only" consensus, a hypothetical history-of-what-might-have-been.

Thus, for instance, the Jameson Raid ("a tragic error") "interrupted the natural growth of unity in South Africa." Had the Liberals only come to power in England a few years earlier, the South African War "might never have been fought" and republics and colonies "might have been left to accomplish amicably and in due time a federation from within," accommodating "race and colour differences" and allowing "diversity and freedom."[25] Similarly, the Union of South Africa was predicated upon a profound political flaw, a flexible constitution: the national convention failed to provide "the only sound basis for concord in South Africa"—a constitution on the U.S. rather than the British model.[26] Again: "if the South African League had risen to the occasion in 1896 and created . . . a multi-racial political party" the Cape liberal tradition might have triumphed at the National Convention.[27] At times, consensus is asserted even without the suppositional or conditional gesture. Le May concludes his study of "British Supremacy" with the claim that "Campbell-Bannerman gave to white politics in South Africa nearly half a century of moderation."[28]

By the 1960s, convergent with this liberal variant of consensus history, a new direction was being charted in Afrikaner historiography. The earlier almost exclusive preoccupation with Afrikaner identity, was supplemented by exploration instead of white identity, white unity. This reflected the politics of the late 1950s. The challenge by organized African nationalism, the decline of the "English" opposition party, and the clear-cut electoral victory of 1958 all provided a platform on which to construct a "conciliatory" interpretation of the past. As early as 1958, van

Jaarsveld called into question the traditional Afrikaner historical self-image. It was simplistic and lacking in universality; it over-emphasized military history; it ignored blacks and reduced English-speakers to a stereotyped antagonist. A new interpretive framework was needed which would "promote unity between the two white language groups" and thus "accord with the situation of our time." In 1961, van Jaarsveld hailed G. D. Scholtz (in words that could equally be applied to himself) as a "prophet of repentance whose mission it is to bring this changed world to the Afrikaner's notice."[29]

Kruger took further the project of a consensual or conciliatory Afrikaner historiography. He wrote when a booming economy and the routing of underground resistance had combined to shepherd significant numbers of English-speaking voters into National Party polling booths. Transparently approving of this trend, his prose and his political purpose have all the subtlety of an advertisement hoarding. From its title (*The Making of a Nation*) to its final sentence ("White South Africa had at last achieved a national solidarity . . . cemented by a common loyalty and patriotism") he traces how the "mellowing process of time" brought Afrikaner and English to a common destiny, a referendum vote both for republican status and for "the maintenance of the political hegemony of the white man."[30]

Kruger's book appeared in 1969. The same year saw the publication of *Class and Colour in South Africa*, by the veteran communist intellectuals, Jack and Ray Simons—which can be viewed either as a precursor to, or as the vanguard of, a wave of revisionist history. Also in 1969 two important "liberal Africanist" works appeared—a collection of essays on black societies, and the first volume of a major liberal overview of South African history. Much of the early revisionist work, discussed below, cut its teeth on reviews of the *Oxford History of South Africa*.

> (iv) . . . but to know
> That which before us lies in daily life
> Is the prime Wisdom
>
> (Milton, *Paradise Lost*)

Since the mid-1960s, a "historical whirlwind" has gusted through the academic discipline in the United States.[31] Its velocity and direction have been abundantly charted by others; here, the barest summary must suffice. First, the subject matter of history has been massively expanded. New methodologies, new sources of evidence, new themes and concepts have not only transformed existing specialist fields of enquiry but also called into being entirely new genres and sub-disciplines. Secondly, within this broader change, social history made especially dramatic gains: at some point in the 1970s it shed its status as the leading growth industry and became instead the overall market leader. Aspects of the past were deftly lassoed by historians from the corrals of other social sciences: crime and deviancy, health and medicine, sport and leisure, sexuality in all its diversity. Thirdly—and feeding into both developments already mentioned—radical, Marxist, and feminist approaches won larger acceptance within the academic profession.

For the purposes of the South African comparison that follows, it is worth pausing to ask what the impact of left-wing scholarship has been in the United States. In some respects it has been substantial. Leading Marxist and feminist scholars have taken their place in the form rank of the profession whether measured by award or election to honorific office. It is scarcely necessary in the pages of *Radical History Review* to identify particular fields that have been decisively reshaped by radical interpretations: the history of slaves, the South, and African-Americans; urban, labor and immigrant history; the history of the family, sexuality, and gender relations.

Particular mention must be made of the achievements of feminist historians, and the extent to which they have helped reshape visions and versions of the U.S. past. (Their contribution to radical scholarship is contradistinctive to South African historiography: a point considered later.) Without overlooking "a long tradition of female historians studying the history of women," the burgeoning feminist scholarship of the past twenty-five years is clearly rooted, politically and historically, in the emergence and consolidation of the women's movement since the early 1960s.[32] New forms of militancy, of collective conscientization, and of autonomous mobilization stimulated and accelerated research—in history as in other fields. The project of "restoring women to history" was overtaken by that of "restoring history to women"—or, in Gerda Lerner's terms, "compensatory" and "contribution" histories of women were followed by a feminist historiography challenging basic historical assumptions.[33] It is no longer the recovery and reassessment of women's agency and autonomy in history, but an insistence on gender as a central category of analysis that directs feminist history; it is not merely the content of the discipline that is redefined and expanded, but "the premises and standards of existing scholarly work" that must be examined anew.[34] The call is for "not only a new history of women, but also a new history."[35]

Less clear cut are the overall advances made by Marxist history within the mainstream discipline. Estimates range from the hubristic ("A Marxist cultural revolution is taking place today in American universities") to the pessimistic (American Marxism "remains still marginal to the historical discipline"). A recent, authoritative assessment concludes:

> The left presence within the historical profession from the 1960s onward was substantial compared to previous periods, but its strength is often exaggerated. In no important historical specialty were leftists a majority; in no major history department were they more than a small minority.[36]

Novick identifies ways in which radical scholarship has been blunted and/or assimilated in the profession, and reminds us that "All of this . . . took place within a larger context which saw the center of gravity of American political culture steadily move ever farther to the right."[37]

To an outsider peering in, there are two predominant features of contemporary historical study in the United States. One is the fertility of the field and the massive harvest it has yielded (products of the historiographic dynamism outlined above.) The other is a pervasive sense of crisis within the discipline. "Crisis" is a sorely put upon concept, its knuckles rubbed raw through overwork and ill-usage by many employers. In the context of U.S. history the term has stretched from pessimism about graduate numbers and employment prospects through to claims of epistemological exhaustion—with a host of other anxieties in between. Diagnoses and prescriptions have come from right, left, and center.

A source of great concern for over decade has been the fragmentation and compartmentalization of academic history. To a degree, this is basically the price to be paid for the enormous expansion of the discipline in the 1960s and 1970s, the cost of "methodological democratization."[38] In part, it is sheer volume that created confusion. "Only a besotted Faust," lamented Bailyn, "would attempt to keep up with even a large part of this proliferating literature in any detail." But the problem is compounded because the literature has simultaneously proliferated and fragmented. "Over the last twenty years," declared Degler recently, "American history has splintered." It has fractured into sub-disciplines and sub-specializations, and in doing so has generated "intensely parochial, nearly hermetic discourses."[39] Over-specialization is first cousin to self-indulgence. There is a tendency within "new" social history to issue licence of approval to almost any topic, no matter how recondite or arcane. Peter Stearns argued in the mid-1970s for the equal importance of the history of menarche and the history of monarchy. A decade later, he made the earlier project sound positively Gibbonian. "We have," he laments, "no history of sleep habits, and only some hints about the history of boredom."[40]

A related, but separate, issue is the specific critique mounted against the "new social history." The core of the charge is that "all the new social history has a tendency to be too apolitical, if by 'politics' we mean the relations of power."[41] The case has been elaborated by Marxist and radical historians, most robustly by Genovese and Fox-Genovese, but also by Foner, Montgomery, Henretta and others. Their critique has been endorsed by senior liberal historians. Leuchtenburg pointed out that at an OAH convention on the theme "To Study the People," papers at a hundred panels had ranged "from the boll weevil to Chicano murals, while virtually ignoring national politics, as if this were irrelevant to the People's experience."[42]

Further, there is a concern over the absence of any synthesis of the new findings, a prevailing incoherence, and the breakdown of interpretive frameworks or structures. The new scholarship has yielded no deeper knowledge: "depth of understanding is a function, at the least, of coherence, and the one thing above all else that this outpouring of historical writing lacks is coherence."[43] The cry is raised by conservatives, liberals, and radicals. They compete to find words to express the gravity of the situation. History displays "a disintegration of credibility," a "disintegration of a coherent synthesis," a view of the "parts" with "no image of the whole." Confidence in the integrity of the discipline, notes Novick, "fell apart" in the 1970s and 1980s—"not, to be sure, in history alone, but in history more than in any other discipline."[44] One is put in mind of Milton's gloomy realm "where Chaos umpire sits,"

And Tumult and Confusion all embroiled,
And discord with a thousand various mouths.

Finally, there is a fear that academic history is losing a wider audience, failing to communicate with non-historians, and suffering from a "declining significance . . . in the general intellectual culture of our time."[45] The amount of history taught in high schools is shrinking; in the 1970s the numbers of university history majors in the United States fell by almost two thirds. Scholarship has become so specialized and arcane as to speak "not to youth or to laity, but a priesthood of elders."[46] Radical historians fear that the study of the past is being so sundered from the realities of the present as to deprive history of broader social and political functions. Many left-wing historians in the United States share David Montgomery's concern to be "doing work that has some sort of meaning to politics and to the daily lives of working people"—but not all feel that they achieve it. They "often lament [their] own relative lack of political engagement today, compared to a decade or two ago."[47]

> (v) When there is much desire to learn, there of necessity will be much arguing, much writing, many opinions . . .
>
> (Milton, *Aeropagitica*)

There is an international context to the more or less contemporaneous emergence of new left scholarship in the United States and a radical revisionist scholarship among expatriate South Africans. Vietnam radicalized a generation, outside as within the United States, and an eclectic counterculture celebrated the May Days of 1968 as an international phenomenon. Personal experience and intellectual influences also linked the two sets of revisionist work. Of the five authors identified by Marks as first contributing to a paradigmatic shift in South African history, one was a North American, one had studied and taught in California from 1964 to 1969, and one had completed in 1970 an Oxford dissertation on new left interpretations of the origins of the Cold War. Genovese, Barrington Moore, and Wolf provided theoretical points of departure for some of the pioneering South African radical history of the early 1970s.

Several accounts already exist of the recent growth of South African radical scholarship.[48] They trace the expatriate origins of this work in the early 1970s and identify various tendencies that shaped it. They show how by the mid-seventies new theoretical approaches were eagerly taken up inside the country, and note the subsequent growth and diversification of such scholarship, domestically and internationally. They have begun to sketch a periodization of this stripling historiography, showing the interplay between changing thematic concerns and the riptide sequence of events in South Africa since 1973. In tones that range from intemperate hostility through even-handed appraisal to approbation, they have logged its main directions and its achievements. There is no attempt here to discuss or even to summarize these studies. Instead, a kind of stock-taking is ventured of the study of history in South Africa as it appears in the late 1980s. To assist this audit, reference will be made to current U.S. historiography—as sketched above.

Martin Murray may be premature in claiming that Marxism is the "dominant intellectual perspective" in South African history and heralding "Marxist scholarship in . . . its ascendant hegemony." Nonetheless, assessments in more measured language do not differ widely in their findings. Johnstone, in 1982, spoke of South African studies being "transformed" by work "within a new and radically different paradigm";

Marks, in 1986, wrote of "what has in some sense been a shift of paradigm" in South Africa. And in 1988, Saunders and Smith (neither of whom writes from "within" radical scholarship) agreed that "no serious historian could ignore class or a political-economy approach" and, more guardedly, that the new approach has succeeded in "calling attention to very important areas which have thus far been overlooked."[49] Beyond such historiographical judgments, the salience of radical and Marxist history in academic structures and practice is readily apparent. In the English-language (and predominantly white universities, and more tentatively on some black campuses), the arrival of a left scholarship is visible in appointments, syllabi, reading lists, publications, conference proceedings, and (especially) in graduate research.

The advances made by South African radical scholars sprang partly from historiographical factors. The liberal and nationalist schools arraigned by South African revisionists were not as sophisticated or resilient as mainstream U.S. history. The radical attack was also abundantly armed. Emerging only in the 1970s, South African radicals perhaps benefitted from their late start: they could draw simultaneously upon French structuralists, E. P. Thompson, and comparative studies of resistance, peasantries, slavery, and so on. Most fundamentally, the South Africanists were operating in a very different political context. The years of resurgent conservatism in the United States and in Britain saw popular mobilization and mass political resistance in South Africa, with significant inroads made upon ruling-class unity and hegemony. While the metropolitan intellectual left experienced isolation and anxiety, radical scholars in South Africa sensed a support and purpose for their work.

A further advantage of historiographical under-development is that fragmentation and over-specialization is not yet a major problem—and it seems unlikely to become one in the short to medium future. With huge areas of basic spadework still needed to excavate the past, research students are not attracted or pushed into esoteric minutiae. Nobody is urging a history of boredom. (Although some may experience a twinge of misgiving a the idea that "needlework and the role of clothing in conversion . . . constitute one of the great unresearched subjects of South African women's history.")[50]

None of this is an unqualified benefit. On the contrary, it means that entire areas of the past remain blank. The most glaring instance is the meager presence of feminist history in South Africa today. In 1983 Belinda Bozzoli observed that "the recent radical revision of South African history, sociology and politics" had for the most part not "been interwoven with feminist re-interpretations." She urged a self-conscious

"two-way interaction between Marxist and feminist concerns," suggesting ways in which concepts of domestic struggle and types of patriarchy
might be applied to a whole range of historical enquiries—in the precolonial, early industrial, and more recent periods.[51]

Since then, feminist and gender-sensitive historical research has been
conducted and published; but it has not, in South Africa, stamped its
concerns firmly on the broader discipline. An interdisciplinary feminist
academic journal has been launched; but, as its editors observed in its first
issue, in South Africa "the urgency of national and worker struggles has
often resulted in a neglect of the specificity of women's position and
experience."[52] Bozzoli remarked that the lack of interplay between
Marxist and feminist scholarship might "in part be attributed to the absence of a significant South African feminist movement."[53] Strikingly
evident since she wrote has been the continuing tendency for women's
organizations to subordinate specifically feminist issues to anti-apartheid
politics: one of the contributors to the opening issue of *Agenda* argued
that since the great Women's March of 1956, "women's position in the
[national liberation] struggle has become weaker both in terms of their
real participation and in terms of issues taken up."[54] The tendency to
subsume feminism in anti-regime politics is typified by no less an authority than novelist Nadine Gordimer in a review of a biography of Olive
Schreiner, radical and feminist:

> Yet the fact is that in South Africa, now as then, feminism is regarded
> by people whose thinking on race, class and colour Schreiner antici-
> pated, as a question of no relevance to the actual problem of the coun-
> try—which is to free the black majority from white minority rule.[55]

Apart from the limited response to Bozzoli's agenda for feminist
challenges to both Marxist and bourgeois historiography, there are a
number of other fields in which as yet relatively little exploration has
occurred. A start has been made, but not taken very far, in demographic
history, the history of the family, of youth, old age and death; much the
same is true for the history of crime, leisure, health, education and law.
Major episodes of conventional South African historiography like the
Great Trek and the coming of Union "cry out for reinterpretation'" so
does the social history of Afrikaners.[56]

Is there, in South African radical history, a retreat from politics, and
an over-privileging of experience and culture at the expense of more
rigorous class analysis? At first glance, this is unlikely: Marks comments
acutely that in the South African case "it is perhaps more difficult than
elsewhere to ignore the realities of power and domination."[57] At the

same time, there has been real intellectual tension between social historians and social theorists. The former accuse the latter of abstraction, economistic reductionism, anti-historical bias, and not least a deafness to nuance and diversity. Equally, there have been ripostes by those who felt that social history is being seduced by the idiosyncratic, the unique and the subjective to the point of estrangement from broader processes and structures. They warn that a preoccupation with localism blurs perceptions of what is occurring nationally, and are unhappy with work that loses the centrality of production and obscures the labor process. This exchange is very similar to debates within U.S. radical scholarship. The critique of social history parallels that levelled against Herbert Gutman's "strategic retreat" from class.[58] Irrespective of nationality, there may well be, inherent to the social history approach, a methodological centrifugalism, in which microstudies spin off and away from central issues of power and modes of production.

Then there is the question of synthesis. Can new finding be fitted together so as to provide an alternative, coherent interpretation of South African history, and is there an urgent need for such an outcome? Every major review of South African revisionist historiography makes the point that as yet no new overview is available. Most suggest that these are early days and implicitly hold out the prospect of such a synthesis, but a "constant process of rebuilding, refinement and reconceptualization." Smith is less sanguine: as the number of micro-studies proliferate, "a synthesis appears all the more difficult and unlikely."[59]

Indeed, among Afrikaans-language historians the prognosis is quite as angst-ridden as some of the American *cris de coeur* quoted earlier. Van Jaarsveld began thirty years ago, and has persisted indefatigably ever since, to warn his colleagues of the vulnerability of the classic nationalist paradigm. The Afrikaner version of history no longer addressed present realities. It was rigid and insular to the point of "petrification." His solution is twofold. First, he urges methodological innovation and for a reorientation of enquiry toward social history. On the other hand, van Jaarsveld calls for a present-minded approach sensitive to the demands of a "new," "industrialized," and "modernized" South Africa. He envisages an interpretation of the past consistent with the constitutional "reforms" of President Botha. The 1983 constitution is more important than that of 1910, he claims, and has made the "old" past dated and irrelevant; there is need for a "general" history of South Africa which finds a place for all politically legitimated "groups."[60] Grundlingh, one of the few Afrikaner historians whose own work has been directly influenced by radical scholarship, argues that van Jaarsveld's methodological panacea is unattainable.

It is not merely that Afrikaner history does not wish to embrace social history. It is unable to: its basic concepts "are fundamentally opposed to the tenets of modern social history with its emphasis on class conflict and 'history from below.'"[61]

Finally, there is the broader issue: what is the place and weight of history within contemporary South African culture—and what is the political and social function of the discipline? Here, those familiar with the U.S. picture may experience double vision: at once *deja vu* and a glimpse of something quite different. The resemblance is there—for the ruling-class intellectual culture. White supremacist politics is on the retreat; so is confidence in this history as explanation and justification. In 1966 an Afrikaans research report drew attention to the languishing of the subject in the (white) school system. In the Cape province, the number of white matriculants (final year high-school students) taking history fell from over 51 percent to under 28 percent between 1970 and 1986.[62] Bozzoli's depiction of "the dominant philistinism and anti-historical character" of South African culture accurately portrays high/bourgeois/white culture.[63]

Against that must be set a remarkable hunger for history among black South Africans. This is not entirely new. Even before the youth risings of 1976, history in black schools carried a potent charge. A decade earlier, in 1966, a visiting British educationalist taught the French Revolution in a Soweto school, and was struck by the intensity and subtlety with which his students drew contemporary inferences. An observer in Soweto classrooms in 1975 noted that while their textbooks depicted blacks only as "useful labour, dishonest bargainers, foolish farmers, or homeland citizens," pupils and teachers developed their own discourse:

> The questions [about history] came from a high degree of awareness of current events. In a lesson on the French Revolution, the teacher was asked, "How can the rich have no power? Were the palace servants paid? Couldn't the king imprison the thinkers? From which estate came the soldiers?[64]

Today, an appetite for the past is but one component of the mass political and industrial struggles waged since the mid-1970s. The Black Consciousness movement of the seventies instilled a new assertiveness among the oppressed; the youth revolts that have flared periodically since 1976 developed a root and branch critique of their own schooling; while the mushroom growth of black worker organizations and the proliferation of radical community associations have also politicized the educational and cultural domain. A leading "Coloured" educationalist remarked in 1988 that "Today there seems to be a renaissance in regard to the subject [history]." In African schools, between 1982 and 1986, there was an increase of 69 percent in the numbers of matriculants studying history.[65] Recently, an experienced "Coloured" teacher told teacher trainees how he transcended the limits of syllabus and textbooks: "For half of every lesson, I teach the syllabus—and then I teach them real history. Don't worry—they can tell one from the other!"[66] Angry that their own history has long been denied to them, resentful of distorted syllabi and texts, aware of the ideological alternative constituted by radical findings, many black school and university students have begun to press a collective claim—for reparations, for reconstruction—upon the historical profession.

Left historians in South Africa are now under palpable pressure to generate "relevant" work of immediate political utility. Their call for an intellectually independent scholarship is countered by demands for "accountability," and their insistence upon rigorous standards of enquiry is frequently dismissed as pedantry. At times these tensions spill over into outright hostility and mutual non-communication between academics and activists. But the links between political commitment and the production of knowledge can also generate much more positive outcomes. Historians responding to demands for their wares encounter audiences larger and more appreciative than those normally met in their profession. They see their publications or lectures devoured, debated and disseminated in unanticipated settings and in a variety of forms.

The emergent black trade unions of recent years have seen worker education as an important activity—and history has bulked large. Radical academics helped set up the Institute of Industrial Education and the *South African Labour Bulletin*; they provided lectures and papers to worker and shop steward classes; they wrote a series on "The Making of a South African Working Class" for the *FOSATU Worker News*. Zwelakhe Sisulu (son of an ANC leader sentenced to life imprisonment at Rivonia, and editor of *New Nation*, a radical weekly newspaper circulating mainly in African townships) approached the History Workshop and commissioned a series on South African history for the paper's educational section. Academics have provided a weekly page of history since November 1986 (except for the three months that *New Nation* was banned under State of Emergency regulations). Community and "alternative" education groupings also exert a steady demand for talks and material on history. In the week spent revising this article, my departmental colleagues and I have delivered talks at black schools on Sharpeville Day; addressed 900 school students, seated en masse in the schoolyard, on "Why Study

History?"; discussed the French Revolution at a local community study group; lectured on "The History of Resistance" to an anti-conscription group, and given "expert" evidence for the defence in a trial of fourteen alleged ANC members in Cape Town.

The relationship between politics and scholarship in South Africa is immediate and pervasive. The ivory tower has already been breached by popular pressures; grappling-irons promise further to scale its walls, and its base of academic autonomy is being undermined. Some of the occupants of the tower, who identify with the struggle against the status quo, welcome the invaders and try to provide them with a scholarship at once committed and intellectually honest. But there are also more sinister assaults on their edifice. Historians are denied access to sources by state censorship. They see their own work banned, their colleagues deported or refused entry to the country, their students imprisoned and exiled. The last decade has seen an Afrikaner historian tarred and feathered for a mildly heterodox approach to the national past; a liberal social scientist fire-bombed, and activist academics subjected to a variety of anonymous harassments. Richard Turner, a pioneering radical political scientist, was assassinated on his doorstep in 1978.

South African radical historians inhabit a present that makes comprehension of the past seem peculiarly important. Their society's history does not present itself meekly for examination. It intrudes, fierce and feverish, baring its deformities, and demanding immediate attention. There is constant tension between scholarly discipline and social existence; the criteria of academic excellence and political relevance often chafe against one another. By and large, South African historians do not wander in the "studios walks and shades" of "the Olive Grove of Academe." That, remember, came only after Paradise had been Regained.

Chapter 6 / Literature and History in South Africa

Stephen Clingman

Jonathan Shapiro

Towards the end of Nadine Gordimer's *Burger's Daughter*, and to an extent not immediately apparent, the normal conventions of fiction are set aside unceremoniously. Suddenly, into the midst of the narrative is interpolated a document purporting to have been written and distributed by the Soweto Students' Representative Council, which in 1976 orchestrated what came to be known as the Soweto Revolt. The document is presented in seemingly authentic form, replete with linguistic naiveties (for English), spelling and grammar mistakes:

> Black people of Azania remember our beloved dead! Martyers who were massacred from the 16th June 1976 and are still being murdered. We should know Vorster's terrorists wont stop their aggressive approach on innocent Students and people who have dedicated themselves to the liberation of the Black man in South Africa—Azania. . . .[1]

Readers may be unsure of how to take this. What is the status of such a document appearing in a work of fiction? Paradoxically, if it is fictional it may also be reprehensible, representing a rather patronizing attempt on the part of the author to mimic the youthful voices of a body of people going through a grave historical experience. This, however, is where the conventions have been set aside more dramatically than may at first appear, for the document *is* actually authentic: in point of fact it was a pamphlet which appeared on the streets of Soweto during the revolt, and was soon after prohibited by the government; it has been reproduced in *Burger's Daughter* in its exact form. As Gordimer put it later, she evidently felt she neither should nor could mimic or "improve" on it; its presence becomes a kind of tribute in the book.[2]

If the pamphlet's inclusion means the conventions have been dropped, then at a moment such as this the relationship between history and literature is also unusually direct: the novel becomes a social and political archive for preserving a document which might otherwise have disappeared. We hear the voices of real historical agents in all their unmediated presence, and historians can turn to literature for a verifiable piece of the past. In matters of literature and history, however, things are seldom that simple. Indeed, if one were to look through the pages of the general mass of fiction for evidence as straightforward as this, the search by and large would be hard and long. At the same time, however, no one would want to abandon the idea of a central relationship between literature and history—a relationship which seems to promise so much, and which is yet so notoriously hard to pin down. Above and beyond "obvious" examples such as the SSRC document, therefore, we need to think about what literature can offer us historically. Even in this case, the issues seem to deepen immediately. For example, the reasons why Gordimer felt compelled to include the pamphlet, and in this form—may not these constitute a kind of history too? The ideological codes into which it is incorporated in the novel, the very field of debate in the work, the underlying concerns which have provoked the novel into being—these too may have historical dimensions. But to recover them we would have to think of why and how they should be approached.

What is the legitimate use of fiction for historiographic purposes? Moreover, what can South African literature, in particular, tell us about the history from whose context it emerges? Few literary critics these days will uphold the idea of an autonomous domain of literature, whole and replete in itself, in which the only distinctions to be made concern the relative merits of particular works. Yet even those unsympathetic to any form of idealism will still be troubled by residual problems in the idea of relating literature to history: questions of specificity (what is specific to fiction *as* fiction) and value (the *value* of fiction as fiction) may seem especially elided in what appears to be the *secondary* use of literature as "documentary" historical evidence. From a different angle—though originating firmly within the idealist camp—deconstructionist argument will put it that there is hardly any such thing as history at all: the whole world is on the contrary "textual," and "history" is one discourse among many.[3]

Facing both of these positions, this discussion will suggest that, on the contrary, in the South African setting literature is deeply historical; further, that in seeing it this way one by no means reduces a sense of its specificity or value, but tangles with the former and enhances the latter. Indeed, the argument here, put simply, is that the real value of South African literature is that, in its nature *as fiction*, it gives us a specific kind of historical evidence, allowing a particular kind of history to be written.

This controverts the literary purists and the deconstructionists, but it may controvert conventional historiographical practice as well. For, while it is by no means true that the whole world is simply "textual" (as the deconstructionists have recently discovered to their consternation[4]), nonetheless textual elements do constitute a part of the historical evidence that literature can offer. More to the point, the essence of the argument here is that literature (*pace* the example from *Burger's Daughter*) does not just provide a kind of *documentary* evidence; nor is it *supplementary* to something else, more real, called actual history; nor is it *illustration* of any kind for historical facts and patterns already understood. In short, literature offers not historical shadow, but *substance*; it offers a specific kind of evidence within a domain of cultural history.

It is one thing to assert this, a more complex matter to establish particulars: in brief, what kind of evidence does literature offer, and what do we mean when we talk of "cultural" history? The second question is more difficult to answer, but we might begin with it anyway, offering a negative definition as a minimum: we are not talking of "culture" in the "exclusive" sense, having to do with the status of literature as a specific cultural institution. Rather, if literature is to have a real historical value, we must regard it in the inclusive sense, having to do with its larger significance in embodying the ways of life, patterns of experience, and the structures of thought and feeling of communities and classes at large.[5] What then are some of the cultural issues that may be revealed through fiction? A short list would include notions of identity, definitions of self and other, projections of past, present, future, and of value, and apprehensions of the varying problematic areas of social life facing such classes and communities.

As to the kind of evidence literature offers within this sphere, it of course varies widely. Of certain interest to historians will be the kind of social history which emerges through fiction, having to do with patterns of behavior and interaction, modes of dress, speech, and so on, all of which can be mined for a nuanced account of sometimes fairly intricate social interrelationships.[6] While using literature in this way is undoubtedly legitimate, historically considered, one has to say that this is not necessarily specific to what fiction has to offer; evidence of this nature can be found in other sources, though literature is often very good in this domain. As soon as one makes the transition from "what is observed" in the literary work to its *modes* and *forms* of observation and imagination, however, one approaches a level of greater specificity: this has to do with the social and historical *consciousness* embedded in the work—its framework of reality, codes of thought, and structures of perception and vision which shape and add meaning to its observation. Moreover, the significance of the individual work may then resonate more widely: insofar as these features derive from broader social and historical patterns, their presence can become direct evidence of the presence and nature of those patterns in society more generally. In short, at this level one approaches a different kind of history through fiction—a *history of consciousness*, not only of individuals, but of groups, communities, classes, and societies at large.[7]

Such an approach must guard against assumptions of a one-to-one relationship between the individual work and its wider social setting; that relationship may be asymmetrical and "symptomatic" as often as it is fully expressive and coherent.[8] Yet even at this level, and with these qualifications in place, one is bound to say that we still have not reached an understanding of the *specific* nature of the evidence literature can offer: for instance one might look for frameworks of reality, codes of consciousness, patterns of perception and imagination—also asymmetrically, symptomatically, or more coherently represented—in a succession of newspaper editorials, or on its letters pages. But why is it so important to look for what is specific to literature in the first place? Surely—it might be argued—the truly radical thing to do would be, instead of *constructing* boundaries between what is fiction and non-fiction, to *dissolve* what may be only conventional and arbitrary. Then, using whatever historical and literary techniques there are at one's disposal, one could analyze all sorts of documents in complementary ways, be they works of fiction, newspaper editorials and letters, or foreign office or missionary communiques. Works of fiction could be used for sociological information, while the techniques of literary criticism might be applied with benefit to sources of opinion or "fact."

There seems to be much truth in this argument—that historical writing has a lot to gain from an interdisciplinary mixing of methods and sources in its approach to a more completely "total" history than would otherwise be available. But, from a literary point of view, what is it that would really make that history more "total"? Unless we take a purely arbitrary view of human behavior, the presumption has to be that fiction fulfills a need of some kind—and not just an individual, but a social need, otherwise it might not survive. Certain needs may be varying or contingent, having to do, for example, with markets for one kind of fiction or another (which may also be sociologically relevant) or the programmatic intentions of individual writers in relation to those markets. But if there is a need which is more or less "essential" to the form, which overrides or obtains through various contingent manifestations, then we should be able to arrive at a sense of what is specific to literature, in terms of the kind of historical evidence it offers.

Let us take, then, a working definition which is very simple. Following the logic of the argument so far, if certain people in society feel compelled to write fiction (rather than any other form of literary endeavor) and other people to read it, then it can only be because fiction offers them the scope of "writing out" and "reading" certain problems and issues which other forms do not, or at least not in the same way. On the one hand we might say that fiction is where the psychological meets the social: this is where writers address those complex issues linking their subjectivity with broader social realities—for instance where repression and oppression are conjoined.[9] On the other we might say that fiction deals with that area where *potential* history meets the actual—where writers and readers address in indirect ways what is happening to their lives, what might happen, and what their obligations, evasions and responsibilities are.[10] This would seem to be true of popular fiction as much as it is of "high" literature, of oral literature in its various forms, from fairy tales to "praise" poetry, as it is of written work (though a range of cultural mediations needs to be taken into account in each case). From these points of view it appears unarguable that fiction writes out, within its hypothetical and potential frame, the normally hidden issues, complexities, and deeper perturbations of a society. It is this area of a history of consciousness that it corresponds to, this domain of cultural history. It cannot be properly discerned without close attention to the specificities of fictional writing, and in all these respects fiction is *never* simply historical "illustration."

We can be sure that the boundaries are blurred. Not all works of fiction address these issues in the same way or with the same degree of intensity. Similarly, not all elements of a single work of fiction are equally "fictional" in this sense—hence those aspects of a more straightforward social or political history one finds, as in the *Burger's Daughter* example (though even here, as suggested before, in thinking of why Gordimer felt compelled to include the SSRC pamphlet, one notes the transition from a documentary to a more "fictional" history). By contrast, works which claim to be fact may also contain elements of the fictional: even historians may "write out" (in every sense of the phrase) problems in their texts of which they may be only indirectly aware; narrative and its attendant displacements enter in. Newspaper editorials, letters, or communiques may similarly be fictional in this sense, symbolically or allegorically addressing otherwise concealed topics, and historians are no doubt alert to this when it occurs. For the moment, however, my claim is a lesser one: that fiction, especially in the South African context, will *tend* to offer the kind of evidence I have suggested, while historical writing would do well, in my view, to *attend* to it—and not as subordinate, but as a central kind of evidence for our history.

Having made this assertion it is incumbent upon me to show in what ways it is true. In support of this view, then, what I propose to do is select specific literary-historical instances from the body of South African fiction of the last hundred years or so, and enumerate some of the themes that emerge through them for which the fiction is significant evidence. The choice of the time-frame is not accidental, for it seems to me that a remarkable history could be written through the literature of the past century. If one sees that century as beginning with the discovery of diamonds and gold (initiating South Africa's modern industrial era) and takes it up to the present day when (partly because of the way the economy thus instituted has worked) a very different political and cultural future seems to be looming, it is clear how remarkable a period it is. Similarly, South Africa's modern fiction, which everyone more or less sees as beginning with Olive Schreiner in the 1880s, has, by the 1980s, taken us to a very different historical "place."

At every stage, South African fiction has provided an inner history of the country's larger social, political, and cultural development, and it is this which we can set out to trace. But how would such a history begin? Of the many approaches which suggest themselves, perhaps the best is by way of an opposition, in order to indicate that histories of consciousness are in themselves dynamic affairs. One particular opposition concerns Olive Schreiner and Sol Plaatje, each of them in their way founders of modern South African fiction. Schreiner burst upon the literary scene in 1883 as the author of *The Story of an African Farm*, and has remained a continuing inspiration to South African writers ever since (as well as, in another sphere, to feminists internationally).[11] Plaatje has been an equivalent inspiration, both politically, as a founder and leader of the South African Native National Congress (later the African National Congress), and in literary terms, as the author of *Mhudi*, probably the first novel in English by any African.[12] The one writer was white and female, the other black and male. Their lives were distantly connected; but their respective works of fiction constitute a study in contrasts. In many ways both novels are, historically considered, transitional, to varying extents looking over their shoulders to the past, and in different ways rooted in their present moments. It is fitting, therefore, that between them they should set up what we might think of as the "colonial problematic"—the question of who belongs in South Africa and who does not, a theme which carries over from the preindustrial era, but still very much with us today.

Schreiner's novel purports to be firmly "settled" in its African setting; it is after all the story of an *African* farm. Yet, as I have suggested elsewhere, the tale it tells is by contrast one of *alienation* from its environment, though—perhaps unsurprisingly—it naturalizes that colonial condition by seeing it in "universal" terms.[13] A different kind of alienation in the novel is more specific, having to do with the gender of both its author and of its chief character, Lyndall. Here it becomes apparent how, in the colonial setting, it is white femaleness which marks out the boundaries of the licit and illicit; and how, for those who venture beyond those boundaries, the threat of mental destabilization appears. This is something which affects Lyndall in the novel, and affected Schreiner in her own life; appearing in different forms thereafter, it is another crucial theme in this period.[14]

From its first pages, Plaatje's novel (written by about 1917, though it was published only in 1930) makes a different kind of claim—that of *belonging*. Retrospectively casting back into the pre-colonial period, it finds *ab initio* an essential harmony there, with community and landscape fitting one another as a hand fits a glove. Here is a very different image of the place of women: not only does every person appear to have his or her proper position in society, and to be valued in that capacity, but Plaatje actively venerates women in his novel—something Schreiner certainly would have envied. The presentation is no doubt idyllic and idealized, but if one thinks of fiction as "writing out" certain problems, this in itself should be suggestive for the historical mind.

Plaatje's novel is indeed extraordinarily rich historically. The very way it modulates language and literary convention—mixing traditional oral and European literary modes in complex, synthesized textures—becomes the definition of an identity, a meditation on cultural transition, and as such the implicit basis of a political claim. Commentators have pointed out how much of the allegoric function of the novel relates to the 1913 Land Act, a traumatic moment of land-dispossession for Africans which Plaatje travelled the country witnessing at first hand, to record in his other major work, *Native Life in South Africa;*[15] hence, one might point out again, the force of his claim to legitimacy and belonging from the first pages of his novel. There is one theme in the novel, however, which has not received much commentary, though I should like to raise it here because it illustrates perfectly the idea that fiction provides specific and relatively unique kinds of evidence.

Mhudi is set in the 1830s, in the period of the *Difaqane*—the "great scattering" of the peoples of southern Africa in the wake of the Shakan wars—into the midst of which the Boers moved on their Great Trek into the interior. Plaatje locates the novel in (what is now) the western and northern Transvaal, where an arena of relatively fluid conflicts and alliances between Boers, Barolong, and Matabele provides scope within the work for a complex articulation of social and political possibilities. One aspect of this has to do with the racial and cultural hierarchies which Plaatje sets up. Top of the ladder, by his account, are the Barolong, who are shown to be morally more advanced and socially more mature than any of the competing groups; next come the Boers, with whom the Barolong set up a strategic alliance against the Matabele, but who are evidently more cunning and barbaric; lowest of all are the Matabele themselves, who wander around naked, are on occasion described as "very black" and who are in general shown as markedly savage. Obviously the key code Plaatje is working with here is that of "civilization"; this is no surprise because it was the standard by which Africans were being measured at the time (though usually only in negative terms) as well as one which Plaatje and his colleagues in the newly formed SANNC (ANC) accepted as a legitimate measure of their worth in their quest for political rights. Within his own cultural traditions, which Plaatje retails in the novel, it is evident that it would have been an acceptable measure. All that he is doing is turning the tables on the conventional category by showing how much more "civilized"—and therefore more *deserving* of a political alliance—than anyone else the Barolong are.

Yet in the aftermath of the defeat of the Matabele by the alliance of the Barolong and Boers, there is a shift in sympathy in the novel: the routed Mzilikazi (chief of the Matabele) makes an impassioned speech prophesying the future betrayal of the Barolong by the Boers (probably a reference to the 1913 Land Act) and it comes to appear that a broader, nationalist combination against the invader might have made more sense. What else can this be but Plaatje's construction of various allegoric scenarios in his fiction? If the "civilized" alliance between a black elite and white power does not work, there are always the "masses" (symbolically the Matabele) out there; the allegory is both a threat on Plaatje's behalf, but also, it would seem, something deeply troubling to him, for his distance from and suspicion of those "masses" has also been indicated in the novel. The significance of this resonates beyond Plaatje's individual consciousness: nothing could better represent, I would suggest, the psychological and political ambiguities facing the small group of ANC leaders, of whom Plaatje was one from the inception of the organization in 1912, than this threatening but troubled allegory. In this way the novel addresses a problem it can scarcely formulate consciously, and provides a rare form of insight historically considered. At the same time, the "colonial problematic" has been transformed from the question of *who* belongs in South Africa to its much more productive historical form of *how* and *on what terms* that belonging should occur—an issue still being worked out every day inside the country.

Other fiction of the 1920s provides a different kind of evidence, having to do with further major historical themes. As South Africa settled into its patterns of modern development in that decade, racial legislation proliferated, regulating everything from labor relations on the mines and industry to living areas and sexual relations.[16] In this setting, as David Rabkin pointed out, it is no surprise that two major novels of race emerged—Sarah Gertrude Millin's *God's Stepchildren* and William Plomer's *Turbott Wolfe*.[17] Millin's novel is written, in the precise sense, as an "experimental" narrative in that it sets up a social experiment to see what happens over the course of four generations when miscegenation takes place. What the book reveals along the way are its rather seamy racial obsessions, the product of evident repressions, projections, and displacements. Yet one should not deduce from this simply a personal mental instability on Millin's part, for the fact of the matter is that the book was extremely well received—in the United States and Nazi Germany, for example, as well as (though after some delay) in South Africa, where Millin was hailed by at least one putative authority as "the greatest of all South African novelists," apparently because of her "dignity and sanity."[18] From this point of view, everything about the book, from its pseudo-scientific framing to the squalid nature of its imagery, is evidence of the inner workings and usually hidden patterns of a broader racial framework at large. Here the psychological, and indeed the psycho-biographical, truly meet the social, suggesting not only the force of the South African racial framework in this period, but also its acute mental violence, both for the subjects and objects of its propagation. William Plomer's novel, by contrast, is apparently intended to *promote* miscegenation as the solution to South Africa's problems, but as soon as this is actualized in the novel it descends, for complex reasons, into incoherence—again, at minimum, evidence of the force of a surrounding framework and of its inner malevolence.[19]

But what is happening on the other side, as it were, of this class and racial line? Fiction emerging from the 1930s and 1940s assists in giving us some answers. As works such as Modikwe Dikobe's *The Marabi Dance* (published in the 1970s, though it derives from the 1930s) help establish,

this was in any case an era of major transition.[20] With the time-lags attendant on cultural transformations, by the 1930s a now-settled urban black
proletariat had to encounter major shifts in its forms of existence, not
least by way of fashioning meaning and a new sense of identity in dramatically changed and changing circumstances. Thus, the shift from a
rural to an urban status; changes from a traditional to a transitional culture; the imbrication of newly-forming class and cultural patterns: all of
these are represented in *The Marabi Dance*, not least because it includes
three generations in indicating what fundamental transformations in
their lives mean to its male and female characters. From this point of
view, discussion as to whether *The Marabi Dance* is South Africa's first
"working class" novel is slightly beside the point.[21] Rather, the work
indicates how closely class, culture, gender, and generation are involved
in the highly complex processes of forming, and experiencing, new social identities. The very fact that Dikobe felt the need to address these
issues in this way is evidence of the force and significance of these transitions: we deduce the social perturbations to which it is the fictional address and attempted "solution."[22] While *The Marabi Dance* is not the only
evidence for these themes, it does, on closer inspection, give an extraordinary inner account of the major issues of its period.

South African fiction is of course also ideological evidence. Thus,
where writers such as Dikobe or Peter Abrahams (in his novel, *Mine Boy*,
for instance[23]) see the troubled but in some ways triumphant construction of new black urban identities, a work such as Alan Paton's *Cry, the
Beloved Country* sees only destruction and demotivation.[24] This novel—
whose fame in Europe and the United States itself requires ideological
analysis—concerns a black pastor from Zululand whose son has murdered a prominent liberal in what is represented as the fallen, teeming
city of Johannesburg; the father is unable to save the son from the gal-
lows, but in turn finds his own form of understanding, back in Zululand,
in relation to the God-like father of the son his own son murdered. The
cadence of the novel is biblical, and everything about the work is revealing. In Johannesburg black politicians are typologically represented as
liars, cheats, and cowards, while the moral of the novel seems to be that
the slow shall be rewarded and that the meek shall inherit the charity of
the high and mighty (this is what the father of the murdered son ultimately provides for the black pastor's community). Indeed, the barely
hidden keyword of the work is "communion": if the black father of a
murderer and the white father of his victim can find it, so the logic of the
novel seems to run, then who can't? In this way, though presented in a
rather intense, religious form, the novel establishes its wider historical

significance—for it was undoubtedly the logic of some kind of interracial "communion" that saw the South African liberal opposition to apartheid into the 1950s, founded as it was primarily on moral principles. Paton of course became a leader of the Liberal Party; when his novel is analyzed with care—and one has to stress "with care," because there is no direct line between the work and Liberal Party policy—*Cry, the Beloved Country* lays out some of the major codes and workings of white liberal consciousness in this period, its allegories of power and love, what it feared and what it desired.

Incidentally, the tremendous success of the novel establishes its historical significance in another form. The common approach to a sociology of literature often asks about the intended audience of a particular work. Here one sees how, by contrast, Paton was evidently "authorized" by his audience to say certain things in certain ways, that "audience" can, in this sense, be "author." This again underlines the value of fiction in historical terms, however, insofar as it takes us back to a broader social consciousness at large informing the work.

By now my basic points should be getting across, and it might be clear as to how one could take the story further. Thus, the black short fiction and journalism of the 1950s (often a thin dividing line between the two) takes us into the inner moods of the period. Whereas the common mythology of the decade is of a glorious and boisterous black cultural revival accompanying the political renaissance of that time, accounts such as Can Themba's "The Bottom of the Bottle" indicate that there was a darker and much more anguished side; the story ends with Themba's journalist/narrator figure staring cynically into the "bottle" which drains him of any social or political solidarity.[25] In the same period Nadine Gordimer's *A World of Strangers*, delving into Johannesburg's ethos of racial and cultural fusion, lays out in an extraordinarily embracing way the dominant social and historical codes of the time.[26] In the 1960s, writers such as Gordimer, Alex La Guma, Richard Rive, and C. J. Driver were drawn to the political upheavals of the period, exploring its meanings in what were now much more deliberately focused political fictions.[27] Alex La Guma is particularly interesting: as a member of the Communist Party (and later the ANC), he explores, in works such as *In the Fog of the Seasons' End*, points of conjunction between everyday struggle and broader political commitment within the "Coloured" community of Cape Town.

As far as the politics of the 1970s are concerned, they simply cannot be understood without reference to the literature of the period. Historically, the decade itself seemed to spiral around the Soweto Revolt when, from 16 June 1976, and for more than a year afterwards, the schoolchildren of Soweto (and then, cumulatively, of the country at large) took on the *force majeure* of the state, initially over the issue of language.[28] Though the lines of transmission were not direct, the underlying ideological ethos of the revolt was that of Black Consciousness, and one of the main bearers and vehicles of the Black Consciousness movement was poetry. Moreover, when we look at it now, the poetry reveals an unexpected side to the movement. Whereas the dominant impression of Black Consciousness was one of assertion—of the confident achievement of dignity through the liberation of the black psyche and of a return to black cultural roots—the poetry shows the devastatingly honest self-inspection of vulnerability and wounding by oppression, the thorough knowledge of which, it seems, had to preface any revival. Reaching into the depths of humiliation and dehumanization afforded under apartheid, the poetry shocks with the extremity of its grieving, bitter, and ironic self-consciousness. Njabulo Ndebele begins one of his poems with the lines, "I hid my love in the sewage/ Of a city . . ." and ends it with "I am the hoof that once/ Grazed in silence upon the grass,/ But now rings like a bell on tarred streets."[29] Mongane Serote begins a poem which is eventually about revival in the following way:

It is not the steaming little rot
In the toilet bucket,
It is the upheaval of the bowels
Bleeding and coming out through the mouth
And swallowed back,
Rolling in the mouth,
Feeling its taste and wondering what's next like it.[30]

Nothing can be more honest, or graphic, than this. If Black Consciousness was about cultural assertion, here we understand, in a way that little else can tell us, the sheer psychological agony that was required and woven into that assertion. Again, the point is of central importance that the poetry was not *incidental* to Black Consciousness, but part of its very *substance*. Despite specific complications in assessing it, the period cannot be understood without the poetry.[31] Incidentally—returning to the point where this paper began—an awareness of the poetry adds vast dimensions to our understanding of Gordimer's *Burger's Daughter*: for instance, of her need to address the voice of the children at that time, and of the hidden arenas of psychological experience underlying their heroism, of their actual use of *words* in the document.

What then of the current period? If we cast our eyes back over the century, an interesting shift makes itself apparent. As has already been suggested, both Schreiner (implicitly) and Plaatje (explicitly) looked over their shoulders to the past while confronting the present in which they were writing. Thereafter, from the 1920s through to the 1970s, it was successive moments in the present which engaged South African writers. Now, however, there is a different topic: in South African fiction, as in South African life more generally, it is evidently the *future* which is the presiding question that must be addressed. This in itself is an index of a major shift of consciousness.[32] The fictional response has inevitably been a varied one, from the guarded welcome of a revolutionary future by Nadine Gordimer (*July's People*, *A Sport of Nature*), to its guarded rejection by J. M. Coetzee (*Life & Times of Michael K*), to a deliberate and purposive meditation on the part of Mongane Serote as to how that future may be brought about (*To Every Birth its Blood*).[33] But common to all three is that allegories of the future are being written. Jeremy Cronin (a white poet who himself spent seven years in jail for ANC activities) has recorded how, in the townships, new modes of poetic performance are actively calling that future into being.[34] All of this yet again reinforces my feeling that it is in fiction that individuals, consciously and even unconsciously attuned, write out for their communities the presiding issues of their worlds, of the histories that confront them. I have no doubt that in another hundred years the fiction of the 1980s, as well as cultural production of other kinds, will be among the most significant bodies of evidence as to what was happening and about to happen a century before.

Chapter 7

Charters from the Past:

The African National Congress and Its Historiographical Traditions

Tom Lodge

New Age, Thursday, April 17, 1958.

This article is about the historical writing that can be associated with the intellectual formation of the African National Congress. On the whole, the texts discussed here are not the work of professional scholars; the emphasis is rather on material which reflects the way the ANC as a community (or at least its leadership) understands the South African past, whether viewed through the lens of its own institutional chronology or more broadly. In this sense, the ANC has generated a substantial body of historical literature, yet as a political movement the ANC is somewhat at a disadvantage when these texts are examined as a "tradition." It is not that the ANC lacks a well developed sense of its historical identity. The very rhythm of its present day political and military activity demonstrates a deeply etched collective memory expressed through an annual calendar of commemorations and anniversaries. ANC speeches are larded with historical references, to pre-colonial societies, to primary resistance, and to its own previous campaigning. ANC recruits are drilled with a basic chronology of the ANC's own development. The ANC frequently legitimizes present decisions by referring to historical precedents, both from its own past as well as an international revolutionary tradition. Yet when the ANC as a movement writes its own history, it is difficult to discern from what emerges an understanding of the past that seems shaped by intellectual traditions that flow from the movement's own cultural base. To be sure there are certain unifying themes—especially evident when writers working within the ANC discuss the history of the organization itself—but in the written historical works the efforts to construct an alternative national interpretation about the past seem half-hearted in comparison to the work generated by other politically motivated groups of South African historians. This paper is about these historical texts but it needs to be said from the beginning that they are probably an inadequate reflection of the way people within the ANC have perceived the past.

This may be partly because of the ambivalence in the manner in which the ANC over the years has constituted itself as a nationalist movement. In the 1940s, Youth Leaguers emphasized a national identity in which race pride and African culture were central constituents. Youth League Africanists were very conscious of the need to *construct* a national culture and their program included a call for the foundation of an African Academy of the Arts and Sciences. By the mid 1950s, though, adherents of "exclusivist" ethnic nationalism were an isolated minority within the organization's leadership. The ANC's adoption of the Freedom Charter in 1956 represented a deliberate eschewal of racial, linguistic, or culturally-based nationalism. Indeed, if nationalism is essentially "the political expression of shared ethnic consciousness" then it becomes questionable whether since then the ANC can be considered a nationalist movement at all.[1] Such a definition of nationalism, though, is an extremely confined one. It fits at best awkwardly the African nationalisms that developed elsewhere on the continent. Yet these anti-colonial movements drew heavily upon cultural components to constitute their "imagined" national communities. In contrast, ANC theorists argue that "class, political and economic issues" can supply an alternate sustenance for the formation of national identity in place of cultural and ethnic resources.[2] That may be the case, but a program based on, for example, the Reverend Z. R. Mahabane's notion of "full and free cooperation of all the white and black races of the land" is one which cannot easily accommodate an African nationalist reconstruction of the past.[3] Of course, there is plenty of material which can be employed in a historiography which emphasizes non-racial traditions in South African history. Modern ANC writers acknowledge the importance of both Christian liberalism and socialist class analysis in influencing the intellectual development of their movement.[4] But these are traditions which have both been dominant at different times in English language South African scholarship and so it is not surprising that it is difficult to distinguish a set of historical perceptions that are peculiarly characteristic of the ANC's depiction of the past.

A nativist, or, to use its own terminology, "Africanist" tradition does exist within the ANC. Certainly, it has found its most forceful expression among groups and personalities who have at one time or another broken away from the organization. Before they went into exile, Pan Africanists talked of the need to "recreate a set of values that will give meaning to the lives of our people." Robert Sobukwe, by profession a university teacher of African languages, used to preface his vernacular speeches with peasant folk wisdom: "I am the son of Sobukwe, born in Graaff-Reinett—that land of goats, the animal which we often have to quarantine when it has scabies." Gerhart suggests that central to the PAC's efforts to promote an Africanized political culture was its popularization "as a nationalist rallying point the memory of eighteenth and nineteenth century African heroes."[5] They were not alone in this; Transvaal ANC President E. M. Moretsele's speeches at meetings conducted in African languages were laced with martial references to pre-colonial Pedi history. This was at a time when the ANC was seeking to extend its rural influence through Sekhukune migrant worker networks. Nelson Mandela was formally photographed by Eli Weinberg in Xhosa costume and later at his trial Mandela described a communitarian ideal which drew its inspiration from his own perception of the precolonial political structures.[6] Even today the ANC deploys symbols, conventions, and language drawn from the period of primary resistance to reinforce its identity as an *African* organization. But this popular historical discourse surfaces very intermittently in the historical writing produced by ANC intellectuals and leaders.

The ANC has not yet commissioned an official history of itself and has only recently begun to sponsor the production of historical textbooks for use in its classrooms. It is possible, though, to distinguish a literary testament associated with the ANC that includes historical narrative and analysis. Within this tradition there are also works which if not primarily historical nevertheless contain important assumptions about the past. This historical testament can be assembled from four groups of writings. First there is a series of fairly substantial works of biography, historical fiction, and social reportage which come from the earliest phase of the ANC's development, when the organization and the men who led it were still rooted in a rural culture. This is followed by a rich vein of autobiography produced mainly in the milieu of 1950s townships and locations, some of it written by people who were active within Congress or close to it. A third category is represented by a succession of more analytical books written by 1940s and 1950s participants in the affairs of the Communist Party as well as the Congress Alliance. The final contribution is from a more recent generation of ANC historians whose academic training and intellectual formation have been influenced by the circumstances of exile. Whether this body of writing can be brought together to constitute a coherent and distinct ANC historiography is a question which will be addressed later in this paper; first more needs to be said about the texts themselves and the people who produced them.

It may not be coincidental that the two foremost historical writers who can be associated with the ANC's early development, S. Modiri Molema (1891–1965) and Sol T. Plaatje (1876–1932), both grew up within Barolong communities, chiefdoms scattered across the northern

Cape, the western Transvaal and the Orange Free State. By the turn of the century, the Barolong inhabited regions which were comparatively lightly settled by white farmers and while retaining a largely intact pastoral economy they were affected by an extensive missionary presence. The two men were born into prosperous peasant families, were intellectually formed by a mission-transmitted literary culture, and lived their childhoods in largely autonomous African chiefdoms, to which, in Molema's case, he could claim close recent kinship. Of the two, Molema can be more conventionally considered a historian while Plaatje was more conspicuous as a politician. Plaatje wrote extensively, of course, as a journalist, novelist, and social commentator and much of his work exhibits historical sensitivity. This is especially evident in his novel *Mhudi*, set in the 1830s during the strife between Mzilikazi's armies and the Barolong. The historical events which supply the framework for the plot begin with the killing by the Barolong Chief Tawana of two of Mzilikazi's tax collectors. Their murder provokes a ferocious attack by Mzilikazi's soldiers on Tawana's clan. The survivors of this massacre join forces with the incoming Voortrekkers to expel Mzilikazi's regiments from the Transvaal.

As a work strongly derived from Barolong oral tradition, *Mhudi* merits serious attention as history. It includes one of the earliest published African correctives to prevalent European stereotypes which depicted precolonial African societies as uniformly barbaric. Plaatje portrays a "community life" in which "abject poverty was practically unknown" and "none could be so mean as to make a charge for supplying a fellow tribesman with the necessaries of life." Plaatje's presentation of this society is not sentimental; he acknowledges its insularity and its economic shortcomings and he concludes that in certain respects Mzilikazi's occupation "might have worked well enough" with its "fresh discipline" but for "manners that were extremely offensive even for that primitive people." Modern commentaries on *Mhudi* have emphasized its central theme of prophecy, reading in Mzilikazi's warning to the Barolong of the fateful consequences of their alliance with the Boers, "these marauding from the seas," a contemporary historical lesson, that violent retribution is always the inevitable aftermath of tyranny. There is a conspicuous moral ambivalence in the plot's treatment of Mzilikazi's kingdom, a society which can generate the perceptive vein of social criticism in the speech of Mzilikazi's heroic general, Gubuza. Plaatje concedes that Mzilikazi's expansionism represented "a beautiful ideal" in which the "overpowering and annexing of adjacent tribes" would lead to the "establishment of an idyllic empire, stretching from the sandy woods of

Bechuanaland to the corals of Monomotapa." Alone among the Matabele, Gubuza was distinguished by wearing sandals similar to those used
by the Barolong. In his life he "has sat at the feet of many a wise man"
and had journeyed "to Zululand, to Swaziland, to Tongaland, and to
Basutoland." He represents in the text a historical antecedent for the
pan-South African political identity which was such a cardinal preoccupation for the ANC's founders. The resolution of the novel's sub-plot,
the enduring friendship between the Barolong Ra-thaga and the Boer
de Villiers, expresses a Christian brotherhood in which "there is neither Greek nor Jew, bond nor free, male nor female, white nor black,
but all are one in Christ Jesus." It reflects the ANC's concept of a racially
inclusive nation based on common values, an ethic which for African
intellectuals such as Plaatje found powerful historical resonances in
the hospitable capacity of both the Barolong and Matabele to absorb
outsiders.[7]

Comparisons between Plaatje's and Modiri Molema's historical perceptions are illuminating. In Molema's posthumously published *Montshiwa*, the depiction of the Matebele state contains few subtleties. Mzilikazi is a fitting representative of the "Tshaka school of blood" which
reduced South Africa to a "seething cauldron of intertribal violence and
bloodshed." The agencies of historical progress were the Christian missionaries whose presence among the Barolong alleviated "the density of
darkness in their minds."[8] *Montshiwa* was written late in Molema's life,
when such views were more widely questioned than when Plaatje recalled in 1915 "the happy reign of Queen Victoria, during which (Africans) were led from the thralldom of heathenism and their native darkness into the enjoyments of social, economic, and spiritual benefits
through missionary enterprise."[9] Montshiwa was Tawana's son; for Molema his greatness lay in his tolerance of an alien faith and his willingness to embrace the secular knowledge which accompanied that faith.
This made him a hero "beyond the limits of his tribe." Notwithstanding
Montshiwa's early fears concerning the spiritual challenge to his authority represented by the Christians (led by his brother Molema, Modiri's
grandfather), ·he later discovered in the Christian converts "the most
loyal and industrious of his people." For Molema, Montshiwa's statecraft
embodied a creative synthesis in which the chief's "constancy" and
"primeval assumptions" combined with an acceptance of Christian modernity in which "his tribe made considerable progress materially, socially, and intellectually." His reign was more akin to "an advanced
modern democracy than that of any chiefdom of his time . . . he was a
constitutional monarch . . . ruled by his councillors." In part, this

achievement was attributable to Batswana traditions, ones which "do not hold with dictatorship," but ones which the Barolong could not have sustained unaided. For the Barolong state was built on a "fitful and precarious material base," "boundaries only (becoming) important with the advent of the European idea of individualism." It was the "individual ownership of landed property" which served as "a motive force for industry, progress and civilisation." But Molema's understandings of Montshiwa's statecraft and missionary ideals are essentially tragic, for both were to be eclipsed in the conflict among British imperialism, Cape colonialism, and Transvaal republicanism.[10]

Plaatje and Molema knew each other well, they read each other's writing, and both held high office in the ANC, Plaatje in the years following its founding, Molema somewhat later, in the 1930s, when he served as treasurer under Pixley ka Isaka Seme's presidency. As writers they expressed a historical consciousness which was probably generally typical of the early generations of Congress leadership. Most early ANC notables shared a family background of wealthy peasant proprietorship, kinship with the chieftaincy, and an awareness of belonging to the vanguard of social progress, though at the same time remaining sensitive to the civic virtues of a "purely African outlook."[11] Plaatje was exceptional in being largely self educated after leaving school in his teens; most of his colleagues were members of an academically nurtured intelligentsia, often trained at European or American universities (Molema qualified as a medical practitioner in Glasgow). This group was by the 1920s producing a prolific and leisured literary culture of newspapers (the ANC published its own newspaper, *Abantu Batho*), letters, polemics, and debate. It was a culture supported by a rural material base which, of course, from 1913 was under constant attack and which, after the First World War, was to undergo almost complete destruction.

By the late 1930s, with a younger cohort of black intellectuals, the modernizing "progressivism" which was such an important component in the worldviews of men such as Plaatje or Molema, had begun to be supplanted with antipathy to white liberal efforts to influence the course of black politics. In the writing of H.I.E. Dhlomo (1903–1956), teacher, journalist, and from 1943 editor of *Ilanga lase Natal*, the author's enforced resignation as organizer for the Carnegie Non European Library helped to crystallize this feeling. In Dhlomo's dramatic epic, *Cetshwayo*, it finds expression in the Zulu king's sardonic distrust of missionaries—"white Christian spies." Cetshwayo's eventual downfall is partly the consequence of his misplaced trust in "English friends." In the words of his "field marshal," Dabulamanzi: "Had the black man trusted himself as he has the white man we would have much achieved." In Dhlomo's play, Cetshwayo dies heroically at the hands of the treacherous white trader, John Dunn; in fact the historical record attributes his death to either heart failure or poisoning after an undignified restoration as the ruler of a rump Zulu kingdom. In the play, though, Cetshwayo ends his life as a pan-African prophet shouting defiance: "We shall be free! / Each race its lord and clime! / An Africa for the Africans remains! / Black Kings shall watch over vast domains! / Black bulls! Black bulls! / No power their rush can stem! / No force can conquer them!."[12]

In 1945 Dhlomo helped to found the Durban branch of the ANC Youth League. His work from that period contains some of the most substantial literary expressions of an "Africanist" nationalist conscious-ness. As a historical vision it is much more romantically idealized that Molema's or even Plaatje's evocation of precolonial societies. For Dhlomo discerned in the wars of Shaka and his successors the will "to unite all the races into one nation . . . a nation slow to leave the past, a nation that can fight and last."[13] It is a theme which has persisted since Dhlomo's time: Bernard Magubane writing in exile in the 1970s argues that "at one point the Zulu empire was about to unite the whole of South Africa under its rule."[14] More generally, Youth Leaguers adhered to the notion of a pristine communitarian precolonial society whose governing principles could be resurrected in modern state forms.[15] It was a vision of the past which outlived the duration of the Youth League's existence as an active political force. Nelson Mandela eloquently ex-pressed these ideas at his trial in 1962:

> Many years ago, when I was a boy brought up in my village in the Transkei, I listened to the elders of the tribe telling stories about the good old days, before the armies of the white man. Then our people lived peacefully, under the democratic rule of kings. . . . The names of Dingaan and Bambata among the Zulus, of Hintsa, Makana, and Ndlambe of the Amaxhosa, of Sekhukuni and others in the North, were mentioned as the pride and glory of the entire African nation. . . . The structure and organisation of early African societies in this country fascinated me very much and greatly influenced the evolution of my political outlook. . . . There were no classes, nor rich or poor, and no exploitation of men by men. . . . In such a society are contained the seeds of a revolutionary democracy in which none are held in slav-ery. . . . This is the inspiration which, even today, inspires me and my colleagues in our political struggle. . . .[16]

Significantly, when nineteenth-century African kings appeared in the Youth League pantheon, it is as warriors and resisters rather than the amenable conciliators and gentle Christian converts commemorated by Plaatje and Molema. But though the heroic perception of precolonial history may have predominated in the oral discourse of political meetings, it did not find frequent expression in the historical writing which can be associated with the ANC in the 1950s and subsequently. Indeed, very little history at all was written by ANC predisposed intellectuals during the decade of Congress's transformation into a mass movement. The ANC's own transition toward becoming a more activist and militant movement often seemed to make its leaders impatient with what they termed "intellectualism." Ezekiel Mphahlele complains of that period that the ANC "never really interested itself in educational and cultural matters as an important front of our activities." Though formally educated men still prevailed among the ANC's upper echelons, its leadership was more socially heterodox than hitherto and certainly included many people who were not immersed in the culture of letter writing, polemical journalism, and imaginative fiction that distinguished men such as Sol Plaatje. It was also true that in the 1950s, African writers were beginning to emerge as a distinct group with a corporate perception of themselves as an intelligentsia standing apart from the broader community. Additionally, writers and activists were together usually much more profoundly shaped by an urban industrial culture than the ANC scholar-statesmen of Plaatje or Molema's generations. To be sure, some would have shared with Mphahlele the memory of a childhood membership of a community in which "we learned a good deal at the fireplace."[17] But for Mphahlele such folk wisdom could not nurture any meaningful sense of nationhood. As he wrote in 1956:

> Non whites live in locations, or in the reserves, or work for whites in towns and on farms, where they are either labour tenants or squatters. There can hardly be a healthy, common culture in conditions that isolate whole communities and make social and economic intercourse difficult or impossible. And the problem of national culture is *per se* the problem of national liberation. It must remain sectional or sterile as long as such conditions prevail. . . .[18]

The defining experiences of Mphahlele's intellectual contemporaries included the bitter contrasts between the squalor and indignity of their living environment and the exhilaration of claiming as their own a "great tradition" of Western high culture.[19] The culture of "multiracialism" reflected in the Congress Alliance was widely influential and for Johannesburg's African writers extended well beyond the confines of organizational politics. It helped to stimulate an exciting and powerful literature of short stories, social reportage, and personal testimony, but it worked against any nationalist-inspired exploration of the past. It was a literature which was set in the present and which centered on the everyday experiences of working and living in the tightly cohesive freehold communities of Johannesburg, according to them a culturally cosmopolitan glamor which has since assumed almost mythic proportions.[20] Many of the major literary talents of the 1950s avoided burdensome political associations partly through inclination but also because of the penalties involved: both teachers and journalists were forbidden or discouraged from joining political organizations.

Chief Luthuli was fairly exceptional among ANC leaders of that time in recording a full length autobiography, dictated to the Reverend Charles Hooper who arranged the transcribed material for the chief to revise. About half the text of *Let My People Go* comprises a chronology of the ANC's campaigning during the 1950s with very little detail on Luthuli's own contribution as president. The narrative depicts an ANC carried along on a wave of popular militancy, often taking it well beyond its organizational capabilities—the shortcomings of which Luthuli candidly concedes. The first part of the book is more personal, describing the Chief's upbringing in a "home (that) was conducted as a Christian home should be." Luthuli was the son of a famous missionary and teacher who had served with British soldiers in suppressing the 1896 Ndebele uprising. His grandfather was one of the first converts at the American Board Mission at Groutville. Both these forebears worked as chiefs on the reserve, an office to which Albert Luthuli himself was elected in 1935. *Let My People Go* is recognizably the voice of a historical identity which was on the defensive by the 1950s. Luthuli writes of his schooling (at Ohlange and the Edendale Methodist Institute) as an experience in which "two cultures met . . . both profited." Political office, church responsibilities, and higher education did not isolate him from "the ordinary life of the village . . . I remain an African." The community which Luthuli perceived to be threatened by the state expressed African values regulated by "Christian standards." It was a community which lived through a non racial ethos; at school, taught largely by whites, "we were not particularly conscious they were Europeans." For the chief the ANC's activities in the 1950s were directed at the reconstitution and extension of such a community; the Congresses' 1951 Joint Planning Council brought the movement "one step nearer to the day when race will be of only incidental importance." In *Let My People Go* it is easy to document the continuities from the optimistic modernizing syncretism which characterized the social project of the ANC's founding fathers. But such beliefs were becoming less persuasive among African intellectuals.[21]

On the one hand romantic nationalists sought a reconstruction of an Africanist culture and polity. One of the strongest literary/historical expressions of such a mission can be located in the writings of Jordan Ngubane. Ngubane was one of the founders of the Youth League and during the 1940s and early 1950s edited *Inkundla ya Bantu*.[22] His hostility to communists prompted a break with the ANC which he left in 1955 to join the Liberal Party. By the end of the decade he was known to be sympathetic to the Africanists, though he never joined the Pan African Congress. In exile from 1961, his first book, *An African Explains Apartheid*, is very largely an acrimonious attack on the impact made by communists on the evolution of African organizations. In subsequent work, though, Ngubane is concerned to develop an idealist theory of South African history as essentially the conflict of two philosophies, in which "race and colour are merely vehicles for the collision . . . not themselves . . . causes of conflict." Racial (and, by implication, class) conflict is explained by the clash between two ideals of fulfillment. One of these Ngubane characterizes as derivative of Greek, Roman, and Hebrew traditions, with its emphases on individual achievement, original sin, and the attainment of power and wealth. Counterpoised to this is an "evaluation of person," according to Ngubane conditioning most sub-Saharan African cultures, in which "the best possible use of life" is the realization "of the promise and glory of being human." Ngubane believes that these values were intrinsic to the notion of Zulu citizenship embodied in the Shakan revolution. Here a humanist respect of others supplies the cultural cement for a community in which "no man is good or evil . . . each responds to the necessity that is within him" and yet "no person has what his neighbour does not have." To recreate this, Ngubane urges a return to African cosmology and law and conversely a repudiation of the organizational, religious, and technical principles of colonial culture. By the time these ideas had reached their fullest development in Ngubane's work, he, logically enough, had returned from exile to assume a role as an ideologue within Inkatha.[23]

More attractive, though, at least among historical writers associated with the ANC since the 1950s, have been the ideas supplied by Marxism. The construction by trade unionists in the 1940s of an organized working-class constituency, and the simultaneous development of a township political base by the Communist Party, strengthened the enticements of a social analysis derived from Marxist theory. Despite the suppression of the party, communists continued to supply vital resources to African opposition politics including a range of publications which became the essential medium of printed communication for the Congress Alliance. More active recruitment within younger ANC leadership may have enhanced communist intellectual influence and certainly it is the case that such SACP principals as Moses Kotane made an important contribution toward defining ANC strategy throughout the decade.[24] But even among ANC personalities who favored liberal welfare democracy, Marxist sociological constructions provided a convincing conceptual vocabulary; Nelson Mandela would be a case in point.[25]

During the 1950s, African communists were conspicuous in the leadership of the ANC in the Eastern Cape, especially in Port Elizabeth. Govan Mbeki, the son of a deposed Transkeien chief, teacher, journalist, and secretary of the Transkei Organised Bodies, was, of this group, the most intellectually creative. Mbeki joined the party perhaps as late as 1961 but it was during the mid-1930s, through a meeting at Fort Hare with Eddie Roux that "for the first time Govan explored the Marxist point of view."[26] Holding two degrees, one in economics, in the 1950s he worked briefly as a teacher before becoming a journalist for the left-wing weekly *New Age*. Before his capture and subsequent imprisonment as an Umkhonto leader, Mbeki managed to complete a book on Transkeien politics. *The Peasants' Revolt* is largely a work of contemporary social and political analysis; unfortunately its historical substance is limited. It does refer to the "long history of Transkei resistance" but traces this back only as far as 1942. Some of the most interesting comments concern the institution of the chieftaincy. Mbeki refers to a "golden age of African chieftaincy . . . when the power of the paramount chief derived directly from the people," but in his text this phrase is surrounded by quotation marks, indicating, perhaps, a degree of skepticism. In the case of the Mpondo, he suggests that a reinvigorated and popularly acceptable chieftaincy had managed until the 1950s to "exercise real power," largely thanks to an effective modernization of the office, an accomplishment Mbeki credits to the influence of Wesleyan missionaries. What Mbeki does not explore are the more popular historical continuities manifested in the Mpondo revolt: the mountain committees, the people's courts, store boycotts, hut burnings, and tax embargoes all suddenly appear in the idiom of peasant struggle without any reference to any historical precedents. Indeed, in the case of the refusal to pay taxes, Mbeki asserts that "not since the Bambata rebellion in 1906 had there been any attempt by the national movement to call for the non payment of taxes."[27] Of course, it is unfair to be very critical of the apparent shortcomings in Mbeki's historical memory; the book could not have been written in more trying circumstances. Part of the explanation, though, may be attributable to a disinclination to discern specifically peasant traditions of revolt. Mbeki's purpose in writing the book was to make the case for "the importance of peasants in the reserves to the entire national struggle." The text hence highlights peasants' modernity rather than their retentions from the past. Therefore, in most cases "people have developed to a stage which discards chieftainship," their "social development contradicts the need for such an institution." As much as urban workers, Mpondo peasants belong to "a single common society."[28]

Connections between Congress and the Communist Party solidified with the formation of Umkhonto we Sizwe as well as with the later reconstruction of an organization in exile. From the 1960s onwards, the Communist Party's own sense of history would help shape and be shaped by the ANC's intellectual heritage. The theoretical basis for the party's alliance with the ANC was to be codified in its 1962 program, *The Road to South African Freedom*. The Program held that there were "no acute or antagonistic class divisions, at present, among the African people." In its phraseology, South Africa from 1910 represented "a new type of colonialism . . . in which the oppressing white nation occupied the same territory as the oppressed people themselves and lived side by side with them." Such oppression, suggests the 1962 document, was virtually synonymous with class oppression, occurring as it did within the context of a modern economy based on "highly developed industrial monopolies" and on agriculture "along capitalist lines, employing wage labour, and producing cash crops for the local and export markets." As they advance to "the formation of a single modern nation" millions of "new peasants" transform the African rural population from "a reserve of conservatism into a powerful ally of the urban working class in the struggle against white colonialism, and for freedom, land, equality and democracy."[29] It is true that the party's conception of "Colonialism of a special type" has not been without its internal critics. Harold Wolpe, one of the saboteurs who succeeded in escaping from police custody after arrest at the Umkhonto headquarters in Rivonia to become a professor of sociology in Britain, contended in 1974 that in the 1962 program "class relations" were simply "assimilated to race relations." Wolpe suggested that internal colonialism would only acquire any explanatory utility when it was linked to the argument that within South Africa a dominant capitalism subordinated but simultaneously perpetuated the existence of earlier non-capitalist modes of production.[30] Wolpe's work was unusual in representing a linkage between the programmatic Marxist tradition embodied in the SACP in the 1960s and a new "revisionist" historiography which drew heavily upon French and British academic Marxist theory. On the whole, though, his proposed refinements do not feature in the work produced within the internal colonialism framework.[31] Here social relationships within the oppressed communities are hardly characterized by the ideological complexities implied by the existence of several modes of production; instead all share a common solidarity, irrespective of "non-antagonistic" social distinctions.

There is a substantial body of texts that can be associated with the SACP's philosophical genesis in the 1960s and 1970s and which can also be seen quite properly as constituents in an ANC "tradition." Foremost among these is H. J. and R. E. Simons's *Class and Colour in South Africa*, written from exile in Zambia. Jack and Ray Simons were key figures in the development of the Communist Party in the 1940s. At that time the two lived in Cape Town, Jack Simons holding the Chair of African Law at the University while his wife established the still enduring Food and Canning Workers Union. Politically active within the clandestine SACP both left South Africa in 1964 to make their home in Lusaka. *Class and Colour*, more than any work considered up to this point, is a work of scholarship and as such represents a monumental achievement. It also contains a powerful element of autobiographical experience which helps to explain the emphases and selectiveness of those parts of the text that describe events occurring in the 1940s. But the narrative should also be read as a legitimizing historical commentary serving to underpin the programmatic formulations adopted by both party and Congress between 1961 and 1969.[32] Its central plot is the convergence and growing mutuality of socialist and nationalist politics which would be destined ultimately to pull together a movement "national in form, socialist in content." This is a reading of popular political history which has interpretive implications which have since attracted heavy criticism from revisionist historians—particularly the Simonses' emphases on mass susceptibility toward revolt and on the underplaying of class interests as a motivating force for early national leadership. This latter factor, the Simonses suggest, could hardly have been "more than negligible." Instead, the Simonses blame all the perceived defects in the ANC's early conduct the on "confusion," "political immaturity," and "backwardness." Paradoxically, though, backward leaders co-exist in the text with an African working class which at least by 1920 was "mature and ripe for organisation." The Simonses are extremely critical of early communist prescriptions because of their "undervaluing of the radical bent of the African middle class" and they insist on this class's willingness to make "common cause with the masses." Their narrative reaches its teleological conclusion in the late

1940s at the point when "the class struggle merges with the movement for national liberation." This climax is reached in the communist/African nationalist alliance prompted by the 1946 African mineworkers' strike, "the biggest strike in South Africa's long record of oppression."[33] A subsidiary and related theme in the Simonses' account is what they contend to be the indigenous roots of South African radicalism. This is exemplified in the CPSA 1928 Native Republic resolution, a document which, in sharp contrast to the perceptions of earlier historians,[34] is celebrated as "a great advance in the analysis of relations between national and class forces in the liberation movement." In the broader discussion of South African society, depicted in the text as a colonial order complicated by capitalist industrialization, there are also present the elements of a strategic charter for the immersion of the class struggle in a nationalist insurgency. The South African state is "degenerate," a decadent excrescence of imperialist greed, rather than the logical consequence of a self sustained internal capitalist development—a historical option which the Simonses believe existed in the Transvaal Republic ("well equipped for capitalist revolution"), and which was preempted by the Anglo Boer War. Modern South Africa exhibits fascist totalitarianism, a social order which can be supplanted only through "a strategy of insurrection, guerilla warfare and armed invasion."[35]

With this formulation the Simonses were echoing an orthodoxy in Communist party characterizations of the apartheid state which party theorists had depicted as fascist since 1948. On the whole, though, South African communists used the term descriptively rather than analytically. Brian Bunting's *Rise of the South African Reich* emphasizes the intellectual influence of German nazism on Afrikaner nationalist thought in the 1930s, at a time when, in his view, Afrikaner nationalism was "deeply rooted in the countryside . . . dominated by the outlook and needs of farmers." From 1948, according to Bunting, an ideologically motivated state capital was locked in conflict with secondary industry and mining; "for ideological as well as economic reasons, the nationalists will spare no effort to subdue them and compel them to conform at last to the demands of the state." In doing so, "megalomaniac" Afrikaner nationalists were pushing against the "forces working for integration" which remained "tremendously strong," a conflict which by 1963, Bunting believed, was producing all "the symptoms of social breakdown."[36]

When set beside this kind of analysis, the internal colonialism model deployed by the Simonses offers an explanation of South African political economy which is of considerable sophistication. *Class and Colour* still provides the richest general survey of the South African left. Its most serious drawback is the absence of any exploration of the relationship between the networks of organizations and activities which constitute its narrative and the broader context of the communities within which they functioned and happened. For all too often, the culture of activism could not ignite popular insurgency. Naboth Mokgatle, once an African trade unionist active in the Pretoria branch of the CPSA, offers this poignant description of the 1950 May stay-away in his superb *Autobiography of an Unknown South African*:

> On the Sunday evening the police, accompanied by the army, began to transport workers to their place of work to sleep there. I went to the bus terminus to see what was happening. There I found the workers being taken away from their families to sleep at work, escorted by the army and police motor cycles. When the workers passed me by into the buses their heads were hanging down. The next day, Monday May the first, I got up early and went back to the bus terminus. I found a long queue of workers lined up by the police and the army getting into buses. Their bus fares were also being paid by their employers. Those who usually travelled to work on bicycles were also being paid by their employers. I passed very close to the queue and again the police said, "Here he is, the troublemaker," but I uttered no word. . . . Later some workers at Atteridgeville came to me to apologise, but they told me that they were pleased that I did not say anything when I passed them in the queue. They said that if I had ordered them to return home, they would have fallen over each other running away.[37]

Since the 1960s, a fresh generation of historians has flourished within the ANC's international diaspora. In contrast to most of the writers considered up to now, the exiles are usually equipped with the scholarly training and research skills of professional historians. The ANC's contemporary intellectual leadership is largely drawn from a group of men, many of them classmates, whose political experience dates back to their involvement in student organizations at Fort Hare and the "open" universities at the beginning of the 1960s. In exile, individuals within this group emerged at the end of the decade with doctorates or other advanced academic qualifications; several were to embark careers of university teaching and research. Through the 1970s, the ANC itself was to construct an organizational apparatus which would include military training camps and educational centers, as well as a range of regularly produced publications. Notwithstanding the hardships, the experience of exile supplied the institutional resources and philosophical inspiration needed to create an ANC school of historiography.

Bernard Magubane's work can be situated within this genre. Magubane was born in Durban in 1930 and graduated from the University of Natal in 1958. He subsequently received a sociology MA from Natal before working for a Ph.D. at the University of California in Los Angeles. Magubane's *Political Economy of Race and Class in South Africa* represents for its author the outcome of "a long and close relationship" with members "of the African National Congress and its allies." Magubane explicitly cites the influence and inspiration of the Simonses and indeed there are strong resonances between his *Political Economy*, and their *Class and Colour*. An explicit commitment to a "Marxist methodology" helps to bring out in a more developed fashion themes and contentions which have only a latent presence in the Simons' text. For Magubane, South Africa's "racial social structure . . . is inseparable from capitalist economic development . . . capitalist economic development and racial oppression are inextricably linked; the removal of one ensures the removal of the other."[38] The corollary of this view is, of course, that national struggle is essentially a struggle against capitalism. In this context, as Magubane argued in an earlier article:

> One cannot speak of social classes among Africans but of social strata, the difference being that members of a stratum can stem from diverse social origins which is true for the educated African, while the great majority (though not all) of the members of a class are born in it.[39]

Those few individuals "who escape from the ranks of unskilled labour" are precluded from developing their own separate class consciousness "because they are forced to live with and among the proletarians and share their difficulties." If their actions and behavior are at odds with the interests and predispositions of popular classes, then the explanation, for Magubane in *Political Economy*, lies in the "psychological enslavement" which resulted from mission education. Educated Africans were "victims of deculturation," they lacked the means "to control cultural identity"; it was this sterilizing experience which in the early years of the ANC's existence explained the leadership's "weaknesses in political strategy," the "intellectual errors," and the "curious reformism and unrealism." Not that proletarians were initially in a position to draw upon more sustaining cultural resources. Magubane suggests that "conquest and enculturation cut short the historical development of the African people." Through the institutions of migrant labor the African working class could be maintained in a state of "permanent disorientation." The well-springs of revolutionary protest had to be uncovered through "a series of ruthless object lessons by means of which history drummed into the heads of the working class the character of their oppression." By the 1950s, the ANC was suitably equipped to perform this didactic vanguard function: "any of the campaigns the ANC waged in the decade 1949–1960 must be looked upon as part of an overall attempt to arouse a radical political consciousness among the masses of the African people."[40]

Magubane's characterization of the South African state is shaped by his observations of the contemporary development of South Africa's political economy during the 1960s. He draws attention to "the close interdependence between the economies of South Africa and those of America and Europe," arguing that "any threat to the stability of the status quo in South Africa could endanger the short and long range interests of foreign capital." In this view, the institutions of Afrikaner nationalism, notwithstanding their "narrow, petty bourgeois" character, become a vital "bargaining force for capital accumulation." White party politics are merely the expressions of conflicts between "fractions of capital." Here Magubane's argument reflects the structuralist orthodoxy which characterized the early "revisionist" historiography. It is not an argument with which he himself seems entirely comfortable; earlier in the book he suggests that "what is known as the Boer character began to crystallize as the settlers . . . moved further inland." For Africans, though, the text seems to suggest, there can be no moral or intellectual legacies from precolonial eras no matter what their glories may have been.[41]

Magubane's work reflects a social vision which is intellectually consistent with the radical thrust of ANC polemics in the early 1970s. Oliver Tambo's speeches at the turn of the decade emphasized the "greed and resultant disunity of imperialist forces" and an "internal crisis within the imperialist countries" which created especially favorable conditions for "the success of armed struggle in South Africa." In its 1969 political report, the ANC's national executive described an international capitalist system characterized by "political weakness" caused by the imperialists' "constant struggle to divide markets."[42]

Since the appearance of Magubane's text, at least two substantial historical books have emerged from within the organization. The first of these, *South Africa Belongs to Us: a History of the ANC*, is the work of Francis Meli. Meli's own standing within the ANC is such that the book is likely to substantially both reflect and influence the organization's current perceptions of its heritage. Francis Meli has edited the ANC journal, *Sechaba*, since 1977 and has been a member of the ANC National Executive from 1985. He holds a Leipzig doctorate. He attended Fort Hare in the early 1960s and was at that time active in the African Students' Association.[43]

The main argument which runs through all seven chapters of *South Africa Belongs to Us* is that "any dichotomy between the leaders and the masses in the ANC is artificial." Hence while Meli would, generally speaking, adhere to a materialist understanding of history, there is no justification, in his view, for suggesting that social or class related tensions can help in any explanation of the ANC's internal development. So, for example, if the ANC leadership in its formative phase appeared to be "reformist" this was only because "the interconnection between colonialism and imperialism was not properly understood." During this phase, Meli concedes, the ANC's programmatic concerns were flawed by an essential "weakness"—the omission of any reference to "equality and national liberation of Africans." But that there may have been material considerations affecting the disinclination of pioneer ANC notables to advocate social equality is not an argument Meli is willing to pursue. If the ANC in the 1920s demonstrated a trend "away from the politics of liberation to the politics of reformism" this had nothing to do with the social predisposition of ANC leadership. Instead the explanation was entirely attributable to the influence of white liberals. And if some ANC leaders were hostile in the early 1920s to efforts to mobilize the working class, for Meli this tells us nothing about the ANC's overall social orientation, but simply helps to "prove that the ANC . . . has always consisted of people with different political views."[44]

By the late 1920s, these people would include communists who assume an important presence in Meli's narrative after (unspecified) "problems in relation to theory and practical questions" were "solved thanks to the assistance rendered by the Communist International." Thereafter, any lingering ANC/CP tensions are singly ascribed to communist advocacy of atheism. By the mid-1940s, Congress, Party, and proletariat have fallen smoothly into step: the 1946 African mineworkers' strike, for example, evoked "widespread support among the ranks of the African working class and national liberation movement." The "Africanism" of the early Youth League was merely a feature of philosophical immaturity; by 1947, CYL founder Anton Lembede had "discarded anticommunist tendencies." Those who failed to register such progress consigned themselves to historical irrelevance, acting out futile paroxysms "against the laws of social development." Meli gives short shrift, for example, to the emergence of the Pan-Africanist Congress. In 1960, the extent of popular response to the PAC's anti-pass campaigning was entirely due to the fact that "the masses of oppressed people were successfully mobilized for the (ANC's) March 31st Anti Pass national stoppage of work." Meli's standpoint as a chronicler is loyally protective; this is the closest the text gets to being an "inside view" of liberation history.[45] In fairness to Meli, *South Africa Belongs to Us* does accommodate a more ideologically eclectic range of figures within its pantheon of legitimate ANC heroes than would be the choice of some less forgiving authorities within the exile movement. An *African Communist* contributor in 1981 was much less willing to take a benign view of the Youth League's founding father: "Many contradictory characters, many opportunists over the years of struggle have proved to be unable to accept or adjust to our hard-won revolutionary perspective. Because of the ambiguous role such men have played, we would hesitate before uncritically extolling the contribution of Anton Lembede."[46]

Despite the professed intention to write a book which would "show the roots of the ANC which run deep in the history of the people," *South Africa Belongs to Us*, is fairly traditional institutional "history from above." A significant feature of the text is the brevity of the narrative is devoted to a description of the 1950s struggles, the phase in the ANC's history when it really began functioning as a popular movement. Here we are confined to a sparse chronology of the major campaigning with the emphasis on the ANC's role in "sharpening the weapon of mass action."[47] Absent entirely is any hint that there were any difficulties in this task or that, as Luthuli suggested in his autobiography, at times popular susceptibilities may have run ahead of ANC organizational capacity.

Meli is writing in his private capacity; his book does not have the status of an official history. Nevertheless it exhibits analytical features which seem to be widely generalized in the kind of history taught in ANC classrooms. A secondary school textbook, *National Struggle, Class Struggle*, produced by John Pampallis, a teacher at the ANC's Solomon Mahlangu College, has solid merits as a synthesis and teaching instrument. Predictably, though, it treads respectfully through the courses and contours of the post-1949 defiance in much the same fashion as Meli's text, with a similar discounting of the possibility of class divisions functioning as a motivating force in the ANC's chronology. History is presented as a series of revelations in which individuals and groups acquire a progressively sharper sense of social purpose and identity.[48]

In its more popularist forms this is a version of the past which comes close to iconography. In the 1980s a succession of books have reflected the revival of Congress as a political force inside South Africa. In these texts the events and personalities of the 1950s supply the elements of heroic epic which is as much about the present as about the past. One of the most compelling of these works is Fatima Meer's biographical tribute to Nelson Mandela, *Higher than Hope*, published in celebration of the

leader's seventieth birthday. Earlier biographical portrayals have emphasized Mandela's development as a public figure, drawing largely on his
speeches and polemical writings to emphasize his position at the center
of the ANC's ideological and strategic evolution in the 1950s.[49] This
volume is, according to Winnie Mandela, the "real family biography."
This is true in two senses. First, the portrayal is as much of Mandela the
private man as it is about him as a public figure; it describes the unhappy
course of his first marriage and is openly honest about Mandela's contribution to its breakdown ("Nelson was extremely attractive to women
and he was easily attracted to them"); it takes as a central theme the preoccupations of its protagonist as a father and head of "a large household
of dependents." But it is also about family as lineage, succession, dynasty,
and inherited greatness. For this is a book about a royal leader, the de-
scendant of kings who "ruled all the AbaTembu at a time when the land
belonged to them and they were free." It is about a man who learnt his
patrimonial history in "silent veneration" at the feet of his elders and is
inspired with a lifelong mission to recapture for all South Africans "the
ubuntu (humanity) of the African kings." Without a father from the age
of ten, he was brought up by "a member of our clan" for whom "according to our custom I was his child and his responsibility." His second,
more successful, marriage is to another representative of aristocratic lineage, to the daughter of a line of "marauding chieftains." Winnie's upbringing owed much to the influence of her grandmother, a reluctant
convert to Christianity. From her, she learnt "things that my mother had
taken care to see I'd never learn":[50]

> She took me into the ways of our ancestors, she put the skins and beads
> that had been hers when she was a young girl on me and taught me to
> sing and dance. I learnt to milk cows and to ride horses and to cook
> mealie porridge, mealie with meat, mealie with vegetables, and I learnt
> to make umphokoqo the way Makhulu made it.[51]

In Fatima Meer's book, it is this world which defines the Mandelas'
moral center. For though Nelson learns to "manage" and "integrate"
Johannesburg "from the standpoint of Orlando," the city was never
home, he remained "intensely rural," "it was the first half of his life that
really mattered when it came to roots." Notwithstanding his wider political and social loyalties, "there were deep-rooted historical identities that
could not be denied . . . the first experience of human solidarity . . . in
the family, in the clan, in the tribe . . . constituted the real identities, the
nurseries for larger solidarities." His leadership is patrician and inborn,
gifted with powers of "breathtaking oratory," compassion "for the

poor," and above all the social empathy that enables him to assume a "rough and ready disguise" and move unrecognized in the crowd ("it felt good to be one of the people"). His social universe is one which is organic, in which, to cite his early mentor, Anton Lembede, "individual parts exist merely as interdependent aspects of one whole." Political conflicts in this world can be intensely personal, involving as they do betrayals between kinsfolk, betrayals which recur dynastically: "Sabata's great grandfather . . . had been betrayed by his brother Sabata; now the grandson, K. D. Matanzima was betraying Sabata and would eventually depose him. They were all Madibas, and should have stayed together at all times; but Madiba was split from Madiba." Authority is also personal; in 1960, Nelson receives at his Orlando home deputations of Tembu and Mpondo tribesmen to report on the Mandelas' errant kinsfolk's terrorization of an "illiterate region . . . not deemed worthy of literate recording." For Mandela can listen to them with the sympathy and insight of a personality "whose instincts were still rooted in rural politics."[52]

Mandela as rural notable and communal patriarch is not an uncontested interpretation of his personal greatness and its broader social meaning. Other versions of his biography situate the events of his life in alternative historical traditions. For example, within the National Union of Mineworkers, according to one of its spokesmen, after the union's election of Mandela as its honorary life president, "work was done to inform workers of Mandela's history and the struggles he waged as a mineworker in Crown Mines."[53] Mandela did stay at Crown Mines for a short period after his arrival in Johannesburg in 1941. Here, according to Meer, he enjoyed the hospitality of an old *induna* of his uncle's, an overseer at the mine, who made him welcome as a member of the royal kraal. Mary Benson's biography, though, tells us that Mandela "was taken on at Crown Mines as a policeman with the promise that he would soon be promoted to clerk." She also suggests that his reason for leaving the Transkei was to escape an arranged marriage: "My guardian . . . was no democrat and (he) did not think it worth while to consult me about a wife. He selected a girl, fat and dignified; lobola was paid, and arrangements were made for the wedding." Benson argues that Mandela's rejection of the marriage symbolized a deeper rejection, "for by this time he had realized he was being prepared for chieftainship and he had made up his mind never to rule over an oppressed people."[54] Communal patriarch, working-class hero, and liberal democrat: even within the context of a devotional epic, the contending understandings of Mandela's life point to the ideological complexity of the movement he so effectively represents.

Conclusion

This article has brought together a significant number of historical works which can be associated with the ANC's ideological and philosophical evolution. As might be expected from a movement which has in nearly eight decades of existence attracted a large and heterodox following, what emerges is a mosaic of different thematic continuities rather than any single "tradition." In its early genesis, the ANC was led by a rural gentry, representatives of a modernizing peasant elite drawing sustenance from both aristocratic kinship and mission school enlightenment. The literary interpreters for this leadership celebrated the African past with circumspection, balanced as they were between a defensive reaction against European denigration and admiration for imperial technological achievements. They understood their role to be cultural synthesizers, welding "tribal" democratic traditions purged of the "thralldom of heathenism" to the benefits of literacy and property ownership. In their writings they commemorated an African tradition of hospitality, adaption, and integration. The material base for this generation was rapidly disappearing during the ANC's first two decades as a consequence of the effects of the 1913 Land Act, but its ideology was to continue to resonate, finding echoes in Chief Albert Luthuli's efforts during the 1950s to reconstitute a non-racial community informed by "Christian standards" and the cultural integrity of the "ordinary life of the people."

Competing with this understanding of a past which could accommodate modernity, was the more polarized perception of a pristine precolonial social order which died heroically, culturally and philosophically at odds with what followed it. Unlike an earlier generation of political leaders, ANC intellectuals in the 1940s sought a language of empathy with the urban poor; they believed they had found it in a nativist nationalism, or Africanism, which celebrated a communitarian nation "slow to leave the past" in which "there were no classes, nor rich nor poor, and no exploitation of men by men." Though they looked forward to an ultimately non-racial African humanism, Africanists believed that indigenousness was a privileged component of African national identity.

Africanism has been an intermittent element in the historical consciousness of the ANC's intellectual community. From the 1950s, it has had to contend with a Marxism that has emphasized a common society formed by industrialization and urbanism in which there can be few mandates drawn from the preindustrial rural past. It is a Marxism which is heavily economistic, in which culture and consciousness tightly correspond to a series of stages in economic development. The oppressed society has no internal topography, all share a common experience and all resist equally in response to the calls of a prophetic vanguard. The society is ideologically uniform and socially homogeneous, its struggle is national because the ruling class in certain respects resembles a colonial order, not because it has specific cultural characteristics. In this view, culture becomes epiphenomenal, something which can be taken virtually for granted, "national in form, socialist in content." At its best, this intellectual tradition has sought to incorporate into the ANC's historical heritage a sensitivity to traditions of working-class radicalism. Too frequently, though, it has been employed to explain the history of organizations not people, and of institutional alliances rather than social relationships. It is an "official" Marxism which is more about programmatic formulations than social investigation. It has, since the 1960s, been shaped by the circumstances of the ANC and SACP's exile and the schooling in Eastern Europe of an intelligentsia in a Leninist vanguardist tradition.

The ANC's historical discourse has also been complicated by the disjunctures in its own history: its emergence as a force representing a nascent rural African bourgeoisie; its transformation into a mass organization after the Second World War and the subsequent tensions within it between nativist communitarians, non-racial liberals and populist socialists; and, finally, its suppression as a mass organization and its renaissance as an exile guerilla bureaucracy. Through this history, to be sure, there are continuities—the persistence of certain leadership dynasties, the lingering influence of Eastern Cape educational establishments, a surviving meritocracy based on academic achievement. But, notwithstanding these constants, the ANC's historical memory has been subjected to abrupt paradigmatic shifts. For example, the generational revolt represented by the Youth Leaguers' ascendency in the late 1940s—not a process which has yet been sufficiently illuminated in the existing historical treatments—was a movement which was profoundly disruptive intellectually. The experience of exile in the 1960s represents another reinforcing rupture separating the social experience of postwar political leadership from the world of its predecessors. On the one side of this divide was an African middle class which could conduct its cultural affairs around the professional distinctions, the educational qualifications, and the property bases which gave it a distinct sense of social identity. If it sought popular legitimacy it did so through a discourse which was derived from folk identity: the celebration of African language and those elements of nativist culture which did not conflict with Christian ethics. The ANC's movement from 1950 toward nonracial alliance politics and the state's assault on African middle-class values as well as the government's own ideological incorporation of African ethnicity reduced the attractions of such a discourse. In any case, by the 1950s, many of the younger ANC leaders were drawn to strategies which emphasized the mobilizing capacity of working-class identity.

The implications of this were that potential components of a distinctive tradition were suppressed or repudiated: the celebration of African bourgeois social achievement, ethnic cultural identities or resistance traditions, mission school concepts of social integration. These were the fundamentals of pre-Second World War African literary culture but by the 1960s they had lost their moral significance for the ANC 's activist intellectuals. In their place was substituted the conceptual categories of an industrial society in which politics mechanically corresponded with a perceived level of economic development. This, though, was not the kind of analysis which could easily explain popular cultural expressions that did not obviously reflect proletarian class identity. Nor was it one which could explain the motivation of the non-proletarian ANC leadership. So the central conflict in South African history came to be perceived as something both more and less than class conflict, as involving concerns and ideas which are "national." The content, though, of these "national" preoccupations is never clearly defined. Instead the ANC's "national" character is expressed through a series of symbols or icons or forms. These lend themselves to the different interpretations which are suggested by the diverse historiographies discussed in this essay. The ANC has not one but many historical memories; its past yields no single charter of unified tradition.

Chapter 8 / **The Unity Movement Tradition:**

Its Legacy in Historical Consciousness

Bill Nasson

History Workshop

I remember my message was always, "Class, you may be bone-idle or your brains may be in deadhorse gulch when you're messing around in geography or biology. But for heaven's sake, this school has a mission to teach you history which will liberate you. We are here to make sure that you aren't contaminated by the *Herrenvolk* poison contained in your textbook. Even if you've only one, miserable, functioning brain cell, the *real* history you learn here will help to equip you to resist the perversions of our society. We as the oppressed cannot *afford* colonised minds. Our history, our liberation are inseparable. Because it teaches us that we should *never* salaam before this country's rulers." That, I think, was more or less my general message. You yourself shouldn't need to be reminded.[1]

The social power of such coruscating schoolroom rhetoric has, since the 1940s, occupied a peculiarly commanding place in the historical lexicon of independent South African Marxism in its home territory, the Western Cape region. An outstanding feature of its organizational presence in the shape of the Unity Movement has been a characteristic intellectual and scholarly tone and a distinctive pedagogical setting. The role of teachers has always been crucial; over the past four decades their Unity Movement influence has waxed and waned, but their persistent ubiquity has continuously drawn numbers of high-school pupils into their ambit.

During the course of the 1960s, when I experienced my own high schooling in Cape Town, the Unity Movement had passed the peak of its popular influence. Yet, an ideologically articulate minority of activist teachers continued to sustain its ideas. Mostly older men of towering personality and effective educational organization, they poured out a vivid freewheeling rhetoric, the tone of which is captured by the quotation with which this article opens. Above all, as socialists, they had an intuitive grasp of the primary value of "history" and of their own histor-

ical function. Whatever their specialist teaching subjects—history, literature, physics, or biology—they constituted a collective forum which
molded a process of historically-aware learning among pupils. That history was of a very directive kind; it found its essential voice as much
through a language of oral tradition as through the alternative South
African historiography of books such as "Mnguni's" *Three Hundred Years*
or Nosipho Majeke's *Role of the Missionaries in Conquest*. Furthermore,
the voice of the teacher was sometimes also an authorial voice. This
mode, and the constant radical vision of Unity Movement history, can
for example be seen in the person of Willie van Schoor who, in a published 1950 speech, declared that "we who have thus far been the victims
of South African history, will play the major role in the shaping of a new
history. In order to make that history, we must understand history. A
people desiring to emancipate itself must understand the process of its
enslavement."[2] Throughout the post-Second World War era, such industrious Unity Movement intellectuals have set out, like Jack London's
fictional *Martin Eden*, to become "drunken with comprehension" in order to help achieve the historical liberation of South Africa's oppressed
people.

Any evaluation of the Unity Movement heritage in South Africa's
alternative historiography is naturally linked to political evaluations. The
story of the Non-European Unity Movement (NEUM) is complex,
convoluted and often bitter; while I cannot hope to provide more than
a bare sketch of its historical origins here, some outline is necessary if we
are to understand the broader context and inner quality of a self-consciously vanguard strain in South African historiography. If the Western
Cape region was the early seedbed of South African Trotskyism and has
been flatteringly judged the continuing "stronghold of the left," the
NEUM has long been inscribed within its dissident political culture as its
most influential independent socialist force.[4] Its partisan historical repertoire has been inextricably part of the intellectual milieu of left politics in
the area for over forty years, and its fertilizing presence is still manifest
today in the discussions and fleeting publications of small socialist sects
and adhering community or civic associations. It exemplifies a gritty and
articulate tendency which, following E. P. Thompson, we might aptly
identify as "a very substantial minority tradition."[5]

The formation of the NEUM in 1943 was largely a product of resistance against segregationist consultative and administrative bodies con-
fected by the state in the late 1930s and early 1940s, especially the
Coloured Advisory Council and the Coloured Affairs Department
(CAD). A preceding anti-CAD mobilization against the imposition of

the latter, which secured widespread support among directly affected "Coloured" teachers, accentuated the leadership role in the new NEUM of a radical middle-class intelligentsia as "the educated orators."[6] For the Unity Movement, the attitudes, values, and loyalties of this sector have always been of key significance to political struggle. This rests on a belief that "intellectuals in the colonial context . . . have an essential community of interest with the rest of the oppressed and exploited," their moral imperative being the articulation of the political position and interest of another class. The question is always: "who has captured them? On whose side are they? Those who have deserted their historic mission become servile parasites or 'policeman-intellectuals,' ensnared by the rulers as collaborators and quislings."[7]

Laying great emphasis on a unity of the oppressed, the NEUM identified itself as a united front rooted in non-sectarian principles; its statement of position was its "Ten-Point Programme" of fundamental democratic demands, the implementation of which would amount to a dismantling of the racist social order. While the NEUM's program stopped short of any explicit demand for the abolition of capitalism and the building of socialism, it bore the unambiguous imprint of a class and non-racial purpose.[8]

Two guiding principles came to carry great weight in NEUM strategy. One was the line of non-collaboration with the regime and a prescribed range of associated interests, which included conservative and liberal forces alike. It also meant boycotting segregated institutions and pillorying the perceived careerism and mendacity of all those who willingly colluded with the dominant white capitalist classes in the hope of securing incremental reform for those classified by statute as "African," "Coloured," or "Indian." As Gavin Lewis has noted, "by isolating and rendering impotent the 'Quisling' black collaborators and their institutions, the . . . NEUM hoped to remove the pillars supporting the white *Herrenvolk* democracy."[9] The other principle was an abiding commitment to non-racialism. This was not only a tactical imperative to overcome "enslaving" ethnic divisions (between "Coloured" and African) people—artificially imposed by colonialism and fostered by the regime—in order to build a principled unity of the oppressed, but also a fierce and uncompromising rejection of the very construct of "race" or ethnicity itself.

This non-racial strand of NEUM philosophy can be witnessed in the words of Cape Town author, the late Richard Rive, who, in response to being classified as a black writer, retorted, "I don't believe in this whole concept of race . . . I am as anti-white as I am anti-black or anti-pink or anti-blue. I do believe entirely in non-racialism as a tenet where color is no criterion at all."[10] The same conception is to be found in the expressions of the intellectual and political activist, Neville Alexander, who stresses that "when we speak of non-racialism we mean that 'race' is a non-entity. We do not merely mean that 'race' is irrelevant, because such a position still admits of the reality of 'race.'"[11] The traditional position of Unity Movement thinkers has always been that race or racialism is a mere "excrescence of capitalism," its existence the bondage of forms of false consciousness.[12]

Historically, the NEUM must therefore be recognized as a highly distinctive South African liberation organization which, while making its greatest popular mark in the politics of the 1940s and 1950s, has continued to carry its ideological fixities into the 1980s, virtually regardless of external circumstances. Its principles and tactics have always been strongly articulated and adhered to uncompromisingly, and it has remained independent and mostly derisive of other more prominent national opposition forces. In the anti-apartheid campaigning milieu of the 1950s, it saw the African National Congress and the South African Communist Party as chronically susceptible to the various reformist contaminations of Popular Frontism, revolutionary "stageism" or Africanist and other derivative forms of bourgeois nationalism. The NEUM carried its strategic isolation from the larger resistance movement of the ANC and SACP to quite vituperative lengths, to the extent of disputing the former's legitimacy as "the African national party."[13] The movement was implacably hostile towards the Congress Alliance's acceptance of "multiracialism" (embedded in the 1955 Freedom Charter which accepted a "Four Nation" theory of South Africa as "African," "White," "Coloured," and "Indian"), and its selective use of boycotts and non-collaboration as tactical strategy rather than as a stiff principle of political struggle.

While there is general agreement among academic historians that the NEUM contribution to the postwar liberation struggle was of significance, analyses have tended also to emphasize the inherently contradictory character of its material situation and the self-defeating qualities of its more vanguardist illusions.[14] Thus, while there is no reason to doubt the cogency and morality of its overriding non-racialist thinking, the cult of programmatic unity and principled abstention from what it called the competing "adventurist" tactics of a racially mired Western Cape ANC, meant that it conspicuously failed to integrate itself into a local and broader black liberation movement. As Colin Bundy has stressed, the NEUM's historical claim to the status of an authentic national liberatory movement has always rested more in its "theoretical claims" than in any "actual organic strength."[15]

Unity Movement authors, in various fragmentary and journalistic "histories" of black political movements of the 1930s through the 1950s, always claimed that these bodies were retarded by petty chauvinisms, wilful mischance, and the false illusions of their leaderships. In particular, they criticized leadership assumptions that genuine liberatory struggle might be conducted on the basis of ascribed "African," "Coloured," and "Indian" identity rather than that of a class constituency.[16] Yet, although the NEUM itself was never a "purely Coloured organisation" its tangible social identity became that of an almost entirely "Coloured" body.[17] To this we would also have to add that for an organization which saw its program as implicitly enabling the realization of the historic mission of the South African working class, the NEUM leadership had precious little direct contact with trade union or other working-class organizations. Its leadership and much of its core activist constituency was, as we have already noted, drawn from the ranks of "Coloured" professionals and other white-collar workers, especially schoolteachers. The NEUM's identity, reflecting its social location as an overwhelmingly petty-bourgeois formation distanced from the pressing realities of wages and production, was both overwhelmingly middle-class and intensely intellectual.[18]

As a grouping of intellectuals holding court among the dominated classes in the broad Gramscian sense (and often living cheek-by-jowl within or alongside working-class households in segregated suburbs), its bid for ideological leadership of South Africa's oppressed tended to be enacted mostly in a propagandist sphere. As one individual recalls of the NEUM's articulate singleness of purpose in Cape Town in the 1940s, it was "more politically ahead. They became more influential than other organisations because they could express themselves. They knew their subject better."[19]

Rhetorical production encompassed protest meetings and lectures; the molecular growth of reading groups, fellowships, and associations; and sophisticated yet brutal polemic in small circulating tracts and journals, such as *Discussion* and *The Educational Journal* of the Teachers' League of South Africa. Here was the anchorage of an independent, lively, and critical left tradition. Here was an autonomous development of a pre-eminently "Coloured" intelligentsia outside white universities. Here was a cluster of tough-minded amateur scholars working outside the seclusion of campus seminars at least three decades before the emergence of academic Marxism in the 1970s. Yet, as trainee teachers and undergraduate students, this little fraternity also intersected with the dominant liberal intellectual culture of the racially "open" English-language University of Cape Town, embracing critically its teaching of such subjects as philosophy or literature. A fine evocation of this left atmosphere, at its zenith in the 1950s, is provided by Rive's novel *Emergency* in which, through the "Modern Youth Association," the hero encounters, "'Colonialism and the African Stage.' . . . Imperialism as the highest development of Capitalism. Secondary industry in South Africa. The dilemma of class and caste . . . a crazy vortex of theorizing, moralizing, generalizations, invectives, stock phrases, cliches. To quote Lenin . . . Plato prescribes Communism for his Guardian Class."[20]

Essential to the NEUM's loose coherence—even in the teeth of internal rupture in the late-1950s over interpretation of the NEUM's revolutionary program, and even with the dogpaddling forced on it by decline—was the particular ethnic, social, and economic structure of the Western Cape. Since the turn of the century this area has contained South Africa's largest concentration of people classified "Coloured," with an elite cultural milieu distinguished by a traditional cluster of intellectually excellent high schools and a politically alert and articulate coterie of sharp petty-bourgeois radicals. Here was a natural anchorage for the minting of an historical consciousness that could best take an expressive form through Trotskyist formulations. Arguably, a minority of NEUM radicals in an "ethnic" "Coloured" group which was itself a national minority, had need of the kind of inculcating, programmatic theory and method which went with a rigorous non-racial and Trotskyist position. Weary of white "herrenvolkism" and wary of African nationalism, what more urgent a task could there be than to get shot of race, and to build the "larger unity of the intelligentsia with the oppressed workers and peasants." To this end, efforts were made by NEUM-linked Cape African Teachers Association members to spread this political message into Eastern Cape and Transkeian rural areas in the early 1950s; in some peasant communities, teachers led agitation against Bantu Education.[21] Equally important was to gear this extrusion of racial concepts to historical awareness, so that no critique of early colonialism should rest upon the fact that the early Dutch were "white . . . or began the white colonisation of South Africa," but ought instead to focus upon "the motor force of history," the "social systems . . . whereby people produce the necessities of life and the social and political relations into which they enter in this very economic process."[22]

Along with the ANC and Pan-Africanist Congress, the NEUM was to become a casualty of the state offensive against popular opposition forces of the early 1960s, harried into an exile existence as the Unity Movement of South Africa. There, smoldering discord between the anti-capitalist heritage of the Unity tradition and nationalist or popular congress alliance politics made common political action as improbable in exile as it had been at home. Yet the fracturing of Unity Movement leadership and its derisory significance in the world of South African exile politics did not erase its fecund deposit in the historical conscious-ness and levelling doctrines of professionals, students, and other adher-ents through the 1960s and 1970s. And, retaining some impetus on the left in the struggles and repression of the 1980s, new bodies consciously derived from the NEUM position have arisen in Cape Town to try to apply its customary principles and tactics to the strategies of the demo-cratic movement.

For decades, mostly in select "Coloured" South African schools, and in reading rooms and halls, radical Unity Movement stalwarts have been teaching a hidden or half-hidden historical tradition which has always coexisted sulphurously with the state-provided or other public histories which it has contested and undermined. Here it has achieved a popular local hegemony, even as students have had to half-obligingly respond to the official demands of an *apartheid* schooling curriculum.

At one level, this alternative tradition has expressed a mocking inter-pretation of large moments and movements in world history as self-delusion—the bourgeois snares of Popular Frontism in 1930s Republi-can Spain, the capitulations of reformist Labourism in Britain, or the deformations of U.S.-inflected Pan-Africanism in West Africa. At an-other, the Unity Movement has developed and transmitted its own re-interpretations, definitions, content, and pedagogies for a South African history placed in an international and anti-imperialist context. Thirdly, Unity Movement teaching practice has from the start been conducted as a component of a liberationist political strategy and program aimed at a transformation of South Africa. As high-school students we were taught to try to understand South African history as a rather craggy materialist representation of class domination and exploitation of the oppressed, with decisive implications for conduct in the present; salutary histories of resisting workers and peasants and compromising or collaborating petty-bourgeois leaders provided moral markers against which present and fu-ture political action was and is to be measured and judged.

This non-academic left historiography has always been a wide-rang-ing construction, mediated through both oral and written forms, and commanding the allegiance of predominantly, but not exclusively, ur-ban, educated, English-speaking "Coloured" people rather than an Afrikaans-speaking working-class majority. While in its contagious history the Unity Movement has drawn in rural Afrikaans-speakers and also some Xhosa-speaking Africans (the latter through the Cape African Teachers Association and the All African Convention in the 1940s and 1950s), English has always occupied a leading place and enjoyed a special nurture. And a particular English vocabulary came to play a constitutive role in shaping the expression and identity of Unity Movement speech and writing. Part of this vocabulary, as Neville Alexander has emphasized, derives from an inherited political tradition, the heritage of a European anti-fascist resistance: hence the fixed, exclusive categories of "Herrenvolk," "quisling," "collaborator," or "puppet" and the inclusive appropriation of "partisan" or "masses."[23] Another part derives from the mobilizing language of apartheid—hence the contemptuous neologisms of "Bantuize" (for the creation of Bantustans or "Homelands") and "ghettoize" or "locationize" (for the forced settlement of blacks in segregated townships).

Like the significance of Chartist language, so elegantly analyzed by Gareth Stedman Jones, it was by virtue of its grid of connotations and adhesions that Unity Movement rhetoric addressed and mobilized its constituency; it too may be seen as representing what Stedman Jones defines as "a complex rhetoric binding together, in a systematic way, shared premises, analytical routines, strategic options and programmatic demands."[24] As an ordering of historical consciousness through new terms of understanding, this radical discourse assiduously cultivated an understood code based on its own English word-play, laced with ceaseless insinuation, mordant humor, powerful irony, scorn and wit. Its polemical scrutiny is free of encumbering nuance or ambiguity; if we wish to find a succinct characterization, it is perhaps best provided by Gwyn Williams's statement that an exemplary "dialectical analysis demands a confrontation in virtually every sentence and a permanent revolution in demystification."[25]

Both inside and outside the organizational sphere of the Unity Movement, this historical thinking and practice has enjoyed a long run. Its language and concepts have survived over whole stretches of our history, from the early 1940s to the late 1980s. In the 1950s, it was "The Contribution of the Non-European Peoples to World Civilisation," scampering from the "neolithic period of cultivation, domestication and production of a surplus giving rise to social classes," to the "leprous psyche . . . of an 'Anglo-American civilisation, . . . bourgeois wastelanders whose epoch of civilisation opened with Leonardo da Vinci and produced a Goethe and a Beethoven and now ends with Johnny Ray and classic comics."[26] In the 1970s, on the evident assumption that history repeats itself, if not as tragedy then as farce, Unity Movement intellectuals situated emergent Black Consciousness in South Africa against the historical experience of the civil rights struggle in the United States. Inevitably, they perceived a pernicious affinity between what they saw as the bourgeois democratic perspectives and racial basis of the civil rights movement and that of Black Consciousness, with its Africanism and accommodation with "communalism" instead of non-racialism as a basis of liberation struggle. Black Consciousness adherents were failing to learn from the bankruptcy of a black American emancipation movement which had failed to place class and a critique of capitalism and imperialism at the heart of its analysis. Therefore, wilfully blind to the rooted relationship between capitalism and racism, oppressed Americans were impaled by "dodges, pious stratagems and legalistic pettifogging," leading to the licensed chicanery of "Black Power folk heroes . . . falling over themselves to get onto the chuck wagon with Uncle Andy Young and other agents plying their wares in the service of U.S. neo-imperialism, especially in 'black' Africa."[27] And in the late 1980s the focus was on a current history: the role of global capitalist forces, prospects for movements of national liberation (Palestine), Third World debt crisis, Poland, the current terms of South Africa's insertion in the world economy, and so on.[28]

We were taught our range of such historical understandings through constant repetition. Some of us were occasionally impatient with this method but rarely disparaged it at the time, which was the bleak and bleached grand *apartheid* phase of the 1960s. With the benefit of hindsight I now see that the extra-curricular anti-racist, anti-capitalist, and anti-imperialist treatment of South African and other histories was actually a spiritual exercise. Sufficient incantation would produce appreciation of a Unity Movement reading of history as adolescent epiphany.

To put the matter more positively, the educative force of the Unity Movement's historiographical outlook may best be understood as forming part of "the long and honourable tradition in which South Africa's historians have been burdened by concern for their role as citizens of its present."[29] This position, as Christopher Saunders has recently underlined, could scarcely "be otherwise, when the moral and political issues are so clear-cut, and the meaning of the past is so contested in the present."[30] And, like academic liberal Africanist historiography of the 1960s or Marxist historiography since the 1970s, the radicalism of Unity Movement historical practice has been pitted against various dominant constructions of the past; its classical embodiment, the bark of the radical schoolteacher, has carried what Alessandro Portelli terms, "the great literary *refusal* of existing history: uchronia." As formidable purists, their often self-educated, systematic view of the past has always been deeply ingrained in "their self-esteem as narrators and their sense of their own past."[31] This remains more than ever true today. It is not to be thought that the explosion of materialist and other progressive scholarship by professional historians of the 1970s and 1980s has necessarily earned much acceptance and approval by Unity Movement thinkers. Not at all: unhesitatingly, noses continue to wrinkle at an all-encompassing "stream of manufactured history that has continued to flow from English and Afrikaans universities," and particularly "people's history workshops," to which is added "several varieties of 'ethnic' history from the newer bush colleges."[32]

Sharing something of the doctrinaire mode of orthodox Communist party historiographies, the Unity Movement's polemical interpretations of South African history cannot be properly appreciated outside a long-standing, combative intellectual practice in which contemporary political commentary and debate consciously spills over into historiography. As in Communist party history, as Perry Anderson has suggested, it is partly a question of assimilating both a particular reading of history as a schematic succession of difficulty and failure in ultimately realizing working class influence and power, and a particular doctrine of group politics.[33] A key feature is "the *active* construction of conceptions of the past as a continual and defining moment in practice, engaging with and deconstructing reactionary 'memories' and histories."[34] For the Unity Movement tradition is the ideological historical inheritance of a left movement; its analyses have always been grounded in both "totalizing" polemical historical scholarship and sectarian recrimination.

For decades the Unity Movement's founding fathers have left an intellectual legacy which stands for a whole, and subsequent history. In the 1950s, the newspaper *The Torch*, the journal *Discussion*, the New Era Fellowship and the Forum Club disseminated the sometimes demotic output of a subculture of socialist intelligentsia; known historical polemicists like Kenny Jordaan, A. C. Jordan, Benny Kies (*Background to Segregation*), Willie van Schoor (*The Origin and Development of Segregation in South Africa*), I. B. Tabata (*The Awakening of a People*) and Edgar Maurice (*The Colour Bar in Education*) all offered pioneering—if crude and deterministic—interpretations of key processes of South African history within a materialist paradigm. And in the later 1980s, the New Unity Movement (notably its Youth League) and the Cape Action League have become the new instruments for the continuing transmission of the

Unity Movement's historical creed. The Cape Action League's "Workbook" series for "community activists," focusing on such familiar themes as the development of "'Race' and Racism," exemplifies the mold of this alternative radical historiography. Its stress is upon the functional causality of capitalist productive forces, in which

> capitalist classes were naturally determined to bring the diamonds and gold to the surface and to make all the profits that these opportunities presented them with. In order to do so, they had to ride roughshod over centuries-long customs, traditions and property relations that existed among the Boers and the peasant cultivators. To obtain labor, they had to dispossess the latter and to obtain food and other supplies as well as the necessary infrastructure they had to break the power of the former. It was a straightforward question of establishing both the dominance and hegemony of capitalist relations.

After an "intense class struggle" involving "LOCAL AND FOREIGN CAPITALISTS" and "precapitalist BOERS and African PEASANTS," the "racialist patriarchal relations of the period before the Mineral Revolution" were honed "into the racist structures and practices thereafter." As in the readings of Kies or van Schoor in the 1950s, we again encounter Marxist notions of conjunctures, crises and structural transformations, and also the contradictory tugs of the iron law of capitalist evolution. Thus, the different rhythms of "PRIMARY INDUSTRY" (mining and agriculture) and "SECONDARY AND TERTIARY INDUSTRY" in relation to the utility of "the migrant labour system, pass laws, locations, compounds, etc." set the terms of ruling-class politics, in which "'white politics' after World War II" consisted in the "working out of this particular contradiction." Pressures were resolved through *apartheid*, "the strategic choice of the 'white' electorate in 1948."[35]

While long on mechanical reductionism and short on the sophistication and allusiveness of much post-structuralist academic Marxist historical discourse, the Unity Movement outlook has also matured over the years. Here and there the reader may even detect a whiff of qualification. To continue to read racism as merely "a consequence of capitalism . . . invented by capitalists as an ideology . . . [to] divide workers against one another," is now seen as too determinate, for "it reduces the whole complex process" and "distorts the reality."[36] And the overall conception of these circulating, explanatory Unity Movement style "histories" has also begun to be informed by more academic and also analytical "popular" modes of historical materialism. For example, in the first of the Cape Action League's workbooks, the writings of Frederick Johnstone and

Luli Callinicos are acknowledged as an influence upon the portrayal of skilled white labor and the color bar in the formative industrialization era.[37]

But this 1980s historiography still embodies a characteristic vision, perhaps a certain essentialist logic, tempered in the 1950s in studies like "Mnguni's" *Three Hundred Years*. Then,

> elements from all previous systems in South Africa—tribalism, slavery, feudalism and capitalism . . . "created" the unified basis of the present-time system of exploiting and oppressing in South Africa. The elements of the past reacted in the vast crucible of the mining revolution to form the compound of monopolistic exploitation and its consequences—totalitarian oppression.

The means to "unburdening ourselves of the decaying monster" was "the awakening of the people" as those "conquered and held in thrall for 300 years . . . become metamorphosed into potential liberators."[38] Now, the current of teleological history is still running; South African history is like an acorn which cannot escape its destiny to be an oak. Thus, "the system of racial capitalism which holds the people of Azania in bondage for the benefit of the small minority of white capitalists and their allies, the white workers and the reactionary sections of the middle classes" awaits the "historic task of the black working class" and its "independent organisations" to lead "a united front for liberty and victory" over "the system of oppression and exploitation by the white ruling class."[39]

The historiographical instincts of the Unity Movement therefore still cohere around the hardened tradition set by a radical, self-styled national liberation ideology. Allowing for permutations here and there, its present shape derives from the power of continuity. The old compulsions are mirrored in the recent resuscitation and reintroduction to "independent" left political culture of two books which constitute the nearest thing to a historical manifesto of the Unity Movement—the early 1950s *Role of the Missionaries in Conquest* by Nosipho Majeke, and *Three Hundred Years*—in a new Unity Movement History Series. The republication of these books and the reaffirmation of their outlook serves to highlight the close association in the Unity Movement between historical production and national liberation struggle. In these cases, the relationship between "scholar" and "active political partisan" is quite different from that implied in "mainstream" academic Marxist economic and social histories or, even more so, from that in nationalist-inscribed people's or popular history.

One might have expected that by the end of the 1980s, the republication of these studies by Majeke and "Mnguni"—now at last publicly identified by the Unity Movement as the white Trotskyists, Dora Taylor and Hosea Jaffe respectively—would stand as some kind of epitaph for a particularist, sectarian, and astringent Western Cape-based cultural tradition. Instead, works which first emerged in insignificant numbers in "semi-underground fashion" over three decades ago, are apparently now being repossessed by some black students on the campus of the University of the Cape Town and by a handful of nonconformist radical intellectuals at the University of the Western Cape.[40] There, these and other reprinted historical essays (such as the 1950s classics by Kies and Van Schoor) may be seen as providing "history from below" with another meaning: that of contesting dominant "high" university history—including its Marxist mode—with a polemical "low" intransigent history which has its own provenance, form, and effectivity. Certainly, this is ultimately a question of seeing these critical practices not merely as a representation of an autonomous form of radical history but as a contesting and constitutive *part* of that history.

In those older Cape Town schools which remain "historic sites of apprenticeship in Unity Movement ideology,"[41] graduating students are still animated by such approaches as a radical bicentennial reinterpretation of the French Revolution. But an equally rooted reality is that this pungent historiography remains a relatively marginal movement. And it is to our introductory conception of it as a hidden or half-hidden historical tradition that we might now return to offer some concluding reflections.

It is now a commonplace—but one which bears repeating—that prickly and self-righteous Unity Movement intellectuals should berate what are sometimes snidely termed "official and academic historians," for marginalizing or deliberately ignoring the pioneering historical materialism of studies such as *Three Hundred Years* and *The Role of the Missionaries in Conquest*. Thus, Bundy has been rapped over the knuckles for suggesting in 1986 "that the Marxist historical method was an innovation of historians (academic, of course) who emerged in the 1970s—two decades *after* the appearance of 'Mnguni's' work."[42] A rather stretched comparative example might be a barb against David Montgomery for surveying the genesis of U.S. Marxist historiography and omitting Leo Huberman or perhaps E. P. Thompson surveying British Marxist historiography and omitting A. L. Morton.

It is undoubtedly true that academic historiographical writings have generally left the radical antecedents of Unity Movement histories unacknowledged, although there are some notable exceptions of late: Julian Cobbing has argued that the most aggressive conceptual criticisms of white nineteenth-century sources on major transformations within South Africa's precolonial and precapitalist societies were "products of Unity Movement intellectuals," notably Majeke and "Mnguni." While acknowledging that both Taylor and Jaffe's writings are polemical (in the sense of debunking what they present as settler or liberal historical fallacies) and empirically rather wishful, Cobbing boldly claims that they are "scientific treatises" compared to the embryonic colonial fabrication and myth-making "on which liberal courses in the white universities continue to be based."[43] Christopher Saunders and Ken Smith, for instance, have both pointed out that the materialist perspectives of Majeke and "Mnguni" anticipated the professional "revisionist" or "neo-Marxist" radicalism of the 1970s.[44] Callinicos has identified the (occasionally psychopathic) historical temper of *The Educational Journal* as falling squarely within "a rich tradition of liberal, national and radical popular history . . . much of this forgotten, or eroded by censorship, like much of our history in general . . . these writings were all outcomes of struggles personally experienced during . . . years of active opposition to the class and race system in South Africa."[45]

These acknowledgements, however, add up to a somewhat belated, passing recognition that Unity Movement historiography was not merely an idiosyncratic or anachronistic amateur "school" centered upon schoolteachers and lawyers, but a lively and vigorous dress rehearsal for so-called alternative or radical historiography in South Africa today. This is not the same as saying that the Unity Movement agenda for history should be seen as a direct precursor of the radical structuralist literature of the 1970s or of contemporary materialist social history in South Africa. Undoubtedly, in certain respects these three perspectives share common assumptions: the salience of class, the exploitative nature of the capitalist mode of production, and the historical evolution of imperialism. Nevertheless, "activist" Unity Movement historiography has still to be defined as an alternative, *oppositional* creed to university-based progressive histories. The most obvious tension is between, say, an academic History Workshop radical history (which may explore the shifting expressions of categories such as class, race, and ethnicity in the structuring of South Africa's social relations), and a lay scholarly view (holding that in comprehending only class and denying the existence of race, it is merely theorizing actual reality). We have already noted the brusqueness with which hard-nosed Unity Movement intellectuals have dismissed the paradigms of an alternative, social historical movement.

This underlying, submerged educative tradition has carried much wider connotations than that of a set of texts that have simply been pushed out to the edge of approved historical discourse, or History with a capital H. For it is certainly true that through the 1960s and much of the 1970s, publications like *Three Hundred Years*, *The Role of the Missionaries in Conquest*, or Benny Kies's "The Contribution of the Non-European Peoples to World Civilization" were themselves historically invisible. But Unity Movement schoolteachers exercised an influence out of all proportion to their small number, as the standard-bearers of a dissident historiography ultimately derived from no visible or accessible texts. Majeke was not even in the library, let alone a set study piece. It remains a puzzle to me, even allowing for the obvious political constraints of the state educational inspectorate and security police vigilance, why the Unity Movement intelligentsia did not do more to make such texts available to students in the 1960s and 1970s. Large numbers of us in high schools which carried an awareness of themselves as Unity Movement enclaves, learned about capitalism and South African history under the diffuse influence of writers and works we never knew existed. Here was an argumentative, occasionally ranting history arising out of the undergrowth, its scope and purposes essentially those of achieving national liberation through ideological penetration and osmosis.

At the same time, we certainly cannot discuss Unity Movement historical practice without a retrospective glance at the concrete historical content and formulations of its most representative products of combative scholarship, *Three Hundred Years* and *The Role of the Missionaries in Conquest*. It is impossible to go into all the dimensions of these historical polemics, which are almost blinding in their conceptual totality and ferocious grasp for an alternative epistemology. These works are obsessed with the need for raw historical dissection and "unmasking," and driven by the insistent human idealism of a liberated and liberating history as a tool of self-knowledge, embodying what Majeke called "a new vocabulary" to purify an historical language "which has become distorted in the service of herrenvolkism."[46]

For our purposes, we might usefully highlight a few important characteristics to situate Jaffe and Taylor and help us to appreciate their early contribution to the contemporary making of a radical South African today. Here two issues emerge which point in interesting directions. The first is that Majeke and "Mnguni's" endeavors represent white writers embracing an African name and identity in writing for a predominantly Western Cape "Coloured" constituency which, by the 1950s, was increasingly isolated from "wider campaigns embracing 'Coloured' and

African people."[47] Yet here was the ideology of unity in *ideal* form, on the understood terms of "Non-European unity, non-collaboration with the oppressor and full democratic rights."[48] In a sense, the disavowal of a European identity expressed the full integration of these white movement associates into this culture; while they performed seminal intellectual functions, they always did so within a subordinate social role. It is quite clear that the Unity Movement did not mirror the white-black authority hierarchy of South African society. The other point is that Jaffe and Taylor's studies are best considered not as innovative, *individual* compositions, but as representative of the intensity of the Unity Movement's collective historical polemic. In other words, the rhetoric of *Three Hundred Years* and *The Role of the Missionaries in Conquest* is that of the movement, practised and developed in a coherent and fairly extended scholarly form. This is no less true of the books' materialist analysis of South Africa's historical development, which distilled and extended many propositions already developed by teachers such as Kies, van Schoor, or Maurice.

Rooted in a hardening Unity Movement world, *Three Hundred Years* and *The Role of the Missionaries in Conquest* were created as bold counter-histories. Their coda was that of the histories of proletarian autodidacts, like the U.S. Marxist Daniel de Leon or Mark Starr, the leading Plebs League propagandist in early twentieth-century British socialist politics. Both books appeared in 1952, the year in which the three hundredth anniversary of the "founding" of South Africa by Jan van Riebeeck of the Netherlands East India Company provided the occasion for a lavish, quixotic, Van Riebeeck festival in Cape Town, officially trumpeted as a "great Historical Pageant" to "symbolize the South African nation entering the future with courage, faith and strength."[49] While the costumed whooping and dancing may have caught the heart of a white nation, it stuck in the gullet of most black Capetonians. Black responses locally and elsewhere took the form of protest rallies and a successful boycott of the Tercentenary festivities. As one anti-festival Unity Movement activist recalls, "It was quite simple. We said no. No to that orgy of herrenvolk culture and nationalism. It was just a case of them trying to inflict a rulers' brand of history on the oppressed."[50] So what "Mnguni" and Majeke represented was an appropriately adversary ideological history. *Three Hundred Years* meant "a history of 300 years of struggle between oppressors and oppressed."[51] For Majeke, the Tercentenary year was a moment to "strip the tinsel and velvet from those puppets who strut the stage of history from Van Riebeeck onwards, the reverends and governors, soldiers and politicians—the heroes of herrenvolkism."[54]

But possibly more striking still was the paradox that such steely anti-racist histories were produced under the most remorselessly racist conditions of cultural accumulation. If primary-source research distinguished Majeke's book from Kenny Jordaan's published 1952 essay, "Jan van Riebeeck: His Place in South African History," this was at least partly because of what would appear to have been the effective exclusion of black scholars from government archives in the early post-1948 era of Afrikaner Nationalist *apartheid*. As Baruch Hirson has recently noted of the accessibility of manuscript records, "it is not certain whether Coloureds were allowed to use such material in the late 1940s, but it was certainly unusual for any but whites to have access to the state archives."[53] Seen as a Unity Movement response to this situation, Jaffe and Taylor provided a solution to the predicament of racial exclusion from material needed to construct a historical autonomy. There had been nothing quite like their books before. And there has been nothing exactly like them since.

While written as blunt counter-histories, and bearing all the rigidities and crude schematizing of their time and political context, both works were based on original scholarly research. To read them is largely to enter a world of history defined almost entirely in forceful terms of "conquest, subjugation, dispossession, enslavement, segregation and disfranchisement of the oppressed Non-Europeans of South Africa." An Africanist interpretation of South African history is distinctly audible, but as an accompaniment to a highly instrumental materialist interpretation of historical process. *The Role of the Missionaries* and *Three Hundred Years* were Africanist in the essential sense of interpreting South African history from the standpoint of the colonized majority, and in attempting to provide black dominated classes with a record and a sense of their own histories under centuries of what Jaffe termed "despotic divide and rule conditions." The splintered history of African societies is a central feature in each. The primitive or savage black leaders presented in racist or still ethnocentric white historiography are sculpted anew; nineteenth-century African actors include the chiefs Tsaka, "a military genius of his time," and Hintsa, "a man of pride and dignity." This new composition is also free of orthodox European labels of racial contempt, like "Bushmen" and "Hottentot," coining instead the positive neologisms of "baThwa," "!Ke," and "Khoikhoin" for precolonial societies which academic historians were later to term Khoikhoi and San. And this incipient Africanist point of view did not simply filter rosy images of an egalitarian, static, precolonial past. "Mnguni's" approach recognized evolving gender and property inequalities and forms of social differentiation and conflict.

Taylor and Jaffe's volumes were recognizably Marxist in inspiration, and thick with its most conspiratorial applications. Although, as Christopher Saunders has correctly stressed, "neither work used class analysis at all systematically," their materialist approach mapped out a kind of historical autonomy of form, language, and resolute scholarly polemic which was separate from any pre-existent South African historiographical tradition.[54] *The Role of the Missionaries in Conquest* portrayed missionaries as the willing cat's paws of imperialism and colonization, interpreting religious "evangelism" in the broad metaphoric sense of asserting control and instilling ideologies of subordination and deference. As "the agents of an expanding capitalism," British missionaries were the transmission belts to ease "the transition from tribalism to capitalism," their devious stratagems of protection and trusteeship of conquered people a first step on the long march to segregation:

> Such were the links, then, between Christianity, commerce and labour. . . . Christianity did not exist in a vacuum. Its evangelists spoke freely of heaven and hell, but its roots were planted firmly in the capitalist civilization of their masters, an industrial civilization that was sending its many agents into Africa, Asia and India in the search for new markets and raw materials, for new lands to conquer and countless Black hands to labour for it.[55]

What Majeke and "Mnguni" were concerned to show was the logical cohesion of the historical relationship between racial domination and segregation and capitalism. Ruling-class interests were therefore harmonized. Atavistic traditional Afrikaner racism did not come into contradiction with British liberal institutions, practices or morality; instead, a united white ruling class was simply periodically reconstituted, adapted and strengthened to further expropriation and the reproduction of cheap labor for capital. The pulse of historical growth was that of capital accumulation. As *Three Hundred Years* thundered, "Rhodes penned the African miners into compounds, just as Shepstone had herded the conquered into rural locations. . . . This oppressive cheap labour system created immense wealth. . . . Out of Kimberley's diamond mines arose the dominance of monopoly capital in South Africa."[56] The book mirrored the argument of an earlier essay by Jaffe, published in Cape Town in 1946, in which he defined

> the colour bar as the cement of the capitalist system. . . . The colour bar policy of the Chamber of Mines sets the standard for the whole country. Its ratio of skilled to unskilled wages influences the whole economy. Its compound system radiates out to all towns. Its pass laws grip the Africans in every corner of the country. This great monopoly

capitalist institution, surrounded by the stock exchange, banks and finance houses, is the might behind the state in South Africa. It is one of the most prized possessions of British imperialism.[57]

Where nineteenth-century liberal missionaries were deceitful or villainous, liberal socio-political blocs in the twentieth century further reinforced what Jaffe, a writer instinctively given to the invention of startling conceptual categories (like "Negative Surplus Value"), termed the institution of the South African color bar as fascism or colonial fascism. For Jaffe, since the 1910 Act of Union, which officially consecrated the "colour bar," the preconditions of fascism ("monopoly finance capital. . . . Labour regimentation . . . the Herrenvolk outlook") have been "present in high degree." This totalizing critique is directed no less at a "South African Liberalism" which, "under the guise of race-harmony, and racial unity, preaches and practises White Supremacy and preserves the united front of Europeans as it brings forth the fascist measures against now this, then that, then all, sections of the Non-European toilers."[58] This bilious contempt for the history of South African liberalism remains undimmed in Jaffe's most recent writings in exile in Western Europe, in which, for example, the "economic content of South African liberalism" derives from the all-pervading "racialist Chamber of Mines."[59] On a brief return to South Africa in 1990 after a continuous absence of three decades, his lectures to young undergraduates reflected the iron laws of uneven development and a zealous dismissal of race as a descriptive category. Not much had gone soft.

Inevitably, such a stark and uncompromisingly radical interpretation of South Africa's historical development trod on the corns of both established professional liberal scholars and that of maturing liberal modernization theorists of the 1950s and 1960s. Both schools, to varying degrees, subscribed to the view that capitalism and racial discrimination were dysfunctional. What John Lonsdale has called "capitalism's colourblind bourgeois revolution" was predestined to snap "the traditional bonds of racial repression" and, as in the United States, usher in "the era of the melting-pot thesis."[60] What Unity Movement historiography hammered at was the proposition that capitalist exploitation and racial domination had forged a cast-iron relationship. Racism was simply the squalid local expression of capitalist class exploitation. "Race and racialism" thus represented "an economic factor, that is, as the ideological reflex of basic contradictions in the productive processes of a heterogeneous society."[61]

Since these words were penned, radical historical scholarship in South Africa has proceeded at a considerable pace. Yet its seminal early traces and intonations ought not to be overlooked. To do so would be to leave this picture of historical memory and understanding to gather dust in the attic of political defeat. Clearly, as Cobbing notes, the contributions offered by the materialist and determinist accounts of Unity Movement authors "have not been taken seriously by the Universities."[62] As little attention has been paid to historical analysis by other 'independent' socialist intellectuals of the 1950s; Ciraj Rossool has highlighted the existence of a further historiographical increment, more explicitly theoretical in its Marxist logic of class struggle, generated outside the nicotine clouds of Unity Movement reading rooms.[63] Yet Movement chemistry has remained tangible since its historical vision always derived much of its intellectual impetus not from classical texts but from the debates and discussions pursued by a tiny vanguard of teachers, solicitors, doctors, and other professionals. As long as there is a body of activists who adhere explicitly to the heritage of Unity Movement practice and politics, analysis and activism, that tradition, as a tradition, is unlikely to be exhausted. Its legacy in historical consciousness has been shaped by, and has also shaped, the history of the liberation struggle in South Africa.

Unity Movement Postscript

When the Europeans came to South Africa it was in a state of wild barbarism, but after 300 years and particularly after 100 years of close contact, what do we find in South Africa today? We find a half-civilised barbarism and a half-civilised barbarism is more dangerous than wild barbarism.

M. C. de Wit Nel,
National Party Member of Parliament,
South African House of Assembly,
June 18, 1951

We do not believe that the Native is really a communist at heart. He is not able to form a conception of the ideology and of the dialectical materialism of this doctrine.

N. Diederichs,
National Party Member of Parliament,
South African House of Assembly,
September 9, 1948

Source: Ben Maclennan, *Apartheid: The Lighter Side* (Cape Town, 1990).

Chapter 9 / **South African**
Labor History:
A Historiographical
Assessment

Jon Lewis

South African labor history, and labor studies more generally, experienced something of a rebirth during the 1970s.[1] The growth of contemporary labor studies has continued unabated in the 1980s, reflected, for instance, in the expansion of industrial sociology courses. While the output of labor history in the same period has been considerable, it has not coalesced into a strong school in its own right, and remains peripheral to the concerns of history departments.[2] This situation has not fundamentally changed despite the impressive growth of social history in South African universities during the 1980s. Indeed, a bifurcation has developed within South African radical historiography: while labor history focuses on the workplace, industrial relations, and working-class organization, social history considers the fate of the working class and other oppressed groups outside of industrial production. This article aims to explain this trajectory, arguing that the specific and rather circumscribed form that labor history (and labor studies more generally) took in the 1970s, largely determined this outcome. In particular, labor history was tied to the immediate concerns of the emerging trade union movement, a link that proved a source of both strength and weakness.

Labor History and Social History

Elsewhere in the world, the criticism of traditional labor history has been that it was overly concerned with the institutions of labor and their leaders. While, at times, it carried a powerful moral condemnation of capitalism and exploitation, this history actually ignored the majority of the oppressed groups that often fell outside the ambit of the organized working class.[3] Traditional labor history was often highly economistic and reductionist: deducing labor organization and activity from the structures of oppression; assuming a monolithic and homogenous working class on the road to socialism; and ascribing the failures of the movement to lack of class consciousness or the machinations of reformist and opportunist leaders.

Over the last twenty years or so this picture has changed considerably. Social history, "history from below," new methodologies and questions have transformed our understanding of the past (and the present) and rescued the oppressed majority from, in E. P. Thompson's phrase, "the enormous condescension of posterity."[4] The rise of social history in South Africa has focused on such issues as: processes of proletarianization and class formation as they were experienced and molded by the participants themselves; the continuing traditions of resistance and creativity among the oppressed; the role of social groups usually shunned in the orthodox histories; and working-class culture and community.

However, with that said, there are very real differences between the practice of social history in South Africa and developments elsewhere in the world, particularly in relation to the traditional concerns of labor history. In Europe and North America, the rise of social history was marked by an *increased* interest in the history of labor organization and social relations in the workplace.[5] This has been especially true since the publication of Braverman's *Labor and Monopoly Capitalism* in 1974 and subsequent interest in labor-process research. Indeed, Ely and Nield, in their critique of social history define their field as comprising a "culturalist" wing often inspired by both the work of E. P. Thompson and a parallel labor-process approach concerned primarily with the history of work and work relations.[6] It is significant that South African social history is largely identified with the first approach.[7] Because of this identification and the lack of historical research into workplace relations, it seems necessary in the South African context, to justify the retention of the terminology "labor history," despite the possibility of a more all-embracing social history.

If labor history is defined too narrowly—say as the history of the labor movement—it betrays the narrowness of a previous approach. But a wider definition begins to approximate the concerns of social history and, thus, renders the terminology redundant. Somewhere between these points lies the terrain occupied by South African labor history: crucially concerned with questions of working-class organization and consciousness at the point of production, while recognizing that organization and consciousness are formed within wider societal structures which themselves are determined by the outcomes of previous struggles. More specifically, South African labor history and labor studies locate their subject within the broader framework of industrial relations, loosely defined as the relationship between workers, employers, and the state. This point perhaps needs to be emphasized. Indeed, recent contributions within the much richer field of British labor history have decried the tendency to ignore the institutional framework within which labor movements operate.[8] That South African labor history has developed within this broader framework is directly due to the fact that this is precisely the arena within which the emerging black union movement has had to operate in order to survive. I will argue below that while this framework adequately reflected the world of the 1970s, on its own it has not proved adequate to the political tasks of the more recent period.

The continuing concerns of labor history rest on largely political assumptions. First, organization is a prerequisite for oppressed people to bring about a change in their situation. Second, the character of that organization will crucially effect both the course of social struggles and their eventual outcomes. Third, in industrialized and industrializing societies, the working class or sections of the working class may be in a position to influence the course of events by virtue of its position at the point of production. Fourth, the workplace organizations established by workers have a specific importance: they are relatively permanent as a result of the socialization of labor and their competence to deal with issues of immediate concern to the membership; they represent specifically workers' interests, and resist the dictates of capital; they are potentially highly democratic and participatory in character since their major source of leverage lies in the mobilization of their membership. In the South African context we might add a fifth assumption: these organizations can play a leading role in the process of political change and social transformation.

Labor History in South Africa: Past Traditions

Activist History

The earliest (and still among the most influential) contributions to labor history emanated from within the labor movement itself. The works of Eddie Roux and Jack and Ray Simons particularly stand out.[9] Roux helped organize the first black industrial unions in the late 1920s, and was a member of the South African Communist Party until his expulsion during the "bolshevization" period of the early 1930s. Ray Simons was a prominent trade union leader in the non-racial South African Congress of Trade Unions (SACTU) formed in 1955, and forced underground or into exile in 1964; along with Jack Simons, he had remained active in the South African Communist Party and the wider national liberation movement. The strengths of the early activist works include an intimate knowledge of and sympathy for their subject. In the case of the Simons, the theoretical issues that concerned them, reflected in the title of their book, *Class and Colour in South Africa*, still exercise activists and intellectuals in the 1980s.

At one time I might have been more inclined to stress the limitations of their work: the early activist historians readily accepted, in E. J. Hobsbawm's words, "a framework of chronological narrative and a pattern of interpretation which was itself the product of the movement's history as much as of research into it."[10] For example, Jack and Ray Simons were preoccupied by the threat to trade union unity posed in the 1940s by Afrikaner nationalists, a very vocal group that in fact represent a small minority within the trade union movement. As a result, the Simonses said little about the role of the English-speaking craft unions, arguably the main culprits in the collapse of the multi-racial Trades and Labour Council (1930–1954), an event which heralded a period of more rigid racial division within the South African trade union movement. Yet today (and in the light of what I shall say below about contemporary labor history), it seems to me that these limitations—the tendency for labor history to reflect the current concerns of the labor movement—are both inevitable and not without some positive import.

The Liberal Tradition and Its Critics

The bogey of Afrikaner nationalism was also taken up by liberal historiography as an explanation for the divisions among South African trade unions. Liberal historians such as M. Horrell say that Afrikaner nationalism was one aspect of a wider problem of race and race relations which lay at the root of disunity.[11] These analyses were in the tradition of liberal economists such as S. T. van der Horst, for whom the greatest crime of white labor organizations was their attempt to circumvent market mechanisms to prevent employers from making the most "economic" use of cheap African labor.[12] According to C. W. de Kiewiet, a liberal economic historian, race had obscured the traditional conflict between capital and labor in South Africa.[13] This approach was simply ahistorical since it ignored the role of employers and the state in structuring the division of labor along racial lines, and treated white labor in an undifferentiated manner, both over time and in relation to the different sectors and categories of labor.

The liberals assumed that the free working of the economy would break down racial barriers and create a multi-racial workforce and, by implication, a unified multi-racial society. Moreover, they saw racism as economically irrational and inimical to economic growth and development. The liberal orthodoxy both promoted race as the primary explanatory factor in any analysis of South African society while refusing to accept any linkage between institutionalized racism and the country's successful economic development.

In the 1970s, however, class analyses of South African society and history prospered. The new historical work emanating from the English-speaking universities and overseas centers of southern African studies, was inspired by the revival of Marxism, the renewed activity of class-based organizations among black workers in South Africa, and by the growing evidence of class cleavages within the white monolith. This work was associated initially with Trapido, Legassick, Wolpe, and Johnstone—all based in universities outside of South Africa, all except Johnstone South Africans by origin.[14] Their work sought to show that racial oppression was conducive to capitalist development; that racism in South Africa was not an unalterable given; that racism did not provide an explanation of South African reality but itself required explanation; and that class analysis provided a useful tool for these purposes. For our purposes, and for labor history, Johnstone's work was particularly important. Analyzing the mining industry, Johnstone showed that color bars were not simply the result of the selfish racism of white miners. He considered how racism intersected with the social relations of production to constitute "exploitation color bars"—the often repressive means adopted by mine employers to secure a cheap black labor force—as well as "class color bars" erected by white workers as a specific response to the conditions created by the employers. As these historians of South Africa demonstrated, a class analysis was not only appropriate to South African society, it was essential.

In retrospect, the preoccupation of the 1970s with issues of class represents something of an over-reaction to the conventional wisdom. Labor historians—and other radical academics—were slow to come to terms with issues of national oppression and racism. Their neglect was due, in part, to the re-establishment of black trade unionism in the late 1970s which suggested that class-based, economistic strategies were succeeding. The growth of broad-based popular movements in the early 1980s, forced academics to confront their previous assumptions and to grapple with questions about community-based organization and the relationship of class struggle to the struggle for national liberation. The work of Philip Bonner and Rob Lambert, both university-based academics who have also been involved in worker education, provides a barometer of the changes taking place within labor history from a narrow concern with trade unions toward addressing broader social and political issues.[15]

The 1970s: Labor History Takes Off

The growth of academic interest in labor history followed hard on the heels of the revival of South African trade unionism in the early 1970s. Indeed, some of these first efforts in labor history were prompted either directly by the needs of the new unions, or were clearly inspired by similar concerns.[16]

FOSATU

The rapid economic growth of the 1960s and the expansion of a semi-skilled black working class had created the conditions for mass industrial unionism. But when large-scale strikes broke out in Durban in the early 1970s it was under circumstances of extreme repression. The new unions of the time adopted what later became known as a "survivalist" strategy, later associated with the Federation of South African Trade Unions (FOSATU) formed in 1979: they concentrated on immediate economic and basic recognition issues and, while seeking to build up grassroots organization, maintained a low political profile and deliberately avoided any confrontation with the state. Such organization was to be factory-based and worker-controlled. The aim of this strategy was to build a working-class leadership in the factories and an organization that would have a better chance of surviving repression and the removal of union leaders. (The continuation of this policy into the 1980s—in a period that witnessed the re-emergence of open, mass political protest—brought forth charges of syndicalism, economism, and worse from the radical nationalist organizations.) But, for our purposes, the character of the new unionism exercised a profound effect on the research agenda of labor historians and helps explain their abiding concern with issues of organization and democracy and with analyzing the machinery of industrial relations.

It should not be forgotten that during the 1970s, Black Consciousness was the most vocal political position among the oppressed, a position that at least initially took little account of class and instead sought to mobilize on the basis of common racial oppression. Indeed, animosity existed between the black consciousness, Black Allied Workers Union and those unions that were to establish FOSATU. Among the leadership of the FOSATU unions, an alternative vision had emerged: one that was class-based and non-racial and concerned with organizational issues of democracy and worker control.[17] This alternative vision certainly inspired the writing of labor history and labor studies at the time. In fact, most contemporary research focused on FOSATU unions. In sharp contrast to their treatment of FOSATU, radical white academics largely ignored those unions initiated or supported by the Urban Training Project that would establish the black consciousness-inclined Council of Unions of South Africa in 1980—despite CUSA's numerical superiority over FOSATU, at least in the period 1984–85.[18]

Why has CUSA been ignored, and why are there so few blacks in the field of labor history and labor studies? Educational discrimination against blacks has resulted in disproportionate representation by whites in all areas of progressive intellectual work. In the 1970s, black university-based intellectuals were largely confined to the "homeland" universities where ideological and other forms of control were more severe than at the liberal English-speaking universities. The home-land universities have not, by and large, established a labor studies tradition and, in any case, class-related issues remained tangential for black consciousness-inclined intellectuals who were engaged in important cultural and ideological struggles at the time. This situation—the lack of research and writing on labor studies by black scholars—is now changing as large numbers of black students enter the formerly whites-only universities.

CUSA's poor coverage in the literature may partly reflect radical white intellectuals' preference for non-racial, class-based unionism along the lines of FOSATU. But CUSA also had its share of white (liberal) intellectuals who staffed the Urban Training Project and assisted in the organization's education program. Criticism, thus, seems to have been engendered by more than white approval of nonracial unionism *per se*. Rather, criticism levelled against CUSA at the time focused on its methods, which were inherently reformist, dependent upon management good-will, and unsuccessful compared to the major organizational gains made by the non-racial unions. Further research is needed to establish the truth of such assertions, and we still know very little about how CUSA operated on the ground. At the very least, the continued survival of CUSA unions in the face of the great numerical superiority of the Congress of South African Trade Unions (COSATU, formed in 1985) and the dominance of Congress tradition (i.e. the tradition of the ANC and its allies), requires further explanation.[19]

At times, the labor history of the 1970s had a didactic quality, evidenced in its emphasis on demonstrating the relevance of class in the South African past and its search to establish the historical presence of organized labor traditions. Some of these historical articles were written with an eye to the present: my own work, for example, investigated the origins and argued for the advantages of industrial unionism; Philip Bonner's article on the Industrial and Commercial Workers Union (ICU) of the 1920s castigated that organization for failing to organize the small nucleus of workers in the towns, and warned about the dangers to organization of a vague political populism.[20] Later, more critical research modified some of these early pronouncements: Bonner was criticized by Helen Bradford for having brushed aside the ICU's true character as a mass-based rural organization representing black peasants and tenants faced by the threat of dispossession.[21]

Resistance and Control

The labor history of the 1970s was also marked by new work on mine labor, forms of control, worker consciousness, and early resistance.[22] Charles van Onselen's *Chibaro* represented, in the words of one reviewer, "a pioneering attempt to create historically the social world of the compound in the early years of the mining industry of Southern Rhodesia." This work, analyzing an early phase of working-class formation during early industrialism—"when an industrial working class with an independent way and view of life emerges from the former 'lower orders' or 'labouring poor'"—was much less concerned with the institutions of labor organization (which of course barely existed) but rather sought to uncover the prior history of informal worker resistance.[23] For South African history, similar themes appear in the works of Peter Warwick (early African worker resistance), Peter Richardson (Chinese labor on the mines), Philip Bonner (the 1920 miners strike), and Sean Moroney (the compound system and informal resistance on the mines).[24] But the history of early informal South African worker resistance and organization within the workplace, both in the mines and especially in secondary and tertiary industries, remains to be written.[25]

The Poulantzians

The growth of academic interest in class analysis was at times tangential to the development of a South African labor history. A group of South African scholars at Britain's Sussex University applied Poulantzas's theories of the state to the South African situation. By the 1970s, their work had become extremely influential in South African studies. Foremost among the so-called Polantzians were David Kaplan, Mike Morris,

Rob Davies, and Dan O'Meara.[26] Although their work covered a number of historical areas, the Poulantzians shared an approach that periodized the changing state formation according to the relations between different factions of capital. The Poulantzians were criticized by Duncan Innes and Martin Plaut—South African scholars then based at Warwick University—for their tendency to ignore the struggles of workers and oppressed groups and the impact of such struggles on ruling-class strategies, focusing instead on secondary contradictions within the power bloc.[27]

The Poulantzians did make a positive contribution to the study of labor history. First, at a general level, Davies's work pointed to the possibility of explaining segmentation within the working class in other than purely racial terms. O'Meara's work on Afrikaner nationalism and its relationship to trade unionism demonstrated the salience of a class analysis: even Afrikaner workers could remain loyal to their class-based organizations and, on occasion, adopt militant industrial tactics. Particularly significant was Davies's article on the history of South Africa's industrial conciliation machinery—with its aim of bureaucratizing the registered trade unions—and David Lewis's account of the state's and employers' responses to the efforts of African trade unions to gain legal recognition in the 1940s and early 1950s.[28] These studies were early indications of what was to become one of the central interests of the new labor history and labor studies: the field of industrial relations, understood broadly as the relationship between workers' organizations, employers, and the state. Not unexpectedly, the Poulantzians focused particular attention on the role of the state. This subject was also a crucial concern of the emerging unions, still battling to gain recognition from hostile employers and constantly facing government harassment. The issues raised by Davies and Lewis (an active trade unionist)—around the threat of bureaucratization and incorporation—became starkly relevant when the unions were faced with the dilemma of accepting or rejecting the restrictive conditions of legal recognition offered in the new labor legislation of 1979.[29] This focus on the state's role in industrial relations points to the clear links which existed between contemporary and historical research and analysis.

These contributions and others which analyzed state strategies and the industrial relations-machinery within which labor organizations were obliged to operate, established a clear focus within South African labor history and industrial sociology that has survived until the present. As we have seen, such a framework of study reflected the strategic interests of trade unionists who did much to influence the agenda of research.

The 1980s: The Dispersion of Labor History

The re-establishment of mass nationalist political protest in the early 1980s had a considerable influence on progressive work within the academic establishment, bringing to the fore questions about the relationship between community and workplace struggles, between the struggle for national liberation and the struggle for socialism, and the appropriate forms of political organization to adopt.

Within South African studies, the effect of events was apparent: Poulantzian as well as structuralist explanations generally lost influence; and social history and historical research into class formation in the countryside began to predominate. This analytical reconfiguration in turn influenced labor history, particularly evidenced in the use of oral history methodologies.[30] However, some historians effectively applied social history questions to the study of the working class, exemplified in the work of Philip Bonner on the formation of a working class on the East Rand, William Beinart on consciousness among migrant workers, and Ari Sitas on "moral formations" among hostel dwellers.[31] Certainly, working-class history flourished within the ambit of social history with the development of history of working-class culture and community and the growth of women's history.[32] Nevertheless, during the early 1980s, a distinct labor history persisted which, by and large, confined itself to studying the workplace, while the new social history turned to the oppressed groups which fell outside the organized working class.

However, labor history, as such, during this period failed to cohere into any agreed project. This outcome was in part due to the changed political climate of the 1980s, in particular the powerful re-emergence of the Congress tradition and the ensuing acrimony between "workerist" and "populist" camps. Labor history became generally associated with a narrow workerist political tradition which reflected its origins in the 1970s. The limitations of a survivalist economistic strategy were reflected in academic labor history that treated trade unions as self-contained entities without reference to the wider arena of black resistance politics. On the other hand, the growth of popular political mobilization and community organization was conducive to the concerns of social history with its similar stress on community (though social history generally maintained a low political profile).

The subsequent "dispersal" of labor history in the 1980s may be viewed as a series of attempts to augment and move beyond the limitations of the labor history of the 1970s. This involved, in some cases, a process of investigating the alternative questions and methods of research posed by social history and, above all, beginning to forge tools appropriate to the changing political environment in which unions found themselves.

It should be stressed that the 1980s have witnessed a considerable outpouring of labor history in the form of papers, theses and, increasingly, publications. Below I will review some of the main influences, methodologies, and concerns which have governed labor history in the recent period. I will make two distinctions: the form in which work is presented and the major questions addressed in that work.

Most scholarly work in labor history has taken the form of case studies, either of institutions such as trade unions and federations, of particular sectors such as metal and engineering, of particular regions, or even of a particular event (usually a strike). Each individual study has addressed its own questions and employed its own methodology.

There also have been works that take a wider view or attempt to synthesize existing work. These have taken a variety of forms. Least successful have been attempts to deal with the whole sweep of labor history, usually drawn from secondary material. The best of these overviews is Steven Friedman's *Building Tomorrow Today*. Friedman's account of the re-emergence of trade unionism in the 1970s (which includes a lengthy historical introduction covering the main episodes in South African labor history) reflects the author's intimate knowledge of recent events, based on his years working as a labor reporter. Yet, Friedman refuses to consider historical developments in their context. Unions and federations are judged according to the degree to which they adhere to modern trade union (specifically FOSATU) practice.[33]

Like Friedman, Denis MacShane, Martin Plaut, and David Ward's *Power!* is mainly concerned with the fortunes of FOSATU—with the result that the role of the Council of Unions of South Africa is significantly undervalued.[34] The authors were in any case concerned to espouse FOSATU at a time when it was under attack internationally by the exiled South African Congress of Trade Unions (SACTU). From another perspective, Ken Luckhardt and Brenda Wall's *Organise or Starve* offers an informative but uncritical account of SACTU's activities particularly in the 1950s.[35]

Popular labor history represents another significant development of the 1980s. The most important example of this genre is the *Peoples' History* volumes written by Luli Callinicos. This series draws on recent academic work from social and labor history, effectively addressing questions of presentation and language raised by popular history advocates to provide a genuine and very accessible synthesis.[36] The strong presence of labor history in her work, according to Callinicos, suggests how much the emergence of popular history was closely linked to the growth of worker education, usually trade-union-based.[37] This is further evidenced by the wide circulation given to labor history through trade union newspapers and publications. *FOSATU Worker News*, the labor federation's newspaper, brought together a comprehensive labor history series in successive issues during the early 1980s. The National Union of Mineworkers carries material on labor history in its newspaper and produces historical booklets on mineworker history for its members. The Commercial Catering and Allied Workers Union of South Africa also uses its newspaper to teach the past and, on one occasion, invited a speaker to address its members on the history of black worker organization in the distributive trades during the 1940s. (This particular encounter subsequently led to an interview between the researcher and a surviving relative of the deceased Dan Koza, the 1940s leader of the black distributive workers union.) The desire among trade unionists to research their own history and to record current struggles is widespread. When the *South African Labour Bulletin* was established in 1974 by the trade union-linked Institute for Industrial Education, one of the tasks the editors set out for themselves was to record and analyze trade union struggles as they occurred, establishing a coherent historical record for the future. Labor history—and indeed primary historical research—is also an important feature of the dozens of worker plays that have been produced by trade unionists during the 1980s.[38]

Questions about industrial relations machinery, first raised in the 1970s, became a central focus of labor history and labor studies following the passage of the 1979 industrial relations legislation which granted legal recognition to black trade unions.[39] Analysts also delved into the nature of trade union structure, with particular attention to furthering internal union democracy. Maree's study of the internal dynamics of the emerging trade union movement, for example, analyzes relations between trade union leaders and their members.[40] Even where such specific industrial relations issues were not a central focus of a particular piece of work, such questions were nonetheless implicit. Perhaps this continued concern with concrete industrial relations issues should come as no surprise. The South African trade union movement grew rapidly during these years, despite recession from the early 1980s (and in contrast to international trade union trends, particularly in the First World).[41]

The Influence of Labor History

For labor history conducted within the ambit of social history, the melding of two approaches prompted scholars to raise new questions and apply different methodologies. A number of important new areas of study emerged, particularly in relation to questions about ideology and culture, class and community, and the role of women and the family.[42] For example, the rise of trade union organization among metalworkers on the East Rand in recent years is a main focus of Ari Sitas's study of migrant hostel dwellers. But when investigating the conditions that promoted trade union development, Sitas's attention moves well beyond the workplace. He analyzes how changing conditions in the countryside have influenced migrants' strategies at work. He explores the world of the hostels with its complex collective morality. He shows how the concentration of workers in hostels facilitated rapid unionization, and how the union acted to maintain social and moral order in the hostels in the midst of desperately dehumanizing conditions. Sitas's work, in drawing heavily on oral testimony, demonstrates the important influence of social history in the area of methodology.[43]

Perhaps the clearest indication of the unique cross-fertilization of labor history questions and social history method, can be found in Helen Bradford's work on the Industrial and Commercial Workers Union of Africa (ICU).[44] Although Bradford mentions the ICU's origins as a Cape-based urban trade union, the focus of her book is on struggles in the countryside after 1924 and the ICU's role in coordinating mass resistance to intensified racial oppression and dispossession. But in following the ICU's shift into the countryside, Bradford also carries over some of the major concerns of labor historians (if only, at one level, to demonstrate the inadequacies of earlier interpretations). Issues considered include: the organizational strengths and weaknesses of the ICU; the role of national and local leaderships and their relationship to the rank and file; the degree of democratic practices within the union; as well as the political implications of the above. Bradford's concern to analyze the relationship between local activity and higher levels of leadership adds a vital dimension to "history from below."

Other issues raised in Bradford's book parallel some of the newer concerns of labor history in the 1980s. Her discussion about the ambiguities of cultural symbols in Natal—to be found in the support for the ICU among traditionalists—is reminiscent not only of Sitas's work, but of the actual ideological battles currently being waged between the trade unions and Inkatha, a Zulu ethnic organization operating largely in the Natal area. (Indeed, in recent years COSATU has established its own cultural unit in the region partly to promote political redefinition of traditional symbols.) A dominant theme in Bradford's work is the ICU's success in combining—in a dynamic way—nationalist and class interests.[45] In the end, Bradford argues, structural conditions—South Africa's incomplete capitalist transition and the lack of political integration in a nation state that was less than twenty years old—fatally undermined the ICU's progressive project.

The Labor Process

The 1980s inaugurated new directions in South African labor history and labor studies. In North America and Europe, labor history has been reinvigorated by an explosion of research into labor processes and the history of work and workplace relations. This research rests on a systematic materialist approach that allows us to penetrate the hidden abode of production and throw light on issues of resistance, control, and accommodation. In addition, labor-process theory has revealed insights into the causes of trade union sectionalism and working-class division, and on the development of trade union and political consciousness. In the South African context, a labor-process approach has helped cut through previous ideological and racially-based accounts.

In my own work I have investigated the relationship between trade union strategies and labor processes to better understand the roots of working-class division in South Africa. The conditions most conducive to class unity existed in the secondary consumer products industries from the 1920s when deskilling had already occurred and workers were largely undifferentiated by skill or remuneration. It was white workers in state-run industries or the mines who were most likely to adopt strategies of racial exclusion and look to the state rather than to their own organization to maintain their relative privilege. The position of skilled workers (mostly white) was very different: their security was guaranteed, at least initially, by their technical indispensability to production, and maintained by traditional craft union techniques. The position of craft-unions was ambiguous: conservative in defence of their conditions against all unskilled workers, white and black; militant in response to threats of deskilling by management. Most important, the craft unions did not rely on the state for color bars to protect their members. As a result, they retained their membership in the Trades and Labour Council—which maintained an official stance of non-racialism, albeit at times largely rhetorical—for twenty years (roughly 1930–50). But, when deskilling intensified during the Second World War, craft unions increasingly adopted explicitly racial strategies. Labor-process analysis demonstrates that racial division within the working class is neither inevitable nor unchanging, and also indicates the role of employers in promoting racial hierarchy in the workplace.[46]

Arguably labor-process analysis remains within the general parameters of labor history established in the 1970s, with its focus on trade union structure and strategy. Although labor-process analysis tends to analyze the material constraints within which trade unions have historically operated, it also has revealed the potential for organization and resistance within the workplace, as well as the possibility for workers to exercise control over the very process of production.

If there are any unifying or dominant themes among the different approaches mentioned so far they would include, first, a shared concern with analyzing organizational structures and the conditions within which they have to operate, and secondly, an attempt to analyze the roots of sectionalism within the South African working class—involving considerations of skill, labor markets, gender, ethnicity, and ruling-class strategies.

Political Unionism

Another approach to emerge in the 1980s, an analysis within a framework of political unionism or social movement unionism, definitely marks a break with the labor history and labor studies of the 1970s. In part the result of growing academic interest in community issues, this development reflected what was already occurring on the ground. Mark Swilling's research into the growth of the shop stewards' movement on the East Rand in the early 1980s demonstrates the shift from an exclusive concern with workplace issues to involvement in community actions; for example, in 1983 shop stewards took up the plight of shack dwellers in the Germiston township of Katlehong whose homes were to be destroyed. Such a shift was dramatically confirmed in the 1984 Transvaal stay-away, jointly organized by trade unions and student organizations to protest the continuing crisis in education and to call for troops to be withdrawn from the townships.[47] Rob Lambert considered similar shifts in the relationship of trade unions to political organization and activity in a reassessment of the South African Congress of Trade Unions in the 1950s. He argues that the close links between SACTU and the ANC were not necessarily detrimental to workers' interests, a view contrary to the conventional wisdom of the 1970s arguing that working-class issues were subordinated in the interests of a middle-class-led ANC.[48] Indeed Lambert has shown that in certain areas the growth of trade union membership went hand in hand with the expansion of political organization.

In his reassessment of SACTU, Lambert has adopted a comparative international approach—rooting his discussion of political unionism in theoretical debates current in the early twentieth century between Leninism, revisionist social democracy, and syndicalism.[49] Lambert rejects each of the three models in turn: the pessimistic Leninist tradition which counterposes the leading political role of the party to the inevitable economism of trade unions; revisionist social democracy, the starting point of which is the absolute separation of politics and economics, preventing any fundamental challenge to the status quo; and syndicalism which collapses political action into workplace militancy and refuses to face the question of the state. Lambert suggests that conditions in South Africa have facilitated a fourth option, that of political unionism. Repression and the political exclusion of blacks have necessitated a vastly expanded role for trade unions which now combines militant workplace organization with an increasingly leading role—in alliance with other groups— within the broader national liberation movement. Finally, this perspective clearly has much in common with the "new international labor studies" that also has influenced the South African field.[50]

The theoretical and political issues raised in Lambert's work deserve amplification. He reiterates that nationalist and socialist projects are not necessarily incompatible; indeed, in South African conditions they may be mutually reinforcing. However the relationship is a complex one which Lambert sees as currently being played out in the search for appropriate political alliances linking the trade union movement to the broader national liberation movement (or with only some sections of it, in some versions). Broadly speaking, it is envisaged that the struggle for working-class leadership and hegemony will take place within the alliance process. This analysis remains at the level of general process and Lambert does not specify the forms of political organization appropriate to such a project— although such debates do continue elsewhere about the possible political role of the unions either alone or as the force which will transform the national liberation movement along socialist lines, or of the merits of a vanguard party as opposed to a mass worker party.[51] For our purposes, Lambert's model of political unionism provides a vehicle for the "politicization" of labor history and points to the possibility of viewing the history of industrial relations within a set of wider political issues.

South African labor history and labor studies have followed the rhythm of class and national struggles. The chosen areas of research and the questions asked by academics have been greatly influenced by the contemporary concerns of the labor movement. This is both inevitable and appropriate if academic pursuits are to have any relevance to contemporary struggles. Of course research findings should not be required to conform to the immediate tactical requirements of the labor movement or a particular faction. Such a state of affairs constitutes a disservice both to labor history and labor studies, and ultimately to the workers' movement itself.

South African labor history should now fill in some of the gaps that exist in our knowledge of the past. These include—insofar as trade union organization is concerned—the period of the South African Industrial Federation during the First World War and up until 1922, which saw considerable industrial growth and turmoil within white labor as well as witnessing the major beginnings of black labor organization; the 1940s, a period of very rapid industrialization and urbanization which produced the Council of Non-European Trade Unions, and which set the scene for later resistance and the formation of SACTU; the workings of TUCSA (Trade Union Council of South Africa) 1954–1988, an organization that combined white, "Coloured," and Indian workers under a truncated economism, while its hostility to more radical union initiatives ensured its survival during the most repressive years of apartheid rule.[52] More ambitiously, a need exists for a systematic history of industrial relations in South Africa that explicitly places its subject in the context of the wider society. This includes exploring the links—which clearly exist— with the history of the majority of the oppressed, who remain outside of the industrial relations arena. There is still very little work on early industrial resistance and the initial making of an African working class, its ideologies and social organization. Finally, it needs to be emphasized that in most sectors of the economy, trade unions for black workers were only firmly established in the 1980s. The task, therefore, remains to provide a historical account of the lives and struggles of the vast majority of unorganized black workers. The precondition for the success of such a project is the continued erosion of the artificial "division of labor" between labor history and social history, and the breaking down of these imposed barriers between the organized working class and other sections of the oppressed.

Chapter 10 / **Popular Struggle:**

Black South African Opposition in Transformation

C.R.D. Halisi

Josh Brown

Popular struggle, when adopted as a focus of analysis, permits a distinction to be made between mass movements and the political organizations which seek to harness their energy.[1] Mass movements, which give rise to popular protest, are expressions of such ubiquitous social forces as race, class, religion, ethnicity, gender, and generation. These social forces, more fundamental than institutional structures, can influence the internal dynamics of political organizations irrespective of their stated goals and objectives.

For South Africa, the dominant mass movements have placed themselves under the umbrella of the United Democratic Front (UDF), but they have also given rise to the broader term, "mass democratic movement." The African National Congress (ANC) is the most obvious political organization, but the increasingly important trade-union organizations also fit this category. The political relevance of the distinction between mass movements and formal organizations has been sharpened by efforts to theorize about the emergence of the black working-class movement as an autonomous force within the struggle for national liberation.

The central theoretical concern of South African studies has been the interaction of racial domination, capitalist development, and democratic movements. Three recent books contribute to our understanding of the character, complexity, and pervasiveness of black resistance to white minority rule within the context of South African capitalism. *Popular Struggle in South Africa*, an anthology edited by William Cobbett and Robin Cohen, concentrates on popular struggle as a means for understanding contemporary black resistance; in so doing, the book presents the nuances of popular black political consciousness in a less rarefied form than previous studies, which tended to focus on the characteristics of formal organization.[2] Similarly, Martin Murray's book *South Africa, Time of*

Agony, Time of Destiny: The Upsurge of Popular Protest is devoted to a detailed exploration of the thought and practice of popular resistance during the Botha era.[3] Stephen Davis's book, *Apartheid's Rebels: Inside South Africa's Hidden War*, focuses on the African National Congress (ANC), but he is no less aware of the importance of popular struggles to the success of established liberation organizations.[4] (With the exception of Davis and Murray, other authors discussed below are contributors to the volume edited by Cobbett and Cohen.)

The ANC transformed itself from what a well-known *New York Times* correspondent termed the "world's least effective liberation movement" to an important political force in both domestic and international politics. (Davis, 55.) Stephen Davis's book, *Apartheid's Rebels*, is least concerned with popular struggle as a theoretical perspective, and his effort to place contemporary liberation politics in a historical context ultimately proves superficial. Nevertheless the book is an eminently readable discussion of the success of the ANC as a revolutionary exile organization and as a renewed underground force inside South Africa. Davis is particularly impressed by the organization's increased capacity to conduct sabotage operations and to intimidate black collaborators and spies. In South Africa, as in other revolutionary situations, exile parties have organized armed resistance beyond the reach of the oppressive regime, established underground networks, rallied international support for their cause, and, by so doing, have remained an influential part of the political equation at home.

The ANC's resurgence, Davis recognizes, is the direct result of the "angry new constituency" in the black townships, whose members have literally swamped the organization since the mid-1970s in order to participate in the armed struggle. But his primary focus on the ANC makes it impossible for him to comprehend the full implications of popular struggle. He is sensitive to the ANC's contribution to internal resistance but only unwittingly does his narrative come to terms with the effects of popular struggle on the ANC.

Popular struggles inside the country present both an opportunity and a challenge to the underground activities of the banned nationalist movement. The explosion of popular protests against a host of local grievances in townships, workplaces, and schools has made it necessary for the ANC to find ways to relate to the new social forces and the changing situation inside the country. The ANC, Davis writes, has to "link protest to revolt." However, he often presumes the relationship between the ANC and worker organizations such as the Congress of South African Trade Unions (COSATU), and community and civic organizations, such as the United Democratic Front (UDF)—with its large component of youth and student organizations—to be far less conflictual than it is in fact. For example, Davis acknowledges that the ANC is, at times, uneasy with the hegemony of students in the UDF, yet he does not offer any explanation why (92). Nor does he come to terms with the potential political tensions inherent in an ANC-labor coalition. He simply asserts that conflicts arising between COSATU and the wider anti-apartheid movement will be easily resolved since "the executive would coordinate anti-apartheid actions and positions with the ANC and UDF yet guard COSATU as an independent advocate of the working-class interest" (104).

The ANC's alliances with popular forces have been an asset to the organization, as Davis recognizes, but he sometimes ignores the ways in which popular struggles shape its policies. The tendency to de-emphasize the impact of popular struggles on liberation politics differentiates *Apartheid's Rebels* from the analyses offered by Murray and the essays in Cobbett and Cohen. Still, Davis does stress the importance that the ANC attaches to the political education of recruits who reach its exile bases with attitudes and ideologies that have been formed back home. As he points out, "if recent exiles are allowed freely to espouse ideologies of racial or class exclusivism, it is feared, they could open movement-wide schisms that, for now, lie buried while waiting for liberation" (64).

Murray's *South Africa* provides a more sophisticated treatment; it aims to conceptualize the interaction of race and class dynamics that underpin state and capitalist power. The book's first two chapters situate the emergence of popular struggle within the theoretical context of the "conjoined crises of accumulation and legitimacy" (17). Both Davis and Murray recognize that the reciprocity of interests between capitalist and state elites cannot be mechanistically assumed. Yet, Davis's chapter entitled "The Bunker State" ventures only a straightforward enumeration of the resources the government has at its disposal for the purposes of carrying out its counterinsurgency campaign known as the "Total Strategy." More comprehensively, Murray devotes a chapter to the national, regional, and international dimensions of the "Total Strategy" and the military-dominated body responsible for its implementation, the State Security Council (SSC), whose tentacles stretch across the country in the form of the National Security Management System.

Although Murray contends that the South African state is in essence a capitalist state, he argues, contradictorily, that it rests upon racially-differentiated forms of political representation and that racial domination is the principal mode of social organization. This formulation of the relationship between capitalism and the state does not adequately distinguish the state's crisis of legitimacy from the interests of capitalism. Nor does it directly address capitalists' commitment to reform. Yet both Davis and Murray observe that business often takes the brunt of black anger because it is more vulnerable to pressure than the state, and black South Africans often equate free enterprise with racial oppression. For these reasons, both English and Afrikaner businesspeople have pressed for reforms, despite their dependence on the state for boycott and strike busting. Consistent with his interpretation of the state as capitalist, Murray considers the Botha reforms to be an attempt to replace mechanisms of control based on crude racism with those that can be rationalized in terms of market criteria (108).

Capitalist elites, the authors all agree, are interested in moving toward what John Saul refers to as a "democratically sanctioned capitalism"; few, however, are sanguine about the progressive character of the Botha reforms. Two distinct assessments of government-led reforms emerge from the essays in Cobbett and Cohen. Some of the authors, well exemplified by Jeremy Keenan, see the recent reforms as part of a calculated counterrevolutionary agenda. Conversely, contributions by Eddie Webster and Rob Lambert on trade unions, Jeremy Seekings on political mobilization in townships, Mark Swilling on the UDF, Jonathan Hyslop on student movements, and Saul on the future of socialism appear to recognize that a dialectic exists between reforms and popular struggles. In other words, whatever the motives of its leadership, policies implemented by the state are not based on a perfect knowledge of future consequences and, as in the industrial arena, can unwittingly allow the black opposition greater impetus and flexibility. After all, the constitutional reforms of 1983 gave birth not only to a tri-cameral legislature, but also to the UDF.

Saul's analysis of the ANC, and the democratic movement as a whole, is informed by his concern with the class content of a potential reform deal. He appreciates that the ANC must contend with both racial and class oppression, but fears that its tendency to stress the former over the latter will propel it in the direction of a political settlement favoring the incorporation of segments of the black leadership into the bourgeoisie. The major challenge the ANC faces, according to Saul, is not merely the military battle against the racist state, but rather that of "synchronizing the struggles against racial oppression and capitalism" (215). Saul argues that by institutionalizing working-class leadership, the ANC will continue its own radicalization. He prefers the formulation of "racial capitalism," which makes socialism a prerequisite for democracy, over that of the "two-stage theory of revolution" which disaggregates democratic and socialist phases of struggle. The latter approach is advocated by the ANC and its ally the South African Communist Party while the former has been associated with the rival Black Consciousness Movement. No longer exclusively associated with Black Consciousness, "racial capitalism" has become a uniquely South African approach to socialist thought. From this perspective, apartheid rests equally on the twin pillars of capitalist and state power and can only be replaced by a socialist order. Saul acknowledges the ANC as the leading force within the black opposition but believes that the successful implementation of its goals require the abolition of both racial domination and capitalism.

The perspectives of Black Consciousness groups such as the Azanian People's Organization (AZAPO), the National Forum Committee (NFC), and the National Council of Trade Unions (NACTU) receive the most attention from Murray, although the theoretical issues associated with their position are confronted by several authors. In their introduction, Cobbett and Cohen address the problematic nature of reconciling racial militancy and class consciousness. They observe that several new black organizations no longer consider race to be the determining feature of politics. Despite the non-racialism of the majority of the trade unions, it has not been possible to permanently unite black and white workers. Such an observation is equally true of the black and white middle classes.

Clearly, the central tenet of the popular struggle perspective is the necessity of prefiguring black working-class leadership in the democratic movement. It would be difficult to exaggerate the impact the growth of a black independent trade union movement has had on analyses of extraparliamentary politics in particular and South African social theory in general. Recognizing that the simultaneous expressions of nationalism, racial consciousness, and democratic self-assertion are unavoidable, Saul rejects the simplistic distinction often drawn between so-called "populists" and "workerists." This distinction originated with disagreements between trade unionists and community activists over questions of registration with the government and trade union affiliation with non-working-class black protest movements. Saul contends that participation in popular-democratic struggles will allow black workers to transcend economism, defined as a concentration solely on wages and working conditions.

Anti-populism remains an important political principle of several black trade unions, as Lambert and Webster remind us. The pivotal federation of trade unions, COSATU, has to consummate alliances with non-working-class organizations while seeking not to compromise its political autonomy. Murray, who devotes considerable space to the emergence of the independent trade unions and to their participation in township protests, also recognizes that the labor movement wants to avoid the "temptation to plunge willy-nilly into the maelstrom of popular struggles" (151). Black working-class caution, with respect to involvement in youth-led warfare in the townships, is not evidence of a dearth of militancy, but rather the prevalence of political sagacity, since democratic trade unions are the primary means workers have of protecting their class interests at present and in the future.

Unlike its counterpart in the West, where universal franchise serves as a mechanism of social integration, the trade union movement in South Africa has evolved a strategy referred to by Lambert and Webster as "social movement unionism." Counterpoised to orthodox collective bargaining unionism, this strategy can be seen as a means of reconciling specifically working-class demands with the broader fight against racial domination (20). Lambert and Webster perceptively locate the critical limitation of government labor reform which has extended industrial rights without granting concomitant political rights. Black trade unions are affected by the government's equivocation in that the political gains derived from these reforms have both transformative and conservative consequences (25). The industrial relations system has been shaped by the advent of genuine worker power, but that same system serves to channel worker militancy into institutionalized forms of conflict.

Studies of politics on the shop-floor which do not consider culture and community life cannot fully explain the nature of worker consciousness, according to Debbie Bonnin and Ari Sitas. For these authors, working-class struggle combines tradition, experience, and organization in the lives of actual workers. In their ethnographic study of the black work force employed at British Tyre and Rubber's Sarmcol factory in Natal, Bonnin and Sitas explore working-class politics at the grassroots level, stressing the unique alliances formed around the new democratic institutions growing out of a specific workers' struggle (43). By focusing on the changes in the labor process at Sarmcol, the nature of working-class leadership, and the characteristics of working-class community life in the primarily company townships in the area, these authors capture the fusion of cultural, personal, and uniquely working-class dimensions of a popular struggle. In short, they relate the politics of production to the broader culture of working-class resistance as a means to better comprehend the forms of popular struggle adopted by workers.

Shaped by the process of proletarianization, the identities of black workers encompass the past as well as the present, the rural as well as the urban. Bonnin and Sitas relate the following story, said to be typical for most black workers at Sarmcol and many other places in South Africa:

> I was not born in that township. My ancestors were born on the land, in a place where they could plough and keep cattle. . . . And I was born on the land which had always belonged to my ancestors and their chiefs. But by the time I was born, our land had been taken over by white farmers. . . . (43)

Under the guise of state-engineered ethnic politics in the so-called homelands, the centuries-old processes of land dispossession and proletarianization culminate today in the lives of many black South Africans.

In general, political analyses of groups oppressed under apartheid have rarely transcended the concentration on urban blacks. A deeper understanding of forms of rural protest may prove to be yet another contribution of the literature on popular struggle. In their provocative study of the Herschelites, a group of Sotho from the Herschel district in the "independent" Xhosa homeland of the Transkei, William Cobbett and Brian Nakedi contend that with respect to the distribution of land and population, rural struggles will have a vital bearing on the complexion of post-apartheid South Africa. Due to the "independence" of the homelands in their region, the Herschelites were trapped between the corrupt and oppressive ethnic governments of Chief Mantanzima in the Transkei, T. K. Mopeli, leader of the densely populated minuscule homeland of Basotho QwaQwa, and the infamous Sebe regime in the Ciskei.

In the rural areas, Cobbett and Nakedi conclude, the South African government is able to disguise its own repressive nature by making struggles over land and power, which it precipitates, appear to be ethnic conflicts. Historically, the bantustan system has served to make rural Africans more conservative and politically pliant to government manipulation. As in the case of the Herschelites, it has now become apparent to many rural Africans that the bantustan system does not foster tranquil ethnic communities but rather curtails the full proletarianization of black workers and marginalizes the unemployed and homeless. The politics of "independence" in various bantustans has led to confrontations between rural communities and state-supported ethnic leaders, resulting in the radicalization of segments of the African population in the bantustans (87-88).

Moreover, as the analysis of the struggle against "independence" in Kwandebele authored by the Transvaal Rural Action Committee demonstrates, diverse alliances of popular forces can, on occasion, successfully confront bantustan bureaucracies. A popular alliance of youth, homeland civil servants, the Kwandebele royal family, local white farmers, and the population at large fought against the leadership of the homeland government, its para-military vigilante group, Mbokodo, and the South African Defense Force in order to stave-off the so-called independence of Kwandebele. The ANC, illustrating its ability to intervene in rural areas (thus linking rural, urban, and armed struggles), claimed credit for the assassination of Piet Ntuli, the sinister leader of Mbokodo.

Nevertheless, the urban townships remain the major site of popular struggles in South Africa. From September 1984 onward, violence erupted in the black townships in the Pretoria-Witwatersrand-Vereeniging (PWV) area, the nation's largest industrial complex, where hundreds of people have been killed or injured. When violence spread to other parts of the country, the government imposed the first state of emergency since Sharpeville in 1960. Although angered by the reassertion of white supremacy in the constitutional order, township protestors also expressed a host of local grievances such as rent increases, inferior schools, and the government support of unpopular hand-picked local authorities.

By relating black mobilization in the PWV between 1980-84 to policies designed to restructure the political economy of townships, Jeremy Seeking reveals how the state's crisis of legitimacy encourages local black opposition. The South African state has been unable to promote collaboration or to implement institutional arrangements that do not result in wide-scale protest. Without a non-racial national franchise, it cannot easily impose acceptable municipal-level political structures to represent black urban communities; this helps to explain the often violent attacks on black counsellors. The core chapters of Murray's *South Africa* provide a virtual compendium of popular protest in black townships, as well as in schools, factories, and rural areas. While his narrative vacillates between overly-detailed accounts of township strife and cogent insights into the nature of these struggles, he does convey the complex dynamics that animate popular struggle. In particular, his account of consumer boycotts organized in numerous black communities illustrates the degree to which many white businesses are dependent on black consumers— hence the power of this tactic.

Popular protests are not spontaneous, nihilistic outbursts of black anger and frustration, but rather are structured within a culture of political resistance: that thesis is argued throughout these works. With the UDF as his focus, Swelling argues that black opposition organizations articulate fairly well-defined political principles, including non-collaboration with government institutions, non-racialism, democracy, and direct action (91). Organizations which have emerged out of popular struggles aggregate different black political demands and articulate important policies for dismantling apartheid structures. In other words, extra-parliamentary movements are an inevitable part of the political process. Black protest tactics during the September 1989 elections display a greater awareness and sophistication on the part of the Mass Democratic Movement (MDM) with respect to its ability to confront the white electorate with alternatives to apartheid and to mobilize international public opinion against cosmetic reforms sponsored by the government.

The class composition of black opposition movements has become an focus of analysis. The UDF, Swelling insists, contrary to the assertions of some of its critics, is not solely the organizational vehicle of the politically-conscious black middle class. Its leadership is comprised of individuals with diverse social backgrounds and, as a federation of groups, the UDF depends on its grassroots affiliates for its strength. As both Eric Molobi and Nkosinathi Gwala show in their separate contributions, black schools and universities are sites of radicalization for many members of the would-be black middle class who have been drawn deeply into community struggles.

Perhaps more than any other issue, the problems associated with black education galvanize strong community concern across classes. For example, by uniting students, parents, and the community around a politically realistic approach to educational reform during 1985-86, the National Education Crisis Committee (NECC) worked desperately to consolidate the gains of countless popular confrontations with the state over educational issues. Hyslop stresses that youth and student organizations, which have supplied the necessary input for the majority of township protests, sometimes employ tactics and make demands that jeopardize long-term gains (198-99). Therefore, adult-led organizations have had to work to incorporate youth into more disciplined political structures and to dissuade them from the belief that apartheid will fall in the near future due to the sheer force of their will to struggle. The explosive anger of youthful militants and the expansion of ANC underground activities have been answered by greater state repression. As Murray shows in graphic detail, the police and military have often resorted to occupation of townships, including house-to-house searches.

In the face of intensified repression during the state of emergency, the politics of popular struggle have become more difficult to pursue. On the one hand, many contemporary organizational structures are the product of mass movements whose political inclinations are in the direction of participatory democracy. On the other, overwhelming state re-pression limits the ability of these organizations to operate in an environ-ment in which they are free to express popular demands. Understand-ably, this may encourage leading black organizations to form more tightly-knit, but insulated, cadre and leadership structures. Yet, in the absence of a representative electoral system, the degree to which work-ing-class and grassroots demands find expression in a post-apartheid South Africa may well depend on the impact of present-day popular struggles on the development of genuinely democratic and participatory political institutions within the black opposition.

Chapter 11 / **Buthelezi, Inkatha, and the Problem of Ethnic Nationalism in South Africa**

Chris Lowe

Josh Brown

Mangosuthu Gatsha Buthelezi.

Americans conventionally view apartheid as a system of racial domination and see social conflict in South Africa primarily as racial conflict between blacks and whites. Those on the left recognize the connection between racial domination and class domination. What may be less well understood is the distinctive role of ethnic separation as distinguished from older forms of racial segregation and domination. The strategy of fostering ethnic or "tribal" nationalism through the bantustan system, to divide blacks from one another and to deny them political rights in a united South Africa, is a major defining feature of apartheid.

Consequently, ethnic nationalism is a serious problem in liberation politics. Ideologically, ethnic nationalism undermines the non-racial South African nationalism which most anti-apartheid groups support. Materially, thirty-five years of "separate development" have created ethnically-based networks of patronage and resource distribution, and institutions of coercion and control, which would not quietly disappear if the universal franchise were won tomorrow. The divisive and murderous potential of such politicized ethnicity is amply illustrated by bantustan ethnic discrimination, by the emergence of violent right-wing vigilante groups linked to ethnic politicians, and, above all, by the horrific violence in Natal/KwaZulu between members of Inkatha, a Zulu nationalist organization, and supporters of the United Democratic Front (UDF) and the Congress of South African Trade Unions (COSATU), which espouse non-racialism.[1]

Ironically, the very centrality of ethnic nationalism to apartheid has made it difficult for anti-apartheid activists to think about ethnicity clearly, or to develop strategies for dealing with it. Because apartheid ideologues present ethnicity as the most important social relationship, the temptation has been to ignore it as simply another divide-and-rule ploy. Yet, as Gerard Maré and Georgina Hamilton argue in *An Appetite for Power*, politicized ethnicity plays a crucial role not only in "classical" apartheid but in various conservative strategies for reform proposed as alternatives to popular demands for egalitarian democratic transformation.[2] It is a challenge the democratic left must find a way to meet.

Maré and Hamilton grapple with the problem of politicized ethnicity by focusing on Chief Mangosuthu Gatsha Buthelezi, Chief Minister of the KwaZulu bantustan, the Inkatha "National Cultural Liberation Movement" which he leads, and the Zulu ethnic nationalism which the movement vigorously promotes. Buthelezi is an ambiguous figure, claiming to work against apartheid from inside the system. His refusal to accept "independence" for KwaZulu in the 1970s created serious problems for the central government and gave him some credibility. But most anti-apartheid groups reject participation in apartheid structures and regard Buthelezi as hopelessly compromised by the inherent divisiveness of the bantustans. This conflict is exacerbated by Buthelezi's desire for personal power and his inability to tolerate criticism or dissent.

As Maré and Hamilton show, Buthelezi and Inkatha claim massive popular support among black South Africans, claim in fact to be the pre-eminent liberation movement.[3] They say they are the true bearers of the African National Congress (ANC) tradition, and that the ANC "Mission-in-Exile" (the ANC to the rest of the world) is an apostate rump. In contrast to the ANC, they oppose armed struggle and economic sanctions. They promote capitalism and oppose socialism or even any substantial degree of mixed-economy social democracy in contrast to virtually all other black anti-apartheid groups. They express implacable hostility to other anti-apartheid organizations. Echoing the South African state, they accuse the ANC of being terrorist and communist and accuse the UDF and COSATU of being the ANC's surrogates. In contrast to Inkatha's non-violence toward the state, its members violently attack other anti-apartheid organizations with increasing frequency. In turn those groups often accuse Buthelezi and Inkatha of being stooges, and their members sometimes violently attack Inkatha supporters.

The real extent of Inkatha's support is unclear. Maré and Hamilton skirt the issue. Studies suggest that its membership is mostly rural and female (the two go together due to the migrant labor system) although there is substantial urban membership and most of its active mobilization seems to involve urban men. Inkatha is overwhelmingly (95 percent) comprised of Zulu-speakers, nearly all of whom live in Natal/ KwaZulu or as migrant workers around Johannesburg. This ethnic and geographical narrowness undermines Buthelezi's claims to speak for all blacks.[4]

Inkatha claims to be the largest black political group in South Africa with over 1.7 million members.[5] Apparently any person who ever paid a membership fee is counted regardless of subsequent participation. More importantly, much membership is generated by coercive manipulation of access to land, housing, water, pensions, social services, and jobs controlled by Inkatha. Maré and Hamilton show that Inkatha's leadership and KwaZulu's are virtually the same, composed of rural bantustan chiefs, sections of the Zulu commercial petty-bourgeoisie and urban strongmen or "warlords." Failure to belong to Inkatha can mean loss of crucial material resources in a situation of desperate rural poverty; in towns it can mean facing potentially deadly physical assaults or flight to become an internal refugee. Civil servants and teachers are especially vulnerable to job pressures.

Yet clearly there is some degree of active support. While KwaZulu cannot adequately provide for all who live there, Inkatha does control enough resources to favor loyalists just as it punishes perceived opponents. The rural dominance of chiefs includes some measure of conservative support for "traditional authority" linked to ethnic ideology. In urban areas, Inkatha's authoritarian reaction to worker organization and youth-led community protest appeals to individuals who see demands for radical change as threatening to their material interests or who wish to uphold patriarchal prerogatives of age and maleness. The protests and repression have brought physical insecurity which some blame on the protesters rather than the state. Others may have kinship and clientage ties to individuals targeted as collaborators by radical youths.

While there is doubt about the extent of popular support for Buthelezi and Inkatha, they certainly do have powerful backers among monopoly capitalists, reformist white politicians, and conservative foreign governments. As Gavin Relly, Chairman of the Anglo-American Corporation (which dominates the South African economy) said in 1986, "You can't expect us to run away from the single black leader who says exactly what we think" (Maré and Hamilton, 83). In the mid-1980s, as thousands of black South Africans were being killed in the streets and tens of thousands detained without trial, the United States and Britain dithered over making even low-level contacts with the ANC, but Buthelezi was an honored guest of Ronald Reagan, Margaret Thatcher, and Helmut Kohl. Their promotion of him as a pro-capitalist, anti-sanctions, non-violent moderate willing to engage in "racial compromise" was widely and uncritically echoed in the Western media.

Giving the lie to uncritical and "sycophantic" media treatment of Buthelezi and Inkatha is a major motivation of *An Appetite for Power*.

Maré and Hamilton wish to expose the divergences between Inkatha's self-promoted moderate image and the undemocratic and violent reality of its actions. But they also wish to go beyond moralistic condemnation to provide analysis of the logic and contradictions of Inkatha's politics.

Maré and Hamilton argue that Inkatha's ethnic mobilization undermines efforts to create a genuinely egalitarian non-racial society. The nature of the political alternative Inkatha poses explains why Buthelezi has so much support from big capitalists and conservative politicians at home and abroad.[6] The crucial point is that "Inkatha has, in effect, drawn a distinction between the *apartheid* state and the *capitalist* state, in a manner similar to the Thatcher and Reagan administrations" as well as to white reformists in the South African Democratic and National parties (221). Buthelezi has been "selling the same political goods" for ten or fifteen years, and white reformists have increasingly moved toward his position. These "goods" are a vision of reform through ethno-regional decentralization. Today, both big business and white nationalist reformists want a weak post-apartheid state, the former to protect private property and the basic division of wealth, the latter to prevent "racial domination" and to protect "the white way of life"—motives which are obviously linked.

Inkatha is strong in one region but weak elsewhere, and its membership is drawn almost exclusively from one ethnic group. Regional decentralization would allow it to maintain its local power and give it the strongest possible power in the weak central state. A political system organized according to ethnic/racial "constituencies" and accommodating "group rights" and "group vetoes" similarly favors Inkatha's strengths. Big capitalists and the state even now reward Inkatha's aspirant accumulators for their pro-capitalist stance with access to capital and joint investment schemes; ethno-regionalism would also allow Inkatha's chiefs to retain their neo-traditional authoritarian powers and means of accumulation.

However, this program clearly conflicts with the demands of anti-apartheid organizations for non-racial national unity, for direct, accountable democracy in political institutions, and for social democratic redistribution in a mixed economy or socialist restructuring. Writing at the height of the uprising of the 1980s, Maré and Hamilton suggest that Inkatha might be bypassed by events, being unable to provide the stability required for the preservation of capitalism. Several subsequent years of intense repression have given Buthelezi a new lease on life. One of the signs touted as showing the new National Party leader F. W. de Klerk's flexibility is his willingness to consider Buthelezi's model for a "settlement" in South Africa. In the United States, pressure is growing for a "pragmatic" bipartisan coalition aimed at "abolishing apartheid while preserving capitalism," exactly Buthelezi's line.[7] Thus Maré and Hamilton's critique of Buthelezi and Inkatha remains timely. Unfortunately, their work is marred by stylistic and organizational problems which hamper its usefulness, and despite its wide range it has analytical shortcomings.

An Appetite for Power is poorly organized and repetitive, largely the result of its odd duality of tone. Although Maré and Hamilton do go beyond moralistic condemnation, they do not escape it. The book alternates between dispassionate analysis and flights of passionate engagement. The latter lead the authors into multiple formulations of the same point for the sake of rhetorical flourishes and pointed turns of phrase. In the end one is left feeling that the book could have made its case more effectively in two-thirds the space, and wishing it had because of the significance of the argument.

The duality of tone may in turn be related to an important interpretive ambiguity. Is Inkatha against apartheid or part of it? Maré and Hamilton say both. Of course, the ambiguity is really Inkatha's, and provides its political bread and butter, as Maré and Hamilton argue. But their inability to maintain a consistent characterization of Inkatha's relationship to apartheid, despite their own analysis, illustrates the declining utility of the rubric "anti-apartheid" in an era of conservative reformism. The strengths of their analysis appear when they ask whether Buthelezi is for genuine democratic transformation rather than if he is against apartheid. Positive emphasis on equality, non-racialism, accountable democracy, and socialism if the people choose it has become the order of the day. Insisting that nothing is changing in order to hang on to the convenient target, "apartheid," will leave supporters of the South African democratic movements vulnerable to "the new pragmatism," especially overseas.

Surprisingly, the book's most important analytical weakness is its shallow treatment of the workings of politicized ethnicity. Maré and Hamilton refer to it almost solely as a matter of "manipulation." While Buthelezi and others do manipulate ethnic identity divisively for political ends, and this is dangerous for democratic hopes in South Africa, the fact remains that there is something to manipulate which people value. Maré and Hamilton fail to tell us what it is or why they value it, and therefore do not offer much aid in looking for a political response. Shula Marks does somewhat better in her book *The Ambiguities of Dependence*.[8]

This short book began as a series of lectures delivered at Johns Hopkins in 1982. Its introduction sets the conceptual stage and sketches Natal and Zulu history up to the 1920s. Three main essays try to interpret a moment, Natal in the 1920s and 1930s, through the ideas and actions of three African political figures: Solomon ka Dinuzulu, the unofficial Zulu king; John L. Dube, leader of Natal's "progressive" Christian middle class, newspaper editor, founder of an industrial school modelled on Tuskegee, and founding president of the South African Native National Congress (later the ANC); and A.W.G. Champion, sometime trade unionist, entrepreneur, policeman, urban boss, and ANC leader. The conclusion draws the three essays together and suggests analogies to Buthelezi.

Marks has both historiographical and political aims. She wants to produce a social history sensitive to both individual agency and structural constraints which can inform our understanding of current politics. She uses methods from anthropology and literary criticism to interpret the "ambiguities of meaning" in the actions of her figures against the "structural ambiguities" of their class and institutional positions. Without abandoning structure altogether, she intends to break with structuralist Marxist history that does not treat Africans as subjects of their own history. Politically, Marks wishes to show the relevance of such history to interpreting Buthelezi.

Linking the three figures is their material dependence on the political and economic institutions of colonial capitalism which separated them from a popular base of support and made them politically weak. All three at some point tried to use Solomon's royal charisma to evoke popular support through Zulu ethnic sentiments. Yet Solomon's traditional authority also became ambiguous when the state too tried to co-opt it.

By the 1920s, white dominance had disrupted Zulu autonomy, and Solomon depended on state acquiescence for political survival. Yet the state lacked popular legitimacy and in turn depended on Solomon and "traditional" institutions to maintain its rule at relatively low cost. Dube and Champion, although they attempted to mobilize African nationalism and working-class consciousness (respectively) to challenge the new social order created by segregationist capitalism, were themselves products of that order and dependent on it. Faced with repression, they turned to Solomon and ethnic nationalism in search of a mass base outside that order. Yet ironically, the state and the capitalist interests it represented were striving to incorporate ethnic nationalism into that order as an alternative to African nationalism and working-class consciousness. Marks skillfully dissects the political ironies of the interdependence of these various actors despite their conflicting aims.

Solomon sought recognition as king and financial backing from the state. The state needed Solomon's popular legitimacy to refurbish "traditional" institutions supporting segregation and migrant labor, because local chiefs were discredited as the agents of white rule (or so Marks argues). Natal's sugar barons supported Solomon's recognition, seeing "African communalism" and "tribal discipline" as an alternative to working-class consciousness. Broader white hostility prevented recognition, but the government subvented Solomon's luxurious lifestyle and aided him in making exactions on commoners to pay his debts. Yet appearing too close to the state threatened his legitimacy, inducing him to make subversive public statements and actions. To gain the benefits of Solomon's conservatism (e.g., his attacks on the Industrial and Commercial Workers' Union which was pushing radical wage and land reform demands in the 1920s), the state had to content itself with his private contrition for such public subversion.

For Dube, the growth of segregationism following Union in 1910 restricted the middle-class "progress" he advocated. But he and his constituency of property-holding Christians were also threatened by the intensified class conflict and radicalism that segregationism produced. Forced out of national ANC office by leaders advocating greater activism and support for emerging worker militance, Dube retreated to his Natal base, splitting the Natal ANC. He struck up an alliance with Solomon, helping to organize the first Inkatha in 1924. It brought together traditionalist chiefs and Christian property-holders, and was the inspiration for Buthelezi's Inkatha. Ironically this alliance put Dube in tacit co-operation with the segregationists who caused his dilemma.

Champion, although from the same class background as Dube, responded to segregationism by turning to the popular classes. He became the most successful organizer in the first African mass political movement, the ICU, which organized farm labor tenants and urban workers. But the ICU could not deliver on its promises of land and high wages, which brought harsh repression from the state and employers. The national ICU broke up and Champion, like Dube, retreated to a regional base, the ICU Yase Natal. While repression sapped his rural support, urban workers began demanding a level of militance he found threatening. When he too made overtures to Solomon, the state saw a threat. Where Solomon's alliance with Dube reinforced patriarchy and property, Champion might have drawn Solomon into mass mobilization. Champion was exiled to Johannesburg.

Marks argues that Buthelezi encompasses the ambiguities of all three figures. Like Solomon, Buthelezi draws on loyalties evoked by Zulu royal traditions, depends on the state for material support while gaining credibility through limited challenges to it, and is seen by big business and politicians as an alternative to a more radical threat. Like Dube, he has turned to Zulu ethnic nationalism in the interests of a constituency of conservative accumulators, putting himself in a practical if not always easy alliance with state policy. Like Champion, he prefers the threat of mass militance to its actuality. And like Dube and Champion, Buthelezi faces being bypassed by more radical forces.

This sketch does not do justice to the rich suggestiveness of Marks' interpretations of these men and their times. Nonetheless, Marks falls short of achieving all her broader historiographical ambitions. Despite her hope to capture the connection between action and structure "by bringing together structure and process, process and meaning, meaning and motivation," over the course of the book Marks tends to lose sight of structure and has very little to say about process (9). The reasons for this include her choice of three individuals from the African middle strata, her stress on individual agency rather than collective and institutional agency, and her emphasis on "reading" events using literary and anthropological methods and defining "events" expressly in a synchronic anthropological sense.

In consequence, she spends more time on the ideas and actions of "elite" leaders than on their political relations to their followers, and class appears more as a matter of structural positions than of social relationships. There is not much analysis of the "structural ambiguities" of migrant workers and labor tenants, or of why sections of the popular classes were turning to both the ICU and ethnic nationalist traditionalism (as well as to independent African churches) in the same period. We have little information on how the precolonial social structure had been reshaped by capitalism and colonialism to illuminate the ambiguities of "tradition" and rapid change. How did Solomon actually mobilize support? We get only hints.

So when Marks comes to Buthelezi, she must give us analogies rather than process, despite her warning that the structural position has changed. The only structural differences she identifies are the emergence of mass popular and working-class organizations, and decolonization in Africa. She might also have mentioned the growth of manufacturing and finance capitalism (and the relative decline of mining and agriculture), the growth of cities, and the rural changes caused by the invention of bantustans and agricultural mechanization on "white" farms. These processes have shaped African accumulation and class formation, the class alliances available, and the political institutions which Buthelezi uses.

This is a lot to ask of three lectures, but it is what would be required to meet the goals Marks sets herself. *The Ambiguities of Dependence* stands as a thought-provoking challenge to pursue those goals further. Marks' own further efforts are likely to be illuminating.[9]

Reading these two books together highlights certain issues. One is the question of how ethnic nationalism is mobilized. In rural areas this requires more attention to the chiefs. Maré and Hamilton stress their centrality to the bantustan structures which Inkatha uses. There is internal evidence that Marks underplays their role, for Solomon seems to have relied on chiefs to collect tribute, while chiefs served as popular spokesmen at mass meetings criticizing Solomon. Thus the chiefs too seem to have been ambiguous, agents not only of the state, but of Solomon and of "the people." They may have lost universal hegemony, but, because in rural South Africa "production is deeply integrated with territory, kinship, language and political authority," they retained significant support.[10] Today the issue for many bantustan residents may be survival rather than production, but territory, kinship, language, and political authority remain linked.

The extent of the chiefs' authority and sources of popular discontent with them need exploration. Maré and Hamilton seem to suggest a merging of the chiefs with the petty-bourgeoisie, with the chiefs using neo-traditional powers for accumulation at the expense of the rural poor. Can discontent with such practices be used to counter politicized ethnicity? To what extent do beliefs in the chiefs' spiritual powers over the land still persist?

There is also an urgent need to understand the dynamics of urban clientelism and violence. In the Inkatha case, the "warlords" seem to refer to tradition and ethnicity to some extent (e.g., respect for age, discipline, Zulu martial tradition) but to be only loosely tied to "traditional" institutions. Is politicized ethnicity less deeply rooted in urban settings than in rural ones? On the other hand, there is also a need to understand the violence associated with "non-racial" community groups, to ask where it parallels conservative vigilantism, where it is asymmetrical, and consider what Marks would call its ambiguities (e.g., changes of allegiance).[11]

A more fundamental issue is the meaning of ethnicity, tradition, and nationalism. Marks, looking at royal traditions, writes of nationalism as a matter of "imagined communities."[12] In rural South Africa, ethnicity also involves more visible local communities, built on face-to-face signals of dialect, kinship, status, religion, magical practices, and on the powerful forces of intimacy and fear produced by rural isolation. And traditionalism involves patriarchal relations of gender and age in which even poor men and older women may have a stake, ideologies of authority which ramify upwards. To understand how ethnicity becomes politicized requires connecting those relationships with the materiality of bantustan resource struggles as well as with wider symbols of "tribal" identity and "tradition." On the other side of the question is the problem of nonracial nationalism, of imagining a community *without* the powerful binding forces of language and ethnic myth. Where is the nation in such nationalism? What provides its unity? Perhaps the struggle against politicized ethnicity itself?

Finally there is the question of how to confront "politicized ethnicity" in the longer term. How will democratic movements deal with the bantustans and the chiefs? These days UDF groups work with Enos Mabuza, Chief Minister of KaNgwane and leader of a movement called Inyandza, an erstwhile ally of Buthelezi. One wonders about Inyandza. Does it rely on ethnic, chief-based clientelism like Inkatha? In December 1988, the Inyandza Youth League (IYL) hosted a rally of "the UDF-affiliated Congress of Traditional Leaders" to commemorate Zulu resistance to the Boers in 1838. The IYL said "the main aim is to mobilize as many chiefs as possible into the mass democratic fold." The event celebrated "one of the outstanding ancient revolutionaries, Dingane" (Zulu king in the 1830s).[13] One wonders about the conceptions of democracy and revolution involved. To what kind of accountability will mass democratic chiefs be subject? Can democracy be reconciled with hereditary privilege? What are the consequences for democratic hopes of political thinking which conflates the perhaps admirable resistance against the invasion of a nonetheless autocratic precapitalist ruler with popular struggles against racial and class oppression today?

The power of ethnicity in South Africa is strong; democratic transformation will require de-politicizing ethnicity in the face of formidable obstacles. A democratic commitment would also seem to require treating popular ethnic traditions as more than false consciousness. Progressive intellectuals face the challenge of treating ethnicity seriously in both of these senses.

Postscript, October 1990

Developments in 1989 and 1990 have borne out much of the analysis presented by Maré and Hamilton and Marks regarding the contradictions of Inkatha's politics and the dangers of ethnic nationalism in South Africa. These developments also intensify questions about whether the unbanned ANC and the Mass Democratic Movement (MDM—an alliance between COSATU and the UDF) have developed an adequate strategy to respond to the challenge of politicized ethnicity, as they move to try to negotiate a new political order with the government.

The issue of police partiality in the continuing civil war in Natal has highlighted the repressive nature of Inkatha's involvement in the KwaZulu bantustan arm of the state. Buthelezi controls the KwaZulu police directly as the KwaZulu Minister of Justice. These police are indemnified from prosecution for any actions they take under the State of Emergency which President de Klerk continues in Natal. At minimum they have defended Inkatha backers from attack by MDM supporters, but have stood back when Inkatha has attacked the MDM. There are many accusations of direct police involvement in attacks on MDM-aligned communities. The national South African Police (SAP) are also accused of partiality towards Inkatha, which after all is fighting the same forces which police have seen as the revolutionary enemy for years. In one telling incident, the Inkatha Youth Brigade sent out a denial of police involvement from a fax machine in the Pietermaritzburg office of the SAP. However, right-wing police aid to Inkatha may aim mostly at undermining national talks between the government and the ANC.

The government's opening to the banned organizations also shows that white reformists have moved towards Inkatha's position politically. Speakers from the the ruling National Party (NP) stated this explicitly when the party opened itself to all races at a convention held in Natal in August 1990, saying that Buthelezi had been right all along. This apparent success has, ironically, intensified Inkatha's problems. Like the NP, Inkatha opened itself to all races in July 1990, now calling itself the Inkatha Freedom Party. Inkatha, the NP and the Democratic Party all now say they want to attract supporters of all races who favor free-market ideology, pro-business policies and decentralization of state power in favor of localized (implicitly ethnic) constituencies.

Buthelezi faces a difficult choice. He can maintain his regional base and enter into an unambiguously subservient alliance with the NP, who now treat the ANC as their main negotiating partner. This would weaken his credibility among blacks still further, and would not answer his personal ambitions. Or he can try to compete nationally, but Inkatha's ethnic narrowness and violent image limit his appeal.

Inkatha's options have been narrowed still further by an MDM and ANC campaign to isolate it. Hostility within the MDM to Buthelezi has risen as several peace settlements in Natal broke down due largely to Inkatha obstructionism. Anti-Inkatha sentiment has grown particularly strong in COSATU and the South African Youth Congress (SAYCO), since unionists and youth have been particular targets of Inkatha violence. The campaign aimed to cut Buthelezi off from alliances with other bantustan leaders, to put pressure on the central government to end the Natal Emergency, disband the KwaZulu police and make the SAP act impartially, and to expose Inkatha's violence internationally.

This campaign has been effective. Popular uprisings in the bantustans in late 1989 and early 1990 (tied to a wider MDM Defiance Campaign) led to the overthrow of several bantustan governments. Other bantustan leaders then aligned themselves broadly with the ANC to save themselves. Now seven out of ten bantustan leaders seem to be more or less in the ANC's camp, apparently leaving Buthelezi few potential allies. A one-day national work stay-away in early July backing the call to end the Emergency and restrain the police had broad participation.

However, questions arise about ANC/MDM plans for the bantustans and rural governance. The uprisings took place with the support of militant youth, workers, civil servants and rural communities, but to isolate Buthelezi the historically urban-oriented ANC has turned to bantustan leaders. One MDM spokesman explicitly said at the height of the uprisings that existing structures were needed to maintain rural order. What this points up is that while the militance of economically marginalized youth is useful to the ANC/MDM now, if the ANC comes to power it will be hard-pressed to provide them with jobs and incomes, and that militance could cut the other way. The ANC also knows that disgruntled chiefs have been a key point of entry for Renamo's war against the government of Mozambique.[14]

The risk is that the ANC will respond to its historically weak rural roots, its fears of youth volatility and chiefs' reactionary potential, and its need to isolate Buthelezi by trading off short-term support from bantustan leaders and chiefs for long-term continuity in undemocratic structures of rural governance. There is precedent in independent Africa for such a pattern. The dilemmas are agonizingly real, but true democracy in South Africa cannot exclude the 50% of the people who live in the bantustans.

Pressing the central state to isolate Buthelezi also raises problems. Hard-line anti-Inkatha forces wish to treat him as a strictly regional figure, just another bantustan leader. They have forced Mandela to back off from an offer to meet Buthelezi personally, on the grounds that it would accord him too much status. Yet making the anti-Inkatha strike national (rather than regional) implicitly acknowledged that Buthelezi's ethnic politics are a national problem.

Desire not to lend Buthelezi undeserved status is understandable. Rank and file anger is fierce, based on a perception that Inkatha is trying to force itself onto the national stage through violence against ANC supporters. But peace with Inkatha is ultimately necessary. The only ones who benefit from the continued war are the extreme right wing who are trying to restore apartheid. The longer it goes on, the less credible the claims of either the ANC or Inkatha to be able to lead an orderly transition become.

More profoundly, in trying not to elevate Buthelezi to Mandela's level the ANC and MDM may risk lowering themselves to Inkatha's, by playing politics with the lives of ordinary people. In Natal in the last several years, Inkatha has "won" the war in numbers killed, but lost support because it was increasingly seen to be obstructing peace. The July campaign, in contrast, produced open splits in the MDM ranks in Natal. If Buthelezi is seen to obstruct peace, no amount of talking to Mandela will save him. If the ANC is seen to quibble over peace talks, its own stature will decline.

The scope of the problem became apparent when the fighting spread to the Johannesburg area in late July 1990 and 750 people were killed in eight weeks. In Natal, the bloodshed had been between Zulu-speakers, undermining Buthelezi's efforts to rally support on an ethnic nationalist basis. In Johannesburg Inkatha-linked violence appeared to target Xhosa-speaking communities and migrant worker hostels (barracks), creating a specific ethnic enmity and focus for solidarity. It mobilized Zulu-speaking hostel-dwellers together with others they coerced. The Johannesburg leader of the Inkatha Youth Brigade played a prominent role and was arrested at the site of one massacre.

Increasingly the ANC has blamed a sinister "third force" trying to sabotage peace and negotiations, which it believes to be tied to rogue elements of the security apparatus. That the violence sharply escalated at exactly the time that the ANC suspended its armed struggle lends credence to this. Such a "third force" may have taken advantage of Inkatha's increasing desperation as the campaign to isolate it, movement by the NP into its political terrain, and the ANC's suspension of armed struggle reduced its options and its claims to uniqueness. Other analysts have focused on the dreadful material conditions of migrant and squatter life and increased competition for scarce jobs and resources.

Nonetheless both Inkatha supporters and ANC supporters described the conflict in ethnic idioms. Inkatha supporters described anti-Zulu threats to their security linked to the July anti-Inkatha campaign and justified at their attacks as pre-emptive. ANC supporters characterized their enemies as "Zulu" and themselves as "Xhosa." In Natal the July campaign and the Johannesburg fighting have been seen by some previous opponents of Buthelezi as anti-Zulu, causing them to rally to him on nationalist grounds. Both the potential for anti-Zulu popular sentiment to solidify among ANC supporters outside of Natal, and for anti-ANC Zulu nationalism to solidify in Natal, suggest that the threat posed by ethnic nationalism is still growing.

The temptation will be great for non-racialists to simply reject ethnic politics as manipulation. The experience of other countries, in Africa and elsewhere, suggests that ignoring ethnic perceptions and fears will only give chauvinists inside and outside the liberation movement room to work.

Chapter 12 / *Intellectuals, Audiences and Histories:*

South African Experiences, 1978–88

Belinda Bozzoli

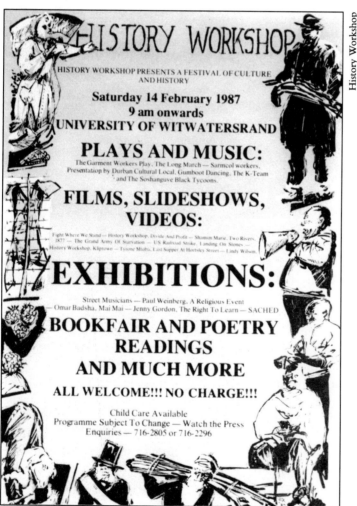

Over the past fifteen years, radical historians have rewritten the history of South Africa. The initiators of this revision in interpretation—Stanley Trapido, Shula Marks, Harold Wolpe, Martin Legassick, Rick Johnstone, and others—were living in England. But as time went on the "new school" found advocates in South Africa itself. A number of British- and U.S.-trained scholars returned to South Africa in the late 1970s and early 1980s, keen to promulgate these new ideas. The South Africa to which they returned was experiencing massive upheavals. The rise of black trade unionism in the early 1970s, the 1976 Soweto student revolts, the spread of the ideology of Black Consciousness, and a whole range of other changes and advances in the consciousness of black and some white South Africans, challenged these scholars of the left. In 1978, the University of the Witwatersrand's "History Workshop" formed, in part to make connections between new historiographical interpretations and the increasingly radicalized culture of ordinary South Africans. This group of university-based and mainly white sociologists, historians, anthropologists, political scientists, and literary theorists had two objectives: The first, to establish a relationship with its intended "audience" of black and white working people, youth, teachers, students, rural dwellers, and the unemployed, whose voices were being increasingly heard in the context of growing trade unionism, populism, and nationalism. The second, to demonstrate to the university itself how it could become a vehicle for a very different kind of education without underplaying the need for the production of more conventionally-trained graduates.

With minimal university support, the Workshop has engaged in four areas of activity since this time.[1] It has promoted the writing of academic studies of "hidden" histories, (an activity which it has vigorously defended as necessary and autonomous);[2] the preparation of a variety of materials for non-academic audiences which convey the findings of this and other research;[3] the development of "write-your-own-history" projects among community and trade union groupings;[4] and the mounting of public occasions—"Open Days." The four Open Days held in the first ten years of the workshop's existence are the focus of this paper.

History and Audience

Knowledge of the past has always been used by political and social movements, particularly nationalist ones, as a means to achieving legitimacy. In the South African case, "history"—knowledge of the past which is written and shaped by self-conscious intellectuals—has been imbricated with the system of social and political domination in complex ways. Afrikaner nationalists have constructed an elaborate myth of origin and of national progress and redemption like the Afrikaner epic of the Great Trek. These and other blatantly ethnocentric and often overtly self-interested interpretations of history have been imposed upon countless schoolchildren of all races for several decades.[5] To black South Africans this dominant history presents images of themselves as passive, savage, tribal, ignorant, and/or warlike, when it presents them at all.

However, this attempt at crafting a successful hegemonic ideology has failed. The dominant ideas, although well thought-out, efficiently promulgated through schools and public media, and backed by a totalitarian state, have not found a secure place in the hearts and minds of ordinary blacks. Most attempts to control their ideas about themselves have been met by black South Africans with disbelief, cynicism, or outright hostility. To some extent this may be attributed to the failure of the ruling classes to embrace those sections of the intelligentsia not of white Afrikaner nationalist pedigree. As a result they have failed to produce any sort of discourse with a symbolic content that even vaguely corresponds to that of the black person in the street. The myths of the Great Trek or of Jan van Riebeeck as the father of the nation, for example, fail to provide for either English-speaking whites or blacks a cultural language with symbols invoking their identity. But the disbelief could also be explained by reference to the rich and ongoing oral traditions which thrive in black communities.

It is in the context of this failed hegemony that we see the attempts (by several other groups as well as the History Workshop) to popularize the "new school" of South African history, to counter the myths and distortions of school and official Afrikaner historiography, and to offer "ordinary" South Africans a different vision of their past. Because hegemonic ideas are weak, such attempts have been welcomed. But the relationship between intellectuals and audiences is far from simple. While some of the complexities are examined in the body of this paper, some need to be mentioned now, as essential background to understanding the whole popularization enterprise.

First of all, popular culture in South Africa is not a culture of literacy, but as implied above, tends to be dominated by oral, visual, and "live" forms of communication. This means that the intellectuals' own means of communicating, the written word, is inadequate to the task of reaching wider audiences—perhaps more so than in Western cultures. At the very least, the gap between the writing of a thought, and its reception by an "audience" may be both wider than, and differently constituted from, the equivalent "gap" elsewhere. And when the intellectuals' first language is English and that of their audiences is not, the gap is wider still. This makes the forum of the "Open Day" a particularly important one for exploring the popularization process, since it relies on non-written forms of communication.

Secondly, popular culture is not straight-forwardly class conscious. It is mainly constituted through community, regional, ethnic, local, gender, or racial categories. For a complex variety of reasons, only rarely does "class" form the significant element in cultural formations. This is not, of course, to deny the analytical value of class as a concept but rather to note that "culture" and "class" are rarely coterminous categories in South Africa.[6] A further difficulty that left-wing intellectuals have in addressing South African blacks is that black popular culture tends to engender and sustain ideologies of a nationalist, populist, "motherist," or racially-defined character.[7] Local traditions as well as broad national movements follow this pattern. This fact presents particular problems for those sections of the intelligentsia who may be wedded to Marxism or a looser form of class analysis. For how do you convey your class analysis to audiences who define themselves firstly in racial or ethnic terms, and only secondly or even thirdly in class terms? This was the problem that confronted us in our first attempts at popularization.

Finally, there is the fact that the popularizing intellectuals are largely white, their audiences largely black. Black nationalism in South Africa has not, in general, sustained itself through the use of a vigorous historical tradition, thus perhaps leaving a gap for a whites to fill.[8] In this light, the nature of the white left intelligentsia requires further comment.

Non-racialism on the South African left is a tradition with a considerable pedigree. Left-wing and liberal whites have played important roles in a variety of struggles in South Africa throughout this century.[9] Only the Pan Africanist Congress and the Black Consciousness movements express as a matter of principle a cynicism about, and rejection of, the role of whites. The ANC explicitly espouses non-racialism, and movements such as the Congress of South African Trade Unions (COSATU) or the United Democratic Front reject black exclusiveness. The existence and involvement of white left-wing intellectuals is not itself a matter for comment. Instead, the debate has been focused elsewhere, namely on the balance between social commitment and intellectual independence within the white intelligentsia. It is this issue that has had direct relevance to the development of History Workshop.

Broadly speaking these intellectuals have fallen into three categories—all of which have, at one time or another, found a place in the History Workshop. Those in the first category have chosen to downplay their intellectual role. During the 1970s, the time of the growth of the Black Consciousness movement, there was a considerable distancing between white intellectuals and black social movements.[10] Those in one category of intellectuals, perhaps to compensate for their rejection, committed themselves to offering their practical services, and virtually abandoned intellectualism. Both Marxist and non-Marxist, these people became organizers in trade unions and active members of major anti-apartheid organizations, playing a vital and often unacknowledged role in the politics of the 1970s and 1980s. One byproduct of their choice, however, was that an anti-intellectualism, echoing that which has always characterized South African society, began to permeate white left-wing culture. Independent thinking, which to many of us entailed independence both from the society at large and from particular organizational "lines" on the left, came under fire from committed activists who (perhaps understandably from their point of view) saw little value in what they perceived as ideas "for their own sake."

The second and third categories of intellectuals, however, sought to retain a certain independence (both from the repressive society and from particular left-wing organizations) and to continue practicing their roles as critics and thinkers.[11] To both of these groups Marxism proved an attractive philosophy. It was Marx himself who said that intellectuals "need to undertake ruthless criticism of everything that exists, ruthless in the sense that the criticism will not shrink either from its own conclusions or from conflict with the powers that be," and it was Marxism that had inspired the "new school" of South African studies which influenced so many South African intellectuals in the 1970s.[12]

Those in the second category found that theoretically assertive Althusserianism offered them a justification for continuing with intellectual pursuits in spite of the generally hostile climate. In their hands, the largely historical and empirically-based work which underlay the writings of such South Africanist innovators as Stanley Trapido, Shula Marks, Richard Johnstone, and Martin Legassick came to be translated into abstractions in the local setting. This grouping did not seek a re-casting of the complexities of South African history in radical terms. Instead they looked for abstract truths—broad statements which gave them a key to reality. It seems that in a context where their own position was subject to increased doubt, Louis Althusser's claims that "the theoretical level" was autonomous and necessary proved unusually appealing. Intellectuals of this type have never sought organic links with popular culture; rather, they have tended to search for theoretical truths to communicate to intellectuals who are attached to organized movements. At times their abstractions have appealed to organizationally-linked thinkers, in that they appear to give clear and unambiguous truths about where movements should go.

The third grouping of white intellectuals espoused a different approach—one which was strongly influenced by the Marxism of Gramsci rather than that of Althusser. To them, the value of the "new school" lay in its historical and empirical work as much as in its overarching insights—perhaps because in the "real" world of fact and history, there lay a potential area for establishing the "organic links with popular culture" which the Althusserian approach eschewed. Gramsci's ideas about consciousness, hegemony, and counter-hegemony provided a framework within which intellectuals could both practice their craft and seek connections with wider constituencies. Forging an alternative set of historical interpretations would challenge hegemony on a high level; but making these new interpretations popular would provide the already-conscientized masses with greater self-insight and understanding of the structural conditions they confronted.[13] The essentially Gramscian aim of raising the capacity of the mass of the people for self emancipation—so that the popularization of history involved a process of empowerment of the people themselves—ran against the Althusserian idea that emancipation would come from above and from "theory." Gramscians stood somewhere between a belief in the subordination of the intellectual to the movement, and one in the subordination of the movement to theory.

As mentioned above, all three types of intellectuals have at one time or another found a home in the History Workshop. Some have had direct links with trade unions, others with anti-apartheid organizations. Some have tended to embrace "theory" and others "popularization." But the "Gramscian" approach has been the dominant one. Naively, at

first, we set out to harness our capacities in support of the cultural assertions of the popular classes, but to do so whilst retaining our commitment
to historical materialism, to truth, and to a critical stance. This complex
self-definition was to breed numerous ambiguities and contradictions in
the subsequent history of the Workshop, some of which are the subject
of this paper. What does it mean to "connect" with an audience but also
to retain an ability to analyze situations objectively and critically? Need-
less to say, the "Gramscian" approach has been consistently criticized by
intellectuals from both of the other left groupings.

The First Workshop—Defining a New Terrain

At first, the Workshop's initiators (Luli Callinicos, Eddie Webster,
Philip Bonner, Peter Kallaway, Charles van Onselen, Tim Couzens, and
myself) stated our aims rather uncertainly: "We hope that the Workshop
will be more than simply academic," ran the invitation to the 1978 conference.[14] Besides a vigorous program of seminars, at which the academic
side of the Workshop was given great impetus, this first conference attempted to reach out. The popular side of the program included public
lectures by two of the "new historians," one on "Class, Race and Gold"
by Rick Johnstone, and another by Charles van Onselen entitled "The
Witches of Suburbia" about domestic servants; a play, also based on
Charles van Onselen's work, "Randlords and Rotgut," performed by
the radical theater group "Junction Avenue Theatre Company" (later to
develop its social history repertoire to include such successful plays as
"Sophiatown"); films on the history of townships on the Rand; slide-
tape shows on the rise and decline of Vrededorp, the history of gold
mining, and the history of garment workers; and a major photographic
exhibition on "Working Class life and Culture on the Witwatersrand."[15]

At the time, these forays into the field of popular history seemed
innovative and relatively successful. With one exception, however, the
kinds of links generated between the intelligentsia and its intended audience could not be described as "organic." While we showed an awareness of the need to use non-literary forms in presenting popular items,
the first History Workshop was a forum where intellectuals presented
research and audiences watched, listened, and learned. The exception
was a talk and slide-show on the history of the Garment Workers'
Union, at which a small audience of mainly white retired garment workers participated excitedly in recalling their own history.

With the exception of those of our group who had active connections with black trade unions, we lacked, at this time, organic links with

the audiences we were seeking to reach. The content of the popular side of the workshop did perhaps reflect a somewhat abstract conception of the popular classes being both addressed and presented. We wrote about and showed pictures of all the right people! There was no shortage of workers, the informal sector, the oppressors and the oppressed. We were self-consciously non-racial in our approach. But these attempts tended to be symbolically cast in ways which drew from an essentially academic culture, even an exile one. We focused quite self-consciously on the question of class; we defined this as the key concept around which popular history should be organized and were a little uncompromising in our definitions of it. Our interpretation of "class" lacked cultural depth and subjective meaning in comparison with that which we evolved in later times.

The form taken by this first workshop was restricting. We had not taken into account the effects of segregation on the audiences we sought to reach. While no breakdown of audience participation is available, it seemed at the time that audiences consisted mainly of white and some black middle-class people. The absence of black working people brought home to us the effect of segregation, cultural deprivation, and colonization which denied black working people any sense of their right to participate in cultural occasions organized by whites and held in primarily white institutions. We learned first-hand of the ethnic isolation of intellectuals and of the encapsulation of black culture within townships (fed by and feeding into the "Black Consciousness" philosophy). The gulf was symbolized by the mundane matter of transportation. We had chosen to mount our "popular" events in the evenings. But Soweto is many miles from the center of Johannesburg, and buses and trains are infrequent, and dangerous at night. Other Rand townships, with the exception of Alexandra, are even further afield. Cultural separation in South Africa is very much tied up with geographical immobility. Large black audiences were not forthcoming, in other words, because they either felt unfamiliar with the cultural terrain the workshop was opening up, or they could not easily get themselves to the venues.

In addition to transportation, other shortcomings became evident. First, only one black intellectual participated in the academic conference; Modikwe Dikobe, a writer and poet whose formative experiences were in the interwar period and did not really speak to the concerns of the 1970s. Second, we had not considered whether black audiences were at that time assertive or self-confident enough to seize what we had to offer. And third, no intermediate group of intellectuals was offering itself to us as brokers, at this time. History and popular education were not on the agenda of most black intellectuals in the late 1970s.

With hindsight, the achievement of this early attempt lay in its opening up of new areas for further exploration, and its collection of valuable materials. History had not yet been shaped by its audience, as it was to be in later times.

The 1981 Open Day—Achieving Legitimacy

Three years after the 1978 workshop, we had expanded and become more confident. We organized a second academic conference, and sought to develop the popular side of our activities. If the first workshop revealed that there was much popularizing to be done, the second gave this exercise legitimacy in the eyes of our intended audiences. The process of legitimation involved not only developing a heightened sensitivity to the audience's own cultural and ideological preferences (an exercise in which most entertainers are expert, but academics somewhat inept), but also overcoming the suspicions of ghettoized black audiences of the middle-class "white" venues at which the workshop was held.

The first way we devised to overcome the problems of transport and black alienation from university occasions, was to draw all the public events together on one day, a Saturday, and publicize it as an "Open Day." Day-time travel would be easier, as would coming to the university for one long non-working day rather than several short evenings after work. Inviting people to this Open Day became a matter of discovering key institutions with a legitimate claim to black audience commitment. We put up posters in carefully thought-out venues, each with a claim to a particular subsection of our intended audience and sent out invitations on a similarly planned basis. The Workshop had made its first attempt at constructing an intermediate set of linkages between intellectuals and audiences, something which was to prove increasingly important in later times, but which would also present intellectuals with considerable dilemmas.

The strategy of finding intermediaries between ourselves and our audience proved successful. At the Open Day held in February 1981, a substantially different relationship between intelligentsia and audience emerged. "Whereas at the last workshop barely 100 people at maximum attended the events we organised," ran the report of the day, "this time 1000 people at least, many from Pretoria and the East Rand townships as well as Johannesburg and Soweto, poured into the campus, during the course of a rainy day and evening." Not only were there simply more items to show (academics and activists were writing and producing more cultural and historical presentations reflecting the beginning of the cultural revival which was to characterize the 1980s), but this time the participation of black township youths and intellectuals was substantial (possibly indicating a more open approach toward education itself, and to education connected with what they perceived as a "white" institution). The atmosphere was a non-racial and comradely one, at a time when the word "comrade" was not widely used in popular vocabulary. It was at this second workshop that we became aware of the importance of the geographical location of the university (near the center of Johannesburg, with reasonable access to both suburban and township transport routes). A space became available within which a non-racialism was possible—going against the general structuring of the segregated society of which we are a part.

Just as geographical space was important to overcoming the physical limitations created by apartheid, cultural and symbolic space which both intellectuals and heterogeneous audiences could occupy was vital. The culturally empty concepts of "class" with which we had approached the first workshop were this time given greater subjective meaning by the inclusion in the Open Day of a number of cultural interpretations of the past and present. This was brought home to us by the anthropologist and Juluka/Savuka performer, Johnny Clegg, who drew on key symbolic and cultural motifs of black culture to establish a rapport with his audience. It was to Clegg's talk on the musical forms of migrant workers that audiences responded rousingly and enthusiastically; it was at his references to some of the telling and universally understood musical phrases of the Zulu migrant minstrel, that people cheered. It was evidence that some cultural language, some sets of symbols, (of black working-class origin) were held in common by all those present—and the realization of this fact was moving to many.

Many of the presentations evoked a nostalgia among the audience—sometimes for something real but at other times for an imagined past. Clegg, for example, tapped into a longing for a common cross-racial heritage; Rebecca Mphahlele, in a talk on her childhood in Vrededorp, an inner-city multiracial area later destroyed by the Group Areas act, drew upon a yearning for the "unknown and unspoken of" Johannesburg. "Suffering" was a further strand of consciousness, perhaps related to the emotion of nostalgia evoked by this Open Day. It was most evident in "Imbumbo," a play devised and performed by Soyikwa, a theatrical group influenced by the philosophy of Black Consciousness. Large segments of the audience were so anxious to see the play that they ran to the theater, and crowded in. The day revealed for the first time that audiences sought and appreciated legitimations of the history of ordinary lives and experiences within local communities. The slide-show "Decade of Defiance" revolved around the idea that the 1950s had been an era of particular significance in the history of black resistance. An air of daring accompanied the enthusiastic cheers given to the show, and its portrayal of the powerful black nationalism which had emerged in the early days of Afrikaner nationalist rule and repression, only to be effectively crushed for twenty years. The slide show conjured a longing for the fifties, and a sense of the potential continuity between the time when that protest was destroyed, and its reemergence in the present of the early 1980s. However, nostalgia seemed to be reserved exclusively for lost possibilities in our urban past; audiences viewing David Goldblatt's exhibition of photographs of an elderly black former sharecropper "Ou Kas Maine," did not respond in a similarly heart-wrenching way. While critics viewed the exhibition with interest and appreciated it in artistic terms, it appeared that while lost townships, lost histories of struggle, and lost possibilities for multiracialism were mourned, lost sharecroppers were less evocative. Was this a purely urban nationalism we were observing?

Nostalgic responses contrasted powerfully with those elicited by the more "workerist" type of production, "The Sun Shall Rise for the Workers," which tended, like many of its genre, to celebrate the struggle for trade union recognition in a particular factory. This play emerged originally as an effort by workers to reconstruct the events surrounding a strike in an East Rand foundry for their union lawyers. The script later evolved through a series of workshops under the guidance of the Junction Avenue Theatre Company. Pragmatism, rather than nostalgia or suffering, characterized this play. As one of the directors commented, "the design of the play is for two types of audiences—it is for co-members of the unions, and offers them another way, a theatrical way, of discussing issues that affect them—[and] the broader township audience, bringing to the attention of the non-unionized worker this kind of struggle and the need for a wider worker unity."[16] Theater was not, in this conception, a means to portray oppression, but to offer and publicize a means of overcoming it.

These workerist sentiments also struck a chord in audiences—but clearly appealed to a very different strand in popular consciousness. The types of audience sentiment apparent in the case of this play were amusement, and in other cases militancy. The audience revelled in the fact that the play was not simply being shown to its main intended audience—

workers themselves—but to a wider group. The occasion provided a way in which a private culture could be made public. The deliberately caricatured characters, both white and black, drew affectionate laughter—a sense of "that's us, that's us on the stage there." Two orientations in a celebratory and more assertive audience consciousness thus seemed to be emerging: one related to nostalgic non-racialism and nationalism, with an orientation toward the local urban community as the origin of subjectivity; and the second coming from pragmatic and forward-looking trade unionism, with the factory as the focus and the union as the source of private meaning as well as public presentation of self. While the trade-unionist form of consciousness had an organizational base, the nationalist one was, as yet, less clearly linked to particular social movements. These two strands—called "populist" and "workerist" by observers and participants—were a puzzle to many. Which was "authentic," we wondered. Would one "evolve" into the other? Subsequent events would help answer this question.

The 1981 Open Day brought home to the Workshop that if we were to tap into popular culture, we would have to take into account the fragmented and interwoven nature of its discourses, and the fact that only some segments of our audience were class conscious. The pattern and symbolic forms that prevailed were to some extent in the process of formation, rather than clearly formed and coherent, but the Open Day gave them momentum and assisted their entry into the ways of thinking of particular groups.

The Workshop's success in connecting with strands of popular consciousness began a process of self-examination among its members. For some, the pull of generally anti-intellectual culture proved powerful. If intellectuals could successfully make these kinds of organic links—where symbolic worlds could be constructed which approached those "inherently" present in the minds of audiences of ordinary people—then would it not be appropriate for us to begin to turn all of our energies away from what the first invitation had called "simply academic" activities? Should we not instead devote our work more completely to the task of finding and constructing symbolic and cultural patterns which the popular classes would find appealing, inspiring, and uplifting? Such arguments were made without a clear awareness of the kinds of complexities in popular discourses. Which symbolic and cultural patterns for which popular classes? Would we abandon our class analysis for the sake of popularity? And what would happen to our independence as intellectuals if we took such a course? For the moment, we were moving closer to our intended audience, but neither group had really reached an awareness of what their potential fusion would lead to. Nevertheless, some had high expectations that this was where the Workshop would lead. There were resignations from the Workshop committee at a later stage, when the majority of members decided to commit themselves to remaining relatively, if not absolutely, independent.

A further sequel to the first workshop was the organization by a group of committee members of a second Open Day, this time in the Benoni township of Actonville. The idea behind this second Open Day—perhaps born of the self-criticisms mentioned above—was that the Workshop would take its wares to the community, rather than expecting the community to come to us. This day, too evoked interest in history and culture. But it lacked the multi-racialism, the emotionalism and the geographical centrality of the original, larger one, providing us with an important lesson in the significance of geographical and spatial factors. In the township/community setting, the white intelligentsia lacked the level of legitimacy and acceptability that it was able to claim in the central venue, while the heterogeneity of audience which had given the original Open Day a lot of its significance was absent.

1984—The Audience Takes Over

Of all the strands of popular consciousness that the first two workshops had tapped, it was to be the most obviously class-based one—that of black trade unionism—that emerged as the most assertive in the next period. By the time of the third History Workshop Open Day, in 1984, black trade unions, but particularly those under the vigorous cultural direction of the Federation of South African Trade Unions (FOSATU), were the most prominent groupings on the South African left.

This time, instead of having one main venue at which all the performances were located, we booked three simultaneous venues, and ran three simultaneous programs. We published translations of the program into two vernacular languages as well as summaries of all the items on show. Building on our experience of the strands of consciousness and awareness which had become evident at the first workshop, we constructed a program which managed (perhaps as much by accident as by design) to reach the variety of audiences we considered likely to come.

Nationalist sentiments were conveyed in many of the productions and performances. They appeared, for example, in "None but Ourselves," a highly emotive and effective slide show on the Zimbabwean struggle for independence and the role of propaganda in that struggle. The play, "Gandhi," performed by the pupils of the multiracial private school Woodmead, depicted in partly heroic, partly questioning terms, the life of one of the heroes of Indian nationalism. A further fillip to the nationalism of this workshop, as well as a presage of things to come, was evident in the performance by a recently released white political prisoner, Jeremy Cronin, who read a selection of the poems he had written while serving several years in jail for ANC activities. His performance, charged with the nostalgia and emotion that comes from someone who has experienced the worst of repression and is now amazed to be released and appearing publicly, reflected the euphoric belief among many that, in the early 1980s, we were witnessing the beginnings of a revolution in South Africa. It provided quite a contrast with the almost furtive enjoyment that audiences had derived from "Decade of Defiance" three years before. His poetry reading was a statement that he represented a different kind of intellectual—organic to the organized movement with which he allied himself.

If nostalgia was a pervasive sentiment, the inner city remained a focal point of interest. Indeed, the sense of locality and loyalty to the history and reality of an inner- or outer-city suburb/township was, if anything, more central than it had been in previous years. "Hell's Kitchen," a slide show on the history of Alexandra Township on the outskirts of Johannesburg echoed the theme of city history and township loyalty which had appeared first in the township film of the 1981 workshop. Reflected in the appearance of stickers such as "I love Soweto" or "Alexandra I love you" on township cars and taxis, the symbol "township" had, by this time, become quite potent. Other films such as "Mayfair" and "Diagonal Street" explored the interplay of working-class culture and multiracialism and the destruction wrought by the Group Areas Act on these inner-city communities.

An internationalism appeared for the first time at this Open Day. We invited the American Working Class History Project (as it then was) to send a delegate; Kate Pfordresher came, introduced the work of the project and showed "Five Points"—a show about early Irish immigrant life, culture and struggle in New York City—to a fascinated audience.

But it was trade union consciousness that prevailed. The day became transformed by the musical performances of such groups as Abafana Bomoya. Its performance of worker songs pushed the day over into one of culture rather than history. Two worker plays, however, kept the occasion more clearly in the mold cast in 1981. "Ziyagika/Turning Point" documented black workers' battle for recognition in the factory; while "The Dunlop Play" portrayed "twenty five years of life and struggle in a rubber factory" (!). Working-class life and culture were also depicted.

The formal program was one thing, but the response to our advertising and sponsored bussing was another. In order to overcome the unending problems of segregation and of cultural distance, we obtained a small grant to subsidize buses. It proved almost too successful a strategy. Trade union members identified sufficiently with union organization for it to be axiomatic that if the union invited them, they would come—particularly if the union supplied a bus paid for by the Workshop. In addition, FOSATU's own cultural program, by now highly creative and well-organized, had included an Open Day, run in August 1983, with a not dissimilar character to those run by the Workshop.[17] An unexpectedly large number of people arrived, most of them trade unionists from all over the Transvaal. Many came thinking the university-based Open Day would take on the form of the FOSATU Open Day—a celebration of the union, its members, its victories, and its culture. The fact that it was held at and by the university was regarded as a sign that even intellectuals were finally coming to realize the power and significance of the union movement (and so we were). The crowds of workers arriving in their FOSATU, Metal and Allied Workers' Union (MAWU), or other union T-Shirts were testimony to the level which the symbolism of political and union affiliation had reached.

The sheer numbers of people overwhelmed the organizers, and so we urgently opened additional large venues to hold the crowds. In earlier times we believed—naive intellectuals as we were—that we were "bringing history" to the audience. But we had not taken into account the cultural and social assertiveness which accompanied the "revolution from below" taking place in South Africa in the 1980s. We had a taste of "counter-hegemony"—for the audience commandeered the history, music, and entertainment. Thus, in cases where slide-shows or films were shown with English soundtracks, workers demanded to know why simultaneous translations into Zulu were not available. In some cases, they insisted on such translations being offered during the performance. Workers brought a raucous, participatory approach toward the rather sedate university milieu, joining in, shouting, singing, and even dancing where they felt this to be appropriate.

It was not only workers who arrived expecting a festival atmosphere. White students, black youths, and middle-class people of all colors, attended. The Soweto Sofasonke Party, knowing that a slide show on its early history was to be shown, arrived in full regalia, asking to be allowed to sing and dance for the assembled crowds. They saw this as an occasion to demonstrate their solidarity and presence. This they did, filling a gap in the program occasioned by the enormous crowds. The Sofasonke Party, however, elicited some yawns from the FOSATU crowds, who saw little virtue in what they perceived as the antics of a group of elderly representatives of a now rather conservative political grouping in Soweto.

Audiences were, it was true, not there to learn as much as to experience and to be entertained. Many of the events were marked by an amateurishness that was only forgivable considering the limited budget available. But large sections of the audience were extraordinarily forgiving of this, (perhaps because they were more than a little drunk?) revelling in the sense, perhaps, that academic intentions had been hijacked by popular methods of participation and behavior. We could not help finding this sense of upturned hierarchies amusing, despite the fact that some drank heavily and the entertainment in some of the venues deteriorated into sleaziness, provoking an angry response from university authorities. The working class, warts and all, had certainly made its presence felt— but not all of the "intellectuals" were impressed.

By 1984 we "knew" both our audiences and our invitation networks better. This was particularly true with regard to the trade union movement. Despite our different interests, a relationship of non-competitiveness between union organizers and ourselves, had come into being. Although a number of invitation networks helped us reach a non-unionized audience, we were still struck by the comparative weakness of organizations which aimed to appeal to the nationalist strands in consciousness. It still seemed that the "populist" consciousness which was emerging was relatively free-floating, or at least found expression in a variety of fragmented forms. The reason perhaps lay in the fact that the black intelligentsia was still operating in the Black Consciousness paradigm of the 1970s, and had not moved sufficiently in the direction of the volatile urban culture of the 1980s, while white intellectuals sympathetic to "populism" had been unable to find a niche in popular movements. By contrast, "workerist" whites had proved central to the growth of black union organization and were sympathetic to the work of the Workshop. In the field of history, it was the more "independent" white intellectuals who were able to make these direct, or moderately indirect, links with popular groupings.

The success of the 1984 Open Day bred a certain amount of resentment among those excluded groups of intellectuals—a presage of things to come. There were clearly real relationships developing between ourselves and a large and varied audience; symbolic universes had been more or less defined, and popular consciousness in the case of several groupings, had reached a stage where it could be tapped.

1987—Populism and Closure

If we had closed down after the 1984 Open Day, we might have ended up believing in a teleological, Lukacsian version of the nature of class consciousness. Had not working-class self-awareness grown in an apparently incremental fashion since 1978, and had it not prevailed in 1984? Such illusions, held by many both inside and outside the Workshop during these years, were soon shattered. During the subsequent three years, populism prevailed. Township revolt and organization reached its peak. Black youths made their most organized, and violent statements of protest. The excitement experienced at the 1984 workshop had indeed been a sign that a revolutionary spirit was abroad. But despite the prevalence of "workerist" sentiment at that Open Day, it turned out not to be a "working-class" revolution but a nationalist one.

The entry into popular discourse of words such as "struggle," "the movement," "power," and "anti-collaborators," the glorification of oppositional and revolutionary political movements, and the elevation of heroes had taken place.[18] At first, the youth movement had been anti-intellectual in spirit. Since 1976, it had advocated the boycotting and even burning of schools: its motivating slogan was "no education before liberation" (perhaps thus leaving the way open to the more educationally conscious trade unions). Schools were seen as an arena, one of the few, in which youth could express their resistance, and even confront the state. It was this period that saw the formation of the broadly-based and "populist"-orientated United Democratic Front, the first organizational expression of popular front nationalism since the 1960s. Before long, an alliance developed between large portions of the black trade union movement and the UDF. The old FOSATU cultural networks declined with the formation of COSATU, a UDF-affiliated federation built upon FOSATU and a variety of other, less "workerist" unions. The rise of the UDF was accompanied by the creation of a complex network of organizations to channel popular consciousness. In this climate, the exiled ANC gained renewed legitimacy as a Black Consciousness strand of thinking and organization reemerged. Township revolt reached its high point in 1985–86, when many were convinced a broader revolution was about to take place.

The State of Emergency, imposed in 1986, revealed that the euphoria of the early and mid 1980s had been premature. Many were forced to modify their almost millennial attitude after the events of that year. The ebullience of 1984 gave way to the tensions of the State of Emergency and the growing civil war. Oppositional movements needed new strategies and different ways of thinking about a state whose power had been so clearly demonstrated. One of the first changes to arise was a new emphasis among popular organizations on education. Now "People's Education" became the watchword. Instead of "No Education before Liberation" the slogan became "Education for Liberation." Township youths halted the burning and boycotting of schools.

Accompanying these profound changes in the form taken by black resistance was a growing assertiveness among many black intellectuals seeking to capture ideological, cultural, and organizational space, and a substantial move among many white intellectuals toward an alliance with those new groupings that would embrace them. Evidence of the growing competition between strata of the intelligentsia lay in the public and private debates about the "role of intellectuals" in the recently formed COSATU.[19] Thus precisely in the field in which the Workshop was attempting to operate, a new intelligentsia was developing organic links with predominantly nationalistic political organizations. Whites of this new grouping continued the tradition of subordination to popular struggles established in much earlier times; blacks were increasingly drawn from the clergy as well as from educationalists, whose role had until now been minimal as a result of the de-emphasis on educational matters.

The Workshop, too, had developed during this time. In the years preceding the 1987 Open Day, we obtained a more secure place within the university and had embarked on a number of projects such as the production of books and slide shows for popular audiences. In planning and working on these, we continued to emphasize our dual commitment: on the one hand to making substantial links with popular culture and public education; and on the other to retaining intellectual autonomy, freedom to criticize, and to continue our research and writing. In the production of these slide-shows and books we set up consultative meetings with audiences and potential user groups to learn about the interests of those we wanted to reach. But the content of these artifacts was designed to provide challenging questions to audiences of all types and affiliations, and to promote the idea that history is a terrain within which a questioning attitude is necessary, in which no fixed, "correct" answers are to be found. While the Workshop had always espoused an intellectual independence, it began now to claim an independent terrain more explicitly.

However, popular organizations and Workshop practice seemed to be moving in opposite directions. In planning and working on these projects, and in arranging our fourth Open Day, we found for the first time that a number of black and some white intellectuals were adopting the role of "gatekeeper" between ourselves and the audiences we sought. Whereas the old FOSATU networks had worked in a non-competitive fashion, the new organizationally-linked intellectuals would claim, for example, that writings must be "cleared" before their organizations would distribute or recommend them. Some trade union intellectuals (not, generally, those from old FOSATU unions) suggested that they may not sanction the participation of their members in the Open Day or might even boycott if the union did not participate in the designing of Open Days or other events. Sets of competing intellectuals were attempting to make links with popular consciousness, and those attached to political organizations tried to shape the terms of the competition by reference to the bureaucratic requirements of their organizations. The tendency for organization members to adopt a strong form of identification with their own grouping (as evidenced by the strong trade unionist loyalties demonstrated at the previous Open Day) made it more likely that this form of gatekeeping would work. We approached our fourth Open Day with some apprehension. Would our "open" approach flounder, given the controls that organizations seemed to seek over ideas?

The Open Day of 1987 turned out to be the most successful of all. An estimated 5,000 people came. The cultural renaissance which had accompanied the growing political struggle of these years had borne significant fruit in the form of numerous films, slide-shows, plays and photographs, videos and poems, stories and books. The amateurishness of some of the productions of earlier years was less evident—we had better goods to offer and more of them. On the part of audiences, it appeared that by the beginning of 1987, the celebratory culture had given way to a sense of seriousness of purpose among many groupings. The slogan "Education for Liberation!" appears to have echoed a need in many people's minds. In addition, despite the existence of bureaucracies and attached intellectuals playing the gatekeeping role, the Open Day provided a forum for cultural expression which many groups could not afford to miss. Ironically, it was precisely the non-organizationally-linked nature of the Open Day which made it an appealing forum for participants. Groups with cultural wares to show wished to exhibit them to everyone, not just to their "own" audiences, and audiences welcomed the opportunity to view the enormous variety of performances on display. At times it seemed as if those coming to perform at the Open Day viewed it as a public statement of their commitment, as a means of informing sympathetic outsiders of the details of their particular circumstances, struggles, and histories.

This desire to communicate gave a sense of legitimacy to variety. Performers and productions included those specifically identifiable as black, white, trade unionist and populist, rural and urban, young and old. Moreover, the day gave a prominent position to youth—whose participation in previous times had to some extent been curtailed by what we may assume was their hostility to educational occasions. The participation and symbolic role played by high-school students made the day significantly different from previous ones. There was little evidence of the nostalgia that had characterized the 1981 and 1984 Open Days; instead many of the items focussed on the historical aspects of present-day struggles.

For the first time, rural struggle entered centrally into the discourse of the histories we presented. We had previously noted the absence of an awareness of issues relating to land and to peasants in our earlier Open Days; now, however, the new assertiveness of those conducting rural struggles was finding its way into what had been and exclusively urban consciousness. The arrival of a delegation from Mogopa, a community engaged in an ongoing and mainly unsuccessful struggle to retain ownership of their land against forced removal by the state, epitomized this renewed sense of self among rural people fighting for their rights. A video of their history and experience of resistance prompted their participation. Their way of engaging with events brought its own particular spirit and language to the day. A group of about one hundred elderly rural people arrived by bus, after a long journey to the university. Dressed in colorful handmade clothing (some of it made by weaving together, in intricate patterns, colorful strips from discarded plastic bags), they carried banners protesting their removal. When they assembled in the Great Hall foyer holding their banners aloft, a security guard tried to stop them, as such behavior was illegal under the State of Emergency. But he gave up in the face of their determination and they began to sing, walking slowly through the university corridors toward the place where their video was to be shown. The large crowds present at the Open Day could not miss them and were greatly moved.

White working-class culture and unionism was more fully explored than previously. The day saw another attempt to recapture the history of white women workers in the garment industry in the 1930s—this time perhaps the most imaginative attempt yet. A play, "Factory Vrouens,"

(Factory Women) drew upon a series of worker plays written by garment workers in the 1930s. While the play did not receive critical acclaim, it was appreciated by workers who learned about their own cultural and social history in the process.[20] A further contribution on the theme of white culture was a dance sequence—Robyn Orlin's performance "What do you think about the countryside around Johannesburg"— which portrayed white decadence and cultural decay in clear and telling contrast to the vigor and spirit of the "medley of gumboot dance, poetry and music by Jeremiah Mofokeng and the Youth Alivers."

Black unions again sent bus-loads of workers to participate and learn from the many worker-orientated productions that were mounted. The play, "Qonda," explored attempts to organize workers in the context of township violence; "The Long March" examined the plight of the surrounding community during a strike at a firm called BTR Sarmcol; the "K-Team," a worker choir, sang; the Granada TV film, "Death is Part of the Process," covered the recent mining tragedy at the Kinross mine; "Night Shift" explored the experiences of a woman shift worker; and "Women without Men" examined the lives of the families of migrant workers in the Transkei. The range and variety of contributions for workers revealed the extent to which the strand of consciousness which we identified with trade unionism had been enriched over the previous three years. Perhaps the loosening of the old FOSATU cultural networks, while itself a loss to workers, enabled intellectuals with varying ideological alignments to offer contributions which concentrated on working-class themes.

For the first time, we explicitly analyzed historiography as a subject. One show, the Swaziland Oral History Project's slide-show on the uses and meaning of oral history, tackled historiographical questions directly, using popular imagery and storytelling techniques. "The Big H," an American Social History Project also tackled questions of the meaning of history while the Workshop/ASHP slide show, "Fight Where We Stand," attempted to portray history in a non-sectarian but nevertheless radical and challenging manner.[21] A useful comparative dimension came from other American Social History Project shows on U.S. history, as well as from one on the history of Bolivian tin miners.

The culminating performance, an unscheduled one by the Shoshanguve Youth Group, had little to do with history—but was more a celebration of youth, of struggle, and of the future. Children of ten and eleven years joined older ones in a riotous song and dance act before a packed Great Hall. Their performance appeared to present symbols capable of drawing upon a broad and varied audience: youth, representing vigor and creativity; symbols of township revolt, epitomizing the day and the times.

One reviewer, noting the innovation and strength which characterized the Open Day, commented:

> You could hardly walk 20 paces without coming upon another group of people dancing in a huddle and singing freedom songs . . . The campus at Wits was transformed. The casual visitor might have been forgiven for thinking that the revolution had already happened—Surprising, to say the least, for the open day at an academic conference. But the History Workshop is no ordinary academic conference, and far more importantly, this is no ordinary point in history. What charged the air on Saturday, what transfixed the proceedings, was an inescapable sense that, far from merely dealing with history, this actually *was* history.[22]

A new seriousness of purpose characterized both the Workshop's contribution to the Open Day, and the audience response to it. Audiences had come to learn rather than to picnic. A move into education rather than entertainment had taken place.

Conclusion

Where did history—and the class analysis that we thought history should embody—fit into this? The 1987 Open Day could perhaps best be summed up as an expression of nationalism: not that of a particular organization (the UDF, COSATU, or the Azanian People's Organization) but of nationalism in its broadest sense, the spirit of common opposition to an oppressive system. Workers, peasants, men, women, the youth, and the elderly, were part of it. The former separation between "populism" and "workerism" had become blurred, just as old "workerist" trade unions had been incorporated into a populist trajectory. While the strength of "workerist" trade unions had declined, that of populism had increased immensely. Was this entirely attributable to the newfound expression of populism through formal organizations?

Although "organic intellectuals" and organizations give voice, coherence, and strength to popular sentiment, as demonstrated by the relative coherence of the better organized "workerists" of the 1984 period, we know that the ideologies of the people are not simply the creations of those who lead them. Populism and workerism have deep roots in both the structural condition of black South Africans and in their past experiences. But of the two it seemed, by 1987 to be "populism"—the broad set of identifications with community, anti-colonial nationalism, and the heroic traditions of the "people" (defined in non-class terms)—that was the stronger. Within the space of three or so years, popular front nationalism swept away the hearts and minds of black (and many white) South Africans, including a large number of workers and trade unionists. The strength of this nationalism was not derived from the resilience and longevity of the organizations through which it found expression, but from the structures of racism, community encapsulation, and experience, which in the minds of many ordinary people appeared to override the particularities of class exploitation at the workplace. No intellectual, however committed to a class analysis, can ignore this fact.

The 1987 Open Day saw the rise of a nationalism whose symbolic form and emotional appeal were irresistible to most who attended, whose frame of reference was the present, or the future, rather than the past, and whose chief exponents were the youthful celebrators of music and dance. On the other hand, it also revealed the rise of an intelligentsia committed to giving organizational expression to these grassroots ideologies, and to influencing their direction and content. We saw a need to distinguish between our responses to these two developments in the nationalist movement.

The fact that a culturally vacant, economistic Marxism is unappealing to most black South Africans in the face of a culturally, experientially, and historically rich nationalism is not surprising. To ignore this fact would be to repeat the mistakes of the German socialists who, in Wilhelm Reich's words, "were offering the masses superb historical treatises . . . while Hitler was stirring the roots of their emotional being." But there is nothing inherent in a class approach to suggest that it cannot include considerations of culture, experience, and community, while also locating these within a historical-materialist analysis. Not only is the creation of a humanistic and culturally sensitive Marxism possible—it may be argued that it is essential if such an analysis is to reach beyond the universities.

And yet the problem presented by the process of enriching and making relevant the categories of historical materialism is that cultural categories are also used by social movements and political organizations to mobilize their members. It was this that rendered all of the Workshop's activities vulnerable to vulgarization and appropriation by crude nationalism and other strategic "lines." It was this that subjected Workshop intellectuals to competition with other groups of intellectuals. Indeed, it seemed from the experience of 1987, that a culturally-informed Marxism disseminated by an independent group of intellectuals is more likely to be accepted by ordinary people than it is by the nationalist and populist intellectuals who seek to lead and organize them. To such intellectuals, popular access to critical thinking and non–organizational interpretations (which may focus on the class differences between themselves and their followers, or may divert people from strictly organizational concerns) needs to be carefully controlled. Middle-class nationalists are a good deal more threatened by Marxism than are their working-class followers. And yet part of the purpose of the Workshop is to continue to involve itself in the very networks that seek to control it, thus placing it in a perpetually ambiguous and vulnerable position. We found ourselves to be both the objects of the living history of our society (this actually *was* history), and the subjects of an attempt to shape it. How this ambiguity and vulnerability will evolve is still unknown.

But 1987 also saw the beginnings of the freeing of history from the teleological constraints placed upon it by the demands of a nostalgic nationalism. In spite of the attempts at gatekeeping by bureaucratically tied intellectuals, we made connections with audiences unmediated by strict organizational discipline, and we drew them into a serious, rather than simply knee-jerk, consideration of the past, present, and future.

Criticism of the Workshop after the 1987 Open Day followed two lines of argument. A letter to the press soon afterwards criticized the Workshop for its "elitism," in that it continued to hold purely academic conferences. The other criticism came from a Marxist academic who lamented the association of Marxist social historians with "romantic populism."[23] The fact that these criticisms came from both sides of the Gramscian position we had adopted, could be seen as confirmation that we were pursuing more or less the middle path we sought. On the one hand, we continued to hold to the idea of a certain intellectual independence (hence the accusations of elitism); on the other, we carried on with our search for meaningful connections with audiences (hence the accusations of "populism"). However, it would be sterile to continue to debate these issues when the realities of our experiences with our Open Days had led us to ask a much more interesting and perhaps important question—what happens to Marxism when it seriously engages with popular consciousness? This question cannot be answered on the level of theory alone.

Part II / *Photo Essays*

Chapter 13 / Labor Tenancy in Bloemhof

Santu Mofokeng

Rainbow after the storm. Sarel Reyneke's farm, Vaalrand, Bloemhof.

The south-western Transvaal lies in the flood plains of the Harts River to the west and the Vaal River to the east and south. It is bounded in the north by the low-lying Bushveld. The landscape is flat and bleak. The soil is of red Kalahari sand, broken in places of chalky limestone. It is an area plagued by frequent droughts.

Bloemhof, a small town on the banks of the Vaal River, forms part of the wedge-shaped south-western Transvaal. The town, in its day to day function, is an example of the classic South African dream of "harmony" between the races.

I have been going to Bloemhof intermittently for the past year for the African Studies Research Institute at the University of the Witwatersrand, to document something of the lives of black tenant laborers who live on a cluster of three white-owned farms in this summer-grain producing region. By visiting these farms at different times of the agricultural cycle, we hope to obtain a detailed record of the social and economic activity of the labor tenants.

There are six families on Piet Labuschagne's farm, Vaalrand, in Bloemhof. Jakobus Maine and his family were allowed to stay on at the Labuschagne's farm after he had retired. He shares his mud house with his wife, six grandchildren, and one great-grandchild.

"When travelling alone on the farm roads at night, be sure to conceal yourself when you see headlights of a vehicle coming," advised September Maine, sixteen-year-old grandson of Jakobus Maine. "Our people have been beaten for no reason."

Jakobus Maine's forebears were successful grain and livestock farmers who came from Lesotho (Basutoland) in the 1890s to settle in the Bloemhof region as sharecroppers. Along with other black sharecroppers, they flourished from the 1920s to the 1950s.

Diyane Maine is in his early thirties, married with two children. He has been unemployed for the past two years; his last period of employment was working underground in the mines. He lives with his grandfather, Jakobus Maine. To pass his time he records radio broadcasts of popular soccer matches and spends hours listening to each recording several times.

Mateatea Maine, fourteen years old, attends school at Vaalrand. There are only two classrooms in this school, a headmaster, and one assistant teacher who each teach three classes. Last December, Mateatea failed sub-standard B for the third time.

The following letter, which I found to be both perceptive and entertaining, was written to Colonel Deneys Reitz, who was the Minister of Native Affairs in the Smuts government in 1940, by Tom McCletchie, an Irishman who came to fight for the British in the South African war and a former Justice of the Peace in Wolmaranstad:

> What about some native labour? There is plenty for all our requirements but it is badly distributed. Those who do little work and the very many who plow on shares and are practically on social equality with them in everything but name and shrieking "Segregation" all the time, have surplus labour galore therefore the natives flock to such farms where they work for only a few weeks in the year and hold illegal beer drinks almost constantly. Suggest that before the end of season, a law be forced thro both Houses, making it illegal under dire penalties, for any white landowner or occupier to have on his farm any native possessing a plow and draft animals. Then, there will be some hope for a white South Africa.

It is remarkable how this archaic relation regenerates. Through the political muscle of the Nationalists and the economic triumph of the tractor the once proud peasant community has been reduced to labor tenants, "surplus labor" trudging the labyrinth, leading a desultory existence outside of the mainstream and thanking God for it.

I am indebted to Charles van Onselen for his "Race and Class in the South African Countryside: Cultural Osmosis and Social Relations in the Sharecropping Economy of the South-Western Transvaal, 1900–1950," *American History Review* 95 (February, 1990).

Tahleho Motshwarsradira is nine years old. He does not attend school. He runs errands and rounds up sheep, cattle, or horses when they stray. His skin is caked with dirt and covered with a rash. His hands and feet are cracked. Piet Labuschagne's farm, Vaalrand.

Jakobus Maine having a morning wash. Labuschagne's farm, Vaalrand.

The bedroom of the Afoor family. Sarel Reyneke's farm, Vaalrand.

Feet of Plaatjie Moss minding the planter. Piet Labuschagne's farm, Vaalrand.

A man picking up mealie crop in the wake of the threshing machine. Labuschagne's farm, Vaalrand.

Harvesting of sunflower. Attie Jackobs's farm, Klippan.

Limbless doll. Derrik Pietersen's farm, Klippan.

Pensioners and their families on the back of a bakkie, en route to a pension pay-point in Bloemhof.

Labor tenants making fodder. Klippan, Bloemhof.

Shebeen, Zevenfontein.

Koelie Moss surveying storm damage.

Chapter 14 / *Promised Land*

Gideon Mendel

Dominee Johan Rossouw of the Dutch Reformed Church delivers an open-air service during the FAK trek festivities at Bonnievale.

The first re-enactment of the Great Trek marked the centennial of the migration of white farmers from the Cape Colony into the interior of southern Africa which ultimately led to the founding of the Boer republics. In 1938, ox-wagons from all over the country trekked to Pretoria and converged on the site of the Voortrekker Monument, where celebrations and ceremonies were witnessed by many thousands of people. The first re-enactment was a key symbolic event in the upsurge of Afrikaner Nationalism that culminated ten years later in the National Party gaining power.

From the outset, the celebrations marking the 150th anniversary of the Great Trek in 1988 were beset with problems. Due to political squabbling, there were two and a half treks instead of one: the Federasie van Afrikaner Kultuur (Federation for Afrikaner Culture) Trek, associated with the ruling National Party; the Volkswag Trek, associated with the Conservative Party (formed in 1982 to protest the Botha government's reforms); and—linked to the Volkswag Trek, yet separate—the Afrikaner Weerstandsbeweging Trek, associated with the far-right Afrikaner Resistance Movement, the AWB. Some participants approached their particular treks with fervor and reverence, but the re-enactments failed to elicit mass white support. Many events were ill-attended, and processions through towns were often more of a curiosity than an inspiration.

The FAK's wagon was to be drawn by oxen from town to town for thousands of miles, preceded by changing shifts of marching youths from the Voortrekker movement. "Step by step, yard by yard, the Voortrekkers will be there—every centimeter and kilometer, from the Cape to the Transvaal," the FAK promised. However, after two weeks of travelling, the difficulties created by trekking over tarred roads proved to be insurmountable. For the next few months, oxen and wagons were transported by truck and off-loaded at every town for a symbolic procession and civic receptions.

The Volkswag decided on thirteen different trek routes, each with its own wagon—strange, pyramid-like structures mounted on trailers and pulled by cars. The Route Thirteen trek was led by Manie Maritz, wrestler turned Brahmin breeder and son of a famous Boer general. He and a team of young disciples rode on horseback from Springbok to Pretoria, a distance of 1339 miles. But the Volkswag and AWB were forced to conclude their trek at Donkerhoek Farm outside Pretoria because the rival FAK had gained control of the Voortrekker Monument site for its festivities.

Nevertheless, under the leadership of Maritz, a group of AWB members gathered at the base of the monument every morning of the week preceding the Day of the Covenant on December 16th, to repeat the vow originally made at Blood River in 1838 by Boer commandos after they successfully repulsed a Zulu army. "I believe we are a white race placed here by God, and it is our duty to stay here as a white race," Maritz said. The AWB wagon was hand-drawn all the way from Blood River in Natal to Pretoria by a full-time team of AWB stalwarts and supporters.

According to the conventional view of the Great Trek, the original Voortrekkers embarked on their journey into the interior in search of their own freedom; trying to find their own promised land. Despite the different characters of the recent treks, each group was still acting out its own vision of a future South Africa; still pursuing its own elusive promised land.

These photographs form part of an exhibition entitled *Beloofde Land* sponsored by *Vrye Weekblad*, a progressive Afrikaans weekly newspaper. The photographs, which are in color, were first exhibited at the Market Galleries in Johannesburg during the Spring of 1989. Their appearance spawned controversy in South African left-wing cultural circles about the proper role of photography in documenting the white establishment. Among left photographers and activists, there is broad agreement about the importance of documenting popular resistance to apartheid, but many questioned the documentation of a mainstream white cultural reconstruction: Should such events be recorded or ignored? Can social-documentary photographers ideologically "frame" such subjects to avoid glorification?

Schoolchildren watch as the FAK ox-wagon approaches Swellendam, a few hours behind schedule due to problems experienced on the trek from Bonnievale. The procession through the town eventually took place well after dark, when most spectators had dispersed. As a result, the attempt to trek from town to town was finally abandoned the next day. The wagon was a movie prop, on loan from the South African Broadcasting Corporation.

The AWB wagon being pulled through the Natal countryside on Kruger Day (October 10), the day of its ceremonial departure from Blood River. This was the only wagon that actually rolled over its entire route without being transported. It was pulled all the way from Natal to Pretoria by a full-time AWB team and occasional helpers.

The AWB wagon is pulled over the last few miles of its long journey from Blood River in Natal to Donkerhoek Farm, about nineteen miles outside Pretoria. At this stage, the team had bloody feet after pulling the wagon for more than 312 miles.

Manie Maritz, an AWB trek leader, reads from the Bible during a gathering at the base of the Voortrekker Monument on the morning of December 15. Maritz and a group of followers gathered at the monument every morning of the week preceding the Day of the Covenant to repeat the vow originally made at Blood River in 1838.

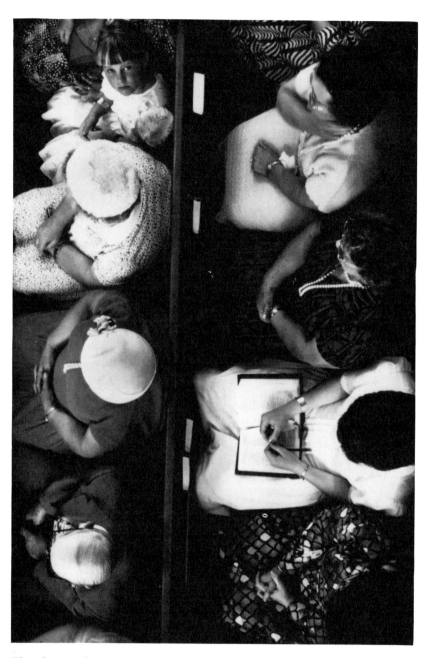

Church-goers listen to a sermon by Dominee Kosie van der Merwe at a special "trek service" held in the Dutch Reformed Church in Uitenhage at the end of a weekend of processions and ceremonies, organized by the Volkswag. Many members of the congregation wore Voortrekker outfits.

A *voorlaaier* (muzzle-loader) is fired during a display of traditional weaponry at the FAK trek festivities held at the Loftus Versfeld stadium in Pretoria in late October. The event was largely attended by schoolchildren.

Residents of Joubertina in the Eastern Cape take part in a tug-of-war against farmers from the surrounding area during a weekend of FAK trek festivities. The farmers won.

A demonstration by the police dog school in the amphitheater at the Voortrekker Monument on Saturday, December 10. The FAK staged a week of events and festivities at the monument prior to the Day of the Covenant.

A lone horseman rides ahead of the hand-drawn AWB wagon during the last few miles of its journey to Donkerhoek Farm.

Part III / Popular History and Popular Culture

Josh Brown

Luli Callinicos

One of the exciting (and problematic) things about being a historian in South Africa today is that history is so hotly contested. Passionate interpretations of the past emanate from a range of activists on the South African scene. To all, from the fascist leader of the AWB (Afrikaner Resistance Movement) to student comrades and worker poets, history is a resource of mobilization, a political weapon activists use to advance current organizational strategies.

Small wonder, then, that in this decade of rapid transformation in South Africa, popular history has become a burgeoning industry. Even Reader's Digest in 1988 published an attractive, comprehensive, full-color *Illustrated History of South Africa*, which spans from the beginning of time to the present day.[1] The panel of Reader's Digest writers consulted closely with some of our most prestigious historians. Clearly, as apartheid rapidly loses credibility among even National Party supporters, the gap in history needs to be filled. And the impact of Africanist and social historiography has been sufficiently impressive to warrant a major commercial enterprise, which can be sold as "the real story," that can now, at last, be revealed. Yet, in spite of its claims, the *Illustrated History* does not in fact tell the "whole story." It leaves out some of the more uncomfortable interpretations of, for example, labor struggles and how South Africa's social structures contributed to apartheid capitalism. But its publication is nevertheless to be welcomed, if only because it explodes in popular form so many of the hoary, racist myths that exist in both colonial and apartheid history. In doing so, Reader's Digest reflects some of the influences that have also had an effect on radical popular history.

In the popular history writings of the 1980s, two approaches can be detected, roughly reflecting the development of the labor and popular movements. The history that has emanated from worker education, on the one hand, is class-based, resting centrally on political economy. The content focuses on non-racial class struggles, and national resistance tends to be played down, if not completely ignored. The history that reflects the popular movement, on the other hand, tends to emphasize organized national struggles, focusing on heroes and leaders, and on state oppression rather than exploitation by the capitalist system. In its aim of "nation-building," class differences are played down.

At the turn of the decade, the dominant influence on popular history arose unquestionably from the independent labor movement that emerged after general strikes in Durban in 1973. By the mid-1970s, worker publications like the Durban-based *Abasebenzi* (*The Workers*) published short history articles in the vernacular, while the *South African Labour Bulletin* printed similar pieces in English. In 1977, a black social and labor history series appeared in the Johannesburg supplement of the black newspaper *Weekend World*. Then in the early 1980s, more substantial historical material began to appear: *Gold and Workers*, a history of the gold industry from the perspective of working men and women, was published in 1981 by Johannesburg's alternative Ravan Press and was soon followed by booklets on key labor history events produced by the Labour History Group in Cape Town.[2] These publications were aimed at a specifically working-class audience, and class struggle was their central focus.

Worker service groups soon emerged to provide educational material about local and international subjects to unions and workers. The International Labour Research and Information Group (ILRIG) published booklets on the history of the working classes of Bolivia, Brazil, Botswana, Mozambique, and Tanzania, as well as an international history of May day. The South African Council for Higher Education, the largest alternative education group in the country, formed a Labour and Community Project (LACOM) to produce accessible material, most recently an illustrated labor history of South Africa, *Freedom from Below*. The Culture and Working Life Project in Durban, where Indians and Africans are employed in roughly equal numbers, published *Divide and Profit*, a history of ethnic labor relationships in the region.[3]

In recent years, trade unions have published labor histories themselves. South Africa's largest union federation, the Congress of South African Trade Unions (COSATU) published *Political Economy: South Africa in Crisis* in 1987. The National Union of Mineworkers' booklet on the 1946 strike appeared a few months before the country's biggest strike ever, the mineworkers' action of 1987.[4] Although the 1987 strike led once more to massive dismissals and a bitter confrontation with the mining companies, the NUM remains the biggest union in the country, with the potential to cause most disruption in the economy. An understanding of this power, learned through lessons in political economy and history, has contributed to the on-going, militant, if uneven organization of the union.

During the period of the first and second emergencies (from 1985 onward) the unions suffered a series of heavy blows. COSATU headquarters, which also housed the NUM and other unions, was destroyed by right-wing sabotage, union officials were detained for long periods, and a prolonged smear campaign was launched against the unions by the state-controlled radio and television networks. During this time, worker education took a back seat while the unions battled for survival. Since 1989, though, some of the education offices of the larger unions are showing signs of recovery. The National Union of Metal and Allied Workers Union (NUMSA) published *NUMSA Women Organize!*, the first chapter of which, "A Historical Overview," was prepared by History Workshop members. A new edition of the former FOSATU's sixteen-part labor history series, *The Making of the Working Class in South Africa* is being prepared by COSATU, in collaboration with the History Workshop.

Popular labor history from trade unions has not been confined to writing. Unions, particularly those in Natal, have also drawn on cultural forms to disseminate their message. One of the most exciting developments has been the flowering of traditional praise poetry in modern idiom. Worker poems in both the vernacular and in English draw richly on struggles and heroes of the past to mobilize and inform members at mass union meetings. Poets such as Mi Hlatswayo, Alfred Qabula, Nise Malange and Mandla Shezi have emerged as popular historians.[5]

In apartheid South Africa, mobilization has not only occurred around the workplace. In 1983, after the government introduced a tricameral parliament—composed of separate white, Indian, and "Coloured" (but no African) divisions, to be staffed by representatives elected in segregated polls—a groundswell of opposition led to the formation of the United Democratic Front (UDF). This popular front of diverse groups of anti-apartheid pro-Freedom Charter activists challenged the notion of the trade unions as the sole form of organized resistance to the system. The UDF position, that workplace and political issues were inseparable, adjusted the focus of some popular history writing to past national struggles, particularly to the mass popular movement of the African National Congress (ANC) in the 1950s. Mass campaigns such as the 1955 Congress of the People, which led to the drawing up of the Freedom Charter, and the women's 1956 anti-pass campaign were recalled and recounted. Raymond Suttner and Jeremy Cronin's *Thirty Years of the Freedom Charter* (1986) is an example of a history of national resistance. Through interviews and documents, the book reconstructs the nature of mass collective participation in drawing up the Freedom Charter, emphasizing the relationship of popular resistance to the rapid growth of the ANC in the 1950s.

A historical focus on organized political resistance has also emerged from the formerly "Coloured" University of the Western Cape, now claimed by its radical Vice-Chancellor to be the "intellectual home of the left." *Let us Speak of Freedom*—a recurring phrase in the Freedom Charter—is an attractive series of booklets in the University's People's History Series. The aim of the series, according to the editors,

> is to encourage the writing of popular history—and to make it accessible to students, workers and communities. . . . *Let us Speak of Freedom* gives one view of the history of the liberation struggle in South Africa. (There are others too, history can be written in many different ways.) We believe it contributes to the historical debate and to the recovery of a neglected aspect of our past.

To that end, the booklet briefly examines the land wars of the nineteenth century, urban political organizations such as the African National Congress, the Industrial and Commercial Workers Union, and the early Communist Party of South Africa. Each booklet is accessibly written, manageable in length, generously illustrated and inexpensively produced.

This series, and UWC's People's History Project which trains students to record oral history in the community, emerged partly as a response to the education crisis which, less than a decade after the Soweto uprising of 1976, again came to a head in late 1984. This time, however, the students' struggles were linked to a broader socioeconomic and political crisis. The November 1984 Transvaal stay-away protesting against, *inter alia*, Bantu education, was widely supported by parents and workers. The stay-away was a turning point for organized labor. For the first time since the 1950s, workers protested en masse over community issues. The action demonstrated the extent of union and community support for the students' demands.

Parents, teachers, and students held a series of meetings and ultimately formed the UDF-affiliated National Education Crisis Committee (NECC). During the course of these meetings, the concept of "People's education for people's power" was developed. Backed by the external ANC, the NECC urged students to organize themselves into democratic

Student Representative Councils, return to their schools and claim them as "sites of struggle."[6]

Toward the end of 1986, the NECC commissioned a group of historians and teachers to work with community representatives to develop an alternative history based on the principles of "People's Education"—that is, a skills-based history that would promote the values of democracy, non-racialism, collective work, and active participation.[7]

The period was characterized by a heady sense of optimism among the leadership of the NECC. It seemed feasible at the time that the state might appreciate the breadth and depth of the educational crisis and try to meet the NECC demand "to deal with the deteriorating situation with thousands of our children condemned by ministerial decree to roam township streets and face our SADF [Defence Force] casspirs."[8]

To demonstrate to both the state and doubting students that an "alternative history" would be feasible in the classroom, the NECC asked its History Commission to prepare an introduction to an alternative history to be ready in less than two months, for the beginning of the 1987 academic year. In that absurdly short space of time, the History Commission produced *What is History?* which they presented as a "history pack," a working draft to be used and then revised in an ongoing process of consultation and negotiation.[9] But the government banned the history material from black schools even before its publication. With the detention of NECC members and hundreds of students, attempts foundered to workshop the material throughout South Africa in street committees, unions, rural and urban student groups. Nevertheless, the history pack was published in March 1987, and its innovative methodological ideas are currently being evaluated for possible further work in curriculum development.[10]

The influence of academics has been important in virtually all popular history. Some popular history publications have emerged from university lecture courses, while other work has been undertaken in collaboration with organizations.[11] The University of Natal in Durban, the University of Cape Town, and the University of the Western Cape have all hosted research programs for the production of popular knowledge.[12] The UWC went further and launched the People's History Project, an ambitious and exciting, if difficult, program which is still in its hectic and formative stages. Currently the project faces the problem of numbers— its 1,200 students are being trained largely by some thirty undergraduate tutors. It is anticipated that with an emphasis on oral history and collective community research, the project should start producing interesting and original work within the next few years.[13]

But the most established example of academic participation in popular history can be found at the University of the Witwatersrand where, since 1977, History Workshop has encouraged the research and writing of an alternative and counter history. The social history or "history from below" approach that has developed from this work explores the uses of experiential and oral history, folklore and popular culture, but still within the paradigm of historical materialism.

The History Workshop is involved in a number of popular history projects. Its Topics Series has so far published two glossy, but inexpensive booklets. The first is an account of a well-known event in popular memory, the massacre in 1923 of a religious group that refused to leave the land which "God had chosen for them." The other booklet focuses on the use of liquor as a form of oppression, survival, and resistance in South African history.[14] The booklets have been very well received, according to the sales in the first year of publication. In South Africa, popular history must be judged as much by its accessibility as by its content since the readership often has little formal education, and speaks English as a second or third language. The History Workshop's plans to produce the series in the vernacular is therefore a great advance.

The History Workshop also has endeavored to present more sustained popular histories. The two published volumes of the projected *A People's History of South Africa* trilogy are much longer than the Topics books. The first volume, *Gold and Workers*, focuses chiefly on the making of a migrant labor system by the mining industry during a formative period of primitive capital accumulation. The second volume, *Working Life*, synthesizes the history of working-class urbanization, survival, and resistance on the Rand up to 1940, featuring a number of case studies to illustrate its themes. To a certain extent, the two books are a reflection of how the thinking of many radical historians developed during the 1980s. *Gold and Workers* is clearly a more succinct counterhistory. *Working Life*, while it examines social structures, explores aspects of experiential and social history more fully, combining it with class struggles.[15] Both books are used as a resource by union education officers, popular history writers, and teachers, whose school textbooks have by and large failed to provide meaningful classroom material.[16]

The History Workshop endeavors to convey popular history in a variety of forums and media. The Workshop coordinates a history series in the popular, left-wing weekly, *New Nation*. Features focus on a variety of topics, including articles on urban gangs, the defiance campaigns of the 1950s, rural resistance in Natal, and protest literature. The series was published in book form and was so well received that the first impression was sold out within two months.[17] The History Workshop has also produced audio-visual history, its most successful production being a twenty-minute slide-tape program, *Fight Where We Stand*.[18] Produced in collaboration with the City University of New York's American Social History Project, *Fight Where We Stand* is based on a number of interviews and depicts—through tinted archival photographs, and an accompanying soundtrack composed of voices, period music, and sound effects—the urbanization experience in the 1930s and 1940s of a woman driven by coercive labor practices off white-owned farms and into Johannesburg in the 1930s. A companion illustrated booklet contextualizes the events related in the slide-show.

The making of popular history—indeed of popular education in general—has generated an awareness of the importance of presentation, and the use of images in particular. Of course, with the arrival of television in 1975, the visual has become an undisputedly powerful medium. But in South Africa, where written language is so unevenly accessible, particularly to black workers, the image has an additional potency which producers of popular education material are keen to explore. The South African Council on Higher Education's two histories in comic-book form attempt to expose readers to a new medium in education, though evaluation of the response to black-and-white drawings in an age of color remains to be undertaken. Black-and-white line drawings have proved highly successful in the comic-strip adventure of the good-natured and permanently hard-up loser, "Sloppy," that appears in *Learn and Teach*, a literacy magazine aimed at adults.[20]

Historical photographs, too, are beginning to be systematically researched and the Workshop has used them lavishly in the People's History series. The accumulation of these photographs is a useful resource for the publication of other popular education material, and a photographic archive is being developed steadily by the History Workshop. The historical photograph is attracting increasing popular attention. The visual evidence of radical resistance in the past—the opportunity to put faces to the names of local heroes, hitherto remembered only orally by the community, or to see images of the day-to-day social reality of the laboring poor of all races—is fascinating to both black and white readers. But much remains to be explored in this medium. Both writers and readers need to be taught how to look at photographic evidence more searchingly and critically.[21] We hope to learn more about this medium from the rich work being produced by contemporary photographers in South Africa. The nation-wide photographers' collective, Afrapix, has, since its inception in 1982, facilitated the recording and distribution,

through popular and union newspapers and magazines, of powerful contemporary images of resistance and day-to-day life.[22] Photo exhibitions
form an important part of the History Workshop Open Days.

One more type of popular history writing should be noted and welcomed. A rich outcrop of historical autobiography is providing the public with an experiential sense of our particularly eventful recent past.[23]
Some of the autobiographies are individual life stories; other testimonies
locate themselves in organizations. Worker poet, Alfred Qabula, for example, in a fascinating account of his life of rural resistance and migrant
labor tribulations and his involvement in developing worker culture,
recognizes that joining the union was a turning point in his life. From
writings such as these, we learn also how history is conceived—where
the influences of folklore, oral history, and popular memory prevail. For
the History Workshop, one of the most exciting aspects of the Write
Your Own History Project (described by Leslie Witz in this volume) has
been the response from a range of people wanting to record their own
experiences and memories. Personal history is being explored and written. The break-up of rural homesteads and families in the destructive
wake of migrant labor, industrialization, "influx control," and removals,
has spurred many people to search for their roots through knowledge
about their ancestors, their land, and community struggles. The fact that
ordinary people come knocking on our door seeking a personal involvement in their history is for me one of the most satisfying aspects of the
work of the History Workshop.

In South Africa, popular history has many definitions and forms.
And, produced in the context of apartheid and popular resistance, the
field is continually confronted with issues about the uses of the past. At
the 1987 Popular History Day, part of the larger triennial History Workshop Conference, questions of professionalism and accountability were
raised by participants. It was observed that the perspectives of popular
history depend partly on the author's location as well as on the nature of
the audience. University-based writers tend to be more concerned with
scholarship, activists with strategies. Critics of the former pointed out
that academics who are not organizationally-based tend not to directly
address the demand for popular history as a source of empowerment.
Scholars, on the other hand, have deplored the sloganeering and tri-
umphalism discerned in various forms of popular history and worker
education. Problems of the history of socialism in Africa, for example,
have not been fully explored. A hard look at gender relations in South
Africa, despite the increasing attention given to the history of women in
labor and community struggles, has consistently been fudged.[24] The fail-

ure of strikes, the unevenness of the response of mass organizations to grassroots movements, the side-lining of the profound and pervasive ideas of Black Consciousness—such uncomfortable issues have not been taken up.

Of course, popular history, more than academic history, is subject to the vagaries of contemporary struggles. Union education, for example, operates under constant pressure: plans for a book must be approved by committee, perhaps collectively workshopped, and published by the next Annual General Meeting, or National Education Committee Meeting. The constraints under which the NECC History Commission operated brought home to sheltered academics the problems of working under intense political pressure. The claim, and general acknowledgement, that professional historians are best placed to produce rigorous work is countered by the demand that such historians should be actively in touch with their audience and organizationally linked. The advantages and disadvantages of these two positions are constantly being demonstrated, and will no doubt continue to be a topic for discussion at future workshops.

But while criticism of the writers of popular history center around race, class, and accountability, the precise nature of the audience still remains unclear. An informal group of producers, the Joint Distribution Group, which distributes books and magazines through shop-stewards in factories and sets up book stalls at mass rallies, concerts, and union meetings, finds that there is always a keen interest in popular history books.[25] Popular history writers also get informal feedback from the unions and other organizations. History Workshop, through its workshops for history teachers, has gained a strong impression that popular history is being used in the classroom, or at least being eagerly read by thousands of school teachers, black and white. Despite harassment, purveyors of these books also do a brisk trade with passengers on the packed township trains, buses, and taxis.

A systematic evaluation of who reads which particular books urgently needs to be undertaken. But it will not be easy. Migrant labor patterns and the racial, rural, urban, ethnic, class, and cultural divisions in our society have contributed to the staggeringly varied range of potential readers. Yet, in spite of our lack of more precise knowledge, there is the enduring evidence from sales that popular history, in all its forms, is indeed popular. Across the political spectrum, the thirst for history, indeed for knowledge in general in whatever form or medium, does not seem to be satiated.

Popular history took off in the 1980s. But this is only the beginning. In the coming decade we look forward to the emergence of a new generation of black historians. With the re-opening in the 1980s of the "liberal" English-speaking universities to blacks after a generation of exclusion by apartheid, and with the appropriation by progressive teachers of the University of the Western Cape (the major training ground for black intellectuals), it is now possible for black students to engage in radical historical scholarship. The effect of this change on the content and method of historiography is likely to be mutually beneficial, and should help to redress the imbalance in the production of the past, for popular history at present is written predominantly by whites. Above all, we may then be able to overcome some of the gaps and limitations encountered in popular history today and realize our hope for a genuinely non-racial and critically engaged intelligentsia.

Chapter 16 / *History and History Teaching in Apartheid South Africa*

Melanie Walker

Josh Brown

Poster produced in the Community Arts Project, Cape Town, 1986.

When it is all over the rivers run red with blood and the Voortrekkers, who are slowly becoming Boers, pick assegais out of their wagons. They make pledges and vows and covenants. Their leaders give their names to mountains and cities and swimming pools.[1]

In his autobiography, Denis Hirson satirizes his own experience of history at school and vividly captures the constraints and problems of history teaching in apartheid South Africa—the bias of the syllabus, the dominant teaching methods, and teachers' inability or unwillingness to transform history in school classrooms. Hirson's satire demonstrates both how the school syllabus is overtly biased to reflect the point of view of the ruling Afrikaner nationalist elite and the way this content is presented to passive classes in the form of a "monologue delivered at breakneck speed, by a teacher with her eye on the number of periods left before the exams and on the door through which the inspector might come at any moment."[2] The education question (and history teaching as part of this question) is central to any democratic settlement in South Africa given that apartheid laws underpin segregated schooling. Discussion around the form and content of history teaching, and what role school history might play in building a democratic South Africa, must then be situated against a backdrop of political repression and resistance in South Africa.

Since the latest cycle of unrest began in September 1984, government authorities have detained 50,000 people (including many high-school students and some teachers), imposed three states of emergency, and severely curtailed media reporting of civil unrest. Central to the continuing cycles of repression, opposition, and resistance have been the struggles waged by school students in and over black schools since 1976. The students reject apartheid education's attempts "to keep the South African people apart from one another, to breed suspicion, hatred and violence and keep us backward."[3] Black schools have been in continual turmoil marked by shifting regional boycotts and climaxing in 1985 with the temporary collapse of black urban schooling in the face of sustained student action.

Such protests are directed against the segregated system which intentionally disadvantages black youth. South Africa provides separate schools for children classified as "White," "Coloured," "Indian," or "African." Segregated schooling is bolstered by the racial designation of geographical "group" areas and further complicated by artificial "homelands" each having its own education administration. At the last count, there were fifteen education authorities in South Africa. Yet, contrary to what these divisions might suggest, education is a highly centralized affair. Ultimately, it is the white parliament, voted into power by an exclusively white electorate, that enacts legislation concerning education and controls the education budget.

Not surprisingly, the material provision for each "racial" group differs markedly. In 1986–87 the per capita expenditure on each school pupil was: "White," $884; "African," $138; "Coloured," $338; and "Indian," $653.[4] But while colleges of education for whites and some white primary schools are being closed down, leaving millions of dollars in assets unused, black enrolment is climbing and the demand for teachers in black schools is growing. At the same time, a ten-year plan to equalize education funding, triumphantly announced by the government in 1986, has, only three years later, shuddered to a halt because of "economic stringency." In April 1989, F. W. De Klerk declared that the plan was "on hold."[5]

Moreover, education is not compulsory for African children. Of those who do go to school, some 50 percent will drop out by the end of primary school. Of those who managed to continue through to the final year of schooling in 1986, only 50.2 percent passed the examinations, compared to 91.5 percent of white pupils. Classrooms are overcrowded in African schools where the overall teacher–pupil ratio is 1:41, compared to 1:19 in white schools. Crucially, 93 percent of African teachers are underqualified if one takes a three-year post-matriculation teacher's diploma (twelve years of schooling) as a minimum qualification. The majority of African teachers have a Junior Certificate (ten years of schooling) and a two-year diploma: only 3 percent have a university degree.[6]

This grossly unequal education provision is firmly rooted in the barren soil of Bantu education. In 1953, Hendrick Verwoerd, later to be Prime Minister but then Minister of Native Affairs and the architect of "grand apartheid," told Parliament that if the native in South Africa is being taught to expect that he will lead his adult life under a policy of equal rights he is making a big mistake. . . . There is no place for him in the European community above the level of certain forms of labor.

Referring to black teachers, he stated that

the Bantu teacher must be integrated as an active agent in the process of the development of the Bantu community. He must learn not to feel above his community with a consequent desire to become integrated into the life of the European community.[7]

The training of black teachers at state-run colleges is meant to prepare teachers to implement Bantu education policies. In Verwoerd's opinion, "People who believe in equality are not desirable teachers for natives."[8]

Saki Macozoma of the South African Council of Churches, in describing his early schooling, captures something of what it meant to him to experience Bantu education. He started schooling in the early 1960s in East London. Of his first year at school he writes:

As kids we soon discovered that "the mistress" had a problem keeping track of the attendance of the 80 odd Sub A pupils that were in her class. Nobody missed us. So we went to the rubbish dump where we helped ourselves to any edibles that were thrown away and sniffed glue to make the whole thing even more interesting. I had a disadvantage in Sub A that made school a mortal enemy of me. I could read and write by the time I came there. What was I supposed to do when the other kids were still doing their "a e i o u's"? The mistress did not know. I and my friends knew. The rubbish dump was beckoning. With hindsight I now see that apartheid can make even an early start work entirely against one.[9]

The impact of Bantu education has been contradictory. While the student uprising in 1976 demonstrated decisively that Bantu education had been a spectacular political failure, it may nonetheless have been "relatively successful educationally, by controlling and suppressing the intellectual and analytical abilities of black students."[10] The experience of Cynthia Kros, a lecturer at the Johannesburg College of Education, confirms this claim. She describes a conversation she had with a black student at the University of the Witwatersrand who told her: "Bantu Education arrested our development. It deprived us of the techniques." Kros argues that the worst consequence of Bantu education is not that it attempts to teach people to despise their own history, but rather that it denies people the skills to uncover and comprehend the distortions and myths of school history.[11]

For teachers, Bantu education requires acquiescence in the distorted content and form of their own classroom work. Ann Yalesco, a black primary-school teacher, commented recently:

> Well history is actually . . . I mean what they are taught is what the whites have written . . . it's what they want the people to think happened, so then they [teachers] have to teach the kids that because they want the people to think the way they have written history is the correct way.

But when asked whether she points out inaccuracies and distortions in school history to her ten and eleven year old pupils, she said:

> No, at the moment I haven't experienced any . . . questioning from the kids, I just teach them what the Department [of Education and Training] expects me to teach them, and I haven't experienced any problems . . . not problems as such, but I haven't come across any questions that would force me to voice my opinion or what I think of the history.[12]

The textbook this teacher uses includes a chapter entitled "Resettlement following the Mfecane," which perpetuates the myth that the voortrekkers moved into an empty land: "Large parts of the country were depopulated. The area between the Orange and the Vaal Rivers was completely empty." Several lessons later, this myth is reiterated in an account of why the voortrekkers left the Cape: "For many years some of the White farmers had been unhappy about conditions on the frontier. The amaXhosa often attacked the farmers and the British Government did not know what to do. The farmers knew that because of the Mfecane, there were no people living in parts of the interior of the country." This alleged depopulation is then used to justify the existence of present-day homelands: "The Blacks settled in an area the form of a horseshoe. . . . This horseshoe pattern forms the basis of the present-day National States." And of course this book assumes that the voortrekkers who settled on occupied land did so fairly and legally: "The Voortrekkers therefore took the land on which no one lived or else made treaties with Black chiefs who were willing to give them some land. The Voortrekkers looked upon these treaties as legal." Such distorted and dull texts hinder black children and their teachers from using history as a means to critically understand and challenge the present.[13]

Most teachers schooled and trained in apartheid institutions lack the technical and theoretical tools to transform history teaching even though they may recognize the problematic content of the syllabus. A member of a progressive teachers' organization, the Western Cape Teachers' Union (WECTU), writes in a teachers' newsletter:

How is one meant to survive in a system like this? And equally important—how is one meant to provide a meaningful education to the
youth of this country? . . . We are all just teachers and, sitting back, feel
a measure of helplessness as we struggle to find the answers.[14]

And another WECTU member suggests that "many teachers are often
well intentioned but feel threatened when their students make relevant
demands on them."[15]

The syllabus, which reflects apartheid ideology, determines the content of history teaching. A core history syllabus is drawn up for all education authorities, black and white alike, by a central body comprising the
Directors of "White" education in the four provinces and the Director-
General of National Education. History is a compulsory school subject
from Standard 2 or 3 (the fifth year of schooling) up until Standard 7 (the
ninth year of schooling). For the final three years of schooling it is an
optional (and unpopular) subject choice. The content is divided equally
each year between general history and South African history. The general history is heavily Eurocentric: for example in Standard 7, pupils
study the unification of Italy or nationalism in the Middle East, the First
or Second World war, the United Nations Organization, the Cold War,
and one Third World country. Overall there is very little on the history
of Africa. The South African history syllabus overwhelmingly presents a
history made by whites: pupils make their way through the arrival of Van
Riebeeck, the British occupation of the Cape, the Great Trek and Voortrekker settlement of the "empty" interior, Sir George Grey, Carnarvon,
Rhodes, and Kruger, the Anglo-Boer war, and so on. Steve Biko put it
this way:

> The history of the black man in South Africa is most disappointing to
> read. It is presented merely as a long succession of defeats. The Xhosa
> were thieves who went to war for stolen property; the Boers never
> provoked the Xhosa but merely went on "punitive expeditions" to
> teach the thieves a lesson. . . . Great nation-builders like Shaka are
> cruel tyrants who frequently attacked smaller tribes for no reason but
> for some sadistic purpose.[16]

Or, as Dennis Hirson satirically comments:

> Meanwhile, tribes are marauding their way down Africa, trampling on
> all the thorns and scorpions with their bare feet and advancing in the
> form of ox-heads. . . . The marauding tribes, who are the cause of the
> Kaffir Wars and later become Natives and Bantu, line up for health
> inspection and go down to work in the mines.[17]

As Biko and Hirson suggest, the oppressed are not entirely absent
from school history, but make their appearance as "background informa-

tion" to white settlement and capitalist development. The oppressed appear as "problems" faced by the whites, for example in *History to the Point Std 3*: "The first Free Burghers had many difficulties. There were droughts and floods. They had few laborers to help them and the Hottentots stole their produce."

Neatly segregated sub-sections dealing with "the Blacks," "the Coloureds," and "the Indians" show how the language of textbooks underscores apartheid ideology by the uncritical use of these racial classifications. Another textbook series, *Timelines 6*, while offering no physical descriptions of settlers from Europe, says of the Khoikhoi: "Their skins were an olive-yellow color and their hair was short and woolly."

Apart from the biased content, the syllabus is very long and must be completed each year and students are required to pass lengthy examinations in it. This further precludes historical understanding or the introduction of alternative interpretations. A black primary-school teacher, in the course of a discussion on how to introduce alternative content into lessons about the discovery of diamonds, suggested that this would "be a little bit time consuming because you find yourself falling short in finishing the syllabus."[18]

The situation is exacerbated by the requirement that schools use textbooks approved by the education authorities. Inspection copies of those that make the approved list are sent to white schools, which choose a single textbook for use over the next five years. African schools, however, do not choose their own books. They are simply asked to indicate how many books are required and must take whatever the Department of Education and Training (DET) sends. Refusal to do so could mean pupils sitting without textbooks for a further two years as the DET is notoriously slow in supplying its schools with books.

Textbooks follow the syllabus closely. They are mostly descriptive rather than analytical, presenting history as a fixed body of unproblematic factual knowledge with little mention of original sources or the work of historians. All ignore the revisionist contribution to historiography—except for one textbook series, *Discovering History* (primary schools) and *History Alive* (high schools). The editor of the Standard 9 and 10 books in the *History Alive* series maintains that "school history remains sterile in the extreme" and "the official version remains entrenched long after radical changes of interpretation have swept through the academic world."[19] Ideally the textbook should not be the only determinant of history teaching. Nevertheless, in most black classrooms it is the only source of information about the past, not only for the pupil but, importantly, for the teacher too. And these books, carry the authority of printed text in a context where books are largely absent from the pupils' own homes and in very short supply in their schools. In the black primary schools in which I work, teachers are supplied one set of textbooks for all their classes. This means that pupils do not have their own copies and are *never* allowed to take textbooks home.

The *History Alive* series mentioned above, breaks with traditional South African history textbooks. Its authors say they have attempted "to provide a comprehensive vision and interpretation of South African history" incorporating "the rich tradition of African and revisionist history that has informed and enriched the understanding of history in the past two decades." The authors suggest that the current out-of-date approach to school history "constitutes a real danger to the ability of the new generation to adapt to the challenges of the future." They further claim to have incorporated a methodology which develops the students' critical understanding of history, emphasizing analytical and explanatory skills rather than rote recall.[20]

Yet the series is not in wide use in schools. In a recent paper Barbara Johanneson, a graduate student and history teacher at a "White" school, describes the books as providing a "refreshing, up to date, dynamic approach to history teaching." Not only do they reflect some of the current historiographical debates but they also present source material (cartoons, pictures, documents) for pupils to analyze and interpret critically. Yet, she concludes, teachers find the series difficult to use, given syllabus and exam constraints and their own inadequate teacher training. And even where teachers' education may have exposed them to a variety of methodological approaches, the existing school culture makes it difficult to introduce and sustain innovation. "A new definition of history and some attractive new teaching materials have not by themselves forced changes in the teaching of the subject," Johannesson writes of the *History Alive* project. "The project approached the task of curriculum development from the wrong end and should have devoted more time to developing teachers rather than developing teaching materials . . . thus a new philosophy, new materials and well-meant exhortations have together been unable to break down teacher inertia; the project quite simply overestimated history teachers."[21]

The externally-set matriculation examination further constrains innovative approaches to history. These exams encourage rote learning and the ability to write down information quickly and accurately. If examinations inform classroom practice and provide feedback for teachers, then the present form of the examinations provides no incentive to teachers to change existing practice. Students, of course, want good grades in order to gain entrance to tertiary education institutions. As Rob Sieborger, lecturer in History Education at the University of Cape Town points out, if changes in the form and content of the syllabus do not incorporate changes in the form of assessment, most especially in the public matriculation exam, then these changes are unlikely to have any significant impact.[22] Given that history is seen by the ruling National Party as "next to the mother tongue the best channel for cultivating love of one's own," then changing this examination is both a pedagogical and a political issue.[23]

Nevertheless, it would be wrong to say that nothing can be done to begin transforming history in schools so that pupils can understand both the processes by which the world has made them and how they might act upon that world and reshape it.[24] Nor should it be assumed that the official history curriculum is being monolithically implemented. There is often a crucial space between the "official" curriculum and the "curriculum in use"—planned and provided by real teachers in concrete, school situations. Thus, while textbooks like the *History Alive* series are state-approved, they are also a reform worth supporting given the more progressive approach embodied in the series. The struggle by progressive teachers to extend the use of *History Alive* can involve these teachers in learning how to improve their present history teaching as they engage with these books.

Improved teaching is, however, not enough in itself if such reform is to result in "both reforms and the intensification of opposition and contradictions within the existing education system."[25] In the end, alternative teaching techniques are only important if progressive teachers start democratizing the educational process in their classrooms. Changing the methods and content of history teaching needs to be set within a framework of a democratic program for broad structural change. Crucially, this depends on the political, academic, and professional training and retraining of teachers to understand that "to be a full teacher . . . is not only to convey academic knowledge but, far more important, to help mould and produce pupils and students that will want and be able themselves to participate in the struggle for full freedom for all in this country."[26]

Chapter 17 / South African People's History

David Anthony

For over a decade the History Workshop in South Africa has been engaged in a unique task of historical reclamation, placing committed scholarship at the disposal of the social majority of that country. Knowledge of history—of the resistance to oppression before and after the imposition of *apartheid*—has become a weapon in the struggle for a new, more democratic society. The writing of such history is thus an intellectual show of solidarity with the aims of the Mass Democratic Movement. Three new works published under the auspices of the History Workshop and two progressive presses illustrate the degree to which this movement has become a source of power for the mass of the South African people.

Each of the three works is written in plain English, produced for sale as cheaply as possible, and are thus accessible to people of varying educational and income levels, including those radical youth now engaged in People's education on a full-time basis through the construction of alternative, grassroots institutions. In format and affordability, they are designed to be of use to students and makers of history alike. These three works fulfill the function of reinterpreting South African history in complementary ways. Two are by scholars, who have chosen familiar themes in modern South African history, but have treated them in unique and imaginative ways. The third is a compendium of articles—designed for direct communication with the African masses—which first appeared in the *New Nation* between 1986 and 1988.

The book with the largest sweep is the *New Nation* text, the first of a projected two-part series.[1] It is intended to revise South African history in the light of the dramatic reconsiderations of social history and political economy which have revolutionized South African studies since the late 1960s. Viewed superficially, it has a deceptively generic quality which disguises the identities of its contributors, at least initially. Upon closer examination, however, the tactical basis of this approach may be seen. In part it reflects the apparent aspiration of the History Workshop to write a collective history rather than one crafted by individual "stars." But it also reflects the dangers inherent in trying to get out the "real story"[2] while under the scrutiny of seemingly ubiquitous agents of the *apartheid* state, for whom the *New Nation* has been a nuisance since its inception. Thus Zwelakhe Sisulu, editor of the *New Nation*, was in detention for the better part of the period during which these pieces were prepared. He was released after more than 400 days in custody, but was forbidden to practice his journalistic craft. The people's history page of the *New Nation*, prepared under the auspices of the History Workshop, began at the urging of Sisulu, who broached the idea late in 1986. On 23 October 1986, the first edition of "Learning Nation," as the people's history page was called, made its appearance.

Volume 1 of *New Nation, New History* includes nine sections. The first three focus upon regional historical phenomena in the Transvaal, Natal, and Eastern Cape respectively. They each emphasize the position of the rural, preindustrial communities which antedated the mineral revolution as these stood in the years preceding the wars of dispossession and the rise of capital. These relatively brief pieces focus on the theme of resistance to alien encroachment, whether the latter took the form of Afrikaner irredentism or British colonialism. As much as possible they examine events from "inside," i.e., from something approaching the viewpoints of indigenes, rather than those of the settlers, colonial bureaucrats, traders, or missionaries, whose voices tended to dominate the discourse on the "Native Problem" during the imperial era. At every stage these sections show the role played by different types of leading figures who galvanized opposition against efforts to displace, subdue, or incorporate their communities. These leaders range, for the nineteenth century, from Nyabela of the Ndzundza Ndebele to Sekhukhune of the Pedi to Shaka and Cetshwayo of the Zulu. But there are also portraits of mission-educated Christians such as Kgalema Dinkwanyane and the *amakholwa* (believers) of Natal—also known derisively as *amagqoboka* (traitors)—led by John Langalibalele Dube. For the twentieth century, further pieces focus on the Zulu King Bambatha, the rise and fall of the ICU (Industrial and Commercial Workers' Union), and the shift from moderation to defiance in the period following World War II.

Because the book is organized topically and regionally, chronology occasionally suffers. Sometimes it is helpful to flip back and forth in order to gain a full understanding of the magnitude and concurrence of the resistance efforts described. On the other hand, the regional approach effectively demonstrates the surprising degree of unity, in the face of larger threats to local autonomy, of groups so diverse and widely dispersed that they could not have forged alliances with one another. Nevertheless, for people not accustomed to viewing the process of change from the perspective of time, a brief, even one-page time line might usefully have been included.

Sections four and five deal with the destruction of a semi-autonomous peasantry, with the creation of an urbanized contract labor force composed of African, Indian, and "Coloured" workers forced to live in locations on the Reef, and with a parallel process which brought about the growth of poor white slums. If the passage of the 1913 Land Act is the climax of the section on the loss of African control of land, the promulgation of the 1923 Urban Areas Act stands as the pivotal factor in the creation of ghettos during the interwar period. Pass laws and other "influx control" regulations—and their relationship to squatting and other strategies to which homeless families resorted—are also examined within the context of the formation of townships. Beer brewing, the subject of la Hausse's monograph, receives space as well.

The 1950s are treated in section six, focusing primarily on the ramifications of the revitalization of the ANC, the Defiance Campaign, and the formation of the South African Congress of Trade Unions (SACTU). Section seven provides a description of the turbulent 1960s and 1970s—highlighting Sharpeville, Black Consciousness, and the Soweto uprising.

The struggle of women and the role of literature in manifesting and shaping a new South African consciousness are examined in the final two sections of the volume, which contains some of its most interesting material. The articles on women in section eight present female migration and its consequences, domestic labor, brewing, women in industry, and militant agitation undertaken by women's groups. Each of these contain significant information, especially in the context of South African history, where writers have not paid sufficient attention to the contributions of African women. It is to be hoped that the second volume will reflect more of an effort to integrate women's travails and triumphs throughout, rather than concentrate them into one section which could be ignored in favor of others revolving around male leading figures. That said, the fact that the section exists at all is to be commended: it provides a basis for enlarging upon what has already been done. Too much of what women of all backgrounds have done in South Africa remains relegated to the status of footnotes to the history of the country, and it is time that this be acknowledged and corrected, especially by radicals.

Literature is the subject of the final section. It traces the history of both oral and written literature in South Africa, beginning with *lithoko*, the heroic praise poetry of the Basotho, and linking it with the pioneering efforts of prose writers such as Solomon T. Plaatje, Thomas Mofolo, R.R.R. and H.I.E. Dhlomo, and A. C. Jordan. Autobiographers Peter Abrahams, Es'kia Mphahlele, Richard Rive, and Frances Baard also receive special consideration, and two final articles concentrate on the black press. This section shows the ways in which literature has exhibited both continuity and change for African writers, and reveals the deep roots of an authentic and independent African voice, uncompromised and resilient in the face of the fetters of generations of government repression. It is a fitting end to a book published by an institution which seeks to continue this authentic and autonomous radical journalistic tradition, the *New Nation*.

The literature section, nevertheless, shares the flaw of the book overall, treating African literary women on little more than a token basis. One wonders why no attention is paid to such writers as Miriam Tlali or Ellen Kuzwayo: their works are not even mentioned in the otherwise extensive bibliography. Moreover, the heading "women" in the bibliography contains only three titles, and these are insufficiently augmented by inclusions under other sub-headings. There is no good reason for omitting autobiographies of such cultural workers as Miriam Makeba, whose life story is widely available within southern Africa. Nor is it readily apparent why Winnie Mandela's *Part of My Soul Went With Him* or *Sibambene: The Voices of Women at Mboza* are not listed. Also ignored are Beata Lipman's *We Make Freedom*, Richard Lapchick and Stephanie Urdang's *Oppression and Resistance*, and IDAF contributions such as *You Have Struck a Rock, For their Triumphs and their Tears*, and *Women Under Apartheid*. All of this should be remedied as the second volume is prepared.

Robert Edgar's book *Because They Chose the Plan of God* explores a particular subject which had a profound effect upon South Africa.[3] His topic is the slaughter of some two hundred members of a millenarian movement which captivated thousands of Xhosa-speaking Christians, who set up a permanent village at Ntabelanga, near Queenstown in the Eastern Cape, in the years immediately following World War I. The community, known as the Israelites, was led by a charismatic prophet named Enoch Mgijima, a member of the "Mfengu" sub-group of Xhosa-speakers, whose forebears had settled as refugees among the Gcaleka of the Eastern Cape in the wake of the *mfecane* or wars of Shaka. Mgijima was born in 1868, the son of a farmer. The father, Jonas Mayekiso Mgijima, was himself part of a community seeking to adopt Western ideas and culture, including mission education at such schools as Healdtown and Lovedale, and membership in the Presbyterian or Wesleyan

Methodist churches. Enoch Mgijima became a lay preacher with the Wesleyan Methodists.

Unlike his brothers, who attended Lovedale Institution and later Zonnebloem College in Cape Town, Mgijima was unable, for reasons of health, to go much further than Standard 3 (fifth grade). On 19 April 1907, however, Mgijima experienced a vision in which he was taken to the heavens by an angel who commanded that he fulfill his mission by educating his people and encouraging them to worship God according to the old traditions. The vision also included an apocalyptic reference to a war and an impending end of the world from which only the faithful would be spared. Although he tried to resist acting upon the vision, Mgijima's "call" to prophecy was strengthened when he witnessed the passing of Halley's comet in April 1910. He gradually drifted away from the Wesleyan Methodists in the two years that followed.

Edgar firmly places Mgijima within a triple context: the Xhosa prophetic tradition, the creation of independent "Zionist" churches, and the pattern of linkages which developed between different groups of African Christians in South Africa and some black American churches during the late nineteenth and early twentieth centuries. Mgijima's movement was not unlike other South African independent churches which forged links with Afro-American denominations. The leading figures of these denominations, such as those of the National Baptist Convention and the African Methodist Episcopal Church, had themselves started as members of orthodox, white-controlled congregations from which they subsequently broke away to form their own, autonomous groupings. In South Africa (as well as in other parts of the continent), this trend was stimulated by the economic and social oppression endured by Africans, on the one hand, and also by the limited opportunities for career advancement within religious communities led by the established churches. White leaders were often unwilling to encourage African Christians to become full members of the clergy rather than mere subalterns of expatriate priests, bishops, and ministers.

Mgijima sought and achieved affiliation with the Church of God and Saints in Christ, led by the black American prophet William Crowdy, but was subsequently cast out for his continuing, allegedly apostate visions. This excommunication led to a schism within Mgijima's church, his faction becoming known as the Israelites. During 1919 Mgijima had a vision calling him to gather his followers together at his home in Ntabelanga, the site of the annual Israelite Passover held each April. Mgijima's appeal was answered by upwards of 3,000 people, and this brought his followers under official scrutiny, stimulated by white farmers who feared the "Black Peril" they seemed to represent. Thus began a test of wills between the colonial state and the religious community which led ultimately to the Bulhoek Massacre of May 1921, in which hundreds of Israelites were shot down by members of a police force of 800 assembled from all parts of the country.

The widely different interpretations of this event and its significance are discussed by Edgar, who stresses the unity which emerged among African intellectuals who commented on it. He makes the text even more powerful by his generous inclusion of rare photographs of the principals and their localities, giving the piece an immediacy which permits modern readers to return to the Eastern Cape during the early 1920s. In a succinct but scholarly monograph, he has made a lasting contribution to the history of popular responses to oppression in South Africa. Edgar is no stranger to the subject of millennarian movements: this is his third examination of the Bulhoek massacre, and his second book-length study of peasant responses to colonial rule in Southern Africa.[4]

In each study he shows a subtle but persuasive identification with the victims of arbitrary, capricious, and Macchiavellian decisions by authority, without portraying the oppressed as helpless. Nor does he resort to the use of cheap emotional devices to elicit sympathy for the "misguided" or "pathetic" Israelites. In fact, he avoids such judgments, concentrating instead upon showing how one community was able to come to conclusions about itself and what it should do to remedy its condition, and how "God's plan" was thwarted by a government that continually overreacted to any manifestation of African assertion, be it political, religious, or cultural. Many readers will be able to make concrete use of the lessons of this study.

Paul la Hausse's book *Brewers, Beerhalls and Boycotts* is similar to Edgar's in important ways.[5] In his case, the problem under examination is the political economy of alcohol. Like Edgar, la Hausse first wrote about his subject while a graduate student, and his thesis led him into such related areas as the growth of *amalaita* gangs in Natal.[6] While his thesis concentrated almost exclusively on the history of alcohol in Natal, his book covers the entire country. Further, while his thesis was restricted to the first three decades of this century, *Brewers, Beerhalls and Boycotts* takes on everything up to 1976 and beyond. Consequently, he has produced a book with the feel of a popular history of alcohol, which also explores the vital role of alcohol in the creation of a captive African work force.

Alcohol provided the battleground for several generations of resistance to capital and the state in South Africa. Well before the nineteenth century, the brews made by fermenting "traditional" grains had social as well as nutritional value. The most common such drink was known as *utshwala* (Nguni), *byalwa* (Northern Sotho), or *joala* (Southern Sotho). La Hausse distinguishes between brews made from grain and the stronger beverages brewed from honey, marula berries, or the leaves of prickly pears. At the heart of la Hausse's work is an analysis of the development and transformation of a resilient drinking culture among Africans in South Africa. In the early times, fermented beverages made under "traditional" conditions had been viewed as "the food of the people." The colonial and industrial transformation led to a culture which was both informed and deformed by a very different approach to drinking; it was coupled with the much stronger alcoholic beverages brewed from hops and other grains consumed by people accustomed to distilled alcohol.

Settlers and their colonial allies resented the autonomy of women who produced "traditional" alcoholic beverages for their male relatives and friends, as well as what they perceived as the "idleness" of the African men who drank these brews and did not feel the need to be part of the colonial economy. From the 1870s, therefore, settlers began to pressure governments to craft legislation which would limit the rights of Africans to brew and consume "traditional" beer. Simultaneously, they used other means—including the "tot" system of providing partial payment to workers in alcohol—as vehicles through which Africans could become addicted to European beer and distilled spirits, and thereby be incorporated into the colonial economy as consumers of alcohol and sellers of labor. Once a dependence was created, the growing demand for these beverages aided the expansion of liquor syndicates on the Rand and, later, the development of a government monopoly.

African resistance to these trends took several forms. Professionals like Sol Plaatje advocated temperance, and created societies for its promotion. Others, including Saul Msane, advocated outright prohibition. By 1908, meanwhile, beer halls began to appear in Durban, challenging the independent, largely female producers of *utshwala* (sorghum beer), who depended upon brewing either in part or entirely to sustain themselves. Shortly before that time the highly intoxicating *isishimiyana* (an onomatopoetic term reflecting the shimmying of an inebriated man) had begun to appear, in response to a demand for newer and stronger beverages. The efforts of the Durban Town Council effectively curtailed the independent production and consumption of alcoholic beverages by semi-autonomous brewers, and brought the exclusion of Africans from the liquor trade. By the 1920s the ICU had become identified with boycotts and other efforts to limit the effects of alcohol consumption upon already impoverished African working people. For a year from 1929 to 1930 its supporters succeeded in heaping heavy financial losses upon the beer halls.

At the same time, an independent *marabi* culture emerged in the slums of Johannesburg, in which alcohol played a vital part. *Marabi* parties in private houses and shebeens created the context in which South African jazz musicians learned and plied their trade, while they and their audiences drank ever stronger, often toxic concoctions with names like *skokiaan*, *isikilimiqiki* ("kill me quick"—a widely encountered name for home brew in Africa), *quediviki* ("kill the weekend"), and *se pa ba le masenke* ("stagger on the fences").

Africans' simultaneous and paradoxically contradictory impulses, toward and away from alcohol are captured effectively by La Hausse. Alcohol was at once a release from the overwhelming burdens of oppression and the grossest manifestation of the debilitating effects of that oppression. It was clearly responsible for the deaths of some of the most gifted township artists, as well as of countless others who were poisoned by deadly *skokiaan*, or killed as a result of quarrels or accidents exacerbated by drinking. In South Africa, la Hausse indicates (though not explicitly), the consumption of alcohol has had effects that defy description. Alcohol's effects are felt not only by the black population, but by others whose addiction goes unmentioned and untreated. There is no telling what role alcoholism has played in incidents of spouse and family abuse, divorce, abandonment, homelessness, homicide, and suicide in historic and contemporary South Africa.

Alcohol led to a deep and complex wellspring of hostility in opposition groups in the period from the 1950s into the 1980s. An illustration of reforming zeal in the eradication of alcohol is the case of the women of the Mkhumbane section of Durban, home to 90,000 people in 1952. In 1958, after the construction of KwaMashu township, the government decided to relocate the population of Mkhumbane. A part of this process was government liquor raiding. Taken together these measures provoked a popular response from residents outraged at having to move, and especially by the women brewers who were being deprived of their meager livelihoods. The book concludes, in contrast, with a description of the manner in which politicized youth in Soweto targeted alcohol as one of the most potent symbols of both government oppression and African acquiescence in servitude. The full story is quite revealing.

In this book as in *New Nation, New History*, women are beginning to get their due. La Hausse's attention to women, while relatively understated, is always apparent: virtually no aspect of this story may be viewed without considering its impact upon African women, non-producers and producers of alcohol alike. Regardless of whether they stood in support of or in opposition to alcohol, they consistently sought to protect tradition.

These texts mark a new step in historical writing on South Africa. They are implicitly anti-apartheid without focusing on it. Rather they concentrate on recasting the past and the present in terms which may be useful in constructing a viable and inclusive future for all who live in South Africa. Some white readers may be alarmed at the fact that their story is not being told, except between the lines. But this is the converse of looking into a mirror and seeing those whom it is no longer possible to avoid—people of the townships, the black gardener, domestic, chauffeur, cook, or child-care worker—who had previously been taken to be a part of the landscape. Such readers may have to adjust their vision somewhat, to accommodate an ineluctable reality. Americans, too, can learn a great deal from this.

Chapter 18 / ## *A Positional Gambit:*
Shaka Zulu *and the*
Conflict in South Africa

C. A. Hamilton

Introduction

Shaka Zulu, the South African Broadcasting Corporation's (SABC) television miniseries, premiered in South Africa in late 1986. Within a year it had been seen by a remarkable 100 million viewers in South Africa and abroad. Equally astonishing was the series' cost, a staggering $24 million. Hailed by some critics as a rare instance of African history from an African perspective, and slated by others as racist propaganda, the series remained in the public eye well beyond its screening times. In this article I examine the significance of *Shaka Zulu* through reference to the series' production history and to its political setting. I situate the miniseries within the context of the contests over the production of history in South Africa in the 1980s.[1] I analyze *Shaka Zulu*'s script, explore the series' "rich and awkward commotion of production," and assess the multiple intentions of the producers and the possible ways of its reception, both in South Africa and abroad.[2] This provides a lens through which to scrutinize the nature of hegemony and power in South Africa, and "the contests which produce, reproduce and change historical knowledge."[3]

"The Thick Forest of Propaganda and Misrepresentation"[4]

The intimate connection between politics and the production of history needs no introduction, especially in a deeply divided society like that of South Africa, where history has been and continues to be raided to provide justification for successive versions of apartheid. Racism in South Africa is underpinned by a range of ideas about what Africa was like before the arrival of the first whites. The precolonial societies encountered by the first settlers were dismissed as barbarous, backward and warlike.[5] In the 1950s and '60s precolonial history was further invoked to justify the "retribalization" of "surplus" Africans in urban areas, and the creation of nine, supposedly deeply historical, ethnic identities, the bases of the "independent homelands."[6] A range of ethnographic studied and films on "the Zulu," "the Venda," "the Sotho," and so on, were made at this time.[7]

At much the same time, popular accounts of African history began to be produced by a number of white authors. Typically sensationalist and romantic, texts like E. A. Ritter's *Shaka Zulu* and P. Becker's *Path of Blood* stress the excesses and obsessions of African "despots," and detail their sexual practices.[8] The interpretation of the South African past in film mirrored these broad historiographical trends. In a 1968 episode of *Cesar's World* on "the Zulu," identical tracking shots follow both game and Zulu people moving through the bush. The scene shifts to the urban setting of Durban. "Nowadays," remarks host Romero, "the Zulus have been tamed." In films like *Zulu* (1964) and *Zulu Dawn* (1979) about the Anglo-Zulu War of 1979, Africans are portrayed only as naked warriors, brave and noble in the first film, and fortunate victors in the second.

The figure of Shaka, one of the best known precolonial African leaders, looms large in any conception of the precolonial past. He is credited with setting in motion the Mfecane (literally "the crushing," the great upheavals and dislocations of African societies in southern Africa in the 1820s and '30s), which apparently led to the depopulation of the southern African interior.

The stereotypes of "untamed barbarians," "noble savages" and "warrior hordes" have been challenged from a number of directions. Liberal historians, focusing on the interaction of groups in South Africa, affirmed the validity and dignity of African societies, but failed to focus squarely on the historical experience of Africans and their capacity to shape that experience.[9] In the 1970s the black consciousness movement promoted a highly idealized view of life in pre-white South Africa.[10] Not only in South Africa, but throughout the continent, Shaka was selected as the premier symbol of African achievement and aspiration, and the challenge to colonialism.[11] Variations on this theme became embedded in the ideological appropriation of the past by a range of South African political groupings as diverse as the Zulu homeland organization, Inkatha, and the outlawed liberation movement, African National Congress (ANC).[12]

The other development of the 1970s was the fusion of Africanist and materialist paradigms in the writing of what has become known as the "revisionist" history of southern Africa. This historiography explored the internal dynamics of both precolonial African societies and Boer societies, and their articulation with the world economy of the nineteenth and twentieth centuries. The Zulu state, and its precursors in the region, have been particularly well served by this new approach. Historians like David Hedges explain the rise of the mighty southeast African states—of which Shaka's kingdom was only one—in terms of the penetration of mercantile capital at a time of environmental crisis.[13] These factors, it is argued, created a situation in southeast Africa of intense conflict over resources, notably over cattle. Territorial expansion, the military innovations and harsh conditions of existence which characterized Shaka's reign, predated his accession to power and were a consequence of the environmental crisis, not of his personal abilities and shortcomings. However, little of this new scholarship on precolonial history found its way into the popular forms of alternative history which began to proliferate in South Africa after 1976.[14] In *AmaZulu, People of the Sky* (1979) a film by independent director Steven Coan, flashbacks to the time of Shaka, "the Black Napoleon of Africa," still consist only of scenes of warriors, battles and flames.

"The Approaching Appetite of History"

In the mid-1980s, the process of marshalling a challenge to the dominant version of the past accelerated sharply in South Africa. Between 1985 and 1986 student protests involved over 900 schools and nearly 40 per cent of black school students in classroom stayaways.[15] With the establishment of the National Education Crisis Committee (NECC) in early 1986, the students' boycott strategy was superseded by a movement for the creation of "People's Education" to replace Bantu Education. "People's History" was given priority. On the far right, the Conservative Party launched a new monthly cultural publication in 1984, *Die Afrikaner Volkswag*, which sought to refocus attention on the Great Trek and the Afrikaners' historic struggle for survival. In 1986, *Volkswag* began a three-year commemoration of the 150th anniversary of the Great Trek in an attempt to wrest *volkskultuur* from the ruling Nationalist party.

The declaration of two successive states of emergency in 1985 and 1986 inhibited active resistance to apartheid, but the struggle for control over the past persisted. Concerned about history's growing primacy in the crisis situation—what he described as "the appropriating appetite of the discourse of history"—the South African novelist J. M. Coetzee remarked that at this time, so ascendant was history that even the novel in

South Africa was "being colonized—at an alarming pace—by the discourse of history."[16] In a similar vein, a heated meeting in early 1987 attended by proponents of "People's History"—history teachers, trade-union educationalists and progressive academics—and hosted by the History Workshop, a social and labor history forum, gave rise to a perceptive press report noting that moments of the production of history were becoming major events in history itself. "What is at stake," said the *Weekly Mail*, "is not brute fact but which version of this country's past establishes itself within the national consciousness, that of the traditional rulers or that of the people. . . . The rewriting of the past becomes an underwriting of the politics of the present."[17] The production of history had moved centerstage in the contest for power in South Africa. It was into this arena that *Shaka Zulu* plunged headlong when it was first screened in South Africa at the end of 1986.

The Plot

Shaka Zulu is a historical drama centered on the earliest encounter between blacks and whites in southeast Africa. Lieutenant Francis Farewell (Edward Fox) is commissioned by His Majesty's Government in London to journey to southeast Africa, and there to make contact with Shaka Zulu (Zulu soccer player Henry Cele), the head of a powerful and warlike kingdom. In the series, Shaka is presented as poised for an attack on the British Cape Colony some 300 miles to the south of his domain. The British government is unable to provide the forces necessary to defend the Cape. The alternative plan is to send out "a solitary Caucasian" (Farewell), armed with little more than "civilization, years of tried and tested double-talk" to overawe and divert the Zulu monarch from an attack on the colony.

At the Cape, Farewell recruits a band of men, adventurous and true, to accompany him to Shaka's kingdom. Their numbers include a compassionate Irish doctor, Henry Francis Fynn. The party sets sail, and is wrecked off the shore of Natal, on the southern periphery of the Zulu kingdom. Shaka, a shrewd tactician, realizes the possible advantages and strengths of the new arrivals in his kingdom, and orders the party up to his capital, Bulawayo (literally, "the place of killing").

Once at Bulawayo, Farewell finds that his task is not as simple as it seemed in London. Shaka is an intelligent man, ruling a highly organized kingdom, a diplomat well-versed in debate and easily Farewell's equal in double-talk. Both Farewell and Fynn are drawn to Shaka, and are fascinated by the society in which they find themselves. During their stay at the Zulu court, they learn the story of Shaka's rise to power and how the mighty Zulu kingdom was built.

Fynn records all that he hears in his diary. The diary, its contents narrated by Fynn, is the vehicle for a series of flashbacks which tell the story of Shaka's conception and birth, his stormy adolescence as an outcast son of the Zulu chief, and his accession to power. Shaka's lifecourse is believed to be controlled by a prophecy, and he is shown to be destined from birth to rule. The achievement of the prophecy is assisted by the timely interventions of the ancient "witchdoctor," Sitayi. By the time the Swallows, as the Europeans come to be called by the Zulus, arrive in Shaka's kingdom, it has expanded under his leadership from a small, insignificant chiefdom to the most powerful state in southern Africa.

Farewell and company win Shaka's trust by healing him after an attempted assassination at Bulawayo, and by assisting him in a campaign against his most powerful enemies, the Ndwandwe, under Zwide. Farewell is then required to escort a Zulu deputation to conclude a treaty with the British on Shaka's behalf. Farewell and a number of Shaka's most trusted advisors set sail for the Cape in a homemade bark. During their absence, Shaka's mother, to whom he is obsessively devoted, dies, and the Zulu kingdom is plunged by the grief-crazed monarch into an orgy of mourning. One feature of this mourning is a destructive campaign in the direction of the colony. Reports of ravaging Zulu hordes pressing on the borders of the Cape sabotage Shaka's diplomatic mission, already under strain as a result of the derisive and shoddy treatment of the party by the Governor of the Cape and his aides. Farewell and the Zulu chiefs return to Shaka's court to find the kingdom in turmoil, suffering under harsh mourning prohibitions. Farewell confronts Shaka, who realizes that his power is crumbling, but he rejects Farewells overtures. To the end a servant of destiny, Shaka then walks alone to meet his killers, his brother Dingane and others from his inner circle. The series ends with the Zulu kingdom in flames. Chaos prevails.

Historical Accuracy, Dramatic License and Propaganda

Bill Faure, the director of the series, defined its position within southern African historiography:

> Shaka's life was originally recorded by white historians who imposed upon their accounts bigoted and sensationalist values—often labeling

the Zulus as savage and barbaric. It is our intention with this series to change that view.[18]

Faure's statement of intention featured prominently in the official *Shaka Zulu* souvenir brochure provided at the series' press launch and was widely quoted in a host of comments and articles at the time of its screening.[19] *Shaka Zulu* was billed as "one of the most important and dramatic stories in the history of Africa, a story which will soon take its place in world history,"[20] and was widely acclaimed as a revisionist production.[21]

In a number of US cities, however, protests were organized and the series was condemned as "fascist," "violent," "historically inaccurate," and "racist propaganda."[22] More pointed criticisms came from a few isolated sources in South Africa: the mainly black readership *Drum* magazine and the *Weekly Mail*, a publication which describes itself as "the paper for a changing South Africa." "Who's [sic] Shaka is this?" asked *Drum*'s Kaiser Ngwenya. "Why is it written through the eyes of Henry Fynn, the white doctor? Why couldn't one of most famous stories be told simply as a black story?"[23] Under the heading "Shaka Through White Victorian Eyes," the *Weekly Mail* reviewer noted,

> Apart from [the later Zulu king] Cetshwayo's brief words to Queen Victoria [a scene omitted from the version screened in the United States], blacks hardly speak in the first episode. . . . This is not a series made or told by Africans. Control is still in the hands of whites.[24]

The producers responded to these criticisms by claiming that the series was originally filmed and edited in chronological order beginning with the birth of Shaka, and tracing his rise to power. Only then were viewers to see the entry of the whites. They claim that the script was restructured and the flashback device introduced only when "American movie moguls" demurred that unknown black faces and black history would not capture international audiences.[25] If this claim is correct, it is worthwhile to note that international market constraints enjoyed priority over Faure's much vaunted aim of moving away from the original records of "bigoted" white historians.

Fynn's narration in the series is no mere sop to the international market or simply a convenient dramatic device. The series actively positions the audience to identify with this character. Fynn is presented as the figure with the most integrity. He is invited to accompany Farewell because of his concern for the black population of South Africa; he is critical of Farewell, and even more so of the British authorities; and he is enormously sensitive in his dealings with Shaka. Separate from, but privy to the thoughts of both protagonists, his is advanced as an objective account of events. The audience is also positioned to be sympathetic to the other main European character, the able but wily Farewell. Developed as a likable and humane character, Farewell cares for the men under his command and establishes an affectionate relationship with Fynn. He is a loving, if absent, husband to his beautiful wife. Fynn and Farewell stand in sharp contrast to Shaka, who is portrayed as a man without warmth. "Love, love?" Shaka rails against his mother. "We are incapable of that emotion, Mother. All we ever felt is vengeance and hate."

Faure's aim of producing a film that does justice to the African past is further undermined by the emphasis given to the white adventurers far beyond their actual historical roles. Indeed, the Swallows are depicted as playing a decisive part in Zulu history. After the assassination attempt, Shaka is badly wounded. The Swallows heal him and then literally get him on his feet and back on his throne in time to foil a *coup d'état*. The Swallows' finishing touch to the king's health appearance is the application of macassar oil to his head. The oil hides Shaka's grey hair and, he believes, has rejuvenated him. He orders its application to the head of his aging mother. In this way, the Swallows are shown to have gained control over Shaka's body and to have saved his throne for him.

They are also depicted as becoming the key force in the military power of the kingdom. Shaka demands that they participate in battle against his strongest and most persistent foe, Zwide of the Ndwandwe. During the battle, the Swallows, using a single cannon and a few muskets, put the Ndwandwe to flight. They succeed in breaking Zwide's power where previously the full weight of the Zulu army had failed. This incident indicates the extent to which real power, from then onward, is not Shaka's alone. It also serves as a reminder that the numerically inferior party of whites controls the means to wipe out entire African armies if they so wish. "Amazing, isn't it sir," remarks one of Farewell's men, "what a little gunpowder does to 'em." In fact, neither of the above incidents actually happened. Fynn did tend Shaka, but he was not instrumental in saving his life or his throne. The visitors did participate in a Zulu campaign, against a small and recalcitrant Khumalo chief, but not against the Ndwandwe whom the Zulu routed unassisted.

Key episodes in Shaka's reign in which the white visitors played no role are omitted in the series. The decampment of one of Shaka's top generals, resistance to Shakan rule in Qwabe country, the visits to the royal establishments of traders from Delagoa Bay and of the Swazi monarch, Sobhuza, are all events which are represented in the corpus of Zulu oral tradition yet extant, are powerfully and richly narrated, and lend themselves to dramatization. The reason that these events do not occur on screen, while others are manifestly inaccurate, is that, despite protestations to the contrary by its makers, *Shaka Zulu* is not about Zulu history, but about black–white interaction.

Not only is the Swallows' role built up far beyond their actual historical significance, but they themselves are ennobled and their quest romanticized. In real life Fynn was not a doctor of medicine, but a callow youth of 20 when he arrived in Shaka's country. He and Farewell fell out soon after their arrival and Shaka was able adroitly to play off the factions amongst the whites against each other. Farewell had been in the British army during the Napoleonic wars, but had since resigned his commission and become involved in shady dealing with India. He was an unlikely character for a delicate diplomatic mission. He misrepresented himself to Shaka as an envoy of King George and used his assumed status as the basis for securing a grant of land from the Zulu king, and as an incentive to persuade Shaka to help him to collect ivory. In fact, the Europeans were given a specific instruction from the Cape Governor not to make any deals with the Zulu king. They were to restrict themselves to what was their only true motive for journeying into the Zulu kingdom—the less noble pursuit of profit through commerce.

To a man, the European visitors were a rough band of fortune seekers and adventurers. Two of the most colorful members of the original party were left out of the series entirely: the seventeen-year-old Jewish orphan, Nathanial Isaacs, who jumped ship at St. Helena, made his way to Natal, had numerous exciting adventures in pursuit of ivory, and who later became a slave trader; and "Hlambamanzi," the Xhosa interpreter of the party. The historical records suggest that "Hlambamanzi" warned Shaka about some of the whites' less reputable intentions and behavior, finally becoming such a problem to the visitors that they killed him. The inclusion of either of these figures in the series would clearly have posed problems for writers seeking to present the white pioneers as romantic figures.[26]

Historical accuracy was not, in fact, high on Faure's list of priorities. Instead, he allowed the series to establish its authority as a legitimate interpretation of the past through close attention to authenticity. Tons of genuine animal skins, feathers, horns and oxtails were used to make the costumes. Real skulls were favored over papier maché replicas; grass huts constructed by "time-honored means" were manufacture for the thousands of "real Zulus" who swarmed across locations in Zululand, playing the role of their "ancestors."[27]

The search for authenticity enmeshed *Shaka Zulu* in a series of contradictions at the level of production. The construction of sets on actual historical sites, often the places of royal burials, raised serious questions about the filmmakers' respect for the history they were recreating; production of any sort in a South African homeland is connected to the issue of the exploitation of an overabundant supply of labor at excessively low wages; equally questionable is the necessary reliance on the co-operation of compliant homeland leaders, desperate for outside sources of income and reluctant to impose operating constraints on crews. Indeed, it is precisely this set of conditions that makes South Africa an alluring location for foreign movie makers.[28]

"The Rich and Awkward Commotion of Production"

Faure's intentions were doomed from the moment he and his white co-authors began working on the script. "Black history suffers because it is mainly written by whites. . . . I am a South African, and I felt it was time to rewrite the black history books," Faure stated, apparently oblivious of the antinomy in his claims.[29] In the very act of producing the script, Faure repeats Fynn's act of constructing Shaka. For a moment, early in the history of the script's production, there existed the possibility that Faure might yet break free of Fynn, and the "bigoted" constructions of Shaka by "generations of white historians," to offer, if not a Zulu version of the past, a script largely based on one. In 1979 Faure had in hand Mazizi Kunene's just published epic poem, *Emperor Shaka the Great*.[30] Kunene's text constitutes a powerful reappropriation of Shaka by a Zulu writer. Based on Zulu oral tradition, it offers a compelling convocation of Shaka as seen through Zulu eyes. Kunene's text is, however, characterized by a cursory and harsh depiction of the white visitors to Shaka's court.

Faure initially toyed with the idea of basing the script on Kunene's text, but the involvement of the state-controlled SABC in his project in 1981 killed the idea. In the eyes of the SABC, no matter how magnificent Kunene's poetry, it could not outweigh the fact that he was previously an official ANC representative and an outspoken critic of the government. The SABC was likely to have eschewed a script based on Kunene's text for financial as much as political reasons. The need to appeal to the American market through the use of white interlocutors ruled out the use of an Africanist text like Kunene's.[31] In 1982 an American, Joshua Sinclair, was brought in to rewrite Faure's original script. The script underwent yet another change of writers before it was completed. At least two significant changes in the script, which seem to have occurred after Sinclair was fired, were designed to present the Swallows in a better light and to eliminate ambiguities in the series' vision of potential interracial cooperation.[32]

These late changes to the script are useful indicators of some of the forces operating on Faure in the course of making *Shaka Zulu*, and which modified his original artistic and imaginative objectives. Faure began his career at the London Film School where, in 1974, he presented a dissertation entitled "Images of Violence." Faure's study addresses the problem of the ubiquity of violence on screen. The solution posited in the dissertation is not the elimination of violence, but the provision of tools for viewers to deal with it. Faure returned to South Africa and began to work for the new established television service of the SABC. According to Faure, he conceived of the idea of *Shaka Zulu* in the immediate aftermath of the 1976 Soweto Uprising. "It was time we rectified the misconceptions of history," he said, "and we needed to give black history a greater status."[33] *Shaka Zulu* was to be Faure's artistic and emotional response to political turbulence. The series develops his thesis on violence, by graphically portraying violence and then showing it to be misplaced. With *Shaka Zulu* Faure hoped to extend and liberalize the boundaries of consensual discourse in South Africa. In 1977, working with these ideas as an SABC film director, Faure was significantly ahead of his time.

However, as Keyan Tomaselli has shown with regard to other historical productions made for the SABC, the director's "selection of content and sources were governed by a sophisticated understanding (or gut reaction) of what would have been acceptable to the SABC and/or its target audience."[34] Indeed, during the period in which *Shaka Zulu* was made, the SABC was moving in a more "reformist" direction; Faure, in turn, was succumbing to the pressures exerted by his backers—restructuring his script and switching from a Zulu to an English text—and becoming increasingly involved in the production of other forms of state propaganda.[35]

In its final form, the script is ultimately faithful to the diary of the "bigoted white historian," Fynn, who originally recorded Shaka's life, and whose view of Shaka Faure was so eager to contest. To flesh out the areas in which Fynn's text is thin, the script primarily makes use of two other sources: the diary of another of the Europeans present at Bulawayo, Nathanial Isaacs; and E. A. Ritter's popular account of the life of Shaka, published in 1955.[36]

Fynn's "diary" was reconstructed from memory after Shaka's death, leading one historian to describe him as a "fiction writer" and the diary as a "forgery."[37] Fynn did indeed keep a journal of sorts, the original manuscript of which was reputedly buried by accident and never recovered. He subsequently wrote up sections from memory. Finally, in 1950, James Stuart, a resident magistrate with considerable knowledge of Zulu history, edited the final version which appears as the *Diary of Henry Francis Fynn*. The preface to the *Diary* describes its genesis and makes it clear that the text is not an original journal reflecting daily events. In many respects, however, the *Diary* offers a detailed picture of life and events in Shakan times, as Fynn remembered them, that is remarkable and invaluable to modern historians, and certainly a rich resource for a scriptwriter. Isaacs' text is based on the writer's memories and the journal of one of his deceased companions in Natal, James Saunders King. Isaacs' objective in publishing was to encourage investment in Natal. Like Fynn, Isaacs learned to speak Zulu and his account also offers valuable historical data, for he was an intelligent and curious observer and was present at a number of the major events during Shaka's reign. His dramatization of events and his romantic streak are easily discernible to the careful reader.

Nevertheless, both Fynn's and Isaacs' texts reflect their authors' biases as lower-middle-class Englishmen of the 1820s seeking adventure and fortune in Africa. Both sought actively to draw Britain into establishing a colony in Natal, and to that end they stressed social disorder and upheaval in the Zulu country.[38] In a now notorious communication to Fynn, Isaacs, on his way to London to publish an account of his adventures, counselled Fynn, "Make them [the Zulu kings] out as blood thirsty as you can, and endeavour to give an estimate of the number of people they have murdered during their reign, and also describe the frivolous crimes people lose their lives for. It all tends to swell up the work and make it interesting."[39] It was certainly in the subsequent interests of these authors to emphasize the "savagery" of Shaka. While the texts remain two of the most valuable sources for historians of the period, they require a careful disentanglement of their facts from their fictions, as well as close attention to their specific biases and their silences. Perhaps the most significant of these is the way in which they position both researchers and casual readers to look at the Zulu kingdom through white eyes.

Ritter's text is rather different. It purports to be an account of Shaka "as the Zulus saw him." Ritter attributes his knowledge of Zulu history to his boyhood attentiveness to the tales of knowledgeable old Zulu informants, and he demonstrates an obvious respect for Zulu oral tradition. Nonetheless, his book, like those of Flynn and Isaacs, reflects his own particular biases. (He was part of the force that suppressed the 1906 Bambatha rebellion and he later joined the Native Affairs department in Rhodesia.) The book is glaringly inaccurate in places, and characteristically romantic. For Ritter, Shaka was a "despot" and the reasons for his "excesses" were to be found in his disturbed childhood.

> Modern psychology has enabled us to understand the importance in after life, of a child's unhappiness. Perhaps we may trace Shaka's subsequent lust for power to the fact that his little crinkled ears and the marked stumpiness of his genital organ were ever the source of persistent ridicule among Shaka's companions, and their taunts in this regard so rankled that he grew up harboring a deadly hatred against all and everything E-Langeni [the clan name of his tormentors].[40]

Sexual insults are as common in Zulu society as they are in many others, but this explanation for Shaka's rise to power, which is echoed in the television series, has no resonance in any other source, and occurs in none of the many oral testimonies recorded by James Stuart at much the same time, and from at least one of the same informants used by Ritter.[41] The ending of the television series with the murder of Shaka, the suicide of his paramour, and the flames and chaos is drawn straight from the final sections of Ritter's text.

Faure claims that the script also drew on Zulu oral history, but there is little evidence of this. Where it does seem that the script writers may have had recourse to Zulu "tradition" is in the rendition of Zulu ceremonies and ritual. Authentic funeral and wedding scenes are a point of pride for the filmmakers.[42] Great attention is paid to the peculiarities of Zulu corpse preparation, the binding of the body in seated position wrapped in a skin hide, and the practice of burying alive the attendants of a dead king or queen.

Scenes involving the so-called "witchdoctors" of the time are handled in a similarly sensationalist manner. Sitayi, the ancient *isangoma* ("witchdoctor;" pl. *izangoma*) who controls Shaka's destiny, is depicted as a grotesque creature, hundreds of years old. Zulu oral tradition holds that, in fact, Shaka was less influenced by his *izangoma* than his predecessors, and through a skillful trick, robbed them of his influence at his court. Zulu *izangoma* were ordinary people who lived and died under ordinary circumstances, although it was believed that they possessed rare and valued abilities. In contrast to the other-worldly Sitay, they were an integral part of the community, unlikely to command packs of hyenas and maintain dens of dwarfs. In the representation of the *izangoma*, and in a host of other ways, the series presents Zulu ritual as disgusting and frightening. It is difficult to credit Faure's contention that

Irrespective of the impressions and license taken in the execution of this project, always paramount was our intention to place in historic perspective seventeenth-century [*sic*] Africa with its witchcraft and superstition, and to correct the misconceptions of those who judged the beliefs and traditions of Africa—not in the context of Africa—but rather through their own narrow Christian perspectives.[43]

The depiction of Zulu society is another area of significant misrepresentation of the past in the series. Granted, some of the series' greatest appeal lies in its representation of a world and a culture that is strange and "other" to modern viewers, both black and white, inside and out of South Africa. Instead of exploring and revealing a historic culture to the viewer, murky filters and molten colors are used together with clouds of smoke from fog machines to smudge the picture of Zulu society, to make its inner workings dark, barbarous and finally incomprehensible. Whether in dance or at war, all movement in the Zulu kingdom is always within a cloud of dust, stirred by thundering barefoot warriors and maidens. These scenes, mostly of the Zulu court, are complemented by black nighttime scenes, shattered periodically by thunder, rain and lightning in steely shades of blue and white, which occur with the representations of the "witchdoctors"—scary, monstrous and even more incomprehensible.[44] In the Cape Colony, by way of contrast, the air is always crisp and clear; images are sharply defined against blue skies and white buildings. Horseback regiments on parade and the carriages in the main streets raise no dust.

The series' focus on the whites' action, the use of Fynn as narrator, the reliance on Fynn's diary and other texts by "bigoted" white historians, and the sensationalistic treatment of Zulu life point to a sharp contradiction between the series' actual content and the director's stated aims. In order to explore the significance of this contradiction, it is useful to look more closely at the financing of the series.

Shaka Zulu took longer to shoot, cost more money and employed more people than any other production yet made in this country. It was also surrounded by rumor, gossip, and tales of sensationalism. Even now, the facts are hard to find.[45]

The biggest scandal was centered on the production's cost. It seems that Faure initially planned to make the series independently, but as work on the script and the pre-production planning proceeded, it became clear that it would be one of the largest, most costly series ever produced in South Africa. By 1981 the SABC had taken over production and financing. *Shaka Zulu* would take two years of pre-production planning and research, two years on location, and one year of post-production work before it was shown on South African television at the end of 1986.[46]

In late 1983, or early 1984, the production scale expanded still further. It was at this time that American distributors were drawn in. Throughout 1984 and 1985, the original budget of about $1.75 million was rumored to be escalating monthly, and the SABC continually refused to publicize any budget figures. The final figure admitted to by the SABC was $24 million.[47] The sudden pouring of masses of money into the production—"as if into a bottomless pit," as one cynic commented—came at a time when the recession in South Africa was biting, the film industry in South Africa was depressed and the SABC was cutting expenditure on other productions and placing a freeze on new productions.[48] The SABC justified the outlay through reference to the anticipated return to be earned on the international market. The US-based associated producer of the series, Frank Agrama, however, noted that the production was a "calculated gamble." *Shaka Zulu* was, in fact, the most expensive miniseries ever produced for television syndicate in the United States without a precommitment to network or operation time.[49] At this point the vastly extended scale of the series and changed circumstances of production began to have an impact on the series' form and content. Tensions between Faure and his backers were running high, until finally the Americans suggested that he be replaced by an American director. This was firmly rejected by the SABC.[50] When *Shaka Zulu* finally went into production, the key technical expertise was provided by overseas specialists. To explain the appropriation of the series in this way, and why the SABC took the enormous risk and embarked on such an expensive project when it did, it is necessary to look at the wider political context which prevailed when the series was being made.

1984 was a traumatic year for South Africa. The United Democratic Front (UDF), formed in 1983, called for a boycott of the tricameral parliamentary elections (the first step in the Government's so-called "reform" strategy), and en explosive backlash against "reform" swept the country. In 1985 "necklace" killings were reported around the country, government buildings were burned, and hundreds of schools were closed down. Between September 1984 and December 1985 nearly 1000 people died as a result of township unrest. Strike action reached an all-time high, and a super trade-union federation, the Congress of South African Trade Unions (COSATU) was formed.[51] One of the ways the state responded to this moment of crisis was with the increased use of its coercive powers. Troops poured into the townships and thousands of people were detained.

It was widely recognized that the image of civil war which South Africa was projecting, with nightly scenes of violence entering living rooms of viewers all over the world, was disastrous for South Africa's image abroad.[52] "The cameras have a way of only finding the violence and not the positive side," noted Faure.[53] Indeed, within months of the uprising, foreign banks refused to roll over South African loans, and both foreign and domestic capital began to withdraw from South Africa.

One step which the South African government took to change its image was to impose restrictions on the press.[54] The SABC, always the government's hand-maiden, at first reported events with biased glosses, but increasingly it limited visual coverage, and restricted itself to relaying official "unrest" figures for each day.[55] In one striking reversal of this policy, used to justify the increased use of troops in the townships, the torching of an informer was screened in gruesome detail.

Television drama was one way in which the SABC could project another of South Africa. John Cundill, writer of a historical drama on the 1922 mineworkers' strike screened just before *Shaka Zulu*, gave an indication of the kind of thinking in influential quarters within the SABC at this time. "[T]elevision is a powerful medium of communication, and the idea of using TV dramas as reform tools has strong relevance . . ." Cundill said. "The projection of blacks and whites interacting in situations portraying reality and highlighting their common humanity would go far to ease the tensions of mounting racial strife."[56]

Shaka Zulu offered the SABC an opportunity for presenting black and white viewers in South Africa with a drama advocating interracial collaboration and portraying the dangers of its failure. The series also presented an opportunity to give another view of South Africa to overseas audiences, one which could be seen to advocate peaceful co-existence and respect for the African heritage, and which provided, by way of analogy, a comment on the government's "reform plans." *Shaka Zulu* was thus extensively promoted outside South Africa. In the United States, in a piece of sophisticated marketing, the series was shown on a network of independent televisions stations across the country, aimed at between 70 and 90 million viewers.[57] Faure and the show's two leading Zulu stars did a promotional tour of the United States that was timed to coincide with the screenings—and with Black History Month. On tour, Faure and actor Cele made the series' propaganda purposes explicit. "We believe that it is time to shed light on South Africa, correct misconceptions and change the system, they claimed.[58] They made it clear that they saw the series as an analogy with the present. Echoing the words of Farewell and Shaka in the series ("nothing is impossible if two kingdoms truly want to live in harmony"), Faure remarked, "There is a large core of white and black people who want to come together in harmony. People are using our situation to further their own ends [presumably a reference to the work of agitators—a common refrain in the parlance of South Africa's frustrated reformers]. They don't give a damn if our children are killed. But Henry [Cele] and I care," Faure continued, enacting yet again a moment of white interlocution, "and so do a lot of other South Africans."[59] Faure and Cele also used the opportunity provided by the interest in *Shaka Zulu* to speak out against the imposition of sanctions against South Africa.[60]

"The Politics of the Tightrope"[61]

In the turbulent political climate which prevailed when the series was screened, *Shaka Zulu* offered an easily recognizable analogy for modern South Africa. The series vividly conjures up the numbers ratio which is obsessively debated by white South Africans. Farewell's party consists of only eight men. The crowd scenes at Bulawayo show masses of thronging black humanity. "There's an awful lot of them, isn't there?" comments one of Farewell's men on their first sight of the capital. Indeed, at times the series' dialogue makes the analogy less than subtle.

The violence of African society is explored at length. It is *the* problem to which a solution must be found. White society at the Cape is represented as being under threat of attach by Shaka. Farewell's mission is to deflect that onslaught. (In fact, this is a scriptwriter's embellishment, for the Cape was not threatened at this time.) Farewell and his party are also presented as being in danger at Shaka's court. Death is always a possibility. Shaka is shown to be a ruthless leader, dominated by the imperatives of power and revenge. The Zulu are constructed as a highly militarized nation, an irresistible warrior tide. In the series, this militancy is not censured. Rather, the Swallows seek to control it and divert it from attack on white society.

The representatives of British imperialism in London serve as symbols for the far right wing, and a clear distinction is drawn between them and the whites on the spot in southeast Africa. King George IV, who considers the Zulus to be nothing more than "a tribe of savages running around in their birthday suits," is an object of ridicule. The Colonial Office's understanding of how to deal with the Zulus is shown to be way off the mark, as are their ready assumptions of the superiority of "civilization" and the potential efficacy of a "solitary Caucasian" in dealing with Shaka. "If we cannot soothe the savage beast," they say, "we can at least confuse him whilst we mount an effective military defensive." The series makes it clear that Shaka confuses as much as he is confused. "Your Colonial Office has no idea of what it is up against," remarks Fynn to Farewell on their first introduction to the full panoply of the Shakan state. Fynn sees the Swallows' relationship with Shaka as a game of chess between two skilled players. The Swallows realize that their position in southeast Africa is most precarious, and that only the most careful strategy will see them through.

The strong rejection of the Colonial Office's racist attitudes strikes a recognizably reformist note. Farewell's final plea to Shaka to refrain from attacking the Cape is perhaps the most direct call of the series. "That yearning which has brought about everything that has happened was as much your fault as it is mine, but hating my people is not the solution. We must search for another, together."

Part of the solution is seen to lie in greater mutual understanding and respect. Farewell makes this point explicit to the governor of the Cape Colony when he escorts Shaka's diplomatic mission to the Cape.

> In the course of the three years that we have been amongst the Zulu people, I have endeavoured to reconcile Zulu interests with those of the British government. Now there have been many difficulties, of course, most of them related to questions of custom, such as you have just witnessed with regard to the seating arrangements [the deputation had just elected to seat themselves on the floor of the governor's office] and basic misunderstandings which affect communication. But more recently I have had the good fortune to win the confidence and the trust of the Zulu king. The result of which is the king's strong desire to show his goodwill be proposing an alliance with Britain.

At this stage of the drama Farewell has discarded parts of his European garb, donning instead elements of the costume of a Zulu chief. Thus he no longer looks like an Imperial officer. Nor is he acting only in the interests of the British king. He has become a product of Africa itself, ambiguously placed midway between the Colonial Office and Bulawayo. This is the terrain on which the advocates of "reform" in South Africa situate themselves, somewhere between the conservative forces and "the place of killing."

Shaka is constructed as the one Zulu with vision who can see the importance of the whites and their "magic" for the Zulu people. Despite the warnings of his advisors and his *izangoma*, Shaka is determined to appropriate the power of western knowledge. His complete control over his people means that he can enforce a vision of interaction if he so chooses. Shaka's commanders are depicted as being utterly subject to his authority. "We share a common life," remarks Ngomane, the Zulu "prime minister," to Shaka. "My own!"

Shaka is the type of black leader with whom the proponents of reform in South Africa would ideally like to negotiate. Enlightened and authoritarian, his closest contemporary parallel is the leader of the kwaZulu homeland and Inkatha boss, Gatsha Buthelezi. Like the Shaka of the series, Buthelezi personifies Zulu politics. During the 1980s, moreover, Buthelezi has enjoyed a media prominence that exceeds that of any other active black leader in southern Africa. The analogy between Shaka and Buthelezi is a common one in South African discourse. It is a comparison often drawn by Buthelezi himself, by journalists, and by ordinary South Africans.[62]

The South African government's reform strategy is centered around the idea of political confederation. Buthelezi's mobilization of Zulu ethnic nationalism is highly compatible with the reformist vision. In the face of widespread opposition to the government's new constitutional proposals, the cooperation of Buthelezi in "reform" became essential. Echoing Fynn's metaphor of a chess game, Faure remarked, "When the game is set and all the parties come together, it's going to be parties like the Zulus calling the shots."[63] For both Inkatha and the South African state, the 1980s saw the increasing inevitability of their mutual alliance against mounting radical opposition. "For some," explain G. Maré and G. Hamilton, "Inkatha offers the last hope of a peaceful negotiated settlement. For the state it may be the most hopeful partner in the first tentative steps beyond or away from the bantustan policy, steps aimed at bringing African people into the central power structure while maintaining a policy based on 'power-sharing' between 'groups'—a plurality of minorities."[64] Inkatha, under threat from the growing UDF presence in Natal, in its turn, began moving closer to the South African state.

It is not sufficient, however, to see, as have J. Wright and G. Maré, Buthelezi and the SABC simply as acting in concert in *Shaka Zulu* to further the aim of presenting the leaders of kwaZulu as the authentic representatives of African peoples in Nata/kwaZulu.[65] By the time the series was first screened, the South African state was certainly more squarely behind Buthelezi than ever before. But the series is characterized by far greater ambiguities than this simple interpretation allows, ambiguities developed as the script itself evolved from 1979 to 1986.

The series ends in chaos when interaction with the whites is rejected by Shaka. It offers a strong warning to independent black politicians like Buthelezi not to try and go it alone. This is not surprising, since Buthelezi had seized the constitutional initiative from the government through the establishment of the Buthelezi Commission in 1980. The Commission rejected as a "sop" the state's attempt to cater to black political aspirations through the establishment of a Black Advisory Council to the President's Council, and set out to explore constitutional alternatives. In 1986, Buthelezi's most ambitious venture, the kwaZulu/Natal Indaba, began to prepare the way for a multi-racial, multi-cultural legislature for the Natal region.[66] The state, which rejected all of these initiatives, was alarmed at the support which Buthelezi was garnering at the expense of the state's own more fraught "reform" plans. A warning note is sounded in the very first scene of the series. Queen Victoria listens closely to Cetshwayo's account of the life of his ancestor, Shaka, and then remarks, "We are a practical woman, your Highness. We will not make an alliance with a legend."

Shaka Zulu offers more than just a caution to Buthelezi and others of his ilk. It neatly twists the veiled threats that Buthelezi directs at the South African state when it seems intransigent. It suggests by way of analogy that the modern Mfecane, which Buthelezi threatens may erupt if whites continue to ignore him, will be as threatening to the Zulu leadership as to the whites. In the series, Shaka's decision to launch an attack on the Cape Colony is the beginning of his undoing. The lesson is there for Buthelezi, and any other black leaders, that a successful outcome for either party is predicated on close cooperation with the other. The alternative portrayed in *Shaka Zulu* is that everything will go up in flames and chaos will prevail. "Out of ashes will come more poverty," commented Faure, "and children will be denied opportunities to be educated. It will pave the way for Marxism and set the country back."[67] The end of the series is, of course, open to a more subversive reading than Faure allows—that Shaka's failure is the inevitable and only consequence of cooperation with Farewell. The final fires can be seen as the cleansing flames of revolution out of which a new order will arise.

The monopoly of power by the Swallows and the way in which they control the telling of Zulu history, while reassuring to white viewers, is a source of enormous embarrassment to Buthelezi. At a King Shaka's Day rally a few weeks after the special preview screening, Buthelezi attacked white historians, and Fynn in particular, for the distortion of Zulu history, especially the depiction of Shaka as a bloodthirsty tyrant. He railed against the Europeans' indiscriminate scattering of their semen across Zululand.[68] Buthelezi's virulent attack, widely report in the press, successfully obscured a central contradiction between the rhetoric surrounding *Shaka Zulu*—the present Zulu king described it as a production of Zulu history "as seen through my people's eyes"—and the fact that the series portrays Zulu history through the eyes of a white visitor and a white director.[69] Moreover although the series does show Shaka to be a leader of caliber and talent, it also repeats the old stereotypes of his psychological imbalances and bloodthirstiness. It incorporates a host of very "unZulu," untraditional features that had a least some critics wondering how it could have been approved by the Zulu royal house.[70]

In fact, Buthelezi could not afford to disassociate himself from the series, despite its flaws. *Shaka Zulu* is a powerful endorsement of the kwaZulu leadership, needed urgently by Buthelezi at the end of 1986 as the battle for popular support in Natal was enjoined bay the UDF and COSATU. *Shaka Zulu* also put Buthelezi on the spot in another respect. More than any of the other South African "ethnicities," the Zulu identity is founded on "traditionalism." Indeed, Inkatha draws heavily on the symbols and institutions of the past. Inkatha forces are called *impi*(s) or *amabutho* after Shaka's armies. Shaka Day is celebrated as a national holiday. The positions of its leadership are justified through reference to traditional rank. Buthelezi, for example, traces his ancestry back to Shaka on the maternal line.[71] *Shaka Zulu* is virtually the only visual rendition of the Shakan period in existence, and with it, the SABC had vividly and powerfully appropriated the linchpin of Inkatha ideology. Buthelezi could not afford to lose the opportunity of riding on the dramatic success of the series. Its screening provided a chance too valuable to miss for Buthelezi to make connections between himself and his illustrious predecessor. The price was to concede the point about white narration and other objectionable features of the series. Indeed, this compromise reflects the essential compromise of Buthelezi's political vision. In this, and in the depiction in the series of Shaka as "bote the master and the victim of his regime," what Shula Marks has termed the "ambiguities of Buthelezi's dependency" are starkly revealed.[72]

In spite of itself, however, the series shows that whites are dependent in a similarly ambiguous fashion. Their options are limited—as Farewell acknowledges, they have nowhere else to go. In the series, the whites cannot shape the course of events in terms of their interests alone. Shaka falls short of the demands made on him by the presence of the Swallows, and Fynn and Farewell suffer in the process as much as Shaka's own subjects. The South African state is, in turn, itself equally dependent on the cooperation of Buthelezi in the "reform" scenario. As Marks notes,

"[Buthelezi] constantly faces the state with his contradictory presence both as critic and as collaborator extraordinary. . . . He is simultaneously needed and feared."[73]

It is a striking feature of the series, and of the analogy that it sets up, that so much hinges on the abilities of key individuals. Shaka's rise to power, for example, is explained in terms of the prophecy. For those viewers who may doubt the power of magic, an alternative explanation is offered through reference to Shaka's character. He is ambitious, able and successful. All the action revolves around him. Clearly, the centrality of a single leader in the series is an important dramatic device. The "Great Man" theory, however, promotes the idea that history is made by leaders, not by ordinary men and women. It suggests that they, by virtue of their exceptional abilities, can best judge the way forward. This perspective denies the struggles of ordinary people and their capacity to shape their own lives. Moreover, as the series so vividly shows, it implies that whoever controls the leader, controls the people. When the attempt is made on Shaka's life, Farewell comments, "We need Shaka alive. If we can control Shaka's soul, we can control the whole of southern Africa." In denying ordinary people access to power, the South African state and Buthelezi stand united against the radical and militant popular movements.

Keyan Tomaselli has argued that *Shaka Zulu* "endorses apartheid discourse which holds that blacks are 'different' and should develop in their 'own areas,' safely out of white civilization."[74] In fact, *Shaka Zulu* is no mere "racist propaganda;" on the contrary, it advocates interracial interaction and mutual dependency. But it is not a simple rendition of the most progressive or coherent "reform" line coming out of Pretoria. A close look at the production reveals both the promotion of the "reform" vision and its limitation, its confusions as well as its subversion, in numerous and varied ways. The contradictions and ambiguities of the series reflect its production during a period when the political landscape of South Africa was altering rapidly and when the nature of domination itself was in ferment. Rather than a reflection of a dominant ideology, *Shaka Zulu* is actually about the process of a struggle for a new hegemony in South Africa—one which is not fully worked out by any of the parties involved.

Chapter 19 / Musical Form and Social History:
Research Perspectives on Black South African Music

Deborah James

Migrant mineworker making music with traditional instrument.

History Workshop

Recently, audiences in Europe and the United States have responded with great excitement and enthusiasm to black music from southern Africa, especially from South Africa. While this new and unprecedented interest may be a product of growing awareness of the injustices and deprivations of apartheid, it must also represent an appreciation of the rhythmic and melodic qualities of the music itself. A look at research and literature on the music reveals a preoccupation with these dual concerns: on the one hand, the socioeconomic circumstances from which the music has grown, and on the other, the intricacies of its musical form. Although in some studies these two perspectives have illuminated each other to provide a complete picture, most researchers have tended to emphasize either one dimension or the other.

Each of these approaches carries its own shortcomings. The earlier style in ethnomusicological analysis concentrates on the technical aspects of music, and examines musical instruments, scale-types, uses of rhythm, and the way in which these formal characteristics have spread from one "tribal" grouping to another. This perspective is most often associated with an interest in "pure" traditional music, and a scorn for hybrid styles or those which have evolved out of the experience of proletarianized communities. In its most conventional form, then, this kind of ethnomusicology appears remote from the concerns of social historians, and stands accused of irrelevance and lack of concern with the pressing issues confronting communities in present-day southern Africa.

The more recent approach views music as a sociohistorical phenomenon, and is concerned with the way in which social groupings have formed around, and expressed themselves through, musical performance. This style of analysis is predominantly concerned with evolving and urbanizing musical styles. In its preoccupation with musical genres and lyrics as expressions of changing social experience and consciousness, it dovetails, often indistinguishably, with the approach of social history. Its flaw, however, is that it sometimes ignores specifically aesthetic dimensions in favor of broadly social ones. Thus, for example, it provides no insight into why a song or dance better expresses particular sentiments than a political meeting or some other form of popular culture.

The apparent polarization presented here can be overcome. The two tendencies are in fact interdependent, and some of the best scholarship succeeds in integrating them both. From the point of view of social and cultural action, too, there is a need for the two kinds of understanding to complement each other. Black oppositional movements in southern and South Africa are often associated—either officially or informally—with programs of cultural revivalism, in which music has played perhaps the most important emotive and symbolic role. A successful use of music in this way has gained from an accurate record of how "indigenous" music was performed as well as a clear understanding of the fact that much of the music deemed "traditional" is really the product of ongoing processes of social change.

During the 1920s and 1930s there were two notable initiatives in the documenting and recording of African music: by Hugh Tracey and Percival Kirby. Tracey's research has perhaps become more widely known through the pages of *African Music*, the journal he founded, and through his later involvement in broadcasting. His research trips, funded first out of his own pocket and later by the Carnegie Corporation, took him to a wide variety of regions in sub-Saharan Africa. The recordings he made were issued in the Sound of Africa record series.

In 1934, the same year Tracey took up broadcasting, Percival Kirby published his book on South African indigenous musical instruments.[1] Like Tracey's, much of the research was funded by the Carnegie Corporation, but while Tracey had concentrated on making sound recordings, Kirby's approach was to collect and photograph instruments, to document their names and uses, and to classify them by demonstrating broad patterns of similarity uniting superficially different musical and tribal traditions.

What both research programs had in common, however, was a concern with the technical and formal details of performance, rather than the social uses of music.[2] Other scholars shared this interest in the formal qualities of African music and were influenced by the work of Kirby and Tracey. As a professor at Witwatersrand University, Kirby supervised dissertations such as that of Yvonne Huskisson on traditional Pedi music.[3] The fact that Huskisson subsequently achieved an influential position in the black division of the state-run South African Broadcasting

Corporation—which upheld the official policy of ethnic segregation by disseminating suitable music for each of the designated "ethnic groups"—perhaps indicates the politically indiscriminate uses to which a purely formalist approach can lead. Other academics also became interested in the stylistic qualities of South African music. David Rycroft from the University of London's School of Oriental and African Studies, for example, conducted research on the forms and structures of Nguni music, and Deidre Hansen, presently at the University of Cape Town, investigated the music of Xhosa-speakers.[4]

Tracey had no formal academic connections and no institutional backing apart from the opportunities provided by the broadcasting industry. With the continued support of the private sector, he founded the International Library of African Music (ILAM), where he continued his work in research, recording, and documentation. His aversion to modern, urban forms of black music led many people—especially the black South African jazz musicians performing in and around Johannesburg in the 1950s and 1960s—to revile him and his research project. From the criticisms of irrelevance to bitter accusations that he tried to divert the development of black musical forms, or even "stole the people's music," one can see that Tracey has been a contentious figure.

Nevertheless, in retrospect the value of the methodical record kept in the ILAM is evident. Especially useful is the inventive expansion introduced by Hugh Tracey's son, Andrew Tracey, the present director of the library. While this ethnomusicologist shares his father's interest in the formal and structural dimensions of African music, he has made a particularly valuable contribution through the systems of notation he has developed, making the music more accessible to a wide range of would-be performers.[5] His influence in this regard has been very broadly felt: at universities, colleges of education, alternative educational institutions such as the Funda Centre in Soweto and the Kwanongoma College of Music in Zimbabwe, and in many more informal settings.

Also notable are the films Andrew Tracey has made in conjunction with the U.S. producer Gei Zantzinger, which provide clear demonstrations of the cyclical structure and improvisatory techniques used in, say, the music of the Shona *mbira* (a plucked reed instrument sometimes referred to as "thumb piano") and the Chopi *timbila* (xylophone). The films, some of which attempt to depict the total context in which the music is played, also go some way to evoking a sense of its social embeddedness.

The first written accounts to emphasize the social dimension came from scholars with a stronger anthropological bent. One of these was

John Blacking who, at Hugh Tracey's suggestion, conducted research into Venda music in the 1950s. His writings, although not neglecting the formal aspect, emphasize the social basis of the various musical styles. He demonstrates, for example, how the various agricultural phases of the year are accompanied by specific work songs, while periods of minimal agricultural activity allow time for major ceremonies and rituals and the music which accompanies these. Likewise, the life of an individual is divided into clearly distinguished phases, each initiated by a specific set of ceremonies in which music plays a crucial role. Two of these to which Blacking gives special attention are childhood and the songs associated with it and girls' initiation. He also investigates the role played by music in maintaining and perpetuating power and status differences in Venda society, showing how an essentially "commoner" musical tradition has been co-opted by the chiefly group and used to enhance its prestige.[6]

A similar study was conducted by Thomas Johnston on the music of the Shangana-Tsonga people of the eastern Transvaal and southern Mozambique. Like Blacking's, Johnston's analysis looks at every aspect of Tsonga social life and shows how music integrates and enhances it. He gives particular attention to the opportunities provided by musical performance for individual entrepreneurship. An example he cites is that of chiefs whose hereditary claim to office does not afford them much prestige in its own right, who attempt to attract musicians to their courts by offering them chiefly patronage. An even more striking example is that of possession-cult doctors who attract large followings of people—both as cult followers and onlookers—through their impressive ceremonies of which music is an essential part. A particularly weak chief, in a bid to enhance his standing, will try to ensure that one of these doctors becomes attached to his court as a permanent fixture.[7]

In attempting to bridge the gap between formal musical analysis and the domain of social/anthropological studies, these two writers typify what was to become a new approach to the study of music in southern Africa. But neither demonstrates what later became a crucial issue: an awareness that the communities they consider had already been subjected to extensive changes, and were already involved in migrant labor and the cash economy.

Around the same time—the late 1960s and early 1970s—a strong thrust toward a socio-musicological approach was coming from U.S. ethnomusicologists such as Alan Merriam, and it was a student of Merriam's, David Coplan, who came out to South Africa during the 1970s to undertake the first extensive piece of research into changing styles in South African music.[8]

It may seem puzzling that earlier research projects had for the most part excluded any reference to new musical forms arising out of industrialization and social change, and that it should have been an American who first became interested in looking at these issues.[9] Part of the explanation lies in the attitude—strongly held for example by Hugh Tracey—that urban African music lacks the formal integrity of its "traditional" forebears, and that it has been bastardized by its assimilation of Western forms. Coplan's research made it clear that much of the exotic "foreign" music embraced by urban and proletarian communities in South Africa, such as American ragtime and jazz, was itself derived from African roots. Its appropriateness to the black South African urban setting resulted "from the comparable experience of the two peoples under white domination."[10] Whereas those focusing on questions of musical structure and form had concluded that new forms were degraded, those like Coplan focusing on the social processes of urbanization and the formation of new social classes, developed a vision of urban African music as an essential expression of these processes.

Coplan's research encompassed a broad sweep of history, from the early days of colonialism in the Cape right through to Soweto of the 1970s. Perhaps the most insightful chapters of his book *In Township Tonight* deal with black urban performance culture in Johannesburg up to about 1960. Here, from archival sources supplemented by a rich variety of oral testimony, Coplan has reconstructed a picture of a complex world of nascent urban communities. Different groups entering the city brought with them a variety of local musical styles and adapted them to help cope with the exigencies of the new environment. Due to the use of Western instruments with standardized scales, these local styles became mutually intelligible, and were influenced by each other as well as by the music of missionaries and, later, of black Americans. An emerging social stratification in black Johannesburg did entail, to some extent, the development of separate sub-styles of music, with, for example, a mission-educated elite favoring church choir music and enjoying American ragtime, while *shebeens* frequented by poorly-paid industrial workers provided entertainment by *marabi* pianists, whose music had a more indigenous flavor.[11] But Coplan insists that these streams could not remain divergent for long. As music began to be disseminated through sol-fa notation, on record, and by professional musicians who played for audiences irrespective of class or even color, influences were transferred from one incipient social class to another. The result, Coplan argues, was a broad-based black urban music with wide appeal, transcending narrower socioeconomic divisions.[12]

Coplan's seminal work laid the ground for a new interest in the study of black South African music, particularly in its sociological, anthropological, and historical dimensions. Indeed, a shortcoming of his book and of some work in a similar vein was that it tended to de-emphasize issues of musical form and style altogether. For example, Eddie Koch's study of the Johannesburg slumyards presented to the 1981 History Workshop, although containing some observations on the *marabi* piano style, subsumed these within a broader consideration of *marabi* culture in general, and of a class culture in formation.[13]

Another shortcoming of *In Township Tonight* lay in its sheer breadth of scope. Like many pioneering studies which open up a field for research, it was later to be criticised in the light of the more complex picture arising from further study in the field. For example, black jazz and vaudeville between the 1920s and the 1940s have been investigated by Natal University's Christopher Ballantine. He has just begun to publish his findings, which challenge some of Coplan's.[14]

Other scholars examined local musical traditions in more detail. This new interest in local tendencies challenged the earlier view of a universal urban working-class music, reflecting similar developments in the wider field of social historical study. For example, the first book of History Workshop papers, published in 1979, reveals a concern with broad issues of class formation and class-based action, and with the objective material circumstances which underlie these things. In contrast, the most recent History Workshop collection, published in this volume, manifests a greater interest in regional variation, locally-constructed identities, and the subjective, or "emic," conceptualizations communities may have of themselves.[15]

These opposing perspectives are presented in their starkest form in a "popular" work by the journalist Muff Andersson. In this overview of South African music both black and white, Andersson starts by roundly condemning the Traceys' work for its exclusive attention to traditional forms, since this, she claims, amounts to a tacit approval of the South African government's policy of ethnic separation and "separate development." According to her argument, it follows that any black music arising from the urban/industrial experience which is remotely "traditional" in form or content is, likewise, party to this official promotion of ethnicity. For instance, Andersson views in this light the *isicathamiya* music and lyrics of Ladysmith Black Mambazo.[16] The music of which she writes with approbation is that which, in contrast, espouses avowedly working-class causes and uses completely urbanized forms.[17]

That this is a crude and simplistic view is revealed by studies which pursue an alternative idea—hinted at but not fully explored in Coplan's book—that different groups moving to the city were involved in creating their own vital versions of urban musical culture out of traditional form of poetry. Far from representing a quiescent acceptance of government-imposed ethnicity, this music often expressed resistance and oppositional sentiments. The studies concern themselves with groups which, while becoming involved in the urban labor market, nevertheless retained strong links in the countryside. Instead of shedding their diverse backgrounds to immerse themselves in the homogenous urban culture which Coplan described, these groups evolved versions of migrant culture which derived from their particular experiences of deprivation and oppression.

Coplan himself, after completing his broader study, began an intensive investigation into a Sotho genre known as *lifela* (songs).[18] Developing from an earlier, traditional form of praise poetry, this style, evolved by migrants, enabled them to express their anxiety and fear about working in the mines and to recount their bravery under these harsh conditions. A novice poet becomes apprenticed to one who has mastered the art of improvisation required by the genre, and sharpens his talents by engaging in *lifela* competitions held during leisure time in the mine compounds. Winners are those who show their eloquence by cloaking their observations about the problems of contemporary life in metaphors deriving from the heroic Botho past. *Lifela* can thus be seen as expressing a dual identity: of workers who are at the same time displaced rurals patriarchs. If the poems appear "ethnic", they are enunciating a self-created ethnicity rather than one manipulated from above.[19]

Similar observations have been made by Johnny Clegg about the music of Zulu migrant workers in Durban and Johannesburg. As with *lifela*, traditional styles were adapted to urban usage. Mouth-bow and chest-bow songs customarily sung by young unmarried women about the men courting them became the songs, accompanied by trade-store instruments like guitars and concertinas, with which migrants boasted about their exploits in the world of the cities. Again as with *lifela*, an aura of intense competition surrounds the performance of this music, with street guitarists devoting hours of their time to the creation of new variations which they hope will be judged superior to those of their rivals. With these migrants, however, the competition is fiercest at the rural pole of their lives. Clegg recounts how the areas traditionally inhabited by clans such as Chunu and Tembu were overlaid by arbitrarily-imposed white farm boundaries, and how this resulted in intense competition between these groups, for labor contracts on the farms and ultimately, therefore, for the right to remain resident on the land. This rivalry, which at its worst gives rise to bitter and violent feuds, is channelled into *ngoma* (song/dance) competitions and has been the source of some extraordinary inventiveness by particular famous dance-team leaders. While Clegg acknowledges that this creative energy has been harnessed and, in a sense, co-opted by the employers of these migrants in the urban setting (who provide costumes, judges and incentives for the competitions), his implication is that this ethnic divisiveness is not so much a conscious creation of officialdom as an unintended result of colonial processes of land dispossession.[20]

Another aspect of the Zulu musical repertoire is explored by Veit Erlmann. He looks at the style known as *mbube* (bombing) or *isicathamiya*, recently made internationally famous by Ladysmith Black Mambazo. This style has several different sources, among which are the *ngoma* dancing described by Clegg, the Christian genre of *makwaya* (choir) music, and the American minstrel music first made popular in South Africa when Orpheus McAdoo toured with his Virginia Jubilee Singers in the 1890s. Erlmann's study addresses the same, recurring question: how is a class identity based on objective, material conditions integrated with other sources of identity—primordial, religious, or even stylishly urban and modern? Although *isicathamiya* carries a number of apparently paradoxical messages, including an unmistakably Zulu stylistic quality, an emphasis on both traditional values and Christian affiliation, as well as a "self-conscious display of urban status and sophistication," none of these is necessarily incompatible with the expression of a working-class identity. Here, "ethnic music" is not seen as pulling against a sense of proletarian unity, but as providing a medium in which this sense can be expressed.[21]

Erlmann's writings cover a broad range of other topics as well: from South African protest music through to the attitudes of elite Africans about the inclusion of traditional African music in the black education syllabus.[22] In all of these, he demonstrates his ability—due partly, perhaps, to the fact that his training in Germany included high-level courses in musicology, ethnomusicology, and anthropology—to combine the skills of formal analysis and socio-historical investigation.

A different direction is taken by Patrick Harries in his work on the songs of relocated communities in the north-eastern Transvaal. In contrast to the ethnomusicologists cited above, he views folksongs from a historian's standpoint, as did Leroy Vail and Landeg White in their work on Mozambique. His emphasis is thus on lyrics rather than on musical styles, and he views these as valuable historical documents enabling the reconstruction of the history of remote rural communities which would otherwise remain undocumented. Songs are especially reliable as sources of evidence, he argues, since they cannot be manipulated or changed at will as can the oral testimony given by an informant to an interviewer. Rather than being idiosyncratic, they are likely to reflect communally-held beliefs and opinions, and "are only retained if they express popular attitudes and opinions." An issue hinted at by Harries, and more fully explored in his 1987 History Workshop paper, is the extent to which songs—or, indeed, all oral testimony—may project an idealized, "Golden Age" view of the past, or a version of society from which real political tensions and social inequalities are absent.[23]

The studies of particular local traditions mentioned above could be seen, in a sense, to have brought research on southern African music full circle. Like the researchers of the 1920s and 1930s, Clegg, Erlmann, Harries, and Coplan in his recent work are concerned to investigate the specific musical styles and practices of specific groups and communities.[24] But these later writers have brought to their work a sense of the social dynamics of the music they study, and of the way it has changed in accordance with its use as a vital and effective mechanism of social and cultural adaptation.

To return to the point with which this review began: the overseas audiences which have responded so enthusiastically to black South African music may be curious about its social origins as well as being moved by its rhythms and melodies. From the above account it can be seen that this music derives not from a single or monolithic experience of social change but that it is constructed out of a variety of ethnicities, class backgrounds, religious affiliations, and experiences of urban life. A style such as that made popular by Ladysmith Black Mambazo combines elements of Zulu tradition with the influence of Christian hymns and American minstrels. This eclecticism represents neither a bastardization of pure tradition as the early ethnomusicologists would have it, nor a reactionary hankering after the past as might be implied by a simplistic sociohistorical view of working-class culture. Only by combining musicological and historical insights can one gain a comprehensive understanding of the strength and vigor of a musical style like this one; an accurate awareness of its form will lend itself in turn to a more precise understanding of the socioeconomic milieu which generated it.

Chapter 20 / Performing History off the Stage:
Notes on Working-Class Theater

Bhekizizwe Peterson

Cedric Nunn/Afrapix

A scene from the Sarmcol workers' play, *Bhambatha's Children*, Durban.

During the last three decades, black performance culture has re-emerged in South Africa. Perhaps the most significant strand in this development has been the appearance of working-class theater in the 1980s. The social and political ascendancy of the labor movement provided the preconditions for the emergence of worker plays. These plays have generally taken two forms: The first comprises short educational pieces dealing with themes on workplace conditions, exploitation, and disputes. These plays tend to use only a few actors and they are created for specific in-house performances such as shop-steward's meetings. The second variant is more inclusive, comprising relatively large-scale productions which deal with labor, social, and political themes, and include public performances in their itineraries.

The narratives of most of the dramas produced thus far focus on the oppressive and exploitative workplace experiences which lead to strike action, and the workers' subsequent struggles with management, the police and Departments of Labour, familial survival, and efforts to mobilize worker and community solidarity. The other issues raised in these representations reflect larger national issues, including racism, ethnicity, the politics of gender, generational struggles, the breakdown of traditional values, and the alienation experienced in urban areas. The most publicly noted plays in this genre are *Ilanga Lizophumela Abasebenzi/The Sun Shall Rise for Workers*, *The Dunlop Play*, *Ziyajika/The Turning Point*, and *The Long March*.

The making of these worker plays is guided by the tenets of working-class initiative, participation, leadership, and accountability. Participants are drawn from urban and migrant workers and plays are generally improvised or "workshopped." This allows for a greater use of the participants' personal experiences and performance skills. The emphasis on worker participation and control has not precluded the use of the skills and resources of community-based individuals and organizations. *Ilanga* and *The Dunlop Play* were created with the assistance of the Junction Avenue Theatre Company, a non-racial group based at the University of Witwatersrand. The Sarmcol Workers Cooperative, creators of *The Long March* and *Bhambatha's Children*, have drawn on the support of activists, academics, and community groups. The skills of playmaking and performance are also shared with workers and participants from rural areas in theater-for-development workshops that are organized by community-based cultural groups such as the Afrika Cultural Centre and the Soyikwa Theatre Institute.

Worker plays, like black performance culture in general, are circumscribed by social constraints. The repressive social environment is further complicated by "practical" limitations. There is a scarcity of performance spaces, accessories, facilities, and transport in addition to a lack of time for the demanding processes of playmaking and performance. Of necessity, rehearsals and performances occur after working hours and during weekends. The spaces used for rehearsals and performances range from temporarily unoccupied union offices, church or community centers, hostel compounds, university auditoriums, and soccer stadiums. This imaginative use of time and space, no matter how limited, represents a creative defiance of the social constraints encountered and also the desire to organize cultural work in ways which are amenable to worker participation. New tensions and contradictions, however, arise as a result of performing at times and venues accessible to workers. For instance, the need to do cultural work at odd hours can lead to familial tensions and it can also militate against the increased and consistent participation especially of women workers in activities demanding time and travel.

The political significance of worker plays is best appreciated in the light of the performance initiatives which preceded them. In the 1970s black theater was profoundly influenced in its social organization, practice, and content by the Black Consciousness movement. Black Consciousness emphasized the political significance of cultural practices and their potential to contribute toward the realization of the objectives of black self-definition, solidarity, determination, and liberation. In order to achieve these goals, collaborative productions involving black and white artists and performances in city-based theaters were discouraged. This resolution was partially a response to the unequal power relationships which tended to characterize non-racial initiatives, as well as to the state's segregation of urban theaters, audiences, and performers between 1965 and 1978. However in the years after 1978, black performances began to shift to city-based theaters, reflecting the desegregation of theaters in that year and, concomitantly, the government's increased control of performance spaces in the townships and harassment of black artists.

The plays produced under the banner of black theater predominantly explored themes dealing with black people's experiences of social and political oppression. Some of the important plays produced in the 1970s that were influenced by Black Consciousness, though not necessarily ascribing to the movement or ideology, include *Shanti* by the People's Experimental Theatre (1973), *Give Us This Day* by Mzwandile Maqina (1974), *Survival* by Workshop 71 (1976), *Egoli* by Matsemela Manaka (1978), and *The Hungry Earth* by Maishe Maponya (1979). The standard issues highlighted were the various manifestations of racial discrimination, influx control, poverty and the denial of political rights to blacks. Considerations of class and the economy were always latent in the plays but were seldom prominently explored. The class-specific experiences and political prerogatives of the black working class were, likewise, prominently presented but only in so far as they could be reconciled with the envisioned nationalist development of the struggle.[1]

Matsemela Manaka's treatment of the experiences of the black working class in *Egoli* is typical of black theater which attempted to foreground the struggles of black workers. *Egoli* explores the experiences of two miners, John and Hamilton.[2] John is a migrant worker from the homelands while Hamilton was born and raised in Soweto, Johannesburg's sprawling township. The major action of the play occurs in the workers' hostel compound where the characters discuss the hardships of life in the compound, the disintegration of African cultural values and customs, political oppression, and the racist violence to which workers are subjected. These experiences are presented primarily as indicative of national oppression, while their contingent but historical links with capitalism are, at best, merely hinted at. Little is said about workplace conditions and exploitation, or the potential for workers to act to better their lot, either at home or at work. In one scene, Hamilton, who at times seems to be a variation on the "city-slicker," describes (with obvious authorial endorsement) the stoic endurance and apolitical bafflement of the black worker epitomized by John:

> Poor boy. A mineworker from the living grave. Look at his face, glittering with sweat, full of dust. This whirlwind within his muscles is turning Joburg into skyscrapers . . . castles and temples. Look at his sweat, if this sweat could quench his thirst! We must beautify the presence of the men who sweat for this godforsaken country. This man is tired of living. He is not enjoying the fruits of his sweat. He is praying for death to come his way.[3]

In sharp contrast to *Egoli*, *Ilanga Lizophumela Abasebenzi* depicts a working class that is far from simply passive and compliant. *Ilanga*, one of the pioneering worker dramas, was created around 1980 by workers involved in an industrial dispute with Rely Precision Castings foundry on the East Rand of Johannesburg. Fifty-five workers were dismissed from Rely after questioning the dismissal of a fellow worker. *Ilanga* explores the events before and after the dismissals. The broader themes of proletarianization, dispossession, and resettlement move through the play. Starvation in the reserves is compounded by the dislocations of family lives through the migrant labor system. *Ilanga* explores divisions among workers in the workplace and the dangers of the work environment. At the same time as the play presents the ways in which capital controls and exploits life in the workplace and the hostel compounds, it suggests the possibility of resistance through labor organization. A strong sense of historical purpose and optimism informs *Ilanga*. The play starts and ends with a song accompanied by slow shuffle dance steps and mime gestures in a style indebted to traditional performance orature:

> Benoni, Boksburg, Springs, Egoli,
> we make you rich.
> We hostel people make you rich.
> You send us back home to die with empty pockets,
> empty dreams and dust in our lungs, chopped-off hands and
> your machines grinding in our brain . . .
> don't worry brother,
> don't give up hope.
> The sun shall rise for the workers.
> Benoni, Boksburg, Springs, Egoli,
> we shall make the people, all the people rich.[4]

In performance the song illuminates the perspective of the workers, but inscribes their experiences with a profound sense of creative cultural resilience and political hope. As in other worker plays, *Ilanga* serves as a record of experience, operating as a form of popular history for the creative team as well as audiences.

The wide-ranging content treated in worker plays is facilitated by the diverse cultural forms used in performance. Dialogue and mime, song and tableau, sounds and dance provide spaces for escape, when necessary, from the constraints of realistic dramatic representation. The combination of all these cultural forms in a play results generally in an aesthetically appealing total performance.

The use of language in worker plays is often syncretic and imbued with metaphorical significance. Performers generally speak one or more of the indigenous languages, sometimes mixed with English, Afrikaans, or slang depending on audience composition and the situation or characters depicted. The divisions and conflicts among workers and between workers and management are at times symbolically captured through the use of different languages spoken in South Africa. In *Ziyajika*, first performed in 1984, management's inability to speak an indigenous language and its insistence on speaking only English or Afrikaans reflects problems of both communication in the workplace and racial arrogance. The compromised position of a black worker-cum-foreman is depicted through his attempts to use his ability to speak English and Afrikaans for personal gain.

Worker plays attempt to foster audience participation through the use of didactism and the traditional call-and-response form of African cultural performance. *Ziyajika*, a play devised by members of a union affiliated with the Council of South African Trade Unions, provides an illustration of this. The protagonists in the play are three workers and their white manager who is referred to as Paulo or "Lekgowa" (white man). After management arbitrarily deducts money from their wages, the workers recognize their need for a union to advance and safeguard their interests. They organize a union and demand recognition, an end to deductions, safe working conditions, compensation in the event of injury, and uniform wage scales. When negotiations fail, the workers declare a strike, forcing management to enter into new negotiations. This summary of *Ziyajika* suggests a simple plot development and resolution of theme and in performance the play's plot does serve as a straightforward illustration of the struggles of workers and the strengths of organized labor. But the plot also serves as a catalyst for embarking on *another* performance, involving the audience. As the characters debate about what a union is, its role, strengths and weaknesses, ways of mobilizing workers, and the probable responses that can be expected from management and the state, the audience is encouraged to participate through interjections and the singing of freedom songs. Dramatic conflict is thus located both within the performance (as interpreted by the actors) and in the audience; depending upon their responses.

The treatment of trade union strengths in *Ziyajika* and other worker plays sometimes oversimplifies and romanticizes the process of organization. The assumption underlying many worker plays is that trade unions can realize, without much effort, the interests of workers. To be sure, the intention is to illustrate the purposes and potentials of organized labor, but this goal is often achieved at the expense of detailing the *struggle* of organization and its connection to the social and political variables operative both in the workplace and in South African society.

In contrast to *Ziyajika*, *The Long March* is a much more accomplished piece of work and is one of the landmarks of worker theater. The genesis of *The Long March* is the subject of the play itself. The play was created in 1985 by members of the Metal and Allied Workers Union (MAWU) in Mpophomeni. *The Long March* chronicles the experiences of the workers of Sarmcol in Mpophomeni, a subsidiary of the transnational British Tyre and Rubber Company. The Sarmcol workers went on strike in April 1985 over the issue of union recognition and they were subsequently dismissed.

The play opens with a collage of song, mime, and oral poetry performed by workers clad in blue overalls. The montage sketches for the audience the principal contradictions and protagonists of the story. One worker steps out from the chanting group and informs us that theirs has been a "long march." A march, he continues, that has been caused by the economic and sociopolitical contradictions impinging on their lives. This introduction of the broader context of the workers' struggles is followed by a presentation of the more specific conflict which informed their experiences at Sarmcol. While the rest of the workers form a human-machine on stage, demonstrating both the factory locale and the labor power expended in production, one worker steps forward and recounts the history of Sarmcol in South Africa. Sarmcol was established in Howick in 1919 and by the 1980s it was one of the major employers in the area, despite the substantial reduction of staff from 4,500 in the early 1970s to 1,500 in 1985. In the 1950s, workers at Sarmcol joined the Rubber Workers Union, an affiliate of the South African Congress of Trade Unions (allied to the ANC). In 1973, the Metal and Allied Workers Union (MAWU) began organizing but was still refused recognition by management a decade later. After MAWU took Sarmcol to court, the company compromised and, in 1983, allowed union organizers access to the factory and to stop-order facilities. Two more years elapsed without union recognition and on April 30th 1985, workers at Mpophomeni embarked on a legal strike.[5]

The play presents management's recalcitrant attitude through a closely observed characterization of plant manager John Samson. On stage he exudes an arrogant self-assurance and viciousness which stems from his appreciation of the high level of unemployment in the area and Sarmcol's status as one of the area's main employers. As he whistles his way to negotiations with the workers, he nonchalantly tells us that he likes to "crush the unions" and that if he was ever honored with the task to govern the country he would "crush" the youth and unions (thus linking the Sarmcol struggle with other conflicts in South Africa). The following scene amusingly demonstrates workers' awareness of divisions among capital: the three faces of capital—regional, national, and transnational—bicker with each other over the phone, only uniting to safeguard their common interests. Samson consults with Johannesburg Sarmcol headquarters which, in turn, call the parent company in London. The message relayed back from London is "fire them all." Samson caps the scene with a grotesque rendition of a ballad, "That's what I want," delivered with abundant glee.

The dismissal of the workers and their replacement creates tensions between workers, their families, the community, and scab laborers. The remainder of the play explores workers' responses to the new challenges confronting them. They call on the community for logistical support to deter members from breaking the strike. The extension of the strike into the life of the community links their workplace experiences more overtly with the oppressive nature of surrounding South African society. It also leads them into more direct confrontations with the state.

The links between workplace and community are emphasized in scenes where workers mobilize the support of the community, culminating in a consumer boycott and stay-away which elicit a repressive police response. Similarly, *The Long March* shows the interdependency of capital and the state, in South Africa and internationally (and its frequently contradictory implications), exemplified in a scene where the BTR Director in London argues with Margaret Thatcher (played to hilarious effect by a male worker wearing an exaggerated mask)

> Maggie! Maggie! . . . you are losing touch about the Sarmcol workers in South Africa . . . each time you talk about democracy in South Africa I suffer. . . . What is this Commonwealth pressure against South Africa? Do you know what it means to my Sarmcol?

In a traditional convention of black performance, *The Long March* ends with a song of mobilization followed by the performers introducing themselves to the audience. The worker/performers conclude their introductions with a reminder that they are "still on strike." This comment together with the song, "Let MAWU reign/ liberate Africa," leaves the audience with the realization that although the play is finished, the conflict at Sarmcol continues—as does the larger struggle for liberation in South Africa.

The importance of worker plays is that they have expanded and, at times, reformulated the themes of black theater, especially in their depiction of workplace conditions and the experiences of the laboring classes. Worker plays, and black theater in general, negate the state's myths about South African history and society by presenting alternative historical narratives and hopes. There is an attempt to retrieve and reconstruct past history in order to counter Eurocentric distortions and also to delineate the historical processes that have gone into shaping modern South African society. The dramas, then, articulate a politically committed popular history at odds with the narratives of management and the state.

Chapter 21 / *"Bearing Witness"*:

Ten Years Towards an Opposition Film Movement in South Africa

Harriet Gavshon

Gill de Vlieg/Afrapix

Seventeen-year-old Sicelo Dhlomo, 1986.

In December 1988, South Africa's longest-running political trial came to an end. State vs. P. Baleka and twenty others aimed to show that legal internal political opposition, acting for the banned African National Congress (ANC), was responsible for the 1984–85 uprising in the Vaal Triangle, south of Johannesburg. Taking place in a small Eastern Transvaal town called Delmas, and later in Pretoria, the trial had lasted 442 court days, accumulated 565 pages of indictment and 27,194 pages of evidence. During the course of the trial the state named 911 individuals as co-conspirators, presented 152 state witnesses and 14,425 pages of documents, five rolls of film, numerous photographs and maps, and forty-two video and radio tapes as exhibits against the Delmas twenty-one.[1] The video material had been confiscated by the security police several years before, mostly from the offices of a small United Democratic Front-supporting video organization called Afrascope which had fastidiously and enthusiastically filmed two years of UDF meetings during the 1983–84 period. Lawyers believe the presence of the material, some of it already edited, was a crucial element in the state's case. What had been filmed openly and legally in support of the movement some years before, now became the main evidence against it.

Film is well suited to be a witness. It is iconic and it is easy to confuse it with reality. In South Africa reality is often so brutal and alive it is tempting to package and market it directly onto film, and many American and British filmmakers have done just that. Their films have provided the rearguard of international pressure against the South African government, which is why the latter have tried to control them. The idea of film "bearing witness," with all the religious associations of this phrase, has served as the matrix for an opposition cinema movement in South Africa. The same material which has recently been used by the state against opponents of apartheid also is used to fight apartheid itself.

To give evidence against the brutality of the apartheid system is a strong motivation for filmmakers, and thus films that are made not only represent an opposition to apartheid, but are also often part of it. The idea of "bearing witness," however, has both nurtured and starved the development of an indigenous film culture in South Africa; it has empowered the oppressed but also on occasion empowered the state to further its oppression.

An independent film movement opposing apartheid has emerged only in the last decade. Keyan Tomaselli attributes this development to improvements in Super 8 technology, the lifting of an embargo on video technology to make way for the establishment of a national television service in 1976, and the introduction of film and television studies courses at some universities during the mid-1970s.[2] One should add to this the development of a local film festival culture and the growth of foreign public interest in South Africa since the 1970s which produced a market for images about it.

Most South African filmmakers still primarily make films for foreign audiences and there continue to be very few independent black filmmakers, but the tentative beginnings of an independent film industry are significant because of the almost monolithic opposition it faces. Film and broadcast media in South Africa are carefully controlled by the government. The government's imposition of the State of Emergency in 1985, with its restrictions on the media, have most drastically affected the presentation of images. Although newspapers still manage to write about security force action, for example, it is almost impossible to get away with filming it. From the government's point of view, ensuring that the images of unrest and police action were taken off foreign television screens was absolutely crucial and despite the relatively short-lived protest that it caused, removing the evidence of popular insurrection and state response has taken a lot of pressure off Pretoria. In addition, all films and videos are subject to pre-censorship. Whereas books, theater, photographs, and newspapers can only be restricted after publication, no film or video can be shown without a certificate of approval by the Directorate of Publications. Although this is not serious for a filmmaker if his or her primary audience is going to be foreign, it does discourage filmmakers from making films primarily for local use.

Moreover, until recently, distribution channels for "oppositional" films have been limited. There are two television stations. The South African Broadcasting Corporation (SABC) is widely regarded as a propaganda arm of the ruling Nationalist Party's right wing and would never show a film which is critical of the government in any way. In addition, as the economic climate in South Africa deteriorates and SABC money for local productions gets scarcer, an increasing proportion of South African television is filled with American sitcoms, many of which are dubbed into Afrikaans and Zulu or Sotho. Because of the British entertainment industry's union, Equity, ban on South Africa, few British programs are allowed to be shown. The other television station is a pay-channel owned by a syndicate of the major newspaper groups. M-Net's license is dependent on its not screening any South African news, documentary or actuality and although they run a yearly competition for the best South African fiction film, they cannot show anything that has not been given prior approval by the Directorate of Publications. For the most part, it is a conduit for American films.[3]

Although there has been a state subsidy for feature films since 1956, its construction favors films which are already commercially successful. The feature industry itself is dominated by conservative capital and has produced few politically challenging films. There has always been a close relationship between the state and the film industry. The time of the "Information Scandal," that rocked the government in 1979 and forced Prime Minister B. J. Vorster out of power, revealed the payment of secret funds to certain South African companies making feature films for both black and white audiences that promoted the ideology of "separate development."[4] Recently the "film industry" bid farewell to the outgoing state President P. W. Botha with the world premiere of South African Jamie Uys's film, *The Gods Must Be Crazy Part 2*.

Within this climate it is not surprising that ideological outsiders battle to break in. South Africa's best known "serious" filmmaker, Ross Devenish, struggled to make each of his films and did so only with the help of foreign grants and television finance. For many years he was the only South African filmmaker attempting films which dealt with social issues. All three of his feature films, *Boesman and Lena* (1973), *The Guest* (1978), and *Marigolds in August* (1980) were made in collaboration with playwright Athol Fugard, who scripted and acted in the films. They were met with considerable critical acclaim but limited commercial distribution and success. Devenish finally left South Africa to work in Britain and has returned once to make a documentary film about Mbongeni Ngema's play *Asinimali* for British television.

In the last five years the "establishment" film industry has been boosted by U.S. capital as well as local business investment. Companies such as Cannon, with the aid of a loophole in the South African tax system, have until recently been able to take advantage of South Africa's favorable investment climate and shabbily unionized film labor force to produce a vast amount of B-grade movies, most of which will never see the screen, let alone the video shop.[5] Since most of these films were made in order to allow investors to take advantage of the tax benefits involved in export—a system which came to be known in South Africa as the "double-deduct"—few people cared about where the films finally ended up. In 1988 alone, over eighty feature films were made in South Africa. The international distribution deals that these films rely on are generally dependent on concealing that they are made in South Africa for fear of international repercussions. Hence European and American "stars" sneak into the country to play lead roles and the South African supporting cast act with American accents.[6] A few local filmmakers have been able to take advantage of the same loophole in the tax laws to produce refreshing small films like *Shot Down* (1986) and *Mapantsula* (1988), but this seems unlikely to be repeated.[7] The government, irritated by the fact that little political mileage can be made through this huge export industry and justifiably worried about the huge drain on tax revenue, has substantially cut the tax benefits that can be made by exporting films and has introduced a new subsidy system to replace the "double-deduct" system. In the past, the only government agency that had automatic access to the scripts of the films before they were made was the Reserve Bank, but the new government subsidy, which is administered by the Bureau for Information, will obviously mean much more government control. Although evidence of more South African landscape will now appear in the films, it is unlikely that too much will be tolerated.

Although there is no subsidy system for documentary or experimental films, it is in this area that an opposition film movement has grown, despite the fact that there is little local sponsorship for any documentary film production. John Grierson of the Canadian National Film Board was consulted in 1954 by the government before it established a National Film Board; he suggested the establishment of experimental film fund to foster a national cinema. However, when a board finally was established ten years later, it served primarily as a production and distribution arm for National Party propaganda.[8] It was dissolved in 1979, a white elephant on a hill outside of Pretoria. Thereafter, the National Film Archives, the National Film Board's most valuable asset, was forced to wander from ministry to ministry until it finally found a place with the national archives in Pretoria's Union Buildings.

The archives have a wealth of material, collected over twenty years from early newsreels to contemporary "smear films" (sic) about South Africa. The Anglo-Boer War, one of the first wars ever filmed, brought war correspondents to South Africa, who were sent by British companies

such as the Warwick Trading Company, British Mutoscope and Biograph Company, and R. W. Paul to record the events on film. These
films mark a turning point in the relationship between the British people
and their colonial wars as well as the beginning of the complex relationship between war and spectatorship.[9] Although most of this primitive
British propaganda is lodged in British archives, the South African National Film Archives, in financially happier times, tried to buy back as
much material as they could. In 1979, for example, they were able to buy
fifteen reels of Anglo Boer war newsreels from Sothebys in London.[10] In
addition, the archives hold one of the few extant copies of *De Voortrekkers*
(1916), Harold Shaw's epic recreation of the Great Trek which has been
said to have inspired *The Covered Wagon*; interesting early ethnography,
some, such as the *Denver Africa Expedition* (also known as *The Bushmen*),
dating back as early as 1912;[11] and the negatives of work by South Africa's
most interesting independent feature filmmaker Donald Swansen—*Jim
Comes to Joburg* (1949) and *The Magic Garden* (1961). Access to the national film archives is not consistent and only the most intrepid and persistent of explorers succeed. Although the SATV uses archive footage,
and indeed holds the rights to a great deal of it such as the cine-magazine
series *African Mirror*, few independent documentary filmmakers can afford to use these resources on any great scale. Because *Freedom Square and
Back of the Moon* (1987), a film about the destruction of the suburb of
Sophiatown after the Nationalist Party came to power, was a high budget
film financed by Britain's Channel 4, the producers were able to use a fair
amount of archival footage, although as much material came from British
and U.S. collections.[12] Another British film, *The History of Apartheid*,
produced by independent television station Granada in 1985, warranted
probably the most detailed international archive search and use of historical footage. Few South African independent filmmakers have been able
to make historical films, primarily because the funding of independent
films derives from foreign church and development aid sources which
prefer greater concentration on contemporary transgressions of justice
rather than historical ones.

Despite the government's hostility to a critical documentary film
industry and because finance for certain types of documentary films is so
much easier to come by than for feature films, the independent documentary industry has developed with little interaction with state or conservative institutional structures other than the censorship board.

Much of the financing and motivation for films critical of apartheid
comes from the church. Some films like *This We Can Do for Justice and for
Peace* (1981) and *And Now We Have No Land* (1984) were financed di-

rectly by the church, and many others are made with support from church groups in South Africa and abroad.[13] Because so much funding for documentary films comes from religious and development sources rather than art funds or television financing, many of the films produced tend to be instrumental, their purpose, directly or indirectly, to bear witness, give evidence, and show how apartheid has destroyed lives.

There is no doubt that international pressure against apartheid has been fueled by the outrage produced by documentary films and, although the state can control the production of images to some extent, it is still of necessity a leaky system. While international news networks and South African filmmakers are vulnerable to state pressure, individual foreign filmmakers are less so. By controlling the output of serious South African filmmakers and television journalists who would have to live with any repercussions their films would have, the state has left itself vulnerable to filmmakers who are not necessarily responsible to anything save their own sense of moral outrage. It is a situation which cuts two ways: on the one hand foreign "adventurers" often shamelessly exploit South Africa's pain, lay their subjects open to harassment, and get away with less than sound research. On the other, they can often go much further than most South African filmmakers in exposing such things as the brutality of apartheid and security force excesses and hence keep one of the last routes of information open.

The way that the political conflict has been covered by the foreign media obviously determines foreign "reading" of that conflict. Although it is very important politically that the transgression of basic human rights be constantly focused upon, such coverage leads to the impression that South Africa is merely facing a civil rights conflict similar to that which the United States faced in the sixties, and that the "abolition of apartheid" is all that is needed to resolve the conflict. Moreover, the documentary tradition has constantly reinforced the idea of the subject as victim, not able to control his or her own life or future, merely waiting for liberation by foreigners, and, certainly in the light of that, not entitled to demand release forms, the right to "read-back," or any privacy.[14] The irony is that few subjects would ask for and few filmmakers would offer any of the above. Moreover, there is a constant danger of representation being tailored to suit the agenda set by the filmmaker or the audience in the country for which it is intended. The most stark example of this is that the political conflict in South Africa is also constantly in danger of being seen as a narrow, racial one because it is difficult for people 6,000 miles away to understand the complexities of a country they have never visited.

The phenomenon of feature films made about South Africa such as Richard Attenborough's *Cry Freedom* and Chris Menges's *World Apart* is not an entirely recent one. Since the development of the entertainment film, South Africans have been used fairly consistently as subject matter, from the earliest narratives, the travelogues, to what must almost be a sub-genre in early film, "the Zulu film." Between 1908 and 1915 there were at least six American feature films that involved Zulus as subject matter—they were actually white people from New Jersey in "black-face"—most notably D. W. Griffiths's *A Zulu's Heart* for Biograph (1913), Lubin's parody of it in *Rastus in Zululand* (1913), followed by the *Zulu King*, *The Kaffir's Gratitude*, and *Queen for a Day*.[15] This tradition has been continued intermittently with films such as Cy Endfield's *Zulu* (1964) and Douglas Hickox's *Zulu Dawn* (1980).

Both *Cry Freedom* and *World Apart* were met with an enormous amount of interest in South Africa, by the state as well as its opposition. *Cry Freedom*, having been passed by the Directorate of Publications and on review on request from the Minister of Justice by the higher Appeal Board, was seized by police on the day it was released nationally by UIP Warner in 1988. It has not been shown publicly since then, although technically there is nothing to stop its release. *A World Apart* was written by Sean Slovo, the daughter of South African Communist Party executive member and former ANC military commander Joe Slovo and Ruth First (who was killed by a letter bomb in her office at the University in Maputo, Mozambique). It has received permission for a few screenings in South Africa all of which have been filled to capacity with extremely supportive and emotional audiences, including family and friends of the characters in the film. The existence of films of this nature has contributed to a growing political film culture in the country, especially since they have used "true stories" as their source material.

An understanding of the necessity for anti-apartheid South Africans to control their own means of representation has formed the background to the development of small format video groups in the country. Since the early 1980s a number of "community video" groups have been formed with the intention of changing the traditional relations between filmmaker and subject community, observer and observed. They are also made up of filmmakers who are unashamedly politically partisan, who do not see themselves as journalists, but rather as media activists. The first of these groups, the Cape Town Community Video Resource Association (now CVET), established in 1981, was influenced by the National Film Board of Canada's Challenge for Change program.[16] Such groups invite community organizations and ordinary people to participate in the creation of images, often about their own local struggles. The CVET produces material which is not destined for foreign television screens but for user-communities themselves, many of which request a particular program and sometimes work on its production. There are about six similar groups around the country.

The nature of the community video movement is essentially tied to the nature of community organizations themselves and it is therefore inevitable that the genesis of the movement coincided with the re-emergence of organized political opposition in the early 1980s and the formation of the United Democratic Front in 1983. Many groups have miraculously survived through three, nearly four consecutive national States of Emergency even though the community organizations themselves in many cases have not. Others, such as the now-dissolved Afrascope, were caught up in the wave of detentions and harassments of 1983. It was not until later that it became clear why the state considered it necessary to raid its offices, detain its coordinator for six months, and confiscate literally hundreds of hours of material documenting perfectly legal and open meetings, gathered in the process of what the group would have called "reclaiming history" from the government and the foreign media. The state was obviously able to think much further ahead. Some of the material turned up as evidence in the Delmas treason trial which, at the time of writing, has still to be heard on appeal.

Despite these setbacks, the contribution of the small, politically aligned film and video cooperatives as well as small distribution structures, has been a significant. Until the early eighties, the visual media—be it the SABC or the cinema circuit—had played a restrictive role in people's lives. With the development of an opposition cinema culture, the small media has emerged as a force for change. Witnessing one's own struggles on screen is a source for mastery and empowerment. Whereas access to state and commercial media has always been denied to opposition organizations (even to the liberal parliamentary opposition, the Progressive Party, or as it is now called the Democratic Party), the small media has created a culture of resistance over the years which is gradually gaining strength—and thanks to the way in which the international cultural boycott has concentrated the minds of South African filmmakers—is also gradually gaining power.

One of most important tasks for any independent film movement is to try to redress the balance in the allocation of skills and education in South Africa. There are few black filmmakers and almost no black women filmmakers. The one film school in South Africa, the Pretoria Technikon, is open to whites only. Two of the "open" universities have film or video sections within other departments; the drama school of the University of the Witwatersrand, and the journalism school at Rhodes University both have small film components, but since it is only in recent years that significant numbers of black students have been readmitted into the open universities, the impact is not yet evident. As a result, most community film organizations try to run film or video training courses.

But it is not the disparate initiatives in the production of films that have created an opposition film movement as much as the growth of an audience for these films. The audience has grown with the re-emergence of political organization over the last ten years as well as the development of the trade union movement. Although many documentary films are financed by overseas agencies or networks and are therefore often directed toward overseas audiences, they have also found both a formal and informal supportive audience in South Africa. Most significant is the proliferation of the video cassette recorder in many homes, from the northern suburbs of Johannesburg to Soweto. The informal network of viewers often occurs without filmmakers even knowing and it is not easily controlled. To cope with the growing demand for video and film, a few distribution agencies have been established, one of the first being the History Workshop Media Centre in 1986. These distribution agencies have thrived, alongside the growing demand for alternative education, autonomous from the iniquitously poor state structure of "Bantu education." Over the past few years most trade unions have established education officers—some even media officers and groups—and hence there is a constant demand for films and videos not only of South African origin, but also of related struggles elsewhere. Aside from South African material, the History Workshop Media Centre distributes films and slide-tape shows from City University's American Social History Project, and American films which are of interest to workers, such as *Union Maids* (1977) and *With Babies and Banners* (1978).

At the same time there seems to be real desire among worker and community audiences to see fiction, especially South African fiction. Films like *Mapantsula* (1988), Oliver Schmitz and Thomas Mogatlane's extremely successful film about a small-time crook who gets caught up in political events, are extremely popular. Another popular film is American director Lionel (*On the Bowery*) Rogosin's *Come Back Africa* which he made clandestinely in Johannesburg in 1959; it has made a big comeback with South African workers and politically-aware audiences since a print was recently brought into the country. Even film festivals such as The Weekly Mail Film Festival are beginning to draw audiences outside of a certain elite. The 1988 festival ran in a community art center in

Alexandra Township on the outskirts of Johannesburg as well as at the Market Theatre in the town. The theme "Cinema Under Siege" highlighted the issue of censorship around the world and enabled the showing of films like Guzman's *Battle of Chile*, and Biberman's *Salt of the Earth*, which had a profound effect on South African audiences. A film that has proved extremely important to Johannesburg audiences, especially women, is *Mothers of the Plaza del Mayo* about the mothers of the disappeared in Argentina (a subject with tragic parallels in our society).

With growing state control and anxiety over politically sensitive images, it seems that the tendency to witness, document, and archive might have to give way to a less figurative treatment of reality. There are many new lessons to be learned as the state gets less "gentlemanlike" each day in its treatment of films, filmmakers, and their subjects.

The Delmas treason trial is one of the latest and most damaging instances of the abuse of the common notion that images of reality can stand in for reality itself. The same video material had in fact been presented nearly four years earlier in a previous treason trial in Pietermaritzburg. Like the Delmas trial, the Pietermaritzburg trial tried to link legal and open political leaders, in this case the UDF and the South African Allied Workers Union, to the banned African National Congress. In the Pietermaritzburg trial, presiding Judge Milne ruled that video material was a document whose "provenance and authenticity" must be proved. The only way to unequivocally prove the authenticity of an image is to produce its creator, the filmmaker, for cross examination. In this case, the person responsible for the footage, having already spent six months in detention, most of it in solitary confinement, was now studying outside of South Africa and was not available for the trial. Because the state could not prove that the material was authentic and unmanipulated (i.e. edited), the judge would not admit the videos as evidence.

Judge Van Dijkhorst, presiding over the Delmas trial, admitted all of the video material including that which had been edited. Although this also allowed the defence to use video material, the implication that edited film and video can be used in political trials without cross examination and without having to prove its admissibility is disturbing. As we know, there is nothing "true" about images, especially images which have been edited. In addition, it means that these images are being taken as "the truth" without anyone responsible having to authenticate them or stand up to cross examination as to their veracity or their context. It also means that the invisible filmmaker can be turned into an unwitting state witness in political trials.

For the subject of the film or video it means that what he/she utters in a specific context for a specific film can be used to compromise him or her at an altogether different time. This is particularly dismaying in South Africa where what is legal one month might not be the very next. Moreover, as in the Delmas case, not only did the legal status of what was being said change, but so did the entire political climate. When the meetings which were filmed took place, there was no State of Emergency. When the speakers were convicted, South Africa was enduring its third Emergency.

The broad implication of the Delmas trial is that people discussing political events in front of a camera cannot ensure that it will be used in context, the transgressor being not the filmmaker but the court, which, if this judgment is accepted as precedent, does not have to question whether the material is authentic "evidence."

Another trend is equally disturbing. It is almost commonplace for there to be some repercussion for subjects who appear in controversial documentary films of a political nature. Although publicity, especially in the foreign media, often offers a form of protection to opponents of apartheid—witness the untouchable status of people like Archbishop Desmond Tutu—appearance in a film often angers the South African government and security forces. Some subjects are questioned by the police, harassed or even detained. Worse still, there is a nagging unease in the air among filmmakers that a number of recent political assassinations were not unrelated to the fact that the victims had appeared in documentary films, especially films receiving a lot of publicity. These subjects in turn often gave evidence "on camera" about security-force excesses. Doctor Fabian Ribiero and his wife were murdered in the township of Mamelodi outside of Pretoria shortly after he appeared in American producer Sharon Sopher's *Witness to Apartheid* (1986). In the film he presented "evidence" of security force brutality in Mamelodi township. Ribiero's murderers have not been found.

Seventeen-year-old Sicelo Dhlomo "gave evidence" in CBS's *Children of Apartheid* (1987) about his own torture while in detention without trial. Within two months he was found dead in an open lot near his home in Soweto with a bullet through his head. Neighbors heard the shot. Shortly before his death he had been questioned by the police about his statements in *Children of Apartheid* and several other interviews he gave. His murderer(s) have never been found despite public assurances by Minister of Police Adriaan Vlok that the police were doing all they could to bring the perpetrators to court.

Other cases are less well known. Subjects appearing in the BBC's *Suffer the Children* (1987), also about children under apartheid, detention, and torture, have also been harassed. Zweliswa Mhlawni, a journalist from the Cape Town community newspaper *Grassroots* who was interviewed in *Suffer the Children*, was shot in the eye several weeks later while walking down the street.

There is no direct evidence of any of these deaths being the result of the victim's film appearances. But as long as there is any doubt, it must make all documentary filmmakers feel uneasy and perhaps even curtail their activities. That, perhaps, is the whole point. Many filmmakers are prepared to risk their films being banned, or even their own safety, but not many will knowingly put their subjects at such serious risk.

The proverbial moral responsibility of the documentary filmmaker carries slightly more serious connotations, therefore, when applied in the South African context. Filmmakers are not only responsible to their audience, they are equally accountable to the subject who might voluntarily give an interview without understanding the implications of doing so. This dilemma especially applies to children. Since "children under apartheid" seems to be a growing sub-genre of documentary films made about South Africa, South African filmmakers are trying to address this issue, even though the three films mentioned above were made by foreign filmmakers coming into South Africa for a short period of time.

The possibility of film so directly bearing witness and implicating and identifying people is obviously extremely serious. Whereas print journalism can always cite a source "who asked not to be named for fear of repercussions," the equivalent in television journalism has never been as satisfactory. Subjects filmed in the dark, from the back, or South African-style with a balaclava over their heads, are clumsy at best and more often read as shifty or "not quite authentic." Presumably this is because film, being iconic, demands pictures, gobbles faces and sadly often spits them out when it is finished with them. Sicelo Dhlomo appeared on Walter Cronkite's *Children of Apartheid* under a pseudonym, something which would be sufficient protection in print but not on screen. One is reminded of Sol Worth's dictum, "Pictures can't say ain't": they cannot present conditionals or counterfactuals, they cannot say "sometimes"; they cannot say (without the help of a narration), "I am a real witness but unfortunately have to temporarily hide my identity"; they have to speak in the present, positive tense; they must, in fact, bear *direct* witness.[17] That has been their historical role and the locus of their power.

It is this ambiguous relationship to reality, its ability to give evidence with the power and eloquence that has given the cinema its particular position in relation to political struggles around the world. It is the reason why the South African government is prepared, in the middle of an economic recession, to spend 30 million rands on a film subsidy scheme; it is the reason why filmmakers in South Africa and other areas of political conflict are harassed; it is the reason why their subjects are harassed, detained, killed. And it is also the reason why, even knowing the risks involved, people are still prepared to give evidence to the camera, to allow images to bear witness to their lives.

Chapter 22 / Oral History and South African Historians

Paul la Hausse

The Times of Swaziland   Monday, June 22, 1987   5

Mr R.S. Mambo, of the Swaziland Oral History Project, which is housed at the National Archives in Lobamba, demonstrating to students of the Mater Dolorosa School how to conduct an interview, using a tape recorder.

MDS students get into history ... practically

In 1961, Jan Vansina elaborated a methodology by which African oral traditions could be gathered, transcribed, and compared to produce raw material for the construction of a new African history. As the methodological backbone of the new discipline of African history, oral history promised to recover the "lost voices" of the African past. Vansina's seminal work (translated into English in 1965) captured the imagination and helped mold the concerns of a new generation of historians working in Africa at a time when large parts of the continent had only recently achieved independence from colonial rule.[1] David Cohen, Stephen Feierman, and Joseph Miller, among others, employed the techniques of oral history to produce pioneering studies of precolonial African kingdoms which appeared to justify the value of oral tradition as a historical source.[2]

This new concern with oral tradition as history made itself felt among a small but influential group of South African historians, most of whom were based in the School of Oriental and African Studies at the University of London during the late sixties and early seventies. Their collective concern was to explore the emergence and dynamics of African polities in the region and their transformation under the impact of colonial rule. One of the first of these scholars to enter the field was Philip Bonner, whose work on the evolution and dissolution of the Swazi state bore the imprint of a wider Africanist concern with oral tradition.[3] Similarly, the work of Jeff Peires on the Xhosa, William Beinart on the Mpondo, and that of Peter Delius on the Pedi all attempted to weave chiefly, clan, and other oral narratives gathered in the field into their respective studies.[4] All these histories, however, employed oral tradition less extensively than had been the case among scholars of Central and East Africa.

At one level the explanation for this can be found in the nature of the colonial experience in South Africa: one legacy of an extended colonial presence was a uniquely rich and substantial body of government and mission records which historians put to extensive and imaginative use.[5] But it was not simply that historians retreated into the uniquely musty security of South African archives. While field research in the subcontinent exposed rich veins of oral tradition, in many regions this was not the case.[6] Particularly among African communities which had been radically fragmented by industrialization, oral traditions bore traces of written historical sources to a degree seldom encountered elsewhere in Africa. To some extent these more intractable problems associated with oral tradition presaged a shift in South African historians' engagement with oral history: Beinart's research on Pondoland, for example, which extended well into the twentieth century, indicated the value of life histories in exploring broader structural processes of rural differentiation and labor migrancy. Similarly, Delius, on the completion of his research, pointed to life history interviews as "the most potentially fruitful area for oral research in South Africa."[7]

The intellectual terrain upon which early work on precolonial and colonial South African societies had been founded was being rapidly transformed, not least due to the emergence of a critique of liberal South African historiography which changed the face of southern African studies.[8] By the late seventies, South African revisionist historians, variously critical of and influenced by a rising tide of dependency theory, Marxist political economy, and French structuralist anthropology, were already seeking to redefine their original Africanist project within a Marxist mold.

The new body of radical literature profoundly challenged previous explanations of the trajectory of capitalist development in South Africa. At the same time, the new radical preoccupation with questions of capital and the state tended to obscure an understanding of those conflicts, struggles, and experiences through which the African working and middle classes were forged in industrializing urban and rural South Africa. The resurgence of African working-class organization during the seventies provided an impetus for historians to move beyond political economy and to explore the relationships between class formation, political consciousness, and culture. A new "history from below" was thus born of the realization that the black working class had its own traditions, cultural consciousness, and forms of self-organization. The new history also owed an important debt to a particular Marxist intellectual tradition embodied in the labor and social history of British and American scholars: most notably, E. P. Thompson, Eric Hobsbawm, Eugene Genovese, and Herbert Gutman.

For oral history, the implications of these developments were significant. As historical research shifted its focus to industrializing South Africa in the twentieth century, it revealed the rich potential of oral testimony in the writing of histories which recovered the subjective popular experiences of social change wrought within living memory. The value of oral testimony in general, and life histories in particular, was also anticipated during the seventies from a less immediately obvious direction. Thomas Karis and Gwendolen Carter's documentary history of opposition groupings in South Africa—and particularly their biographical profiles of political figures often forgotten or unknown—drew renewed attention to the unevenly explored history of black political organization and protest in South Africa.[9] Perhaps even more significant in retrospect was the extended oral research of Tim Couzens in recovering the life and work of South Africa's first major black playwright, H.I.E. Dhlomo, and that of Brian Willan in his biography of pioneering African nationalist, Sol Plaatje.[10] These efforts to gather oral testimonies coincided with increasing international debate around the practice of oral history,[11] and were rooted in a wider impulse to retrieve the frequently hidden history of largely illiterate underclasses in a society where the past has been suppressed, forgotten, and distorted in a variety of complex ways.[12]

During the course of the eighties, the techniques of oral history, used largely in conjunction with more conventional archival sources, have not only illuminated aspects of popular experience, culture, and political organization, but have also exposed new areas of historical investigation and served to mold the theoretical contours of an emergent South African social history. The value of oral history has been most clearly demonstrated in historical research on the South African countryside, an area in which conventional archival records reveal little about the nature of social relations. In the work of Tim Keegan, for example, oral testimonies of members of the rural underclasses—peasants, sharecroppers, labortenants, and laborers—are used to support discussion of wider processes of social and economic change.[13] Perhaps the most ambitious project in this regard is the current research of Charles van Onselen, which explores rural production and social relationships in the industrializing Southwestern Transvaal for the period 1914–66 through an extensive series of biographical interviews with Kas Maine, a black sharecropper.[14]

Moving beyond biography, the recent studies of Patrick Harries and Jeff Peires record and reflect critically upon regional and community-based oral narratives of particular processes of rural impoverishment and dispossession which have been so central to the experience of black South Africans.[15] In recognizing the uneven impact of industrialization and capital accumulation in South Africa, recent historical work supported by oral testimonies has begun to explore the implications of differential processes of proletarianization for particular forms of rural political organization and struggle. Notable in this regard is Helen Bradford's study of the largest mass movement in South African history—the Industrial and Commercial Workers' Union.[16] Bradford is able to move well beyond the formal institutional confines of the I.C.U. by employing a series of interviews with elderly men and women who witnessed the spectacular spread of the union's branches in the countryside. Used in conjunction with especially rich archival records, these testimonies provide a powerful sense of the variety of ways in which the rural poor in different parts of South Africa interpreted the message of union organizers in terms of local traditions of resistance, inherent ideologies, and particular shared historical experiences.

In situations where people remained fiercely attached to their rural identities and productive resources, the questions of land and livestock dominated their political responses.[17] This was no less the case for labor migrants, as the current research of Peter Delius on the Sekhukuneland revolt (1958–60), and William Beinart on the Pondoland revolt (1960) suggests. Both Delius and Beinart rely on extensive oral evidence as one of the few ways of reconstructing the world of African migrant experience. They explore the often contradictory nature of migrant consciousness, as well as the forms of migrant association which provided a crucial context for the revolts and limited the role of national political organization within them.[18]

The notion of limits imposed on formal worker organization by forms of migrant association and modes of consciousness is at the heart of Dunbar Moodie's reappraisal of the 1946 mineworkers' strike. Supported by the oral testimonies of Mpondo migrant workers, Moodie charts the rise of the African Mine Workers' Union and the events of 1946 within the framework of the particular moral economy, repertoires of collective worker action, and migrant networks which characterized the *milieu* of mine and compound.[19]

The use of oral history has enabled South African historians to construct a culturally sensitive understanding of class, compelling them to relate issues of class formation to those of ethnicity, community, gender, youth, and the family. In Jeff Guy and Motlatsi Thabane's study of the way in which Basotho mineworkers mobilized their rural ethnic identity to gain control of shaft-sinking on South African gold mines, the authors' starting point was to take subjective expressions of such identity seriously.[20] Similarly, Ari Sitas's study of migrant cultural formations and trade unionism on the East Rand during the post-1972 period pays close attention to the ways in which workers understand their world in terms of commonsense ideas and creatively respond to it through a collectively-constituted moral order and the formation of defensive cultural networks.[21] The studies of Jacklyn Cock and Eddie Webster echo Sitas's concern with the working lives of people. Both use individual life histories to uncover the nature of working experiences in the household (in the case of Cock) and the metal foundry (in the case of Webster).[22]

Among a growing number of urban social historians, oral history is being used in an effort to deepen understanding of urban communities and the fabric of their social, economic, and cultural life. Philip Bonner's remarkable research uses oral material to explore the history of a criminal Basotho migrant organization within the context of the changing forms of social life, family structure, youth organization, and political struggle which characterized the Witwatersrand in the post-1930 period.[23] In some of my work I have used interviews to understand the patterns of migrant youth organization in an early urban setting, now largely obscured by the emergence of an African youth culture rooted in South Africa's sprawling urban townships.[24]

Finally, retrieving the history of working-class life in urban communities destroyed by the *apartheid* state after 1960 would have been inconceivable without the insights of oral history. Two such communities have been the subject of research by Iain Edwards and Bill Nasson.[25] Edwards' research on Cato Manor in Durban and that of Nasson on Cape Town's District Six depict socially differentiated communities which nevertheless forged a powerful sense of their own identity, based on largely defensive cultures, networks of self-help, and populist, sometimes undemocratic, politics.

The growing preoccupation with oral history since the mid-seventies has resulted in the establishment of regionally-based oral history projects concerned to document aspects of popular experience in industrializing South Africa—particularly where these have passed unrecorded in archival records. The first oral history project was initiated by the African Studies Institute at the University of the Witwatersrand in 1979. The major part of what is now known as the M. M. Molepo Oral History Collection comprises an oral history of proletarianization in the countryside. For nearly a decade, the life and work experiences of the rural underclasses, as recalled for the period 1890–1945, have been extensively recorded. The gathering of oral testimonies has been concentrated in the Transvaal countryside, where interviews have been used to refract the changing nature of social relations and productive forces in the wake of South Africa's industrial revolution. In the western Transvaal in particular, these processes have been mapped through an extensive and richly detailed series of interviews.

The project also incorporates collections which explore particular dimensions of rural experience. For example, there is now a set of fifty-eight in-depth interviews with African women from Phokeng which explore, among other things, family structures, the economic history of the family, and the nature of migratory experience. The collection now comprises well over six hundred interviews. More than two hundred of these have been transcribed, translated (mostly from Setswana and North Sotho), and typed up in standard format. The second part of the project comprises a more broadly-based collection of around 450 interviews. Among these are trade unionists, political activists, literary figures, urban workers, and township gangsters.

The realization by the Killie Campbell Africana Library in Durban that oral history was a notable *lacuna* in its otherwise rich documentary archival holdings on Natal and Zulu history precipitated the creation of the University of Natal Oral History Project in 1979–80. The project originated in an attempt to "fill out the picture of evolving patterns of conduct of African people in the social, domestic and working spheres in the Greater Durban area and selected rural areas of Natal for the period 1900 to 1970."[26] Between 1979 and 1982 (when the project was terminated), 240 interviews were conducted. During the course of fieldwork, the focus of the project was broadened to include, for example, interviews with members of the Zulu royal family, township administrators, early African National Congress politicians, and members of KwaZulu government. Many of these interviews were conducted in Zulu and all of these have been translated. Most of the interviews have been transcribed, indexed, and, as is the case with other oral history collections, the material is available for consultation by researchers, except where informants have requested confidentiality.

The potential of clearly focused oral history projects to generate particularly useful documentary material is demonstrated by the South African Institute of Race Relations Oral History Project (1982–84). This project comprised three discrete interviewing programs on Hurutshe resistance to state policies in the Western Transvaal during the fifties, African dockworkers in Durban, between 1940 and 1980, and Indian hawkers in the Transvaal from the 1940s. In all cases the interviews were edited and published in booklet form in order to make the collective experiences which they recorded accessible both to the social groupings from which they derived and to a non-academic audience in general.[27]

The attempt to recover the history of urban and rural communities, sections of an emergent working class or members of a fractured middle class—most of whose voices remain indistinct or silent in archival records—is not simply rooted in sentimentality. The historical contribution of many groupings to the making of modern South Africa has been significant but often unrecognized. The Oral History Project established at the National University of Lesotho in 1982 aimed to recover one of these unwritten histories: that of Basotho workers on the South African mines. Its objective has been to record, transcribe, and translate the personal testimonies of men from Lesotho who had worked on the South African mines, "in order to gain not only a greater knowledge of the changing work experience of Basotho miners in South Africa but also new insights into the history of mining itself—from the viewpoint of those who did the mining."[28]

As has been previously noted, the rise of organized labor in the early 1970s encouraged historians to use oral testimony to refine their understanding of the processes and struggles which shaped the development of social classes in South Africa. The massive urban popular protest which characterized the early eighties made this task—particularly the exploration of class in relation to culture and community—more urgent for many historians. In 1985, historians at the University of Cape Town launched the Western Cape Oral History Project which aims firstly, to collect life histories of residents and ex-residents of inner Cape Town, an area of tremendous social and economic change in the last eight decades and composed of a rich diversity of social activities, ethnic groups, self-employed people, and working-class patterns of life. Secondly, the project has undertaken an oral history of African immigration and informal settlement in Greater Cape Town. Bill Nasson anticipates that participants in this project "will hopefully see more and more of the history of [Cape Town's] working people from their own perspectives: not just buckling under the weight of capitalist exploitation and class oppression, but making their own cultural worlds and attempting some self-realization within them."[29] No doubt these are expectations which have been at the heart of the various oral history projects over the past ten years.

If the value of oral history has been increasingly evident in local historical research over the last few years, so too have the problems involved in gathering and utilizing oral material. Where the researcher is unfamiliar with African languages or local *patois*, the question of accurate transcription of recordings and the implications of the use of interpreters have emerged as most obvious problems. In a society where interviewing can be potentially hazardous for both interviewer and informant, the conditions under which interviews have been conducted are seldom indicated in research.[30]

For South African historians who have only relatively recently begun to explore and debate the value of oral testimonies as an historical source, it is perhaps hardly surprising that the local historiography does not evince the same level of methodological engagement to be found among oral historians in the United States, Britain, and Europe. No doubt part of the reason for this also stems from the fact that oral sources have invariably been used in conjunction with a range of more conventional archival sources. Indeed, where oral testimonies have provided the bulk of primary sources for historical studies, South African scholars have been at pains to use this material critically. The tendencies toward the romanticization of the past, the elision of class differentiation in accounts of community life, the blurring of myth and reality and the ways in which evidence has been molded by the ends of both interviewer and informant, have been explicitly raised and explored.[31] Through the practice of their craft, historians have begun to confront a range of complex methodological issues raised in the large comparative literature on the use of oral testimonies as historical sources: the structure of memory and its relation to social process, narrative forms, and conventions; issues of representation; the role of the unconscious in oral history.[32] In the South African context some of these concerns have been raised in the work of literary critics such as Isabel Hofmeyr and Stephen Clingman.[33]

Of course there are still large areas of historical enquiry in South Africa which would benefit from the careful use of oral evidence, perhaps the most obvious being the story of rural Afrikaner proletarianization and the making of South Africa's ruling classes. It needs to be recognized, however, that the use of oral history, while still in its early stages, has established significant roots in a new South African historiography.

Chapter 23 / **Staffrider** *Magazine and*
Popular History:
The Opportunities and Challenges
of Personal Testimony

A. W. Oliphant

Cape Youth Congress meeting in KTC squatter camp, Cape Town, 1986. The photograph was published on the cover of *Staffrider*.

Staffrider, the South African cultural magazine, first appeared in March 1978, almost two years after the Soweto uprisings of 16 June 1976, and approximately six months after the banning of the political, educational, religious, and cultural organizations which, according to the South African government, were responsible for the upheaval. The first edition of the magazine carried a series of personal testimonies of ordinary people who lived in Soweto. Such personal narratives, presented at the time as a way of turning "every man into an author," came to be seen as one of the principal tools of popular historians to uncover the perceptions and experiences of working people.[1]

This paper provides an overview of these personal testimonies and assesses whether, as popular histories, they enhance the historical consciousness of their authors and audiences. After considering earlier popular histories and outlining the origins and aims of *Staffrider*, I will examine some of the interviews published in the magazine. My argument is that oral testimonies or life stories, regardless of whether they are solicited through community or academic institutions, invariably fall short of their declared social transformative aims if they are not consciously situated within the broader historical context. Moreover, the efficacy of popular history depends on the extent to which it is reinserted into the community from whence it came.

The oral testimonies published in *Staffrider* since 1978 were not the first attempts to record and disseminate the experiences of blacks in South Africa. As early as 1916, Sol Plaatje, the Secretary of the South African Native National Congress (later the ANC), published a comprehensive account of the effects of dispossession among the rural African population caused by the Native Land Act of 1913.[2] Between the 1930s and 1950s, an era which saw the rapid proletarianization of the African population, the South African Communist Party (SACP) contributed historical articles to party publications and other journals. Although most of these articles were not oral histories, they aimed to uncover the struggles of workers.[3] In the 1960s, the Nationalist government suppressed these early SACP histories along with the journalistic and biographical writings of Es'kia Mphahlele, Can Themba, Bloke Modisane, Nat Nakasa, Casey Motsisi, and other writers associated with *drum* magazine.[4] This large-circulation tabloid focused on the social and cultural lives of urban blacks.

The apparent acquiescence in the aftermath of these bannings was followed by a resurgence of educational, cultural, labor, and political resistance in the early 1970s. This movement was led by Black Consciousness organizations with strong Africanist orientations. It culminated in the Soweto uprisings of 16 June 1976, precipitated by school pupils protesting against Bantu education.[5]

Following the Soweto uprising, the government banned virtually all progressive black organizations. To fill the gap created by these bannings, Mike Kirkwood, the newly appointed manager of Ravan Press, and Muthobi Mutloatse, a journalist and current manager of the black publishing house, Skotaville Publishers, perceived the need for a community-oriented magazine. The magazine's objective was to provide a forum for the cultural groups that were emerging out of the black townships. Included among these groups were the Bayajula Group in Kwa Themba, the Kwanza Group in Mabopane, the Mpulanga Arts Group in Natal, the Creative Youth Association Group in Diepkloof Soweto, and the Khauleza Group in Alexandra.

Staffrider took its name from those dare-devil commuters who, in the words of Mike Kirkwood, rode illegally "on the fast, dangerous and overcrowded trains that come in from the townships to the city, hanging on the sides of the coaches, climbing on the roof, harassing the passengers."[6] The connotations of illegality, defiance, and risk conveyed the aims of the magazine's founders and situated it outside the institutional forms of South African life.

The magazine strove to implement a tenet of black self-reliance. Accordingly, a system of "self-editing" governed the editorial policy during the early years. The first issue carried a note of explanation: "We hope that the work appearing in this magazine will be selected and edited as far as possible by the groups themselves. The magazine is prepared for publication by Ravan Press but has no editor or editorial board in the usual sense. This is our policy: to encourage and give strength to a new literature based in communities, and to establish important lines of communication between these writers, their communities and the general public."[7] This attempt to overturn the top-down conventional editorial directives of institutionalized publications did however encounter various problems.

First, publication in the magazine was not restricted to submissions form black cultural organizations. Individuals across the country sent in stories, poetry, essays, interviews, photographs, and visual art, and these submissions were edited by a relatively permanent editorial and production staff at Ravan Press. Second, many of the cultural groups gradually dissolved as a result of the state restrictions placed on black communities. By the early 1980s, the *Staffrider* board terminated the self-editing policy and appointed Chris van Wyk, a black poet, as editor. This development coincided with the waning of Black Consciousness, the emergence of a non-racial national democratic movement, and the growth of a labor movement linked to the ANC politics of the 1950s and 1960s. The waning of Black Consciousness and the internal changes in editorial policies did not, however, affect the magazine's focus on the experiences of black South Africans.

In its tenth year, I became editor of *Staffrider*, and together with the staff at Ravan Press decided to reconstitute the editorial policy of the magazine. We set up an editorial board consisting of representatives from the literary, visual, and performing arts, music and theater worlds, and popular history. By drawing on a wide variety of disciplines, the magazine established links with the Congress of African Writers, the African Writers Association, the cultural department of the Congress of South African Trade Unions (COSATU), and other progressive intellectuals.[8]

This broad-based editorial board both provided advice and direction to the editor and served to ensure that the magazine retained a broad popular perspective and upheld the principles of non-racialism and non-sexism. The magazine remained committed to disseminating the views and experiences of all South Africans and attempted to assist in the creation of an inclusive, non-sectarian South African culture.

To facilitate the dissemination of such a culture, various literary and artistic groups took responsibility for the distribution of the magazine. When these groups collapsed, individuals based in the townships together with formal commercial distributors brought the magazine to readers countrywide. In a time of renewed repression, *Staffrider* is now re-establishing informal networks to ensure that the magazine reaches students, workers, cultural activists, and writers' groups throughout the country.

From its inception, *Staffrider* has published stories, poetry, plays, essays, visual art, and social documentary photography as well as interviews with writers, musicians, and working people. One of its most striking features was its regular column "Soweto Speaking" in which the writer Miriam Tlali presented the experiences of various people living in Soweto. The column was later extended to include contributions from the organized labor movement and academic institutions engaged in oral history projects. The personal testimonies can be grouped into four categories: basic life testimonies of Sowetans; stories of trade unionists' lives; testimonies compiled by university-based oral history projects; and interviews with popular performers, musicians, and writers.

In analyzing these various kinds of testimonies, I will examine what differentiates them, assess whether they succeed in providing popular and accessible historical accounts of working people in South Africa, and finally, determine whether such testimonies can empower people and facilitate working-class emancipation. The first two types of testimonies, those solicited by the Soweto-based writer, Miriam Tlali, and those written by workers, share a common feature: both were presented by people with close ties to the communities whose experiences they were recording. The university-based oral history project interviews, however, were generally conducted by people removed from the experiences of the person or community they were investigating.[9]

Tlali's column emerged out of her book, *Muriel at Metropolitan*, based on the author's experiences while working at a furniture store. The book was inspired by Studs Terkel's *Working*.[10] Following Terkel's lead, Tlali published personal testimonies of three Soweto residents in the first issue of *Staffrider*.

The first interview was with a retired driver who had been employed by a sales company. At the time of the interview, he illegally sold vegetables and poultry to supplement his inadequate pension. His testimony recalled his years as a driver for a white salesman. He spoke of their interdependence and relatively close relationship which invariably ran into the alienating forces of apartheid: the white salesman, for example, had access to countrywide hotel accommodation while he, as a black man, had to make do with backrooms and servants' quarters. He tells how after driving all day they would arrive at a hotel: "Then when we get there 'partheid' starts again. He goes to the nice part of the hotel, and I go to the servants' quarters. Sometimes it is cold and there is no fire in those rooms. All a lot of sh— man!" After retirement, the white salesman occasionally visited him in Soweto. This came to an end with the uprising in 1976: "We were just like brothers. He still comes to see me sometimes.

But now since the fighting in 1976 he has not come. He is afraid." The rest of the testimony bears witness to rent evictions, police harassment, and state indifference to the needs and problems of local residents.[11]

Tlali conducted her second interview with a self-employed dress-maker, Mrs. Leah Koane, who embarked on a home industry after working for several years in a factory. "You had to work hard and sew many, many garments per day—but when you get your pay, it would not be the amount of labour you put into your work. It was so little! One day I thought seriously to myself and said, no! No, I can't work so hard for another person. I went and bought my own machine. I stayed at home and worked at home."[12]

Tlali drew the third testimony from the experiences of a market researcher whose field of expertise was black consumer preferences for insecticides. The researcher describes some of the difficulties she encountered in her work, including the tendency of people to regard all enquiries with suspicion: "Sometimes they become suspicious. They ask, 'Why are you asking me all these questions. You want to put me in trouble? You want to put me in gaol? Why are you asking me to sign my name?' But you go on anyway. They're always suspicious. They think everybody is a spy." When asked about her future plans, she pointed to problems she was having in educating her children: "First I'll take my youngest son to boarding school. Anyway outside. In Soweto there is no hope. What shall we do, children have to learn something. But not Bantu Education. We must do the best under hopeless conditions. . . . What is to be done? Personally I cannot see what the wisdom of it is. Taking children from one Bantu Education to another Bantu Education. What's the use of sending your child to a Bantu Education boarding school? That's what happening. Pointless."[13]

These first three testimonies set the tone for much of the content, structure, and orientation of the other testimonies drawn from Sowetans during the self-editing phase of *Staffrider*. Their value resides in the attention they draw to some of the issues which precipitated the Soweto uprisings. The effectiveness with which this is conveyed is, in retrospect, weakened by their dependency on readers' knowledge of the socio-political context. Thus, while the testimonies are most likely clearly understood by people with similar experiences, they fail to convey a coherent picture of the historical period. At most they catalogue some of the grievances that fueled the revolt while remaining virtually silent on the uprising itself. Ironically, no student testimonies were published during this period of intense student political activity. The publication of interviews seemed to operate on the assumption that the common experi-

ences of the black urban population were sufficient to develop a historical consciousness that would facilitate effective opposition to oppression.
It could also be argued, however, that it was imprudent to publish testimonies which contained explicit references to the uprising and the role
of the Soweto community in it. The validity of this reticence is borne
out by the fact that the first edition of *Staffrider* was banned and that one
of several pieces considered "undesirable" by the State Director of Publications was Mariam Tlali's short story entitled, "Soweto Hijack: A Story
of Our Times." The story demonstrates how fiction, rather than personal
testimonies, can more fully convey the repression and resistance of the
period.

The author recounts how the police intercepted buses taking Soweto mourners to Kingwilliamstown for the funeral of the Black Consciousness leader, Steve Biko, who had died in police detention on 12
September 1977. The story recaptures Tlali's experiences of police violence: "The policeman held in his hand a revolver with its mouth pointing into the man's terrified, blinking face. 'I can shoot you now, and
there's nothing you or anyone can do to me!' "[14] Tlali contrasts this brutality with the resolve of the community to carry on resistance, even in
prison: "The floor inside the cell where we were lying seemed to quaver
as the bare young feet thundered on the cement floor outside. They
declared: 'Thina silulutsha/ Singeke sibulawe/ Ngama-Banu—Sililut-
sha' [We are the youth/ We shall never be destroyed by the Boers—We
are the youth]." The Directorate of Publication considered this story to
be subversive since "the authority and image of the police, as persons
entrusted by the State with maintaining law, internal peace and order, are
undermined."[15]

In the early 1980s, a number of factors resulted in a shift in the editorial policy of the magazine. As the cultural groups succumbed to the
government clamp-down on community activities, the editorial board
stopped publishing material under the name of the communities or cultural organizations from which contributions came. Moreover, in response to the growing labor movement, testimonies began to focus on
workplace struggles. *Staffrider* published these stories in a new column
called "Staffworker." The first such story appeared in the April/May
edition of 1981. In light of its relatively early publication of worker stories, it is ironic that criticisms were later levelled at the magazine for the
perceived absence of such stories and of a materialist analysis.[16]

One of these first worker testimonies, "Factory Worker's Story,"
relates the experiences of Simon Kumalo in fighting efforts by white
workers to reimpose segregated ablution facilities at a Colgate-Palmolive

factory. Kumalo noted: "When the signs of discrimination were re-moved we were called in by the liaison committee, and advised that discrimination in the company's facilities had been ended, so we've got the right to use what was once for whites." However, when Kumalo tried to use the shower facilities, he was ordered to leave. He reported the matter to management but pressure from white employees resulted in the building of new "separate but equal" facilities for blacks. According to Kumalo, "up to this date no black goes near the whites-only change rooms or uses the white only toilets. The story all happened to me in 1977." The black workers linked this affair to a general dissatisfaction with the role of the management-initiated liaison committee. When their grievances were not taken up by their committee representative, they decided not to re-elect him or anyone else and to join a union. "We as the workers went out in search of the union," Kumalo stresses, "the union didn't come to us." These factory workers became members of the Chemical Workers' Industrial Union against the wishes of management: "Once we were organized, we wanted management to know that we were now members of a Chemical Workers' Union and we made man-agement aware through a petition which was signed by all the workers who were members of the Union. By this time it was the majority of the workers."[17]

A similar story is told by Lawrence Mshengu, a shop steward in a chain-store in Natal. He too complains of the autocratic nature of super-vision: "In 1977 I was employed by OK Bazaars. From the beginning I had many hardships. The hardships I had was not because I could not do my work but because of the way we were treated by employers, *indunas* and *impimpis. Indunas* are workers but they do not go along with the workers' struggle. They are individualists who tend to side very much with the employers. Their friendship with employers results in the op-pression of workers."[18] Mshengu also testifies to the failure of manage-ment-imposed liaison committees, and the subsequent unionization of the workers as members of the Commercial, Catering and Allied Work-ers' Union.

As union members, Kumalo and other workers learned of their rights as workers as well as the need for unity. He concludes by empha-sizing the purpose of his testimony: "I wrote this story so that those who read it will gain from it, so that you too will have the courage to know about your rights. So that you know that you will not get your rights unless you struggle hard for them."[19]

These worker testimonies differ from the Tlali histories in so far as they focus on workplace struggles. In addition, they do not aspire to turn workers into authors or to make publishing history, but are almost exclusively governed by the desire to impart information and experiences to fellow workers. Unlike Tlali's histories, the worker testimonies make their social transformative aims explicit; in Tlali's stories this aspect is muted and articulated more in the form of personal survival. What, however, is common to these two types of testimonies is the fact that those conducting the interviews shared close community and class links with the people being interviewed. As well as this, both types require a knowledge of the surrounding context if they are to be understood, and neither make any attempt to link personal accounts to the broader society and history.

In 1984, *Staffrider*, in conjunction with the Oral History Project based in the African Studies Institute at the University of the Witwatersrand, published an example of the third form of personal testimony under the title "Popular History." This story on the "Widow of Phokeng" reveals the shortcomings of the first two types of personal testimonies and highlights the skills required to construct popular histories. The story succeeds in integrating the personal testimony of a working woman into broader historical, political, and cultural events.

The history recalls the experiences of a woman who left her home in the village of Phokeng, in the Rustenberg area, for Alexandra Township in Johannesburg. She married in Alexandra and continued to live there for thirty years, from 1930 to 1961. During this period, she worked as a domestic worker in the white suburbs. Because her income was inadequate, she, like many of her Soweto counterparts, combined this occupation with sewing at home and selling apples on street corners. She was also politically active, participating in the Alexandra bus boycotts of 1940 and 1942. In 1955, she marched with thousands of other women to the Union Buildings in Pretoria to petition against the Nationalist government's plans to extend the pass system that regulated freedom of movement, to African women. She was arrested and defended in court by Nelson Mandela.[20]

Unlike the other vignettes, this interview combines personal testimony with historical, political, and cultural contextualization. It also carries a more limiting difference, namely that it was constructed within an academic institution which does not have the same close links with the communities in which this woman lived. While the Tlali and worker testimonies establish a rapport with people who have had similar experiences, they lack historical contextualization and coherence; indeed, they are hardly more than the basic materials from which popular histories are constructed. The academic popular histories, on the other hand, provide coherent historical pictures but are prone to be alienated from the class or community for which the histories are written. If these histories are not returned to the communities, they are in danger of remaining merely scholastic forms of research, accessible only to specialists in the field. The broader historical perspective which these histories provide must become part of the self-understanding of the people they represent.

If popular histories, which rely on personal testimonies, are to achieve their aim of providing oppressed groups with the means of self-conceptualization, then the immediacy of these testimonies must be located in broader historical processes. Since this skill has traditionally been the preserve of academics, the obvious challenge is to render it available to those nonacademic groups involved in popular history projects. In other words, oppressed communities engaged in effective struggles for social transformation must demand the democratization of institutions of knowledge and research, and institutions supportive of these struggles must meet the responsibility both to return the results of their research back to the communities from which they were drawn and make available to these communities the skills that would enable them to go beyond the rudimentary step of testimony. Community publications such as *Staffrider* have a role to play in this process by publishing popular and oral histories which are fully placed within a broader historical setting.

Chapter 24 / **Developments in Popular History in the Western Cape in the 1980s**

Andre Odendaal

John Berndt

Logo of banned cultural festival in Cape Town, 1986.

The Western Cape is today one of the most active South African centers of the writing and production of history. It probably also has the longest tradition of popular history in the country—a tradition closely linked with resistance politics. It goes back, among other things, to the emergence of alternative newspapers such as *The South African Spectator* and *A.P.O.* in Cape Town in the first years of this century;[1] to the newspaper articles of Eddie Roux and fellow workers in the 1930s;[2] to the radical analyses of the Teachers League of South Africa (TLSA) and the Non-European Unity Movement (dealt with elsewhere in this volume by Bill Nasson); and to the *New Age* articles and pamphlets of the 1950s written by people affiliated to the Congress Movement and the Communist Party, most notably Lionel Forman.[3]

As the struggle against apartheid and capitalism intensified in the 1970s and 1980s and a new radical South African historiography started making an impact, a tremendous revival in popular history writing occurred in the Western Cape. A network developed including political and support groups, resource centers, alternative bookshops and newspapers with various degrees of support from college- and university-based academics. These groups focused on reinterpreting the past and making it accessible as part of the contemporary struggle. The emphasis on a long history of resistance has been integral to the political mobilization and resistance process, particularly among the so-called Charterist supporters who lay claim to and call upon a tradition of resistance which goes back to the formation of the ANC in 1912, and before.

The popular history produced during the eighties has emanated from three main areas: community-based organizations, educational institutions, and trade union oriented groupings. Among the latter, the Labour History Group (LAG) and the International Labour Research and Information Group (ILRIG) have been the most important. LAG, formed in

1981, but now unfortunately virtually moribund, aimed "to research, write and publish booklets that tell the history of the labour movement in South Africa for workers whose home language is not English."[4] It published seven booklets: on the Industrial and Commercial Workers Union (ICU); the 1922 white mineworkers strike; working-class mobilization in the 1940s and 1950s; the 1973 Durban strikes; and a more specifically local history of dockworkers in Cape Town. Most of the booklets have been translated into Zulu, Xhosa, Afrikaans, or Sotho.[5] ILRIG was established in 1983 as a resource service "to produce education materials and collect information on international labour issues" for unions and other progressive organizations.[6] Its activities include preparing dossiers for unions and running courses for shop stewards. Like LAG, with which it cooperated closely, ILRIG has published a number of booklets. In its series "Workers of the World," topics covered include the history of May Day and the history of workers' struggles in Botswana, Bolivia, Brazil, and Mozambique.

While the above groups serviced the labor movement, the Educational Resource and Information Centre (ERIC), the *Grassroots* community newspaper, and others fulfilled—on a larger scale—a similar role for the emerging community and political groups that coalesced under the umbrella of the United Democratic Front (UDF) in 1983. They held workshops and produced resource packages, audiovisual material, and articles with a strong historical content. With a circulation of up to 40,000, *Grassroots* and its junior counterpart for schools, *Learning Roots*, reached a wide audience. The activists who staffed these groups played roles as mass mobilization became the order of the day in the mid-eighties. These groups, involved primarily in the national rather than the workers' struggle, seldom concentrated specifically on history writing. The only formal popular history publication written from the national perspective during the early eighties was the booklet, *The Struggle for the Land*, produced by the academically linked Economic History Research Group.

Academic institutions at first lagged behind in making accessible popular material in a politically relevant form. The academics connected with the groups mentioned above were involved informally outside academic structures. An exception in this respect was the South African Council for Higher Education (SACHED). Through projects like Turret College (and later Khanya College, which offers pre-university bridging courses), SACHED experimented with alternate courses and multimedia approaches aimed at challenging conventional ideological bias in the teaching of history.[7] It made special efforts to make education accessible to workers, adults, and disadvantaged people, and published *Up Beat*, a children's magazine featuring regular historical pieces.

There were also popular history activities outside of the more structured frameworks discussed above. As is widely recognized by now, the oppressed have for centuries passed down historical knowledge from one generation to the next, mainly through oral tradition, even though they were excluded from the "South African History" of the ruling classes. People and groups outside the arena of formal university scholarship still draw on this well of historical knowledge. An example of this in the Western Cape is the work of Achmat Davids, whose writing on the history of the Moslem community in the Cape draws largely on the community's own accumulated knowledge. The influence of popular tradition can also be seen in some of the publications produced by religious and community groups that have appeared in recent years. A good example is the people's history booklet on Claremont produced by the United Women's Organization as part of its campaign against Group Areas removals.

While the early 1980s saw the development of various organizations producing and propagating popular history, the insurrectionary climate of the mid-decade provided the impulse for a flowering of popular history in a multitude of different guises. The strength of resistance and organization, manifested in the drive for people's education and people's power, created a great demand for more structured alternative channels to make history available to the masses. It bound much more tightly together the different strands of activity described in the previous paragraphs. People's history classes flourished in schools as pupils took control of the classrooms and decided what they wanted to study. Activists organized workshops and strained distribution networks to ensure that the necessary material reached the schools. Organizations held education and training seminars. Community groups set out to write local histories. School teachers formed organizations to address the history teaching issue. Academic historians were drawn closer into the arena of struggle and started looking at course content and teaching methods—in some cases tentatively, in others aggressively. As Luli Callinicos has observed, "Ultimately, popular history is located in the present . . . it starts from the need to understand and directly *confront*, not the past for its own sake, but present-day situations and problems."[8] Nowhere was this more true than in the heady atmosphere of revolt in the Western Cape in 1985–86.

The most important of the many notable advances was, undoubtedly, the formation in 1986 of the National Education Crisis Committee

(NECC), a national coordinating body which started directing the anti-apartheid school and educational struggles of that time. Its regional affiliate in the Western Cape was very active, and people from Cape Town were also involved in the NECC's History Subject Commission. The History Commission's aim was to help draw up a syllabus which could be implemented in schools in place of the official syllabus, putting into effect the popular slogan of "People's Education for People's Power." The workbook, hurriedly prepared for this purpose, was compiled mainly by Cape Town-based academic activists.[9]

The official school textbooks generally negate, ignore, and distort black history and consist of "great slabs of names and dates and details" constructed upon "a platform of Verwoerdian pseudo-anthropological and thoroughly racist assumptions."[10] The NECC workbook, in contrast, emphasizes a collective, critical, open-ended approach to history. Instead of a question-and-answer format, it consists of thirty-seven group "activities" intended to make students grapple with historical issues and differing interpretations, and at the same time develop their speaking, reading, and writing skills. The experiences of black South Africans form the basis of the material.

The History Commission's regional working group in the Western Cape was working on various follow-up projects to the history booklet when the banning of the NECC, early in 1988, effectively put an end to its work. Before this, the regional NECC and History Commission drew community, school, and university-based historians into a tighter working relationship, and gave political coherence to their work. Here, representatives of the three local progressive teachers' organizations worked together with academics from the universities and activists from a number of community and youth groups.[11] The NECC's profile was boosted by regular workshops, political programs, social activities, and media coverage in which people's history usually featured prominently.

The uprising and the ensuing organizational developments significantly challenged prevailing academic ideas about the nature of historical research, teaching, and writing. The result of this was a flurry of activity at both the radical, black University of the Western Cape (UWC) and the liberal, historically white University of Cape Town (UCT). Academics debated issues such as curriculum content, teaching methods, accountability, and the production of such multi-media popular-history presentations as documentaries, slide-shows, plays, and easily accessible publications. At UCT, for example, the Community Education Resources (CER) project was launched in 1985 with the following aims:

1) To facilitate the use of the research, resources, and skills of the university by progressive organizations and the oppressed community.

2) To bring ideas and experience gained in the process of servicing progressive organizations (in particular the building of links with the democratic movement) back into the university environment.

3) To pursue research and produce material in an accessible form which can be utilized by the oppressed community.[12]

The research has a strong historical bias, focusing on precolonial hunter-gatherers and herders, and the struggles of farm workers as well as struggles around local government. Post-graduate students are employed to rework their research for popular consumption.

At UWC, the Department of History launched a People's History Project in 1986, becoming probably the first history department in the country to identify formally with and attempt to institutionalize at university level the demands of the mass-based democratic movement for people's education. Employing the language of resistance, the department declared that the university could not be politically neutral, and that history had to be made meaningful for its students, who are drawn from the oppressed communities.[13] The project encourages a participatory and collective approach to learning. It stresses "the role of the masses in the making of history and aims to give the students a sense of themselves as historical subjects, as people who have roots and who participate in the making of history."[14]

The two thousand or more students in the department discuss the theory and methodology of People's education before going into communities to do research on the "hidden" history of the oppressed— preferably in cooperation with local organizations. In 1987, the first annual People's History Open Day was held on the campus in collaboration with the NECC, to round off that year's People's History program. The program included films on struggles in South Africa and other countries, workshops for primary-school children and teachers, exhibitions and stalls, music, poetry readings, a play, and a session devoted to oral history. The oral history workshops were mostly run by community groups and involved rural activists from the 1950s, women and youth involved in local struggles, people from country areas who had been dispossessed of land, and family and friends of people who had been killed or jailed for ANC underground activities. Around one thousand people attended, drawn from a wide range of schools and organizations, including more than a hundred people from rural areas such as Worcester. At the same time the first two publications in a UWC People's History Series, *Let Us Speak of Freedom* Nos. 1 and 2, were published. Produced by a community group, they dealt with the history of resistance in South Africa up to the late 1920s. Before they were banned by government censors a few weeks later, several thousand copies of each booklet had been distributed throughout the Western Cape region through the effective alternative political and educational structures which had emerged during the 1980s.

The above developments illustrate the fact that even in the universities traditionally wedded to elitist notions of "history," the discourse of people's education has gained a foothold; and that the campuses are now beginning to interact with and service the community in a much more accountable and relevant way. This is a reflection on the superstructural level of the changing balance of forces in the unfolding struggle in South Africa. These activities also reveal something of the context, growth, organization, style, and political focus of popular history in the Western Cape during this decade. It has been a dynamic process, though not without certain problems and contradictions. Unfortunately it is not possible to "problematize" the process and analyze in depth the material produced in a short overview such as this.

The massive counterrevolutionary onslaught launched by the state in 1987–1988 has undoubtedly rolled back in the short term many of the political and educational gains of the 1980s—in the Western Cape as well as nationally. The experiment in people's education has been temporarily disrupted. The banning of the NECC and the outlawing of people's education in African schools are just two manifestations of this. Yet, despite intense repression, the drive to popularize history and apply it as an instrument of struggle against apartheid continues both on and off the campuses. One of the community-oriented agencies referred to above, for example, is currently involved in a historical project drawing in Youth Congresses and Students Representative Councils in the schools. An organizer has been employed to coordinate the project. The purpose is to galvanize local communities into recovering their own history and to encourage the process of political mobilization.[15] The militancy and historical consciousness of the mass-based opposition in South Africa remains as strong as ever and, in a technological age, the production of alternative historical materials continues to be a powerful weapon of struggle.

Chapter 25 / The Write Your Own History Project

Leslie Witz

The Write Your Own History Project, set up in March 1986 under the auspices of the History Workshop and the South African Committee for Higher Education (SACHED), aimed to encourage ordinary people in South Africa to write their own history. In this sense, the establishment of the project followed the lead of groups set up in Britain and the United States in the 1970s such as the Baltimore Neighborhood Heritage Project, the Brass Workers History Project, the Hackney History Project, and others which attempted to involve communities in the researching and writing of their own history.[1] But in one crucial aspect the Write Your Own History Project was different: it attempted to promote a *critical* engagement with the past. This paper attempts to provide the background against which the project was established, analyze its practice, and evaluate the extent of its success.

The Establishment of the Write Your Own History Project

The mid-1980s was a period of intense political activity in South Africa. This was reflected in the images of violence in South Africa's townships which appeared on television screens across the world (excluding state-controlled South African broadcasts). Behind these superficial images was a great deal of discussion and debate among extra-parliamentary opposition groups about how to develop alternative structures in South Africa, particularly in education. Activists and academics alike placed a great deal of emphasis on history, aware that the evocation of mass anti-apartheid campaigns in the past could serve as rallying points for political struggles in the present.

With the regular use of history in mass political meetings, the relationship between critical history and political activism was, not surprisingly, hotly debated at the History Workshop conference in 1987. When Graeme Bloch, a political activist and academic, argued that the "criteria of academic excellence are, perhaps, only secondary to the task of integrating a historical consciousness in the daily lives of the oppressed majority," many academics were horrified.[2] "In this type of suggestion," argued one academic, "lay the dangers of populist excess."[3]

History Workshop set up the Write Your Own History Project to take this debate a step further. Rather than argue over how the past should be represented, the organizers of the project felt it was far better to give ordinary people the historical tools to engage with the past; to empower ordinary people to become producers of their own history.

It was significant that the two main promoters of the project were the History Workshop and the South African Committee for Higher Education (SACHED). The History Workshop, a group of academics mainly based at the University of the Witwatersrand, had, up until 1986, primarily concerned itself with producing history. Now it wanted to empower ordinary people to become producers of history, producers who would engage with the past critically by examining a variety of sources, detecting bias, and evaluating evidence. Cooperation with SACHED, an educational organization whose major aim is to counter imbalances created by the apartheid education system, was also vital for the project. SACHED is "committed to establishing participatory, non-discriminatory and non-authoritarian learning processes. It seeks to transfer skills and resources in such a way that organizations, communities, and individuals are empowered to take charge of their own projects."[4]

Having committed themselves to the project, SACHED and the History Workshop had to find a way of making historical skills, which previously had largely been the preserve of academics, more widely accessible. Should they, for instance, produce a cook-book type manual with a step-by-step approach of how to research and write history? As anyone who has been trained as an academic knows, there are no predetermined rules that one must follow. Indeed, historians generally learn much more through the actual experience of engaging in research and writing than by following set precepts. How then was the concept of the *process* of researching and writing history to be promoted?

In March 1986, SACHED and the History Workshop appointed me as project coordinator to facilitate this process. My first task was to set up groups of people who would write their histories. Then, through skills workshops, I would assist these groups in writing history. Second, I would make contact with other groups in southern Africa which had been, or were, involved in similar history writing projects. Finally, with the help of the SACHED publishing project and the History Workshop, I would produce a book reflecting the experiences of all these groups, to encourage other individuals and organizations to engage in the process of writing history.

The Practice of the Write Your Own History Project

My first task as project coordinator was to find groups that would research and write history. After discussions with SACHED and the History Workshop, we decided to draw upon as wide a range of people as possible—rural communities, students, workers, women, urban communities, elderly people, and youth. However, there were obstacles to achieving this initial broad outreach. First, the limited resources of the project made it impossible to draw upon different groups with all these different components. The political context also made it difficult to find groups who had time to devote to this project. Although there was a keen interest in history, most groups felt that the political struggle was their primary concern into which all their energies had to be channelled.

Despite these difficulties, we made contact with three groups (workers, students, and rural youth) who decided, in June 1986, to embark on the Write Your Own History Project. The first group came from Kagiso, a township on the West Rand, near Johannesburg. Many of the residents of Kagiso work in the nearby industrial area of Chamdoor, either in light manufacturing industry or in the nearby slaughterhouse. This area has been the scene of attempts to unionize workers over the past few years, with the assistance of organizations like the Young Christian Workers (YCW). The group who worked on the Write Your Own History Project from Kagiso were all members of this organization. "If you are organising in a factory," said Myboy of YCW, "you need to know about past struggles in the industry to help you organise effectively. By asking why things happened we can learn from our mistakes and successes and build up strong worker organization."[5] Myboy, a worker in a ceramics factory, and Pogiso, who worked at the slaughterhouse, therefore decided, with permission from their organization, to write a history of the YCW.

The second group in the project came from Soweto, the massive township which borders on Johannesburg. At the time of the project, they were all studying for their graduation exams at the Witwatersrand Council of Churches (WCC) tuition project in Johannesburg. Although they were very young at the time, the four participants—Rosalee, Myra, Tshepo, and Steve—had all experienced the Soweto riots of June 1976 when there were massive protests against the inferior education to which blacks in South Africa were subjected. Much has been written about the revolt, but Steve, Myra, Tshepo, and Rosalee decided to write about these events from a family perspective. As products of inferior "Bantu education" which virtually ignores the history of South Africa's blacks, they saw writing history as an opportunity to give another version of history than the one which is taught in schools. "We need to find information that has been left out of the school history textbooks and what has been distorted," commented Rosalee.[6]

The group of rural youth came from the settlement of Driefontein in the south-eastern Transvaal, about 220 miles from Johannesburg. Driefontein is a farm that was purchased in 1912 by a consortium of black business people for blacks to live and farm on. It is surrounded by land farmed by whites and is thus, in the government's terms, a "black spot" in a white area. From the 1960s the government consistently attempted to remove the people of this "black spot" to the areas reserved exclusively for black settlement, the so-called homelands. Under the leadership of Saul Mkhize, the community resisted this scheme. In 1984, a member of the South African police shot and killed Mkhize while he was addressing a local meeting. The policeman was acquitted of murder, a decision which the community found difficult to accept. But it did not abandon its struggle against the removal, and in 1985, after sustained pressure from within South Africa and from abroad, the South African government allowed the Driefontein community to remain. The leaders of the community decided that they needed to document this struggle for their land, so they nominated a group of youth belonging to the Driefontein Rebuilders Youth Club (DRYC) to write a history of Driefontein, *Umlando We Driefontein*.

Once the groups were set up, we began to explore the research and writing skills that they would need to craft their respective histories. We were specifically concerned with the skills of making notes, chronological sequencing, defining questions, conducting interviews, and evaluating evidence. In each case, I handled the development of these skills in a different manner, although the underlying premise was that learning is *not* the filling of empty vessels but, rather, the mobilization of the vast resources and skills people have at their disposal, which have not yet found expression.

I held the most structured workshops with members of the YCW group. Activities on the various skills with accompanying worksheets formed the basis of these meetings. For instance, the group had to construct chronological tables and formulate questions on a specific event, the 1946 mineworkers strike. These assignments helped them to define their own topic more closely. In addition to the workshops, we went on a field trip to the archives of the University of South Africa in Pretoria where YCW documents are kept. At the archive the YCW members learned how to find documents and make notes that selected the relevant information.

In the case of Myra, Steve, Tshepo, and Rosalee from the WCC tuition project, the workshops were much less structured. I responded more directly to requests for assistance from the group. For instance, members of the group started interviewing very early on in their project, but found that they were encountering problems. People were reluctant to speak to them, they arrived at interviews only to find that the tape recorder did not work, or when they did conduct interviews there was so much noise on the tape that they could not hear what the interviewee had said. So we arranged a workshop on interviewing techniques where these problems were talked about and possible solutions discussed. After this workshop WCC members were much more at ease when they conducted their interviews.

This group in particular struggled with the issue of critical engagement with the past. Should they include information in their history which would put political organizations in a bad light? At a workshop to discuss this issue, a debate took place between Steve and Rosalee.

> STEVE: All history is written from a point of view and so it has to be biased. To further our cause we can also be biased. Our aim is to achieve a political goal.
>
> ROSALEE: Then what we are writing is propaganda and not history. We must include both the good and bad things if we want people to respect our work.
>
> STEVE: What you are saying could destroy our struggle.
>
> ROSALEE: No, exactly the opposite. By leaving out information, in the future a situation might arise when that information is what we need. What do we do then? We have to learn from our history to help develop our organizations.[7]

Only through discussions within the groups and with other organizations could important issues like these be resolved. Indeed, when this group presented its work at the History Workshop in February 1987, it engaged the audience in debate on this issue rather than presenting a resolution.

With Driefontein located a long way from Johannesburg and the scarcity of telephones in the area it was difficult to keep in close contact with this project. I spent nearly a week at a time in the area and helped the participants in the process of researching and writing the history. In the morning we would go out interviewing people and then in the evening discuss the major points that had come out of the interviews and set the agenda for the next day. In this way, through the actual experience of conducting research, the Driefontein youth developed historical skills.

While these groups were sharpening their skills, they made contact with similar local history projects in southern Africa to learn from their experiences. Particularly close contact was established with the Swaziland Oral History Project, the Transvaal Chinese Association History Project, and the Grahamstown Oral History Project.

In Grahamstown, the history project formed part of an effort to bring about change in the community. The youth were trying to form street committees, clean up the township, and provide parks for people. In their efforts to take control of their own lives, they did not want to wait for other historians to write about their past: "We wanted to explore the history of ordinary working people, their leaders and the ways in which they have organised themselves in their struggle against the oppressive apartheid system."[8] By writing about these experiences, the Grahamstown Oral History Project not only recorded the past but also encouraged others in the community to help them in their political struggles.

The Transvaal Chinese Association Project, as the name indicates, is researching the history of the Chinese community in this region of South Africa. The Chinese community in South Africa is very small, but this project is uncovering a part of the past that is not very well-known, even among the community itself.

The history that the Swaziland Oral History Project is researching stretches way back into the eighteenth century, long before there was any written documentation in the region. They therefore have to rely for their evidence on an exceptionally rich body of oral traditions with a unique chronological depth. A member of the project, Carolyn Hamilton, points out that the survival of these traditions is a consequence of "the relative stability of the Swazi kingdom and its high degree of centralisation."[9] The Swaziland Oral History Project collects these traditions through interviews and aims to make them accessible through history tours, school books, and media productions. They also encourage and facilitate the establishment of write your own history projects in Swaziland, particularly at school level.

After doing their research, all the groups presented their histories. In February 1987, at the Popular History Day during the History Workshop conference, the students from the WCC tuition project and the members of the Grahamstown Oral History Project gave talks about their respective pieces of research. The Grahamstown project, in addition, had prepared a paper on the history of workers struggles in Grahamstown which they handed out to their audience.

Both the YCW and Driefontein groups have written their histories in draft form, the latter in Zulu. Although they have not yet presented these it to a wider audience, various organizations and individuals have expressed an interest in publishing them.

The Transvaal Chinese Association and the Swaziland Oral History Project have both produced slide-tape shows. In the Swazi slide show, *Mr Big Beaten by History*, precolonial Swazi history is presented to a modern world. In addition, the Swazi project has encouraged others to write their own history. Thus, with the assistance of the project, students at Mater Dolorosa School in Mbabane compiled an exhibition in June 1987 about the history of their school.

The Write Your Own History Book

Up until this point, the Write Your Own History Project involved a relatively small group of people. We now wished to broaden the appeal of "writing your own history." This was to be achieved through a book drawing on the experiences of the three groups initially involved in the project.

Regular meetings were held with academics from the History Workshop who provided their expertise on two levels. First, they conveyed their own experiences in mastering technical aspects. In interviewing, for example, they stressed the necessity of conducting follow-up interviews. Second, the History Workshop academics wished to ensure that the producers of history would conduct histories that would critically engage with their sources. An activity which involved the reader in evaluating evidence from a court case, for example, arose out of discussions with the History Workshop.

Members of the SACHED publishing project edited and designed the book, taking particular care to make it accessible to a wide audience. This involved very careful language editing to help those for whom English is a second language. We included photographs and illustrations of the various groups doing the research and writing to enable the reader to identify more closely with the process of historical research.

Prior to completing the manuscript, we sent it out to a wide range of worker, student, community, and teacher organizations for comment.

On the whole, their responses were most favorable. The language of the book and its easy writing style were particularly praised. However, three aspects of the manuscript came in for a great deal of criticism. The first was the relationship between empirical research and theory in the book. The book, many argued, placed too much emphasis on empiricism as the way to write history. Everything seemed to be deduced from the evidence. "There is a great danger in this method of history becoming too empirical—losing sight of trends, analysis, country-wide patterns and becoming an end in itself," commented one of the respondents. The second problem was that the book did not reflect the likelihood of people not being able to finish researching and writing their history. Some felt that the manual should prepare people for this possible eventuality. The last section of the book on presenting the history was perceived as unrealistic and very thin. One person suggested that it would be useful to show different ways of presenting histories.

The SACHED publishing project, the History Workshop, and I reviewed these criticisms. To a large extent we found ourselves in agreement with the points raised and I altered the manuscript accordingly. It was difficult to know how to encourage theoretical considerations in history writing in an accessible manner. Although the book already emphasized finding different sources and trying to work out their bias, this now had to be taken a step further. So we added a new section on evaluating evidence, in which readers are presented with various different versions of a history and asked to choose the most valid. The section is written from a theoretical perspective, inviting readers to build conclusions on their own experiences and ideas, as well as listening to and reading about other people's views. In this way, the book encourages the development of theoretical ideas to engage the past. "It is our point of view which influences how we interpret what happens in our society."[10]

The second criticism proved to be just as difficult to overcome. How could we introduce the possibility that projects may not be finished without discouraging people from starting the process at all? The solution lay in stressing the value of the process of historical research and writing. Thus the book urges people not to be discouraged if they do not have enough time to write up their history: "The information that you have collected is very valuable. You have also learnt a great deal about how to write history. Store your information in a safe place so that you or someone else can use it in the future."[11]

The third issue involved thinking about how history could be presented cheaply. I first suggest that there are many ways to present history: "You may think that because you've written your history you have to put it in a book. But there are many other ways in which you can present it. You can present a talk, stage a play, make a tape for people to listen to, put on an exhibition, write a column in a newspaper, make a slide show or even a movie."[12] Then the costs of each of these different forms are estimated to enable readers to establish the feasibility of making a specific presentation.

Write Your Own History was finally published in 1988, by SACHED and Ravan Press. The book is divided into five sections, each reflecting a different element of the process of researching and writing history: Why Write History?; Starting Out; Collect the Information; Writing the History; and Present Your History. The various pilot groups relate the process that they went through, the problems they encountered, and how they overcame them. Readers are thus able to identify with the experience of people who were involved in the project rather than being presented with prescribed, sometimes abstract, concepts with which they have to deal.

A number of activities accompany each section, each relating to history writing skills. These activities are based on the worksheets which were developed in the skills workshops. There are activities on technical and critical skills, including how to evaluate evidence, draw up an interview outline, and find books in a library. One of the most crucial objectives of these activities is to help develop a critical understanding of the past. One activity asks the reader to find bias in newspaper reports, another is concerned with interpreting interviews, and a third asks the reader to evaluate the evidence that was presented in a court case.

At the end of the book, we have included a list of organizations that people can refer to for help when writing their histories. An extensive reading list of books on southern African history is also provided.

Evaluating the Project

In terms of its initial objectives it would seem that the Write Your Own History Project has been a success. This has been reflected in the distribution of the books, the completion of the project by the various groups initially involved in it, and the confidence gained by the participants. SACHED and Ravan Press are distributing *The Write Your Own History* book through bookshops, at worker and community organization meetings, and at teachers' workshops. The groups that began the project all went through the process of researching and writing their histories. To various degrees they have produced histories, although some of them have not, as yet, managed to present their work. The involvement of the participants in the project also went a little way toward developing the skills and confidence of the participants. Pogiso is now an organizer for Young Christian Workers. Steve and Rosalee are both history students at the University of the Witwatersrand, and Tshepo took up a scholarship to further his studies in Britain. They have begun to acquire more control over their own lives.

It is more difficult to evaluate the success of the long-term objective of the project, namely to encourage other individuals and organizations in southern Africa to embark on history writing projects. But there are clear indications that there is more than a passing interest in "write your own history." At the University of the Western Cape, for instance, students at undergraduate level are involved in a people's history program which entails researching the history of various communities in the region. A similar project is run at Khanya College, a pre-university college with campuses in Johannesburg and Cape Town. At certain schools, like Mater Dolorosa in Swaziland, pupils are doing historical research and writing. *Write Your Own History* is also being used in a trade union education program. A group of people from an asbestos mining area in the Northern Transvaal have started looking at the effects asbestos has had on their lives and their families over the years.

While, at this stage, it might not be true to say that history is being written to any great extent by ordinary people in South Africa, the first steps are being tentatively taken along that road. For, like the many groups in Britain, the United States, and elsewhere in Africa that are writing history themselves, South Africans are starting to realize that writing history will give them power, "power to understand, power to resist and power to work towards change."[13]

Chapter 26 / *Every Picture Tells a Story, Don't It?*

Joshua Brown

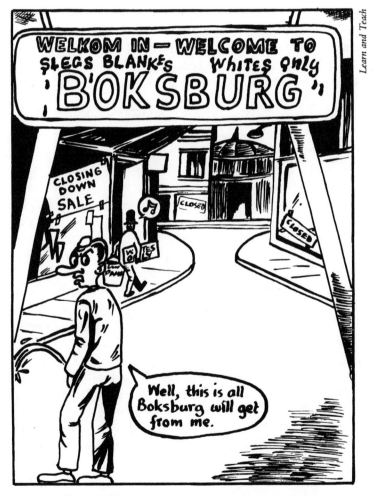

Mogorosi Motshumi's "Sloppy" in *Learn and Teach*.

At the opening of the first exhibition of South African "alternative comix" in 1987, one of the more influential members of the small community of underground cartoonists commented: "The comix scene in South Africa is pitifully retarded." The reasons, Andy Mason concluded, "undoubtedly have to do with cultural isolation as a result of apartheid and censorship."[1]

In light of the impressive array of popular political art that has emanated from South Africa in the last decade, Mason's self-deprecating comment seems apt. Amid the songs, theater, poetry, fiction, photography, posters and t-shirts (perhaps the most ubiquitous of "people's art") that have emerged from the anti-apartheid struggle, the relative absence of alternative comix and cartoons is marked. But if the comix-scarcity is the result of "cultural isolation," as Mason suggests, we might then ask why other popular arts have thrived. Perhaps, paradoxically, the limited appearance of alternative comix is based in part on cultural *influence* from abroad, on the uncomfortable fit between the perceived needs of a South African political movement and a popular art form whose aesthetics and conventions derive from the United States.

The independent cartoonists whose work appears in the two sporadically-published South African comix anthologies, *Pax* and *Icy Blind* (published in Durban and Johannesburg respectively), clearly have been inspired by the American underground comix of the 1960s and 1970s. Leafing through *Pax*'s pages, for example, one immediately sees the influences of Robert Crumb, Gilbert Shelton, "Spain" Rodriguez, and Greg Irons, as well as traces of the so-called "new wave" comics of the 1980s (exemplified in Art Spiegelman and Françoise Mouly's *Raw*). Underground comix in the U.S. were part of a broad, amorphous counterculture that interwove aesthetic and expressive experimentation with the often equally amorphous ideologies of a left political movement. The appellation *comix* indicated the undergrounds' iconoclastic response to the repressed sensibilities evident in the costumed-superhero, code-approved *comics* since the mid-fifties. It was an anything-goes approach that prompted the largely male contingent of alternative cartoonists to investigate the lighter and darker sides of their psyches (aided by ample doses of controlled substances). But, for anti-apartheid activists in South Africa, alternative comix inspired by the uninhibited "personal-is-political" productions of the American undergrounds may appear self-indulgent under conditions where every expression is judged by the political freight it carries. Within a movement culture demanding clear, accessible and programmatic messages, the form and content of underground comix lack the grim determination of "useful" agitprop.[2]

Nevertheless, there have been indications of appreciation for sensibilities that we might loosely term "alternative." Zapiro's 1987 United Democratic Front calendar displayed a lively, full-color cartoon replete with a range of activist "types" doing battle with the state and, to a more limited extent, each other. The calendar was an instant hit, and activists went scrambling for the few available copies once the government, less reluctant to recognize the ideological power of humor, banned its publication.[3] Similarly, thousands of readers continue to enjoy the misadventures of "Sloppy" that appear regularly in the anti-apartheid literacy magazine *Learn and Teach*. Mogorosi Motshumi's Sloppy is a township resident who, originally, possessed certain characterological traits similar to those of Ernest Riebe's "Mr. Block," the capitalist dupe who appeared in the pages of the Industrial Workers of the World's (IWW) *Industrial Worker* during the second decade of the twentieth century. Unlike his predecessor, Sloppy's thinking has matured over the last few years and he has gained a certain amount of political integrity, even though he remains subject to an unconscionable number of pratfalls. Motshumi's cartooning is hardly professional, his rendering is raw (and oddly reminiscent of "Archie" comics), and his compositions unartful, yet Sloppy's trials and tribulations while trying to earn a living or just plain relax within the confines of township life resonate with the experiences of his readership (as indicated in *Learn and Teach*'s letters column).[4]

Some of South Africa's cartoonists have gone in another direction, one that also derives its inspiration from an off-shoot of underground comix in the United States. Educational comics or "nonfiction cartooning" comprise "a scattered archipelago" in the larger field of American alternative comix. They range from the "For Beginners" histories inspired by the Mexican cartoonist Rius (including Larry Gonick's *Cartoon History of the Universe* and the comic books published by Leonard Rifas's

Educomics), to sensational investigative narratives (such as the Central Committee for Conscientious Objectors' *Real War Stories* and the Christic Institute's *Brought to Light*) to autobiographical and oral-history accounts (Howard Cruse's *Wendel* and Art Spiegelman's *Maus: A Survivor's Tale*), to expressionistic agitprop (Seth Tobocman's *World War 3 Illustrated* and Sue Coe's *How to Commit Suicide in South Africa*). "Educational" comics share the one characteristic of experimenting with the form to convey information and political analysis. Yet, these comics—with important exceptions such as Nick Thorkelson and Jim O'Brien's *Underhanded History of the USA* and Ron Turner's *Slow Death*—did not emerge as a trend until the late 1970s, after the heyday of the undergrounds and, more significantly, the period of widespread social and political activism. And, as Leonard Rifas, American educational comics' most outspoken advocate, has sadly concluded, their present-day impact is minimal: "Many comic book fans are repulsed by any comic with even the faintest odor of the classroom about it, and many educators condemn the entire medium as lowbrow."[5]

But contemporary South Africa provides cartoonists with conditions of production that, potentially, could lead to educational comics having the kind of distribution and impact that American "nonfiction" cartoonists can only dream about. In sharp contrast to the United States, South African educational comics are being produced in the midst of a broad, if embattled, social and political movement. One of the important emphases of this struggle is alternative or "people's" education (where the schoolroom in the state-run educational system is a major locus of struggle). And, some of the most prominent organizations dedicated to alternative education have turned to the comic book, as well as other forms such as books and videos, as an accessible and attractive teaching tool.

In the present state of affairs, *potential* remains the key word. The number of educational comic books is small. The ground-breaking comic was Andy Mason and Dick Cloete's *Vusi Goes Back*, a densely-written and illustrated history of the South African countryside published in 1982 by Pre-Azanian Comix (the Durban publishers of *Pax*) in association with the Environmental and Development Agency, an organization dedicated to aiding black community organizing and self-help projects in the "bantustans."[6] In a similar fashion, the largest independent education program in the country, the South African Council for Higher Education (SACHED), has used comics in a number of its educational publications. Serialized comic strips based on popular novels and auto-biographies appear regularly in *Upbeat*, SACHED's monthly magazine designed for black teenagers. And now SACHED has embarked on a new series of "People's College Comics," beginning with two comic books: *Equiano: The Slave Who Fought to be Free* and *Down Second Avenue.*[7]

Equiano is based on the autobiography of the eighteenth-century black abolitionist, *The Interesting Narrative of the Life of Olaudah Equiano, or Gustavus Vassa, the African, Written by Himself*, published in 1789. The thirty-page comic book portrays Equiano's story from his kidnapping by slave traders through his experiences in Virginia, London, and the West Indies, to his eventual self-purchase and dedication to the abolition of slavery. The script by Joyce Ozynski and Harriet Perlman (edited by Helene Perold) presents the story through succinct narration and dialogue, modernizing and simplifying the formal structure of Equiano's eighteenth-century prose—although the dialogue in several key scenes is taken directly from the book. The script necessarily simplifies the "through-line" of Equiano's epic experiences, condensing time to create a coherent and direct narrative. Although one might quibble with some of these changes—adapting from an original text always involves judgments that will not suit every reader—the resulting narrative preserves the integrity of the tale.

Nevertheless, *Equiano* fails to convey the essence of the original book even as it successfully presents the sequence of its narrative. This is not due to the gulf between a complex text and simplified comic book (the old distinction I remember repeated to me *ad nauseam* when I cracked a *Classics Illustrated* comic instead of the classic). The impact of Equiano's autobiography lies, in part, in the passion and evocativeness of his writing, in the images that arise out of his compelling descriptions. It is the kind of writing that should work well in the comic-book form—if the conventions of the form are used inventively. *Equiano* fails to exploit the visual power of comic books to convey information and emotion.

Although this comic book has been handsomely produced—its full-color cover and interior design by Mary Anne Bahr and Zaidah Abrahams are distinctively inviting—much of the problem lies in the work of the artist, Rick Andrews. Cartoonists have their specialties; with the exception of certain virtuoso draftspersons, cartoonists tend to render some subjects better than others. In Andrews's case, broad compositions such as landscapes, maritime scenes and city views are often composed and drawn with skill and interest. On the first page of *Equiano* the reader is immediately attracted to the story by the representation of a West African village, especially the skillful use of chiaroscuro that suggests the harsh light of the midday sun. Or, later in the story, on one of his adventures after he has gained his freedom, we share with Equiano the wonder of viewing Mount Vesuvius erupting (although, as a colleague pointed out to me, part of the dramatic effect seems to derive from a point of view that could only be gained from a plane flying over the harbor of Naples).

........and to Italy, where he saw an eruption of a volcano, Mt. Vesuvius.

At his best, Andrews gives the reader a sense of time and place, endeavoring to engage the reader as a participant in Equiano's experiences through sensitive visualization of the past, filling in both qualitative and sensuous information that the text cannot convey. But Andrews's visualization has its limits and our participation is all too often disrupted by his depiction of people, both their individual characteristics and their physical relationships to one another. The drawing of faces and figures is almost always stiff and inexpressive. Faces lack individuality, are almost generic in their presentation. The faces of characters barely change as they traverse a range of emotions; we only know that characters are happy, scared, or angry because the words in the balloons indicate the emotions (although the lettering in the balloons could have employed the kind of typographical emphases used to great effect in many comic books).

This lack of skill would be less of a problem if the action in *Equiano* was depicted with greater concern for conveying drama. In fact, the first six pages are very compelling as we follow Equiano's kidnapping and experience on the slave ship. The compositions vary from panel to panel and the images successfully present the unfolding of a dreadful experience. But, all too soon, there is a numbing consistency in the compositions, only rarely interrupted by broader scenes. Figures are locked into static poses as they converse. We are dissociated from the story, reading balloons and viewing talking heads that move from extreme close-ups to flat, proscenium-like panels where people gesture stiffly. When Equiano confronts a crowd hostile to his abolitionist message, we see frozen shrugs, outstretched palms and pointing fingers, a panel that suggests hostility solely via the words displayed above the heads of the crowd. And scenes that seem to cry out for the excessiveness of expression, move-

ment, and point of view that characterize the action in superhero comics—for example, when Equiano demands his manumission and is physically abused by his captain-owner—here fail to communicate a sense of threat, intimidation or injustice.

The text carries the message, unaided by the images. By not expanding Equiano's tale visually, using the strengths of the comic-book medium in both telling a compelling story and communicating information, the reader is left with what is largely a reading experience. There are certainly occasions where a cartoonist endeavors to use a style that emphasizes the text (a purposeful strategy perhaps best used in Art Spiegelman's *Maus*), but in *Equiano* the effect suggests a lack of skill and undermines the larger presentation.[8] In a way, *Equiano*'s visualization of history emphasizes the "elementary" quality of the writing, designed for readers for whom English is a second language. The comic book therefore appears condescending, an aspect it does not deserve.[9]

It is striking to compare Equiano with its companion, *Down Second Avenue*. This second "People's College Comic," based on Ezekiel Mphahlele's celebrated autobiography published in 1959, originally appeared in *Upbeat* in 1981. Drawn by Mzwakhe Nhlabati, written by Lesley Lawson, and edited by Joyce Ozynski, *Down Second Avenue* is considerably shorter in length than *Equiano*, yet in twelve pages it much more successfully interweaves text and image.

Perhaps because of its severely circumscribed length, the narrative is much choppier than in *Equiano*; there are virtually no "scenes" that extend beyond one panel so that, in fact, the comic is largely composed of single-image incidents. The result is impressionistic yet the narrative flows, largely due to Nhlabati's artwork which gives the story variation and continuity. His style is more raucous than Andrews's, ranging from punchy, "cartoony" panels—characters' expressions and gesticulations wildly exaggerated—to much more circumspect, illustration-like pictures. The variation works well, despite moments where Nhlabati's skill falters, because there is a panache and wit in his work, a consistent and enthusiastic quality that transmits—anger in one panel and perplexity in another. It may not be the most sophisticated or well-rendered drawing, but when Nhlabati shows a cop slapping the young Mphahlele, it "hurts."

Finally, the drawings tend to fill out the spare narrative, presenting a nice sense of place whether it is a scene in a kitchen or in a township street. This may, in part, result from the artist's reliance on archival photographs, particularly (as indicated on the credits page) resource photographs of the Marabastad location in Pretoria where Mphahlele grew up.

A number of pupils decided to stay out of school to protest against our dismissal.

The class teacher said I was backward. But I could read fast.

I have evaluated these comic books using criteria that are distinctively American, assuming an impact based on pervasive visual sophistication in the United States. SACHED has conducted an evaluation of the effectiveness of *Equiano* and *Down Second Avenue* as teaching tools—including the utility of the supplementary learning "activities" that comprise the latter part of each comic book (which I have not addressed because of my own specific concerns). As one teacher remarked in SACHED's preliminary report, "visual literacy is learned and so is comic literacy and [neither] should . . . be presumed." Whereas the comic book is a familiar form in the United States, it remains somewhat exotic in South Africa, especially for many black students. Comic-book conventions that are accessible to virtually all American readers—such as the distinction between dialogue and thought balloons—are mysterious to many South Africans in a system that has successfully isolated accessibility to information and culture. Therefore, it appears that some of the qualities in *Down Second Avenue* that I've lauded tend to confound student readers while the very simplicity of *Equiano* permits greater readability. *Down Second Avenue*'s impressionistic narrative, where each panel is a discrete scene or argument illustrated by a pivotal moment (whether it shows Mphahlele's grandmother accusing him of cutting school or, as we saw above, a cop's slap), confused some students because the vignettes' resolutions were rarely presented either textually or graphically. These students were more comfortable with *Equiano*'s traditional narrative structure that gave scenes a clear beginning and end (not to mention an explicit lesson or moral).[10]

I am impressed by young readers' response to *Equiano*, but I would suggest that it is largely due to the attributes of the script. The pictures certainly seem to convey information to readers—anonymous comments by students clearly indicate they learned a lot about slavery from reading the comic book—but we are left to wonder how much more information could have been conveyed with greater attention to point of view, visual characterization, and detail.

Down Second Avenue is a much more nuanced and complex work, both pictorially and textually. I hope that the difficulty many students experienced with this comic book will not prompt SACHED to favor simplification or dilution, whether in narrative structure or visualization. On the contrary, if SACHED and other educational cartoonists and publishers take the form seriously, they should be promoting another purpose for the comic book in South Africa. To be sure, there is great value in using the form as a means to teach more traditional material, including reading literacy and historical knowledge. But what about the goal of visual literacy itself? How can the comic book contribute to teaching critical viewing or thinking about images, as distinct from sophisticated visual consuming? The answer does not lie in mirroring R. Crumb or Rius or Art Spiegelman. The very imminence of South African comic-book art is exciting to watch because the context of its production promises future experimentation and expression.

Chronology
South Africa, 1800–1990

1806	Britain takes permanent control of Cape of Good Hope from the Netherlands
1816–28	Shaka presides over formation of Zulu state; Mfecane (war between Africans in southeastern Africa)
1834	Cape Colony abolishes slavery, following lead of British Parliament
1836–40	Boers embark on Great Trek (migrations from eastern Cape to what became Orange Free State, Transvaal, and Natal)
1857	Nongqawuse catastrophe (Xhosa cattle killing)
1860	Indian labor introduced in Natal
1867	Kimberley diamond fields opened
1876–80	British and Boers initiate wars of conquest against Xhosa, Zulu, Sotho, and Pedi
1877	Britain annexes Transvaal
1880–81	Transvaal rebels against British rule ("First War of Independence")
1886	Witwatersrand gold fields opened
1899–1902	South African War ("Second War of Independence")
1900	Chamber of Mines forms Witwatersrand Native Labor Association to recruit black labor for gold mines (WNLA)
1902–10	Lord Milner, British High Commissioner, governs South Africa; reconstructs economies of Transvaal and Orange Free State, spurring industrialization centered on gold mining
1904	Lord Milner permits mining industry to introduce Chinese labor in gold mines

1910	Transvaal, Orange Free State, Cape Colony, and Natal join to form Union of South Africa; South African Party, an Anglo-Afrikaner coalition, forms government
1912	South African Native National Congress formed; changes its name to African National Congress in 1923 (ANC)
1913	Natives Land Act restricts future African land ownership to reserves, ultimately thirteen percent of nation's land
1914	Nationalist Party formed
1917–20	Black labor militance emerges on Witwatersrand
1918	Broederbond, an exclusive Afrikaner cultural and economic society formed
1919	Industrial and Commercial Workers' Union (ICU) formed; organizes urban industrial workers and rural peasants and labor tenants
1921	South African Communist Party (SACP) formed
1922	White workers engage in massive strikes and a revolutionary movement on Witwatersrand
1923	Industrial Conciliation Act grants rights of collective bargaining and industrial conciliation to all but African workers
1924	Nationalists head an alliance government with Labour Party Trade Union Congress, forerunner of South African Trade and Labor Council, formed; combines many white and some "Coloured" and multiracial unions
1924–36	Government passes legislation establishing segregation around nation
1928–30	ICU collapses
1930	White women enfranchised
1930s	Africans migrate in large numbers to urban areas
1932	South Africa leaves gold standard; boom follows
1933	South African Party and Nationalists form a Fusion Government, on basis of a "white labor" policy and maintenance of "white civilization"
1936	All African Convention formed; creates a united front to oppose segregationist legislation
1939–45	World War II spurs substantial increase in black industrial labor force
1941	Council of Non-European Trade Unions (CNETU) formed

1942	Black industrial workers engage in wave of strikes
1943	Non-European Unity Movement (NEUM) formed; establishes non-racialist, socialist movement led by western Cape intellectuals
1944	ANC Youth League formed; emphasizes boycotts, strikes, civil disobedience, indigenous leadership, national self-determination, and hostility toward communism
1944–50	Squatter campaigns on Witwatersrand proliferate
1946	Black mine workers strike
1947	India raises South African racial policies at United Nations; initiates international pressure on South Africa
1948	Nationalist Party wins national elections under slogan of apartheid or separateness; elected with a minority vote
1948–55	Government builds major black townships, including Soweto
1950	Suppression of Communism Act passed; Communist Party of South Africa disbands
1950s	Government tightens legislative framework of apartheid; passes Bantu Education Act, Separate Amenities Act, Group Areas Act, and Native Laws Amendment Act
1952	ANC launches Defiance Campaign against six laws, including: pass laws, Group Areas Act, Voter Representation Act, Suppression of Communism Act, and Bantu Authorities Act
1953	Nationalists win election with a comfortable majority for the first time
1954	South African Communist Party reconstitutes itself and goes underground
1955	South African Congress of Trade Unions (SACTU) formed; creates first formal alliance between independent African trade unions and those representing other races Congress of the People adopts Freedom Charter; Charter embodies ANC principles including affirmation of South Africa's multiracial character, nationalization of mines and banks, redistribution of land, universal franchise and provisions for labor laws and welfare benefits
1956–58	Women campaign against extension of pass laws to include African women
1959	Pan-Africanist Congress (PAC) formed; PAC adopts an anti-communist line, focusing on white and Indian influence in Congress Alliance

1959 (*cont.*)	ANC calls for international sanctions against South Africa Government launches its separate development theory; bantustans created as prospective "national states" for Africans
1960s	Most African colonies gain independence
1960	Police kill 67 African anti–pass law demonstrators at Sharpeville Government bans African political organizations
1961	ANC forms an underground military wing—Umkhonto we Sizwe ("Spear of the Nation") South Africa becomes a republic and leaves Commonwealth Albert Luthuli, president of ANC, awarded Nobel Peace Prize
1964	Rivonia Trial leads to imprisonment of ANC leaders, including Nelson Mandela and Walter Sisulu
1965	Government imprisons SACP leader Bram Fischer
1966	Prime Minister H. F. Verwoerd, architect of apartheid, is assassinated
1966–68	Lesotho, Botswana, and Swaziland become independent
1968	South Africa first excluded from Olympic Games
1969	Black Consciousness student movement forms South African Students Organization (SASO)
1973	Black labor movement re-emerges following large scale strikes in Durban
1974	Portuguese revolution led by armed forces who refuse to fight further in Angola and Mozambique Chief Gatsha Buthelezi revives Inkatha movement (modelled on 1920s cultural organization)
1975	Mozambique and Angola become independent
1976	African nations expand boycott of countries that have links with South African sports; boycott of Montreal Olympics
1976–81	South Africa grants "independence" to Transkei, Bophuthatswana, Venda, and Ciskei "Homelands" (they receive no recognition abroad)
1976–77	Students lead rebellion in Soweto and other African townships
1977	Steven Biko, Black Consciousness leader, killed Government bans Black Consciousness organizations Divestment movement spreads in America

1970s–80s	ANC intensifies its armed struggle
1979	Federation of South African Trade Unions (FOSATU) formed; creates a politically non-aligned union federation with a mostly black membership
	Azanian People's Organization (AZAPO) formed; serves as a Black Consciousness umbrella organization
1980	Black Consciousness-inclined Council of Unions of South Africa (CUSA) formed
	Zimbabwe becomes independent
1980–81	Student uprising in Cape
1981	Human Sciences' Research Council Report on Education in South Africa issued; in response to black educational upheaval, report calls for creation of equal education in South Africa
1982	National Union of Mineworkers (NUM) formed
1983	United Democratic Front (UDF) formed; creates loose alliance of anti-apartheid organizations
	New South African constitution allows limited "Coloured" and "Asian" participation in a tricameral parliament
1984	Bishop Desmond Tutu awarded Nobel Peace Prize
1985	Congress of South African Trade Unions (COSATU) formed; FOSATU and community-oriented unions merge with ex-CUSA mine workers
	Afrikaner Weerstandbeweging (AWB), para-military neo-fascist organization, formed
	Divestment movement revives
	Miners strike; township residents boycott rents; students boycott classes (slogan, "No education before liberation")
	Government declares first partial state of emergency in major urban areas
1986	Government declares second nation-wide state of emergency; renews it annually until 1990
	National Education Crisis Committee (NECC) formed; directs anti-apartheid school and educational struggles
	CUSA and other Black Consciousness unions merge into National Council of Trade Unions (NACTU)
1987	Angolan and Cuban troops defeat South African army in Battle of Cuito Cuanavale (southeastern Angola)
	Government bans twenty-six organizations
	Government repeals pass laws
1987–90	Squatter communities spread around main cities

1988	Government bans UDF; COSATU forms a structured alliance with local UDF groups; alliance becomes known as Mass Democratic Movement (MDM)
1989	Namibia becomes independent
1990	Government releases Nelson Mandela
	ANC and government begin negotiations
	ANC suspends armed struggle
	Black Consciousness and Unity Movement/socialist groupings reject negotiations with government

Compiled by Karin Shapiro

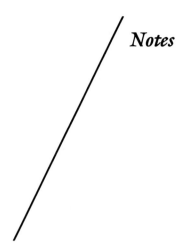

Notes

Chapter 1

1. Our pragmatic definition of the term "radical" refers to work which is concerned, broadly, with these specificities.

2. Our approach differs from that of other recent historiographical surveys, in that we concentrate mainly on the development of a radical tradition, rather than on its differences with other major approaches such as liberalism. For a broader overview see Ken Smith, *The Changing Past: Trends in South African Historical Writing* (Johannesburg, 1988); C. Saunders, *The Making of the South African Past: Major Historians on Race and Class* (Cape Town, 1988); S. Marks, "The Historiography of South Africa" in B. Jewsiewicki and D. Newbury, eds., *African Historiographies: What History for Which Africa?* (Beverley Hills, 1986); and Colin Bundy's chapter in this volume.

3. Sol T. Plaatje, *Native Life in South Africa before and since the European War and the Boer Rebellion* (London, 1917); James Henderson Soga, *The South Eastern Bantu* (Johannesburg, 1930); S. M. Molema, *The Bantu Past and Present* (Edinburgh, 1920) and *Chief Moroka* (Cape Town, n.d.); see also Z. K. Matthews, *Freedom for my People* (Cape Town, 1981) and D. D. T. Jabavu, *The Life of John Tengo Jabavu* (Lovedale, n.d.).

4. See, for example, E. M. Ramaila, *Setlogo Sa Batau* (Pretoria, 1938); M. M. Faze, *Abantu Abamnyama* (Pietermaritzburg, 1922); R. T. Kawa, *I-Bali lama Mfengu* (Lovedale, 1929); and P. Lamala, *Uzulu ka Malandela* (Mariannhill, 1930).

5. This tradition is discussed extensively in Lodge's chapter in this volume.

6. A small number of studies trace the left-wing heritage of South African Jews, notably Taffy Adler, "Lithuania's Diaspora: The Johannesburg Jewish Workers' Club 1928–1948," *Journal of Southern African Studies* 6:1 (October 1979); E. A. Mantzaris, "Radical Community: The Yiddish-speaking Branch of the International Socialist League, 1918–1920," and R. Krut, "The Making of a South African Jewish Community in Johannesburg 1886–1914" both in B. Bozzoli, ed., *Class, Community and Conflict: South African Perspectives* (Johannesburg, 1987). The myriad ways in which Jewish left-wing thought has

permeated the radical tradition requires further examination. Jewish communists, Trotskyists, trade unionists, and academic socialists have played a significant part in a variety of social movements and political and historical writings. See also S. W. Johns, "Marxism and Leninism in a Multi-Racial Environment: the Origins and Early History of the Communist Party of South Africa, 1914–1932," Ph.D. thesis, Harvard University, 1965.

7. The clearest statement of this analysis is to be found in J. Slovo, "South Africa" in B. Davidson, A. Wilkinson, and J. Slovo, *Southern Africa: the New Politics of Revolution* (Harmondsworth, 1976).

8. Discussed in more detail in Nasson's chapter in this volume.

9. Key works of these authors include W. M. Macmillan's *The Cape Colour Question* (London, 1927); *Bantu, Boer and Briton* (London, 1929); *The South African Agrarian Problem and its Historical Development* (Johannesburg, 1919); and *Complex South Africa* (London, 1930); and C. W. de Kiewiet's *A History of South Africa: Social and Economic* (Oxford, 1941), and *The Imperial Factor in South Africa* (London, 1937).

10. Imperialism was seen as "benign" in that it contrasted with settler rapacity.

11. See J. Lonsdale, "From Colony to Industrial State: South African Historiography as seen from England," *Social Dynamics* 9 (1983); W. Beinart and P. Delius, "Introduction" in W. Beinart, P. Delius, and S. Trapido, eds., *Putting a Plough to the Ground* (Johannesburg, 1986); Saunders, *The Making of the South African Past*.

12. This rich tradition is not explored in this volume, although Lodge refers to some of the major works concerned. The works of Tim Couzens and Brian Willan have uncovered a great deal of the previously obscured world of the black intellectual from the late ninteenth to the mid-twentieth century. See, for example, T. J. Couzens, *The New African* (Johannesburg, 1985); and B. Willan, *Sol Plaatje: a Biography* (Johannesburg, 1984).

13. An African cultural renaissance took place in the 1950s, epitomized by the journalism and photography of *Drum* magazine, and the fiction of writers such as E. Mphahlele, *Down Second Avenue* (Johannesburg, 1959); see also E. Patel, ed., *The World of Nat Nakasa* (Johannesburg, 1975).

14. The word "Africanist" is used here to refer to a particular school of historical writing which emphasized the existence of precolonial history and stressed African initiative, rather than political movements with a base in an exclusivist black constituency (the PAC being the central one) which go by the same name. A romanticism about Africa tended to accompany this early Africanism, but so did a powerful humanism and emphasis on human agency, influences which were to permeate later radicalism in South African studies.

15. An important strand of the early Africanism evolved in the United States, where a whole corpus of work on black South African resistance emerged, possibly spurred on by the presence of black nationalism within the United States itself. See, for example, P. Walshe, *African Nationalism in South Africa*

(London, 1970); E. Feit, *African Opposition in South Africa* (Stanford, 1967); T. Karis and G. Carter, *From Protest to Challenge: a Documentary History of African Politics in South Africa 1882–1964* (Stanford, 1972); and G. Gerhart, *Black Power in South Africa* (Berkeley, 1978).

16. Richard Gray, review of the *Oxford History of South Africa*, Vol. 2, in *Race* 14:1 (1972), 84.

17. Examples of these furtively circulated banned books included E. Roux, *Time Longer than Rope* (Madison, 1964); H. J. and R. E. Simons, *Class and Colour in South Africa*, (Harmondsworth, 1969); Govan Mbeki, *The Peasants Revolt* (Harmondsworth, 1964); and a whole series of additional books in the Penguin African Library which explored African history and politics in popularized forms.

18. A long-standing Communist party member who lectured in African Government at the University of Cape Town until 1964, when he was banned from teaching, and went into exile. Simons was a powerful influence on a number of scholars.

19. Thompson's early works included *The Unification of South Africa 1902–1910* (Oxford, 1960); while his more Africanist books include: ed., *African Societies in Southern Africa* (London, 1969) and *Survival in Two Worlds* (Oxford, 1975). He finally emigrated to the United States, where he taught at UCLA and Yale, and headed the Yale Southern African Research Program.

20. Which in Shula Marks's case gave rise to a classic study of the Bambatha revolt of 1906, *Reluctant Rebellion* (Oxford, 1970).

21. Much of the work of this group took a long time to come to fruition, including P. L. Bonner, *Kings, Commoners and Concessionaires: The Evolution and Dissolution of the 19th Century Swazi State* (Johannesburg and Cambridge, 1983); Jeff Guy, *The Destruction of the Zulu Kingdom: the Civil War in Zululand 1879–1884* (London, 1979); M. Legassick, "The Griqua, the Sotho-Tswana and the Missionaries," Ph.D. thesis, UCLA, 1969; D. W. Hedges, "Trade and Politics in Southern Mozambique and Zululand in the Eighteenth and Early Nineteenth Centuries," Ph.D. thesis, University of London, 1978; H. Slater, "Transitions in the Political Economy of South East Africa before 1840," Ph.D. thesis, University of Sussex, 1976.

22. See the chapter by la Hausse in this volume for a discussion of this early use of oral history, and how it differs from that of later oral historians.

23. African studies, African Government, and African Law courses, taught by such critical thinkers as H. J. Simons and Julius Lewin, trained several students who were subsequently to become radical scholars, including Trapido, Suttner, van Onselen, Bozzoli, and O'Meara; later appointments such as those of P. Bonner and R. Hallet added impetus to this.

24. F. A. Johnstone, *Class, Race and Gold* (London, 1976). Johnstone's article "White Prosperity and White Supremacy in South Africa Today," *African Affairs* 69 (1970), was central to the revisionist attack on existing liberal paradigms.

25. Barrington Moore's work was influential here, particularly in its comparative, historical, and materialist dimensions. See S. Trapido, "South Africa in a Comparative Study of Industrialisation," *Journal of Development Studies* 7 (1971).

26. See M. Legassick, "South Africa: Capital Accumulation and Violence," *Economy and Society* 3 (1974); "Legislation, Ideology and Economy in Post-1948 South Africa" *Journal of Southern African Studies* 1 (1974); "The Dynamics of Modernisation in South Africa," *Journal of African History* 13 (1972), and several others, both published and unpublished.

27. The Institute of Commonwealth Studies in London hosted two seminars: one in African History and the other in Southern African Societies. The papers from the latter were regularly published, rendering them perhaps more accessible than the equally challenging and fertile seminar run at the Oxford Institute of Commonwealth Studies by Stanley Trapido.

28. These included Colin Bundy, who set out to explore the "rise and fall of the South African peasantry," challenging dual economy models and notions of the irrationality of African responses to market forces, by illustrating that a substantial peasantry had risen in response to the growing mining markets of the late nineteenth and early twentieth centuries; see C. Bundy, *The Rise and Fall of the South African Peasantry* (London, 1979). Charles van Onselon, like Johnstone, focused on the mining industry (this time in Rhodesia), examining how this industry helped forge a black working class—capitalist strategies of control increasingly prompted working-class strategies of resistance. See C. van Onselen, *Chibaro: African Mine Labour in Southern Rhodesis 1900–1933* (London, 1976); Duncan Innes, who examined the political economy of the major South African corporations in *Anglo American and the Rise of Modern South Africa* (London, 1984); Belinda Bozzoli, who examined capitalist ideologies in her *The Political Nature of a Ruling Class* (London, 1981); as well as the group of precolonial historians mentioned above in footnote 21. Several of the scholars mentioned here and earlier have referred in interviews to the influence upon them of earlier left traditions: those mentioned include Jewish socialism, African Studies courses, NUSAS, the Unity Movement,a variety of forms of white radicalism, socialism and the works of MacMillan, Simons, Roux and others.

29. While Andre Gunder Frank and his critic Ernesto Laclau (then at Oxford) presented suggestive ideas as to how peripheral or semi-peripheral economies such as the South African one were drawn into relationships with the world economy, Eugene Genovese offered insights as to how slave and semi-slave formations may coexist with capitalism, giving a non-idealist explanation for the persistence of racial hierarchies. Lenin and Barrington Moore were appropriated for their explanations of transitions to modernity through different routes, particularly where the capitalization of agriculture took place side by side with labor repression, while the concerns of Gramsci and Genovese with dominant ideologies, and of Hobsbawm and Genovese

again with the cultures and ideologies of the oppressed, provided inspiration for those seeking to see South African cultural formations as more complexly constructed than the self-evident category of "race" would suggest. The Italian Marxist Giovanni Arrighi had also made imaginative and penetrating use of Marxist concepts to explain the means whereby a cheap labor force had been created in Rhodesia, challenging liberal economic theory of supply and demand.

30. Indeed Trapido's earliest work, to whose concerns he has subsequently returned, was on the construction of nationalisms; while Legassick conducted a subterranean debate in some of his papers with this theme; he subsequently came to reject any consideration of nationalism far more consciously when he moved into Trotskyist politics.

31. A term used here and in other chapters in this volume to refer to political and analytical perspectives which focus exclusively on the capacity of the working class (often defined quite narrowly to include only those who have been unionized and whose political consciousness centers upon the workplace) alone to lead the movement for emancipation; its obverse is "populism," used in a quite specifically South African sense to refer to the politics of popular alliances among community, workplace, working and other classes.

32. See van Onselen, "Worker Consciousness in Black Miners: Southern Rhodesia, 1900–1920," *Journal of African History* 14:2 (1973); and Bozzoli, *Political Nature of the Ruling Class.*

33. Our use of the notion of "realism" is derived from the work of J. Keat and J. Urry, *Social Theory as Science* (London, 1986); and Lloyd, *Explanation in Social History* (Oxford, 1986).

34. H. Wolpe, "Capitalism and Cheap Labour Power: From Segregation to Apartheid" *Economy and Society* 1 (1972); Wolpe was also critical, however, of purely "internal colonial" conceptions at the time: see his "The Theory of Internal Colonialism: The South African Case" in I. Oxaal, T. Barnett, and D. Booth, *The Sociology of Development* (London, 1975); and his explorations of the class divisions within South African society, such as "The 'white working class' in South Africa," *Economy and Society* 5 (1976), or the unpublished "The Changing Class Structure of South Africa: the African Petit Bourgeoisie."

35. Its posing of separate but intertwined spheres of "production" and "reproduction" owed much to the work of French structuralist social anthropologist Claude Meillassoux, and echoed the direction of work being taken by a number of Marxists (and feminists concerned with matters of "reproduction") at the time. See C. Meillassoux, "From Reproduction to Production: a Marxist Approach to Economic Anthropology," *Economy and Society* 1 (1972).

36. For a discussion of the re-emergence of the left in South Africa see E. Webster, "Competing Paradigms: Towards a Critical Sociology of Southern

Africa," *Social Dynamics* 11:1 (1985); J. Maree, "Harnessing Intellectuals: Tensions Between Democracy and Leadership in the Independent Trade Unions in the 1970s," *South African Sociological Review* 1:2 (1989); S. Friedman, *Building Tomorrow Today* (Johannesburg, 1987); Gerhart, *Black Power in South Africa*; and S. Nolotshungu, *Changing South Africa*, (Manchester, 1982).

37. These openings were partly created because expansion also resulted in a slackening of ideological control by a liberal old guard—there simply were not enough straight-laced liberals with adequate qualifications to fill the posts; but in some cases liberals welcomed and supported incoming radicals.

38. Turner's background was in existentialism (his Ph.D. was on Sartre). See his *The Eye of the Needle: Towards Participatory Democracy in South Africa* (Johannesburg, 1980). Turner's role as mentor was complemented by that of Sheldon Leader in Johannesburg, a French-trained American also advocating the neo-Marxism (of an Althusserian bent) of the sixties, and anxious to provide theoretical and epistemological backing for the workerist thrust.

39. These studies are examined in Lewis's chapter in this volume.

40. Eddie Webster, for example, surveyed black worker attitudes in the early 1970s, and found that a SACTU leader from the 1950s, Moses Mabhida, and Nelson Mandela figured prominently among those individuals workers regarded as their leaders. See E. Webster, "A Profile of Unregistered Union Members in Durban," *South African Labour Bulletin* 4:8 (July–Aug 1977).

41. Their structuralism is to be distinguished from that of Wolpe in many respects: they placed greater emphasis on the relatively autonomous role of the state, whereas Wolpe's major essay tended to reduce it to a reflection of the economic interests of capital. The key summary of the approach of the Poulantzian school is R. Davies, D. Kaplan, M. Morris, and D. O'Meara, "Class Struggle and the Periodisation of the South African State," *Review of African Political Economy* 7 (1976).

42. Thus O'Meara set out to show that Afrikaner Nationalism's strength lay in its capacity to forge a successful alliance between white Afrikaner workers and their capitalist and petty-bourgeois counterparts. See his *Volkskapitalisme* (Johannesburg, 1983). Davies worked on demonstrating that the white working class more generally was predisposed to support capital because its position in the process of production was radically different from that of black workers; see his *Capital, State and White Labour in South Africa 1900–1960* (Brighton, 1979). Kaplan concerned himself with the construction of the state form itself and its relationship to broader capitalist interests; see his "The South African State: the origins of a racially exclusive democracy," *Insurgent Sociologist* 10 (1980); while Morris set out to suggest that the "Prussian Road" to agricultural capitalism, a parallel originally used by Trapido, had lent to the white farming sector a particularly strong relationship to the state which helped to transform it, in his "The Development of Capitalism in South African Agriculture: Class Struggle in the Countryside," *Economy and Society* 5 (1976).

43. Bradford suggests in this volume, for example, that Morris "reclaimed" an entire field of analysis for historical materialism; while O'Meara's work has had considerable influence on subsequent interpretations of Afrikaner nationalism.

44. See S. Clarke, "Capital, Fractions of Capital and the State: Neo Marxian Analyses of the South African State," *Capital and Class* 5 (1978). Non-Poulantzian analyses of the state which were undertaken during the 1970s included Bozzoli, *Political Nature* . . . ; S. Marks and S. Trapido, "Lord Milner and the South African State," *History Workshop Journal* 8 (1979); and S. Greenberg, *Race and State in Capitalist Development: Comparative Perspectives* (New Haven, 1980).

45. For examples of this see D. O'Meara's key piece, "The 1946 African Mineworkers' Strike in the Political Economy of South Africa," *Journal of Commonwealth and Comparative Politics* 13 (1975), which contributed both to the study of labor at the time, and which made a bold statement about the transformation of the ANC from a liberal elite organization to a mass-based social movement. For another Poulantzian attempt at placing class struggle in a central position see R. Davies, "The 1922 Strike and the Political Economy of South Africa" in Bozzoli, ed., *Labour, Townships and Protest* (Johannesburg, 1979).

46. See D. Innes and M. Plaut, "Class Struggle and the State" and Bozzoli, "Capital and the State in South Africa," both in *Review of African Political Economy* 11 (1978).

47. A. Atmore and S. Marks, "The Imperial Factor in South Africa in the Nineteenth Century: towards a reassessment," *Journal of Imperial and Commonwealth History* 3:1 (1974).

48. Examples of attempts by the earlier Africanists to recast precolonial history in new terms are included in S. Marks and A. Atmore, eds., *Economy and Society in Pre-Industrial South Africa* (London, 1980); S. Marks and R. Rathbone, *Industrialisation and Social Change in South Africa* (London, 1982); and J. Peires, ed., *Before and After Shaka* (Grahamstown, 1981); e.g., Bundy *The Rise and Fall of the African Peasantry*; R. Palmer and N. Parsons, *The Roots of Rural Poverty in Central and Southern Africa* (London, 1977).

49. W. Beinart, *The Political Economy of Pondoland* (Cambridge, 1982); F. Cooper, "Peasants, Capitalists and Historians," *Journal of Southern African Studies* 7 (1981).

50. See, for example, Meillassoux, "From Reproduction to Production . . ."; M. Godelier, "Infrastructures, Society and History," *Current Anthropology* 19 (1978); E. Terray, *Marxism and Primitive Societies* (New York, 1972); M. Bloch, ed., *Marxist Analyses and Social Anthropology* (London, 1975); D. Seddon, ed., *Relations of Production* (London, 1978). See: P. Delius, *The Land Belongs To Us* (Berkeley, 1984); W. Beinart, "Chieftaincy and the Concepts of Articulation: South Africa ca. 1900–1950" and P. Harries, "Modes of Production and Modes of Analysis: The South African Case" both in *Canadian Journal of African Studies* 19:1 (1985). Wolpe had drawn

attention to some of this work, but his analysis was not concerned with the internal dynamics of African societies and was of limited assistance to Africanists themselves.

51. P. Hindess and P. Hirst, *Pre-capitalist Modes of Production* (London, 1975).

52. See, for example, Delius, *The Land*; Bonner, *Kings, Commoners and Concessionaires*.

53. See, for example, Beinart, *Political Economy*; Delius, *The Land*; and P. Harries, "Kinship, Ideology and the Nature of Pre-colonial Labour Migration" in Marks and Rathbone, *Industrialization and Social Change*.

54. Beinart, Delius, and Trapido, *Putting a Plough to the Ground*. Much of the work that was ultimately included in this volume was initiated in 1977 or before. See also T. Keegan, *Rural Transformation in Industrialising South Africa* (Johannesburg, 1987).

55. The main "workerist" strand had also undergone considerable modifications, showing much greater awareness of the world beyond the workplace and the union.

56. See, for example, *Staffrider* magazine which provided a forum for this outpouring of writing and which is discussed in the article by Oliphant in this volume. See also A. Oliphant and I. Vladislavic, eds., *Ten Years of Staffrider, 1978–88* (Johannesburg, 1988).

57. See Kelwyn Sole, "Culture, Politics and the Black Writer: a Critical Look at Prevailing Assumptions," in S. Gardner, ed., *Publisher, Writer, Reader* (Johannesburg, 1986).

58. The public side of the activities of these intellectuals is discussed in Bozzoli's chapter in this volume. See also, for an idea of the kinds of concerns that lay behind the early intellectual work in the History Workshop: Bozzoli, *Labour, Townships and Protest*. Both the revisionist strand of academic analysis and the local "activist" traditions came together in these times, providing a fruitful interplay.

59. The chapter in this volume by Callinicos looks at "popular history" in more detail. Popularization appears to have had two underlying motivations: that of providing trade unions or other organizations with useful information and historical background; or the more Gramscian motive of empowering the dispossessed by returning to them their lost or distorted historical traditions, and giving to them a sense of their contribution to the making of society. Witz's chapter in this volume explores an aspect of this approach.

60. The "photocopying" culture which had characterized the earlier period of indigenization was transformed by the growth and initiative shown by the small alternative publishing house, Ravan Press, in Johannesburg, which came under the direction of Mike Kirkwood during 1977 and which seized the opportunity to publish some of the new academic and popular work locally. Kirkwood's imaginative approach to publishing made the decolonization of academic work possible, and since that time several more local publishers have emerged or become transformed in the image of Ravan, giving great impetus to the creation of a local intellectual tradition.

61. The chapters below by Walker, James, Gavshon, Oliphant, and Peterson give an idea of the kinds of innovations that were being made.

62. This was, we suggest with hindsight, something of a misreading of the original historical materialist thrust, which, we argue above, was not so much about how "class" would always substitute for "race," but about the relatively greater explanatory capacity of the former concept.

63. C. van Onselen, *New Babylon, New Nineveh: Studies in the Social and Economic History of the Witwatersrand* (London, 1982). Van Onselen's local focus on the marginalized and dispossessed of the Witwatersrand has led some to misinterpret his work as a "culturalist" response to the "structuralism" of the Althusserian school. But this is a misnomer, for van Onselen emphasises rather than underplays the power of capital accumulation, profitability and the forces and relations of production in his depiction of the evolution of the city. This is a prime example of the folly of attributing metropolitan labels to local scholars.

64. See, for example, P. Tourikis, *The Political Economy of Alexandra Township*, B.A. Honours dissertation, University of the Witwatersrand (1981); and A. Proctor, "Class Struggle, Segregation and the City: a History of Sophiatown 1905–1940," in Bozzoli, *Labour, Townships and Protest*.

65. Examples of such work would be D. Coplan, "The Emergence of an African Working Class Culture" in Marks and Rathbone, *Industrialization and Social Change*; and his "The African Performer and the Johannesburg Entertainment Industry: The Struggle for African Culture on the Witwatersrand" in Bozzoli, *Labour, Townships and Protest*; Coplan's work is discussed in more detail on James's chapter in this volume; K. Sole, "Class Continuity and Change in Black South African Literature, 1948–1960" in Bozzoli, *Labour, Township and Protest*. E. Koch, "Without Visible Means of Subsistence: Slumyard Culture in Johannesburg 1918–1940" in Bozzoli, ed., *Town and Countryside in the Transvaal* (Johannesburg, 1981); and I. Hofmeyr, "The Mad Poets: An Analysis" in Bozzoli, *Labour, Townships and Protest*.

66. Tim Couzens was one of those doing oral history at this time; see, for an example of his work, *The New African: a study of the life and work of H. I. E. Dhlomo* (Johannesburg, 1985); and also his "The ABC of Research," *Africa Perspective* 6 (n.d). See also Koch, "Without Visible Means of Subsistence." These initiatives are covered in la Hausse's chapter in this volume. Generally, this thrust into community and cultural studies was lent greater legitimacy by intellectual developments in Britain, where structuralist Marxism was being routed by socialist humanists; where cultural studies were being imaginatively consolidated in Birmingham and elsewhere; and in the United States, where oral documentation programs and studies of slave societies and black experience were far advanced. That local scholars were influenced by these developments is undeniable; mechanistic and functionalist formulations (some still paying considerable homage to Althusserian and other functionalist notions, including the pervasive idea that all non-

workplace issues could be explained under the rubric of the catch-all concept "reproduction") were vigorously debated and British "culturalism"
became a reference point for their rejection. But then, so too did Africanist,
Gramscian and other approaches to popular consciousness and ideology.
We cannot understand the South African foray into the field of community
and culture without acknowledging its eclecticism, as well as its strong local
roots, and its powerful connection to a degree of economism which a Gutman or Thompson might well have found unacceptable. The legacy of both
workerism and the basic materialism of the first neo-Marxists was one
which remained present, while the resolute commitment to "decolonizing"
South African studies, freeing it from its unhealthy dependence upon metropolitan influences, ensured that an indigenous and eclectic synthesis,
rather than a mindless metropolitan slavishness, would begin to emerge.

67. See, for example, M. Morris, "Social History and the Transition to Capitalism in the South African Countryside," *Africa Perspective* 5–6 (1987); for a
cogent reply see T. Keegan, "Mike Morris and the Social Historians," *Africa
Perspectives* 1:7–8 (1989).

68. This is discussed at length in Bradford's chapter below.

69. Van Onselen's early work had emphasized this point: see his *Chibaro*. See
also B. Bozzoli, "Class, Community and Ideology in the Evolution of
South African Society," in Bozzoli, *Class, Community and Conflict* (Johannesburg, 1987); and her "Marxism, Feminism and South African Studies,"
Journal of Southern African Studies 9:2 (1983).

70. Johnstone,*Class, Race and Gold*, had first explored this factor; see also
Bozzoli, *Political Nature*; more recent examinations of the historical and social construction of "race" as an ideology include S. Dubow, who con-
structs race as a historical rather than ideal-typical category in "The Idea of
Race in Early 20th Century South Africa," paper presented to the African
Studies Institute, University of the Witwatersrand, 1989; and C. van Onselen, "Race and Class in the South African Countryside: Cultural Osmosis
and Social Relations in the Sharecropping Economy of the South Western
Transvaal 1900–1950," *American Historical Review*, 95:1 (Feb. 1990).

71. See the classic work of Philip Mayer, *Townsmen or Tribesmen* (Cape Town,
1971); as well as the more recent "The Origin and Decline of Rural Resistance Ideologies" in P. Mayer, ed., *Black Villagers in an Industrial Society*
(Cape Town, 1980); and J. Comaroff, *Body of Power, Spirit of Resistance*
(Chicago, 1985).

72. See Beinart, *Political Economy*; Delius, "Sebatakgomo: Migrant Organisation, the ANC and the Sekhukhuniland Revolt," *Journal of South African
Studies* 15:4 (1989), and *The Land Belongs to Us*.

73. Beinart, Delius, and Trapido, *Putting a Plough to the Ground*; Helen Bradford, *A Taste of Freedom*, (London, 1988); and Bonner et al, eds., *Holding
their Ground* (Johannesburg 1989).

74. A growing literature attempts to avoid treating so-called "ethnicity" (ie. in

the African context what used to be called "tribalism") as an ahistorical given, but examines its construction as a form of ideology and identity. See Marks, "Patriotism, Patriarchy and Purity: Natal and the Politics of Zulu Ethnic Consciousness" and P. Harries, "Exclusion, Classification and Internal Colonialism: the emergence of ethnicity among the Tsonga-speakers of South Africa" in L. Vail, ed., *The Creation of Tribalism* (London, 1989); Delius, "The Ndzundza Ndebele: indenture and the making of ethnic identity" in Bonner et al., *Holding their Ground*; C. Hamilton and J. Wright, "The Making of the Lala: Ethnicity, Ideology and Class Formation in a Pre-Colonial Context," unpublished paper, History Workshop, Johannesburg 1984; I. Phimister and C. van Onselen, "The Political Economy of Tribal Animosity: A Case Study of the 1929 Bulawayo Location 'Faction Fight,'" *Journal of Southern African Studies* 6:1 (1979); Beinart, "Worker Consciousness, Ethnic Particularism and Nationalism: The Experience of a South African Migrant 1930–1960" in Marks and Trapido, eds., *The Politics of Race, Class and Nationalism in Twentieth Century South Africa* (London, 1987).

75. See Bundy, "Street Sociology and Pavement Politics: Political Aspects of Youth and Student Resistance in Cape Town 1985," *Journal of Southern African Studies* 13:3 (1987); C. Glazer, "Students, Tsotsis and the Congress Youth League 1944–55," History Honours Dissertation, University of the Witwatersrand, 1986; P. L. Bonner, "Family, Crime and Political Consciousness on the East Rand 1939–1955," *Journal of Southern African Studies* 14:3 (1988); P. La Hausse, "'The Cows of Nongoloza': Youth, Crime and Amalaita Gangs in Durban 1900–1936," *Journal of Southern African Studies*. 16:1 (March, 1990).

76. See Hilary Sapire, *Industrialisation and Urbanisation in an East Rand Town*, Ph.D. thesis, University of the Witwatersrand, 1989; several of the papers in Bozzoli, *Class, Community and Conflict*; M. Chaskalson, "The Road to Sharpeville," and "Apartheid with a Human Face: Punt Jansen and the Origins of Reform in Township Administration 1972–76"; J. Seekings, "Why was Soweto Different? Urban Development, Township Politics and the Political Economy of Soweto 1978–84," all African Studies Institute Seminar Papers, 1988–89; K. Shubane, *The Soweto Rent Boycott*, University of the Witwatersrand Honours Dissertation, 1988; K. Jochelson, "People's Power and State Reform in Alexandra," *Work in Progress* (Nov–Dec 1988); J. Seekings, "The Origins of Political Mobilisation in PWV Townships 1980–84," in W. Cobbett and R. Cohen, eds., *Popular Struggles in Africa* (London, 1988).

77. This is discussed in more detail below.

78. See also Harold Wolpe, *Race, Class and the Apartheid State* (London, 1988) in which Wolpe acknowledges that "classes exist in forms which are fragmented and fractured in numerous ways, not only by the division of labor and, indeed, the concrete organization of the entire system of production

and distribution through which classes are necessarily formed, but by politics, culture and ideology, within the division of labor, for example gender, religion, the mental-manual divide and racial differentiation." (p.53) Wolpe tends to be dismissive of the work of "social historians" yet there is much in his discussion of class which resonates with the work of those discussed in this paper, who have, moreover, sought to show *how* the various divisions have been forged and transformed and their relationship to wider forces.

79. See above, footnote 55.

80. See van Onselen, "Race and Class"; Bradford, *A Taste of Freedom*; Keegan, *Rural Transformations*; Keegan, *Facing the Storm* (Johannesburg, 1988).

81. Bonner, "Family, Crime"; "We are Digging, we are seizing huge chunks of the municipality's land: popular struggles in Benoni 1944–52," African Studies Institute seminar paper, University of the Witwatersrand, 1985; "Desirable or Undesirable Sotho Women? Liquor, Prostitution and the Migration of Sotho Women to the Rand, 1920–1955," in C. Walker, ed., *Essays on the Changing Position of Women and the Organization of Gender in Southern Africa 1800–1945* (Cape Town, 1990).

82. This basic misunderstanding has blighted debates between those misleadingly dubbed "social historians" and those of a more idealist inclination.

83. See Bradford, *A Taste of Freedom*; Comaroff, *Body of Power*; Comaroff and Comaroff, "The Colonisation of Consciousness in South Africa" *Economy and Society* 18:3 (1989); J. Peires, *The Dead Will Arise: Nogquawuse and the Great Xhosa Cattle Killing Movement of 1856–1857* (Johannesburg and Bloomington, 1989); Beinart and Bundy, *Hidden Struggles in Rural South Africa* (Johannesburg, 1987); Delius, "Sebatakgomo." Clingman's chapter in this volume discusses this question.

84. See Bozzoli, "Class, Community and Ideology in the Evolution of South African Society" in Bozzoli, *Class, Community and Conflict*; as well as Bonner, et al., *Holding their Ground*.

85. The study of nationalism had been transformed by the work of Tom Lodge, who based his analysis of African Nationalist movements much more firmly in community, class, and grassroots experience than on the earlier Africanist-romantic tradition, which tended to adopt an organizational and "great man" approach. See T. Lodge, *Black Politics in South Africa since 1945* (Johannesburg, 1983).

86. See D. Posel, "Rethinking the 'Race-Class Debate' in South African Historiography," *Social Dynamics* 9 (1983); and Wolpe, *Race, Class*.

87. The early Poulantzians had made a significant contribution to the understanding of white nationalism by viewing it as a construction of class alliances (echoing work by Trapido as early as the 1960s); analyses since then have tended to give greater weight to the ideological forces at play by looking at processes such as the "invention of tradition," the community roots of nationalism, and the discourses it entails. See for example, I. Hofmeyr, "Building a Nation from Words: Afrikaans Language, literature and ethnic

identity, 1902–1924," and R. Hill and G. Pirio, "Africa for the Africans: the Garvey Movement in South Africa, 1920–1940," both in Marks and Trapido, *The Politics*. O'Meara, in one of his most perceptive but least known pieces, made a bold attempt to address the ideas of Poulantzas. Basing his arguments on the more subtle and persuasive work of the later Poulantzas, he set out to examine the origins of the reformist stance adopted by the state during the era of P. W. Botha's rule, and to analyze, with great skill, internal contradictions within the former monolith: D. O'Meara, "'Muldergate' and the Politics of Afrikaner Nationalism," *Work in Progress* 22 (1983).

88. See J. Saul and S. Gelb, "The Crisis in South Africa: Class Defense, Class Revolution," *Monthly Review* 33:3 (July-August 1981).

89. The quote is from John Lonsdale, "States and Social Processes in Africa: An Historiographical Survey," *African Studies Review* 24:2–3 (1981).

90. However neo-structuralism appears to be emerging in the form of studies influenced by M. Aglietta and the "regulation" school, which see the state and society as forming a "regime of accumulation"; see, for example, S. Gelb and D. Innes, "Towards a Democratic Economy," paper presented to the Social Transformation Seminar, University of the Witwatersrand, 1989.

91. See, for example, Marks, *The Ambiguities of Dependence* (Pietermaritzburg, 1987); S. Dubow, *Racial Segregation and the Origins of Apartheid in South Africa* (London, 1989); Beinart, *Political Economy*; S. Greenberg, "Ideological Struggles within the South African State" and D. Posel, "The Language of Domination 1978–1983" both in Marks and Trapido, *The Politics of Class*; D. Hindson, *Pass Laws and the South African Proletariat* (Johannesburg, 1988); D. Posel, *Influx Control and the Construction of Apartheid 1948–1961* (Oxford, 1987); S. Greenberg, *Legitimating the Illegitimate* (New Haven, 1987).

92. See, for example, A. Sitas, "Moral Formations and Struggles Amongst Migrant Workers on the East Rand," *Labour, Capital and Society* 18:2 (1985); "African Worker Responses on the East Rand to Changes in South Africa's Metal Industry 1960–1980," Ph.D. thesis, University of the Witwatersrand, 1983; Dunbar Moodie, "The Moral Economy of the Black Miners' Strike of 1946," *Journal of Southern African Studies* 13:1 (1986); R. Lambert, "Political Unionism and Working Class Hegemony," *Labour Capital and Society* 18:2 (1985); R. Lambert and E. Webster, "Political Unionism in Contemporary South Africa" in Cobbett and Cohen, *Popular Struggles in South Africa*.

93. M. Kinsman, "Beasts of Burden: The Subordination of Southern Tswana Women ca 1800–1840," *Journal of Southern African Studies* 10:1 (1983); J. Wright, "Men's control of women's labour in the Zulu Kingdom," unpublished paper; C. Murray, *Families Divided; the Impact of Migrant Labour in Lesotho* (Cambridge, 1981) and "High bridewealth, migrant labour and the

position of women in Lesotho," *Journal of African Law* 21:1 (1977); and Walker, *Essays on the Changing Position of Women.*

94. W. Beinart and P. Delius, "The Family and Early Migrancy in South Africa, unpublished paper, 1979; Beinart, "Labour Migrancy and Rural Production: Pondoland 1900–1950" in Mayer, *Black Villagers*; and Bozzoli, "Marxism, Feminism"; van Onselen, in: "The Witches of Suburbia: Domestic Service on the Witwatersrand between 1890 and 1914" and "Prostitutes and Proletarians" (both in his *New Babylon, New Nineveh*) looks at both males and females in the city. See also D. Moodie, "Migrancy and Male Sexuality on the South African Gold Mines," *Journal of Southern African Studies* 14:2 (1988).

95. P. Bonner, "Family, Crime"; "Desirable or Undesirable"; chapter in this volume; C. Walker, *Essays on the Changing Position of Women*; K. Eales, " Patriarchs, Passes and Privilege," in Bonner et al., *Holding their Ground*; and "Jezebels, Good Girls and Mine Married Quarters" African Studies Institute Seminar Paper, 1989.

96. Bradford, "'We are now the men': Women's Beer Protests in the Natal Countryside 1929," and Beinart, "Women in Rural Politics: Herschel District in the 1920s and 1930s" both in Bozzoli, *Class, Community and Conflict*; C. Walker, *Women and Resistance in South Africa* (London, 1982); J. Wells, "A History of Southern African Women's resistance to pass laws, 1900–1960," Ph.D. thesis, Columbia University, 1982. See also Walker, (ed) *Essays.*

Chapter 2

1. Unless otherwise indicated, all references are in my book, *The Dead Will Arise: Nongqawuse and the Great Xhosa Cattle-Killing Movement of 1856–57* (Johannesburg, 1990).

2. J. Rutherford, *Sir George Grey* (London, 1961), 355.

3. J. B. Peires, "Sir George Grey versus the Kaffir Relief Committee," *Journal of Southern African Studies* 10 (1984).

4. Cape Archives, GH 8/48-50.

5. A. W. Burton, *Sparks from the Border Anvil* (Kingwilliamstown, 1950), 70; S.E.K. Mqhayi, *Umteteli waBantu*, 5 Sept. 1931; Interview with Chief N. Bhotomane, Ramntswana, Kentani District, 16 Dec. 1975; Cape Archive, BK 1, G. Grey—J. Maclean, 7 Aug. 1856.

6. Interview with M. Soga, Kobonqaba, Kentani District, 15 Jan. 1976.

7. George Matanzima, cited in A.G.K. Brown, "The Cattle-Killing: an Oral History Questionnaire," unpublished paper, University of Fort Hare, 1983. Buthelezi quoted in *Daily Despatch*, 23 May 1988. Such references are too common to be fully documented; another letter from a conservative black comparing sanctions advocates to Nongqawuse appeared in the *Dispatch*, 20 June 1988.

8. The quote from Xundu was recorded by a person who was present at the

service; the song was collected in Graaff-Reinet by N. Maister and R. Hall in December 1986, but refers to Prime Minister Vorster who resigned in 1978; Chief Bhotomane (see note 5 above) was one of those who said "she was bought."

9. N. Majeke, *The Role of the Missionaries in Conquest* (Cape Town, 1952), reprinted in the Unity Movement Series (Cumberland, 1986).

10. Abdur-Rahmaan Wright, "The Black People of South Africa and the Imported Religions," Johannesburg, n.d. My thanks to Denver Webb of Kingwilliamstown for this document. The AZAPO pamphlet was in the possession of the Grahamstown UDF before its suppression.

11. Brown, "The Cattle Killing."

12. Interview with R. Cakata, Xobo, Idutywa District, 5 Dec. 1975.

13. For a fuller analysis of the structure of Xhosa oral traditions, see appendix of J. B. Peires, *The House of Phalo* (Berkeley, 1982).

14. A full discussion of the lung-sickness epidemic and of Mhlakaza's relationship to Christianity may be found in J. B. Peires, "The Central Beliefs of the Xhosa Cattle-Killing," *Journal of African History* 28 (1987), 43–63.

Chapter 3

My thanks to Colin Bundy and Ian Phimister, without whom this would not have appeared. The usual disclaimers do not apply. It should also be noted that this article was essentially completed in 1989, and has not been able to take account of the most recent contributions to the debate, such as Jeremy Krikler's seminal work.

1. Francis Wilson, "Farming, 1866–1966," in Monica Wilson and Leonard Thompson, eds., *The Oxford History of South Africa,* Vol. 2 (Oxford, 1971), 153. *Platteland* is an Afrikaans term that literally means "flatlands," but refers to farmlands as distinct from African-occupied reserves.

2. Martin Murray, "The Triumph of Marxist Approaches in South African Social and Labour History," *Journal of Asian and African Studies* 23:1–2 (1988), 79.

3. C. Eloff, quoted by Colin Bundy, "Assessing the Harvest: Some Perspectives on South Africa's Rural History (19th and 20th Centuries)," paper given at National Conference of the South African Historical Society, Cape Town, January 1985.

4. Mike Morris, "Social History and the Transition to Capitalism in the South African Countryside," *Africa Perspective* 1:5–6 (1987), 15.

5. Robert Brenner, "The Origins of Capitalist Development: a Critique of Neo-Smithian Marxism," *New Left Review* 104 (1977), 33.

6. Ellen Meiksins Wood, *The Retreat from Class* (London, 1986), 18; Perry Anderson, *In the Tracks of Historical Materialism* (London, 1983), 21; see also Anderson, *Considerations on Western Marxism* (London, 1979).

7. Colin Bundy, "The Emergence and Decline of a South African Peasantry," *African Affairs* 71 (1972), 383.

8. Stanley Trapido, "Aspects in the Transition from Slavery to Serfdom: the South African Republic," in *Collected Seminar Papers on the Societies of Southern Africa in the 19th and 20th Centuries,* Vol. 6 (London, 1975), 24; Trapido, "South Africa in a Comparative Study of Industrialization," *Journal of Development Studies* 7:3 (1971); Henry Slater, "The Natal Land and Colonisation Company 1860–1948," in *Collected Seminar Papers,* Vol. 4 (London, 1973), 49.

9. Mike Morris, "The State and the Development of Capitalist Social Relations in the South African Countryside: a Process of Class Struggle," Ph.D. dissertation, University of Sussex, 1981, iii.

10. Anthony Winson, "The 'Prussian Road' of Agrarian Development: a Reconsideration," *Economy and Society* 11:3 (1982), 384.

11. Mike Morris, "The Development of Capitalism in South African Agriculture: Class Struggle in the Countryside," *Economy and Society* 5:3 (1976), 306.

12. Ibid., 296, 302–08.

13. Morris, "The State," 9; Morris, "Development of Capitalism," 338.

14. Morris, "Social History," 17; Timothy Keegan, "The Transformation of Agrarian Society and Economy in Industrialising South Africa: the Orange Free State Grain Belt in the Early Twentieth Century," Ph.D dissertation, University of London, 1981, 26.

15. These scholars include Rosalynde Ainslie, *Masters and Serfs* (London, 1973); Merle Lipton, *Capitalism and Apartheid* (Aldershot, 1985); Dunbar Moodie, "Class Struggle in the Development of Agrarian Capitalism in South Africa: Reflections on the Relevance of the Natives' Land Act, 1913," paper presented at History Workshop, University of the Witwatersrand, 1981; Stanley Greenberg, *Race and State in Capitalist Development* (New Haven, 1980), 71.

16. Greenberg, *Race and State,* 73; Robert Miles, *Unfree Labour under Capitalism: an Anomalous Necessity?* (London, 1987); Timothy Keegan, "Primitive Accumulation and Class Formation in the Making of Agrarian Capitalism in South Africa," paper given at an agrarian symposium, Institute of Commonwealth Studies, University of London, 3 February 1989, 3.

17. Susan Newton-King, "The Labour-market of the Cape Colony, 1807–28," in Shula Marks and Anthony Atmore, eds., *Economy and Society in Pre-Industrial South Africa* (London, 1980), 198.

18. Helen Bradford, *A Taste of Freedom: the ICU in Rural South Africa, 1924–1930* (New Haven, 1987), 38–41.

19. Tessa Marcus, *Restructuring in Commercial Agriculture in South Africa—Modernising Super-Exploitation* (Amsterdam, 1986), 86–91; Morris, "Development of Capitalism," 327–35; *Third (Final) Report of the Commission of Enquiry into Agriculture,* RP 19/1972, (Pretoria, 1972), 37; Marcus, *Restructuring;* Karl Marx, *Capital* Vol. 1 (Harmondsworth, 1976), 1019. This argument does not solve, however, the thorny question of when (or whether) capitalism dominated in the stage of formal subsumption of labor to capital.

20. Aninka Claassens, "Those who live on the farms and those who come and go: labour tenancy in the south-eastern Transvaal," TRAC paper given at the 1988 Black Sash conference, reprinted in summarized form in *Sash* 31 (1988).

21. Donald Denoon, *Settler Capitalism: The Dynamics of Dependent Development in the Southern Hemisphere* (Oxford, 1983), 37.

22. Martin Murray and Charles Post, "The 'Agrarian Question,' Class Struggle and the Capitalist State in the United States and South Africa," *The Insurgent Sociologist* 11:4 (1983), 50–1.

23. Stuart Hall, "In Defence of Theory," in Raphael Samuel, ed., *People's History and Socialist Theory* (London, 1981); Shula Marks, "The Historiography of South Africa" in Bogumil Jewsiewicki and David Newbury, eds., *African Historiographies* (Beverly Hills, 1986); E. P. Thompson, *The Poverty of Theory* (London, 1978).

24. Marks, "Historiography," 171.

25. Keegan, "Transformation of Agrarian Society," 32, 34.

26. Murray, "Triumph," 83; Charles van Onselen, "Race and Class in the South African Countryside: Cultural Osmosis and Social Relations in the Sharecropping Economy of the South-Western Transvaal; 1900–1950," paper presented at African Studies Institute, University of the Witwatersrand, 1 August 1988, 5, 22; William Beinart, "Settler Accumulation in East Griqualand from the Demise of the Griqua to the Natives Land Act," in William Beinart, Peter Delius, and Stanley Trapido, eds., *Putting a Plough to the Ground* (Johannesburg, 1986), 262; Colin Bundy, "Vagabond Hollanders and Runaway Englishmen: White Poverty in the Cape before Poor Whiteism," in Beinart et al., *Putting a Plough*, 106; Saul Dubow, *Land, Labour and Merchant Capital* (Cape Town, 1982), 6; Timothy Keegan, "White Settlement and Black Subjugation on the South African Highveld: The Tlokoa Heartland in the North Eastern Orange Free State, ca.1850–1914," in Beinart et al., *Putting a Plough*; Peter Richardson, "The Natal Sugar Industry in the Nineteenth Century," in Beinart et al., *Putting a Plough*; Stanley Trapido, "Putting a Plough to the Ground: a History of Tenant Production on the Vereeniging Estates, 1896–1920," in Beinart et al., *Putting a Plough*; Malete Nkadimeng and Georgina Relly, "Kas Maine: the Story of a Black South African Agriculturalist," in Belinda Bozzoli, ed., *Town and Countryside in the Transvaal* (Johannesburg, 1983), 100.

27. William Beinart and Peter Delius, "Introduction," in Beinart et al., *Putting a Plough*, 17; Robert Brenner, "Agrarian Class Structure and Economic Development in Pre-Industrial Europe," *Past and Present* 70 (1976), 32, 56; Morris, "Development of Capitalism," 309.

28. Charles van Onselen, "Randlords and Rotgut 1886–1903," *History Workshop Journal* 2 (1976), 83; Shula Marks and Stanley Trapido, "Lord Milner and the South African State," *History Workshop Journal* 8 (1979), 60; Denoon, *Settler Capitalism*, 123–24; Beinart and Delius, "Introduction," 49.

29. Timothy Keegan, "The Making of the Orange Free State, 1846–54: Sub-

imperialism, Primitive Accumulation, and State Formation," *Journal of Imperial and Commonwealth History* 17:1 (1988), 29; Peter Delius and Stanley Trapido, "Inboekselings and Oorlams: the Creation and Transformation of a Servile Class," in Bozzoli, ed., *Town and Countryside*; Beinart, "Settler Accumulation." In Natal, for example, Cape mercantile firms bought farms for a snippet. By the 1860s, five-sixths of the land was held by absentee owners, the largest was a London-based company, and the entire commercial system balanced precariously on mortgages on land.

30. Peter Delius, *The Land Belongs to Us* (Johannesburg, 1983), 33; Stanley Trapido, "Landlord and Tenant in a Colonial Economy: the Transvaal 1880–1910," *Journal of Southern African Studies* 5 (1978), 35, 43; Trapido, "Aspects in the Transition," 28.

31. Keegan, "Primitive Accumulation," 4; Keegan, "Making of the Free State," 44, 48; Peter Delius, "Abel Erasmus: Power and Profit in the Eastern Transvaal," in Beinart et al., *Putting a Plough*; Karl Marx, *Grundrisse* (Harmondsworth, 1973), 465.

32. Keegan, "Making of the Free State," 47.

33. Keegan, *Rural Transformations in Industrializing South Africa* (Johannesburg, 1986), 198; van Onselen, "Race and Class," 6, 23.

34. Van Onselen, "Race and Class," 9; Robert Ross, "The Origins of Capitalist Agriculture in the Cape Colony: a Survey," in Beinart et al., *Putting a Plough*, 69. "Rich whites" were, of course, also deeply implicated in the creation of "poor whites." Among those who have perceived these black serfs are Ainslie, *Masters and Serfs*; George Fredrickson, *White Supremacy: A Comparative Study in American and South African History* (Oxford, 1981), 38; Wilson, "Farming," 110. Morris first raised this issue of the relation between high land values and relations of exploitation—but he downplayed the roles of merchant and interest-bearing capital.

35. Keegan, *Rural Transformations*, 87; Bradford, *Taste of Freedom*, 25–26, 40; Lenin, *Collected Works* Vol. 1, 216.

36. Keegan, *Rural Transformations*, 197; Keegan, "The Dynamics," 9; See also Beinart and Delius, "Introduction," 28–9; Bradford, *Taste of Freedom*, 31; Dubow, *Land and Merchant Capital*, 13; Beinart, "Settler Accumulation," 262–87; Tony Kirk, "The Cape Economy and the Kat River Settlement" in Marks and Trapido, *Economy and Society*, 230, 236–27; Ross, "Origins of Capitalist Agriculture," 68; Timothy Keegan, "The Dynamics of Rural Accumulation in South Africa: Comparative and Historical Perspectives," paper presented at African Studies Institute, University of the Witwatersrand, 18 March 1985, 9.

37. Beinart, "Settler Accumulation," 276; Robert Morrell, "Competition and Cooperation in Middelburg, 1900–1930" in Beinart et al., *Putting a Plough*, 390; Trapido, "Putting a Plough."

38. Bundy, "Vagabond Hollanders," 118; Ross, "Origins of Capitalist Agriculture," 84; Maureen Swan, "The 1913 Indian Strike," *Journal of Southern*

African Studies 10:2 (1984), 243; Bradford, *Taste of Freedom*, 49; Morrell, "Competition and Cooperation," 395, 408; Timothy Keegan, "The Share-cropping Economy, African Class Formation and the 1913 Natives Land Act in the Highveld Maize Belt" in Bozzoli, *Town and Countryside*, 118.

39. Bill Freund, "Rural Struggles and Transformations," *South African Historical Journal* 19 (1987), 168–73; Murray, "Triumph," 84; Floris van Jaarsveld, *Omstrede Suid-Afrikaanse Verlede* (Johannesburg, 1984), 88 ("dogmatic Marxism" and "modern social"); Keegan, "Transformation of Agrarian Society," 33.

40. Robert Ross, "Capitalism, Expansion, and Incorporation on the South African Frontier," in Howard Lamar and Leonard Thompson, *The Frontier in History* (New Haven, 1981), 226; Robert Ross, "The Rise of the Cape Gentry," *Journal of Southern African Studies* 9:2 (1983), 194; Robert Ross, "The First Two Centuries of Colonial Agriculture in the Cape Colony: a Historiographical Review," *Social Dynamics* 9:1 (1983), 45; Ross, "Origins of Capitalist Agriculture," 79, 73, 56.

41. Jeremy Krikler, "Putting a Plough to the Ground: a Critique," *Journal of Southern African Studies* (forthcoming).

42. Keegan, *Rural Transformations*, 3; "White Settlement," 239; Marx, *Capital* Vol. 1, 998, 999.

43. Krikler, "Putting a Plough," 5–6; Morris, "Social History," 14, 22–23.

44. S. Newton King, "Primitive Accumulation and the Cape Frontier—A Case of Mistaken Identity?" paper presented to the workshop on precolonial history, University of Cape Town, 1986; Keegan, "Primitive Accumulation," Colin Bundy, Shula Marks, Stanley Trapido, and Charles van Onselen, interviewed by Belinda Bozzoli and Peter Delius, University of the Witwatersrand, July 1988, 20–21.

45. Marx, *Capital* Vol. 3, 453. For further discussions on the "merchant road," see also A. de Janvry, *The Agrarian Question and Reformism in Latin America* (Baltimore, 1981); Elizabeth Fox-Genovese and Eugene Genovese, *Fruits of Merchant Capital* (Oxford, 1983); R. Hilton, *The Transition from Feudalism to Capitalism* (London, 1980).

46. Bradford, *Taste of Freedom*.

47. Ben Mazower, "The Transition to Agrarian Capitalism in South Africa: a Review of the Historiography," unpublished paper, University of Cape Town, 1988.

Chapter 4

The financial support of the Richard Ward Foundation of the University of the Witwatersrand and the Institute for Research Development (IRD) of the Human Sciences Research Council (HSRC), towards this research is hereby acknowledged. Opinions expressed in this publication and conclusions arrived at, are those of the author and do not necessarily represent the views of either organization.

1. For a brief review of the literature see P. L. Bonner, *Black Urban Cultures and the Politics of Black Squatter Movements on the Rand*, paper presented to the University of the Witwatersrand, History Workshop, *Radical History Review* Workshop, 22–23 July 1988. For those who have equated black urban squatting with organized squatter movements see, for example, A. H. Stadler, "Birds in the Cornfield: Squatter Movements in Johannesburg 1944–1947," *Journal of Southern African Studies* 6:1 (Oct. 1979); Kevin French, "James Mpanza and the Sofazonke Party," M.A. dissertation, University of the Witwatersrand, 1984.

2. A. Potgieter, "Die Swartes aan die Witwatersrand, 1900–1933," Ph.D. thesis, Rand Afrikaans University, 1978, 58–153; Union of South Africa, *Report of the Small Holdings Commission (Transvaal)* (UG 51'13) 4–30; *Report of the Commission on Small Holdings in the Peri-Urban Areas of the Union of South Africa* (UG 37/1957), 3–10; a similar pattern is found in many towns elsewhere in South Africa. See Paul la Hausse, "The Message of the Warriors: The ICU, the Labouring Poor and the Making of a Popular Political Culture in Durban," paper presented to the University of the Witwatersrand, History Workshop, on "The Making of Class," 9–14 Feb. 1987, 8.

3. See Hilary Sapire, "African Urbanisation and Struggles Against Municipal Control in Brakpan, 1920–1958," Ph.D. thesis, University of the Witwatersrand, 1989, 289–304, 379; J. Cole, *Crossroads: the Politics of Reform and Repression 1976–1986* (Johannesburg, 1987).

4. Ibid., Ari Sitas, "Vigilantism in Durban" (unpublished).

5. Helen Bradford, "The Industrial and Commercial Workers Union of Africa in the South African Countryside, 1924–1930," Ph.D. thesis, University of the Witwatersrand, 1985, 87–97; Edward Koch, "Doornfontein and its African Working Class 1914 to 1945: A Study in Popular Culture in Johannesburg," M. A. dissertation, University of the Witwatersrand, 1983, 103; Sapire, "African Urbanisation," 7–8; P. L. Bonner, "Desirable or Undesirable Basotho Women: Liquor, Prostitution and the Migration of Basotho Women to the Rand, 1920–1985," in C. Walker, ed., *Women and the Organisation of Gender in South African History* (Cape Town, 1990), 18–27.

6. University of the Witwatersrand Library Historical Papers, Records of the South African Institute of Race Relations Basement Archives Collection AD 1715 S,7, "The Urban Native," Memorandum, 11.

7. Martin Legassick and Harold Wolpe, "The Bantustan and Capital Accumulation in South Africa," *Review of African Political Economy* 7 (1976); Daniel O'Meara, "The 1946 African Mine Workers Strike in the Political Economy of South Africa," *Journal of Commonwealth and Comparative Politics* 13:1 (March 1975), 149–152; Central Archives Depot NTS 6687, File 310/332, Vol. 2, Report of the Commission appointed to enquire into the disturbances of 30 August 1947 at the Moroka Emergency Camp, Johannesburg, 11 .

8. J. Cohen, "A Pledge for Better Times: The Local State and the Ghetto,

Benoni 1930–1938," Honours dissertation, University of the Witwatersrand, 1982, 42, 49–52; L. Menachemson, "Resistance through the Courts, African Urban Communities and Litigation Under the Urban Act, 1923–1939," Honours dissertation, University of the Witwatersrand, 1985, 38; French, "James Mpanza," 45, 54; Ray Phillips, *The Bantu in the City* (Lovedale, 1937), 342.

9. UG 8/1940, Report of the Committee to Consider the Administration of Areas which are becoming Urbanised but which are not under Local Government Control; Sapire, "African Urbanisation," 172–3, 216–225, 239–304; NTS 6490, File 125/313 (S), Vol. 2, NTS 6491 File 125/373 (S), Part 4; NTS 6470 File 51/313 S.

10. P. L. Bonner, "'We are digging, we are seizing great chunks of the municipality's land'; Popular Struggles in Benoni, 1944–52," paper presented to the African Studies Seminar, African Studies Institute, University of the Witwatersrand, Oct., 1985; NTS 6687, File 310/332, Vol. 2, Report of the Commission Appointed to Enquire into the Disturbances of the 30th August 1947, at the Maroka Emergency Camp, Johannesburg.

11. NTS 6490, File 125/313 (S), 4; NTS 4828, File 620/313, Details of Natives living at Shantytown, Alberton; NTS 4528, File 620/313, especially, O.J.T. Horak, Deputy Commissioner, SAP, Witwatersrand Division to Commissioner, SAP, 22 Nov. 1944; Interview, S. Sinaba, Daveyton, Dec. 1985, 13 May, 1986.

12. "Skokiaan queens" are illegal beer-brewers, "section 29s" are those considered "idle and undesirable" in terms of that section of the Urban Areas Act. P. L. Bonner, "Family, Crime and Political Consciousness on the East Rand, 1939–1955," *Journal of Southern African Studies* 14:3 (April 1938), 394–8; NTS 6371, File 51/313/S1, Vol. 1, Notes of a meeting between Johannesburg City Council and various government departments, 12 March 1946.

13. NTS 6470, File 51/313/51, Vol. 1, Minutes of the Continuation of a Discussion between Johannesburg City Council, government officials and with the Minister of Native Affairs, 18 March 1945.

14. Laura Longmore, *The Dispossessed: A Study of Sex Life of Bantu Women in the Urban Areas in and around Johannesburg* (London, 1959), 72, 58.

15. Interviews, Mrs. E. Ntlokwane and Mrs. Senosi Wattville, May 1985.

16. Interview, Johanna Mahwayi, Chiawelo, Soweto, February 1988.

17. NTS 6475, File 51/313/5(3), Vol. 6, memo., Moroka Advisory Board Members to Johannesburg City Council, 12 Dec. 1951; NTS 7921, File 520/400, P. R. Mosaka to Secretary for Justice, 26 Sept. 1950; Telegram, L. l. Venables, Manager NEAD to Secretary for Native Affairs, 12 Feb. 1951; Memo. to Minister of Justice and Native Affairs from Johannesburg Advisory Board, 23 Feb. 1951.

18. See, for example, Johannesburg Intermediate Archive (hereafter IA), Johannesburg Municipal Records (hereafter JMR), D1942, "Johannesburg City

Council Supplementary Memo to the Moroka Enquiry Commission," 7; IA, WRAB File 158/8, minutes of meeting of NEAD members with a deputation of squatters 20 Feb. 1947; Interviews, Mr. W. M. Sekhukhune Mapetla, 22 Dec. 1988 and Mr. Methula, Senaoane, 23 Dec. 1988.

19. NTS 4534, File 641/313, General Secretary, Jabavu Township to Native Commissioner, Johannesburg, 28 Sept. 1946. NTS, 6470, File 51/313/51, Vol. I, Director of Native Labor to Sec. for Native Affairs, 19 June 1944; Ibid. T. D. Young, Auditors Report, 13 July 1944, *Rand Daily Mail*, 6 June 1944; *The Star*, 17 June, 1944.

20. P. Walshe, *The Rise of African Nationalism in South Africa* (London, 1979), 145–47.

21. NTS 6477, File 51/313 S(4), Interview Adv. Mendelow with SNA, 10 Feb. 1947; ibid., Part I. Memo, Under Sec. Native Affairs, DNL, Native Commissioner and others, 1950.

22. Interview, Mrs. Moteka, Mapetla, 4 Sept. 1988.

23. NTS 6470, File 51/313/(Sl), Vol. 1, Auditors' Report (T. D. Young) on Sofazonke Township, 13 July 1944; IA, WRAB File 158/8, minutes of a meeting with squatter leaders. BMA, NEAC meeting 8 Sept. 1947. Letter, Native Commissioner, Benoni, Annexure B. Notes of interview with squatter leaders. Interviews, F. Mahungela, Daveyton, 4 Aug. and 6 Oct. 1986; IA, WRAB File 158/8. Minutes of meeting with squatter camp leaders, 20 and 24 Feb. 1947.

24. For some indications of these, see University of the Witwatersrand Library Historical and Literary papers MIC A1157, Johannesburg City Council Memo. For submission to the Fagan Commission of Enquiry into the Riot at Moroka Emergency Camp, 26 Sept. 1947, and annexure: Applications for Trading Sites.

25. NTS 6470, File 51/313 (S1), Vol. I, Report by NEA Committee to JCC meeting, 24 Nov. 1944; IA, WRAB, File 158/4. Minutes of meeting with squatter leaders, 24 Feb. 1947. Benoni Municipal Archives (BMA), NEAC meeting 12 Oct. 1950. Report Acting Supt. Emergency Camp; NTS 6477, File 51/313 (54) Part 1, memo, Under Sec. Native Affairs, D.N.L. Native Commissioner, 1950.

26. NTS 6687, File 310/332, Vol. 2. Report of the Commission appointed to enquire into the disturbances of 30 Aug. 1947 at the Moroka Emergency Camp, 4–10; NTS 6475, File 51/313 S(3), Vol. 3, Porter to Minister of Native Affairs 21 July 1948; ibid., Vol. 6. K. D. Morgan to J. Ntenjane, 27 Sept. 1951; ibid., notes by K. D. Morgan of a meeting with 32 persons, 14 Sept. 1950, and a meeting 20 Feb. 1951.

27. Interview, Mrs. Moteka, Mapetla, Sept. 1988.

28. French, "Mpanza," 77–78; BMA, NEAC meeting 8 Sept. 1947, Annexure "B"; interviews, Mrs. Ntlokwane and Mrs. Senosi; interview, K. S. Komane, Daveyton, 14 July and 7 Sept. 1988.

29. Bonner, "We are digging"; NTS 4528, File 620/313, notes of an interview

with Mr. Jack Behrman, Attorney, 3 Nov. 1944; ibid., Behrman and Behrman, Attorneys to Native Affairs Dept., 30 Nov. 1944; NTS 6491, File 125/313(S), Part I. Sub-inspector, SAP, Benoni to District Commandant, Boksburg, 28 Sept. 1948; University of the Witwatersrand Library, Historical and Literary Papers, MIC A 1157, Johannesburg City Council Memo, for submission to the Fagan Commission of Enquiry into the Riot at Moroka Emergency Camp, 26 Sept. 1947, pp. 52–54.

30. NTS 4534, File 64/313, L. I. Venables, Manager NEA—summary of an address by Mpanza, 4 Aug. 1946.

31. IA, WRAB 158/8, D. F. Hennesy, Asst. to Manager NEAD 6 Feb. 1947; ibid., minutes of meeting with squatter leaders 24 Feb. 1947; NTS 6477 File 5v313 S(4) Emmett to Chairman, Native Affairs Commission, 6 March 1947.

32. JMA, JMr., D1942, Johannesburg City Council Supplementary Memo to the Moroka Enquiry Commission, 27; M. Benson, *The African Patriots* (London, 1963), 113; Stadler, "Birds in the Cornfield"; French, "Mpanza"; B.G.M. Sundkler, *Bantu Prophets in South Africa* (London, 1961), 91, 139–50; Mia Brandel-Syrier, *Black Women in Search of God* (London, 1962), 27–232.

33. For the use of this notion in a similar context, see J. Comaroff, *Body of Power, Spirit of Resistance* (Chicago, 1985), 197–99. Here, following Levi-Strauss, she defines this as "concoctions of symbols already freighted with significance by a meaningful environment."

34. Martin West, *Bishops and Prophets in a Black City* (Cape Town, 1975), 16–40, 76–118; B.G.M. Sundkler, *Bantu Prophets in South Africa* (London, 1961), 180–259, Mia Brandel-Syrier, *Black Women in Search of God* (London, 1962),130–32.

35. Comaroff, *Body of Power*, 182.

36. West, *Bishops and Prophets*, 84–87, 197–98; Mayer, "Religion and Social Control in a South African Township," in Heribert Adam, ed., *South Africa: Sociological Perspectives* (London, 1971), 179–184.

37. NTS 6470 File 51/313/(Sl) Vol. 1, Affidavit H. A. M. Henderson, Senior Social Worker, Johannesburg, 24 March 1945; ibid., Vol. 2, Affidavit H. A. M. Henderson, 15 March 1946; ibid. Vol. 1, Affidavit, Tom Mokete, municipal policeman, 28 Feb. 1945.

38. As when he engineered an assault and attempted ouster of the Basotho President of the African Dingaka (Herbalist) Association when its former Zulu President had been displaced. NTS 7253, File 265/326/1; Hearing of K. D. Morgan, Native Commissioner, 3 Aug. 1951.

39. NTS 4534, File 641/313, L. l. Venables, Manager NEAD, summary of address by Mpanza, 4 Aug. 1946; NTS 6470, File 51/313/51, Vol. 7, Director of Native Labour to Sec. for Native Affairs, 15 May 1944.

40. Sundkler, *Bantu Prophets*, 24, 51, 88–90; Brandel-Syrier, *Black Women in Search of God*.

41. NTS 6470, File 51/313 (S1), Vol. I, Director of Native Labor to Sec. for Native Affairs, 19 June 1944; ibid., T. D. Young, Auditor's Report, 13 July 1944; *Rand Daily Mail*, 6 June 1944; *The Star*, 17 June 1944; NTS 6470, File 51/313 (S1), Vol. I, Director of Native Labor to the Sec. for Native Affairs, 15 May 1944; ibid., report by Non European Affairs Committee to Johannesburg City Council Meeting 24 Nov. 1944; ibid., Notes of meeting 12 March 1946. Ibid., R. Caudwell 13 March 1946, Notes of meeting 12 March 1946; BMA, NEAC meeting 8 Sept. 1947, Native Commissioner, Benoni 7 Aug. 1947, Notes of interview with squatters committee; ibid., 15 April 1947, meeting with Native Affairs Commissioner; NTS 6477, File 51/313/S(4). Director Native Labor to Sec. for Native Affairs, 7 Sept. 1946.

42. D. B. Barrett, *Schism and Renewal in Apra* (Nairobi, 1968), 64–71, 77, 80.

43. Interviews, Mr. F. Mahungela, Daveyton, 4 Aug. and 6 Oct. 1986.

44. Interviews, Mrs. E Simandle, Daveyton, 12 Feb. 1988, and Mrs. R. Nthoba, Daveyton, 21 Dec. 1988.

45. Interviews, Mr. K. S. Komane, Daveyton, 14 July, 7 Sept. 1988; Interviews, Mr. Motshweneng and Herman Zwane, Daveyton, 18 July 1988.

46. Interviews, Mr. M. N. Pukone, Daveyton 10,17 June, 20 Oct. 1986; Mr. P. Tukisi, Daveyton 22 Aug. 1986,19 Nov. 1987; Mr. Putone and Mr. Tukisi late 1987, NTS 7921, File 520/400(12), L. l. Venables to Native Commissioner Jhb, 25 June 1951, K. D. Morgan, Native Commissioner Johannesburg to Director of Native Labour, 20 Feb. 1951, NTS 4534, File 614/313, Supt. Jabavu Township, Precis of case against Ntoi (no date), various affidavits, 16 Sept., 19 Sept, 2 Oct. 1946.

47. This issue is partly explored in Bonner, "Desirable or Undesirable Basotho Women." It will also be the subject of a separate article.

48. BMA, NEAC meetings 14 Aug 1951, 9 Oct. 1951,13 Oct. 1952, 7 Oct. 1949.

49. Interview, F. Mahungela; BMA, NEAC meeting 8 Sept. 1947. Letter, Native Commissioner, Benoni, Annexure B. Notes of Interview with squatters' committee; Interview, Mr. D. Mtshali; Interview, Herman Zwane; Interviews, Mr. M. Pokane; NTS 4534, File 641/313, Record of Enquiry by Carr 16 Oct. 1946; IA, WRAB File 158/8 Memo, D. F. Hennessy to Assistant to Manager, 6 Feb. 1947.

50. Bonner, "Family, Crime, and Political Consciousness," 419; Interview, Mr. K. S. Komane, 14 July 1988; Benoni City Times, 1 April 1955; Stadler, "Birds in a Cornfield"; French, "Mpanza."

51. NTS 6479, File 51/313/59, K. D. Morgan, Native Commissioner, Johannesburg, to Director of Native Labor, 15 April 1946; ibid., Director of Native Labor to Sec. for Native Affairs, 11 April 1946; ibid., File 641/313, Memo on events between 23 and 25 May 1946; NTS 6477, File 51/313/54, K. D. Morgan to Director of Native Labor (Aug. 1946, 7 Sept. 1946, and 29 Nov. 1946). Director of Native Labor to Sec. for Native Affairs, 7 Sept. 1946; Mendelow and others interview with Sec. for Native Affairs

10 Feb. 1947; NTS 7921, File 540/400 (12), K. D. Morgan, Native Commissioner, JHB to Director of Native Labor, 20 Feb. 1951. See, for example, M. Horrell, ed., *A Survey of Race Relations in South Africa, 1956–7* (Johannesburg), 90; M. S. Lebelo, "Sophiatown Removals, Relocation and Political Quiescence in the Rand Townships, 1950–1965," Honours dissertation, University of the Witwatersrand, 1988, 86–88.

52. IA, WRAB File 158/8 minutes of a meeting with squatter leaders, 24 Feb. 1947.

53. Interviews, Mrs. E. Ntlokwane, and Mrs. Senosi, Wattville, May 1985; I. A. WRAB file 158/8 minutes of a meeting with a deputation of squatters, 20 Feb. 1947. Interviews, Maliehe Khoeli Teyateyaneng (Lesotho) and Muldersdrift (Transvaal) 1986–87.

54. NTS 7253, File 265/326/1, Memo on the case of Mpanza, n.d.; NTS 4534, File 614/313, Supt. Jabavu Township, Precis of case against Ntoi (n.d.); various affidavits, 16 Sept., 19 Sept., Oct. 1946; K. D. Morgan, Native Commissioner, Johannesburg to Director of Native Labor, 18 Oct. 1945; NTS 6470 File 52/313/(51) Vol. 1, C. P. Alport, Director of Native Labour to Sec. for Native Affairs, 19 June 1944.

55. This requires a separate discussion in its own right. For one among several suggestive accounts of mass meetings in this period see NTS 6687 File 310/332 Vol. 2, Report of the Commission Appinted to Enquire into the Disturbances of 30 Aug. 1947 at the Moroka emergency camp, 31–32.

56. NTS 6470, File 51/313/51, Vol. 1, Director of Native Labour to Sec for Native Affairs, 14 July 1944; IA, WRAB File 158/8, memo D. E. Hennessy, Assistant to the Manager 6 Feb. 1947; ibid., minutes of 2 meetings with deputations of squatters, 20 Feb. 1947; ibid., minutes of a meeting on the squatter camp 24 Feb. 1947, NTS 6477 File 51/313/5(4) Part 1, minutes on memo Under Sec of Native Affairs and others n.d. 1950.

57. Interview Mrs. Methula Senaoane, December 1988; IA, WRAB File 158/8 minutes of a meeting with a deputation of squatters 20 Feb. 1947.

58. M. Scott, *A Time to Speak* (London, 1958), 158.

59. IA, WRAB 158/4, L. l. Venables, Manager NEA to Dep. Commissioner, SAP 5 Sept 1946; ibid., 158/5, Vol. 1, K. D. Morgan, Native Commissioner, Johannesburg, to D. N. L. 23 March 1949; CAD NTS 6470 File 51/313/(S1), Vol. 1, I. D. Young, Auditors Report 13 July 1944; French, "Mpanza," Chap. 5.

60. Interviews, D. K. M. Mboweni, N. Mbulane, John Ngwenyama, and Mr. Ndlovu Chiawelo, Feb. 1988.

61. J. Seekings, " 'Why was Soweto Different?' Urban Development Township Policies and the Political Economy of Soweto, 1977–1984," paper presented to the African Studies Seminar, African Studies Institute, 2 May 1988, 9–10.

62. J. Cole, "Crossroads," *South African Labour Bulletin* 12:2 (1980); Ari Sitas, "Vigilantism in Durban" (unpublished).

Chapter 5

1. *New Statesman* Weekend Competition, 6 August 1987. One of the winning entries ran:

From the primitive, pre-social horde
Through the rule of the priest and the lord
To the bourgeoisie's sway
Of our own present day
There's been little enough to applaud.

2. Howard Lamar and Leonard Thompson, eds., *The Frontier in History: North America and Southern Africa Compared* (New Haven, 1981); George M. Frederickson, *White Supremacy: A Comparative Study in American and South African History* (New York, 1981); John Cell, *The Highest Stage of White Supremacy: The Origins of Segregation in South Africa and America* (Cambridge, 1982); Eric Foner, *Nothing but Freedom: Emancipation and its Legacy* (Baton Rouge, 1983); Stanley Greenberg, *Race and State in Capitalist Development: Comparative Perspectives* (New Haven, 1980).

3. Karl Marx, "Preface to First Edition," *Capital* Vol. 1 (Harmondsworth, 1973), 92.

4. Leon Trotsky, *The History of the Russian Revolution* (New York, 1980), 5.

5. Peter Novick, *That Noble Dream: The "Objectivity Question" and the American Historical Profession* (New York, 1988), 239, 320.

6. Ibid., 239–40.

7. Ibid., 240; R. Hofstadter, *The Progressive Historians* (New York, 1968), xii.

8. Ibid., 457. On the Progressive historians see also: John Higham, *Writing American History: Essays on Modern Scholarship* (Bloomington, 1970); Gene Wise, *American Historical Explanations* (Homewood, 1973); David W. Noble, *The End of American History* (Minneapolis, 1985); J. Tyrrell, *The Absent Marx: Class Analysis and Liberal History in Twentieth-Century America* (Westport, 1986).

9. Perry Anderson, *Considerations on Western Marxism* (London, 1979), 55.

10. Hofstadter, *Progressive Historians*, 442.

11. Noble, *End of American History*, 44.

12. William M. Macmillan, *Bantu, Boer and Briton: The Making of the South African Native Problem* (London, 1929), vii; Christopher Saunders, *The Making of the South African Past* (Cape Town, 1988), 81 (quoting from private correspondence by de Kiewiet).

13. William M. Macmillan, *The South African Agrarian Problem and its Historical Development* (Johannesburg, 1919), 23; Cornelius W. de Kiewiet, *A History of South Africa Social and Economic* (Oxford, 1941), v.

14. William W. Macmillan, *The Cape Colour Question: A Historical Survey* (London, 1927), 3; for his didacticism see *Bantu, Boer and Briton*, 314–18; de Kiewiet, *The Imperial Factor in South Africa*, 1.

15. William M. Macmillan, *Complex South Africa* (London, 1930), 17–18; de Kiewiet, *Imperial Factor*, 1–3; cf. de Kiewiet, *History of South Africa*, 79, 87, 179–80, 217, 242. De Kiewiet's theme of interaction and interdependence was also pursued by his contemporary, H. M. Robertson, in the mid-1930s; and it was acknowledged as central to the conception of the past in the *Oxford History of South Africa* 1, eds., Monica Wilson and Leonard Thompson (Oxford, 1969).

16. Hofstadter, *Progressive Historians*, 27.

17. Floris A. van Jaarsveld, *The Afrikaner's Interpretation of South African History* (Cape Town, 1964), 57, 62.

18. Petrus J. van der Merwe, *Die Noordwaartse Beweging van die Boere voor die Groot Trek* (The Hague, 1937); *Die Trekboer in die Geskiedenis van die Kaapkolonie* (Cape Town, 1938); *Trek* (Cape Town, 1945). The Turner reference is in W. Keith Hancock, "Trek," *Economic History Review*, second series, 10:3 (1958), 338.

19. Pierre van den Berghe, *South Africa: A Study in Conflict* (Berkeley, 1967), 267.

20. The examples are from: Godfrey H. L. Le May, *British Supremacy in South Africa 1899–1907* (Oxford, 1965), 1; Clement F. Goodfellow, *Great Britain and South African Confederation 1870–1881* (Cape Town, 1966), 261; Leonard M. Thompson, *The Unification of South Africa 1902–1910* (Oxford, 1960), 95–97.

21. David M. Potter, "Tasks of Research in American History," (originally published in 1963) in D. E. Fehrenbacker, ed., *History and American Society: Essays of David M. Potter* (New York, 1973), 33.

22. Kenneth W. Smith, *The Changing Past: Trends in South African Historical Writing* (Johannesburg, 1988), 137; Jeffrey Butler and Deryck Schreuder, "Liberal Historiography since 1945," in Jeffrey Butler, Richard Elphick and David Welsh, eds., *Democratic Liberalism in South Africa* (Middletown, 1987), 156.

23. Frederick R. Johnstone, "'Most Painful to Our Hearts': South Africa through the Eyes of the New School," *Canadian Journal of African Studies*, 16 (1982), 7.

24. John Lonsdale, "From Colony to Industrial State: South African Historiography as Seen from England," *Social Dynamics* 9 (1983), 69.

25. Jean van der Poel, *The Jameson Raid* (Cape Town, 1966), 330.

26. Le May, *British Supremacy*, 213.

27. Le May, *British Supremacy*, 214.

28. Le May, *British Supremacy*, 215.

29. Van Jaarsveld, *Afrikaner's Interpretation*, 66–67, 149.

30. D. W. Kruger, *The Making of a Nation: A History of South Africa 1910–1961* (Johannesburg, 1969), 335, 1, 329. A similar shift from "Afrikaner" to "white" history is exemplifies in C. F. J. Muller, ed., *Five Hundred Years: A History of South Africa* (Pretoria, 1969), see esp. xi–xii.

31. The phrase is from Michael Kammen, "Introduction" in Kammen, ed., *The Past Before Us: Contemporary Historical Writing in the United States* (Ithaca, 1980), 21.

32. Gisela Bock, "Women's History and Gender History: Aspects of an International Debate," *Gender and History* 1:1 (Spring, 1989), 7.

33. Joan Kelly-Gadol, "The Social Relation of the Sexes: Methodological Implications of Women's History," *Signs* 1 (1976), 809 (quoted by Bock, "Women's History and Gender History," 8) Gerda Lerner, *The Majority Finds its Past* (New York, 1979), 145–54.

34. Joan W. Scott, "Gender: A Useful Category of Historical Analysis," *American Historical Review* 91 (1986), 1054.

35. Ann D. Gordon, Mari Jo Buhle, and Nancy Shrom Dye, "The Problem of Women's History," in Berenice Carroll, ed., *Liberating Women's History* (Urbana, 1976), quoted by Scott, "Gender," 1054.

36. Bertell Ollman and Edward Vernoff, "Introduction," in Ollman and Vernoff, eds., *The Left Academy: Marxist Scholarship on American Campuses* (New York, 1982), 1; Tyrrell, *Absent Marx*, 241; Novick, *Noble Dream*, 458.

37. Novick, *Noble Dream*, 438.

38. The phrase is from Charles S. Maier, "Marking Time: The Historiography of International Relations," in Kammen, *The Past Before Us*, 356.

39. Bernard Bailyn, "The Challenge of Modern Historiography," *American Historical Review* 87 (1982), 2; Carl Degler, "In Pursuit of an American History," *American Historical Review* 92 (1987), 1; Thomas Bender, "Wholes and Parts: The Need for Synthesis in American History," *Journal of American History* 73 (1986), 126.

40. Peter Stearns, "The New Social History: An Overview," in J. B. Gardner and G. R. Adams, eds., *Ordinary People and Everyday Life* (Nashville, 1983). But the advance of science is inexorable: cf. Stearns, "Social History and History: A Progress Report," *Journal of Social History* (1985), 323: "New aspects of the social experience remain a bit richer—as witness recent efforts to deal with histories of emotions or histories of beliefs about sleep."

41. Interview with Linda Gordon in H. Abelove, et al., eds., *Visions of History* (New York, 1984), 91.

42. William E. Leuchtenburg, "The Pertinence of Political History: Reflections on the Significance of the State in America," *Journal of American History* (1987), 586–87.

43. Bailyn, "Challenge of Modern Historiography," 3.

44. Richard M. Andrews, "Some Implications of the *Annales* School and its Methods for a Revision of Historical Writing About the United States," *Review* 1 (1978), 165; Herbert Gutman, "Whatever Happened to History?" *Nation*, 21 November 1981, 521; Bender, "Wholes and Parts," 120.

45. Novick, *Noble Dream*, 438.

46. D. C. Coleman, *Whatever Happened to Economic History?* (Cambridge, 1973),

8, quoted in David Cannadine, "British History: Past, Present—and Future?" *Past and Present* 116 (1987), 177; Cannadine's threnody is a reminder that the disciplinary "crisis" is *not* peculiarly American.

47. Interview with David Montgomery in Abelove, et al. *Visions of History*, 180; Jon Wiener, letter to author, December, 1988.

48. Johnstone, "Most Painful to Our Hearts"; Lonsdale, "From Colony to Industrial State"; Shula Marks, "The Historiography of South Africa" in Bogumil Jewsiewicki and Navid Newbury, eds., *African Historiographies* (Beverly Hills, 1986); Martin Murray, "The Triumph of Marxist Approaches in South African Social and Labour History," *Journal of Asian and African Studies* 23:1–2 (1988); Saunders, *Making of the South African Past*, 165–91; Smith, *Changing Past*, 155–221.

49. Murray, "The Triumph of Marxist Approaches," 71; Johnstone, "Most Painful to Our Hearts," 5, 10; Marks, "Histeriography," 168, 166; Saunders, *Making of the South African Past*, 190; Smith, *Changing Past*, 216.

50. Deborah Gaitskell, "Race, Gender and Imperialism: A Century of Black Girls' Education in South Africa," unpublished seminar paper, University of Cape Town Africa Seminar, August 1988, 10.

51. Belinda Bozzoli, "Marxism, Feminism and South African Studies," *Journal of Southern African Studies* 9:2 (1983), 139, 170.

52. "Editorial" in *Agenda* 1 (published c/o Sociology Department, University of Natal, Durban), 1.

53. Bozzoli, "Marxism, Feminism and South African Studies," 139.

54. "Editorial," *Agenda*, 2.

55. Nadine Gordimer, *Times Literary Supplement*, 15 August 1980.

56. Marks, "Histeriography," 175; and see Albert Grundlingh, "Sosiale Geskiedenis en die Dilemma in Afrikanergeskeidskrywing," *South African Historical Journal* 19 (November 1987).

57. Marks, "Historiography," 170–71.

58. As, for example, by David Brody, "Labour Historiography" in Kammen, *Past Before Us*, 265–71.

59. Marks, "Historiography," 175; Smith, *Changing Past*, 216–17.

60. Floris A. van Jaarsveld, "Afrikaner Historiography" in D. Ray, P. Shinnie and D. Williams, eds., *Into the 80s: Proceedings of the Eleventh Annual Conference of the Canadian Association of African Studies* (Vancouver, 1981), 237–39; *Moderne geskiedskrywing: opstelle oor 'n nuwe benadering tot gekiedenis* (Pretoria, 1982), 129, 133, 155–57. Cf. van Jaarsveld, *Wie en wat is die Afrikaner?* (Cape Town, 1981), 72; "Die ontmitologisering van die Afrikaner se geskiedsbeeld" in A. J. Coetzee, ed., *Hulsels van kristal* (Cape Town, 1981).

61. Grundlingh, "Sosiale Geskiedenis," 31. The quotation is from the English summary of the article.

62. C. A. Kapp and A. E. Carl, "Trends and Developmental Patterns in History Education under the Cape Education Department" in A. E. Carl, ed., *His-

tory Education—the Road Ahead, Second National Congress of the South African Society for the Training of History Teachers (Stellenbosch, 1988), 201, 208.

63. Belinda Bozzoli, "History, Experience and Culture" in Bozzoli ed., *Town and Countryside in the Transvaal* (Johannesburg, 1983), 2.

64. The British visitor was the late Sir Robert Birley (personal communication to author); Lynn Maree, "The Hearts and Minds of the People" in Peter Kallaway, ed., *Apartheid and Education: The Education of Black South Africans* (Johannesburg, 1984), 152, 155.

65. Richard E. van der Ross, "The Pen and the Sword: Seeking a New Focus on History and the Teaching of History in South Africa" in Carl, *History Education*, 2; C. P. Jooste, "Perspectives in Distance Education of History at the Campus Further Training University of Vista," in Carl, *History Education*, 238.

66. Observed at the University of the Western Cape, 1988.

Chapter 6

1. Nadine Gordimer, *Burger's Daughter* (London and New York, 1979), 346–47.

2. Nadine Gordimer et al, *What Happened to Burger's Daughter, or How South African Censorship Works* (Johannesburg, 1980), 30. This compilation gives an account of the remarkable process whereby *Burger's Daughter* was first banned and then unbanned after its publication; among the reasons for its original banning was that the SSRC pamphlet was a prohibited document, and that the SSRC had itself been outlawed.

3. For a South African example, see "Coetzee and the Cockroach which Can't be Killed," account of an address by J. M. Coetzee at the Weekly Mail Book Week, Cape Town, November 1987, in *Weekly Mail* (Johannesburg), 19 Nov. 1987, 19.

4. The discovery that Paul de Man—one of the leading lights in deconstructionist literary theory and criticism—had written anti-semitic articles in a pro-Nazi newspaper in Belgium during the war, sent his associates scurrying in search of contextual aspects the theory normally refuses: history (the contingencies of the Second World War); biography (influence on de Man by his uncle); and "evidence" (the hope that his story might turn out to be more complex than it appeared at first sight). For example, see Jacques Derrida, "Like the Sound of the Sea Deep within a Shell: Paul de Man's War," *Critical Inquiry* 14:3 (1988), 590–632.

5. My indebtedness to Raymond Williams should be apparent here. See his *Culture and Society 1780–1950* (New York, 1983), *The Long Revolution* (Westport, CT, 1975), and *Marxism and Literature* (Oxford, 1977).

6. A related area in South African study is the social history of writers themselves. For a fine example, see Tim Couzens, *The New African: a Study of the Life and Work of H. I. E. Dhlomo* (Johannesburg, 1985).

7. This is what I have attempted to explore in my book, *The Novels of Nadine Gordimer: History from the Inside* (Cambridge, 1986). See the Introduction for a fuller explanation.

8. Pierre Macherey, *A Theory of Literary Production* (Boston, 1978). Macherey's account is a necessary complement to any conception of "homology" between the literary work, the "world-view" of a particular class, and the broader structures of society—as put forward in its classic form, for instance, by Lucien Goldmann in his *The Hidden God* (London, 1976).

9. An idea contained within the ambit of what Frederic Jameson explores far more broadly in his *The Political Unconscious* (Ithaca, 1981).

10. Cf. Raymond Williams's remarks on the presence of an implicit "subjunctive" mode in Dickens's work, in his "Forms of English Fiction in 1848," *Writing in Society* (London, 1983), 160–61.

11. Olive Schreiner (pseud. Ralph Iron), *The Story of an African Farm* (New York, 1987; first published, 1883). For her key feminist work see *Woman and Labour* (New York, 1972; first published, 1911). For her biography see Ruth First and Ann Scott, *Olive Schreiner* (London, 1980).

12. Tim Couzens's introduction to Sol T. Plaatje, *Mhudi* (London, 1978; first published, 1930). For a monumental account of Plaatje's life, see Brian Willan, *Sol Plaatje* (Berkeley, 1984).

13. Clingman, *Novels of Nadine Gordimer*, 135–6.

14. For a fuller analysis of this theme see Stephen Clingman, "Beyond the Limit: The Social Relations of Madness in Southern African Fiction," in Dominick LaCapra, ed., *The Bounds of Race: Perspectives on Hegemony and Resistance* (Ithaca, forthcoming).

15. Sol T. Plaatje, *Native Life in South Africa* (Johannesburg, 1982; first published, 1916); for the linkage between this and the novel, see Couzens's introduction to *Mhudi*.

16. Legislated under the Mines and Works Amendment Act (1926), the Natives Urban Areas Act (1923), and the Immorality Act (1927).

17. David Rabkin, "Race and Fiction: *God's Stepchildren* and *Turbott Wolfe*," in Kenneth Parker, ed., *The South African Novel in English* (London, 1978); Sarah Gertrude Millin, *God's Stepchildren* (Johannesburg, 1986; first published in 1924); William Plomer, *Turbott Wolfe* (New York, 1985; first published in 1926).

18. See J. P. L. Snyman, *The South African Novel in English (1880–1930)* (Potchefstroom, 1952), 87. Snyman's own account of *God's Stepchildren* indicates, as might be expected, that *readings* or *interpretations* of fiction also have a historical basis.

19. For further analysis of Millin and Plomer in these terms, see Clingman, "Beyond the Limit."

20. Modikwe Dikobe, *The Marabi Dance* (London, 1973).

21. See Kelwyn Sole and Eddie Koch, "*The Marabi Dance: A Working Class Novel?*", mimeo. This article does, however, give a good sense of Dikobe's

complex life-history from the 1930s on as a vendor, hawker, clerk, trade unionist, political activist, farmer, and schoolmaster, and of the almost equally complicated publishing history of the novel.

22. Jameson, *Political Unconscious*, 77, adapts Levi-Strauss's characterization of the function of myth in this way.

23. Peter Abrahams, *Mine Boy* (London, 1963; first published, 1946).

24. Alan Paton, *Cry, the Beloved Country* (Harmondsworth, 1958; first published, 1948).

25. Can Themba, "The Bottom of the Bottle," in *The Will to Die* (London, 1972) and in Essop Patel, ed., *The World of Can Themba* (Johannesburg, 1985).

26. Nadine Gordimer, *A World of Strangers* (New York, 1958). For analysis of these codes, see Clingman, *Novels of Nadine Gordimer*, chapter 2.

27. Nadine Gordimer, *The Late Bourgeois World* (New York, 1966); Alex La Guma, *The Stone Country* (London, 1974; first published, 1967), and *In the Fog of the Seasons' End* (London, 1972); Richard Rive, *Emergency* (Cape Town, 1988; first published, 1964); C. J. Driver, *Elegy for a Revolutionary* (Cape Town, 1984; first published, 1969).

28. For a summary of other work on the Revolt as well as his own analysis, see Tom Lodge, *Black Politics in South Africa Since 1945* (New York, 1983), chapter 13.

29. Njabulo Simakahle Ndebele, "I Hid My Love in a Sewage . . . ," *The Classic* (1970), reprinted in Tim Couzens and Essop Patel, eds., *The Return of the Amasi Bird* (Johannesburg, 1982), 213–14.

30. Mongane Wally Serote, "What's in this Black 'Shit,'" in *Yakhal'inkomo* (Johannesburg, 1972).

31. For some of these complications—especially those surrounding issues of social and cultural identity—see Kelwyn Sole, "Identities and Priorities in Recent Black Literature and Performance: A Preliminary Investigation," paper presented at a conference on Economic Development and Racial Domination, University of the Western Cape, October 1984.

32. I discuss this issue in "Revolution and Reality: South African Fiction in the 1980s," in Martin Trump, ed., *Rendering Things Visible: Essays on South African Literary Culture of the 1970s and '80s* (Johannesburg, 1990).

33. Nadine Gordimer, *July's People* (New York, 1981) and *A Sport of Nature* (New York, 1987); J. M. Coetzee, *Life & Times of Michael K* (New York and Johannesburg, 1983); Mongane Serote, *To Every Birth its Blood* (New York, 1989; first published, 1981).

34. Jeremy Cronin, "'Even Under the Rine of Terror': Insurgent South African Poetry," *Research in African Literatures* 19:1 (1988), 12–23.

Chapter 7

1. Heribert Adam, *South Africa Without Apartheid* (Berkeley, 1986), 27.

2. Joe Slovo, "The Working Class and Nation Building" in Marie van Diepen, *The National Question in South Africa* (London, 1988), 43.

3. Z. R. Mahabane, "The Exclusion of the Bantu" in Thomas Karis and Gwendolen Carter, *From Protest to Challenge*, Vol. 1 (Stanford, 1978), 290.

4. Pallo Jordan, "The South African Liberation Movement and the Making of a New Nation" in van Diepen, *The National Question*, 119–124.

5. Gail Gerhart, *Black Power in South Africa* (Berkeley, 1978), 202, 201; Philip Ata Kgosana, *Lest We Forget: An Autobiography* (Johannesburg, 1988), 17.

6. Eli Weinberg, *Portrait of a People* (London, 1981).

7. Sol T. Plaatje, *Mhudi* (Johannesburg, 1973), 23, 24, 150, 47, 163. For commentaries see Brian Willan, *Sol Plaatje: A Biography* (Johannesburg, 1984), 349–71; Tim Couzens, "Introduction," Plaatje, *Mhudi*.

8. S. M. Molema, *Montshiwa, Barolong Chief and Patriot* (Cape Town, 1966), 17, 11, 27.

9. Plaatje, "The Late Allen King," *The African World Annual*, December 1915, reprinted in *English in Africa*, Plaatje Centenary Issue 3:2 (September, 1976), 27.

10. Molema, *Montshiwa*, 203, 55, 203, 207, 210, 192, 168.

11. Ibid., 203.

12. H.I.E. Dhlomo, *Collected Works* (Johannesburg, 1985), 121, 174.

13. Ibid., 140.

14. Bernard Magubane, *The Political Economy of Race and Class in South Africa* (New York, 1979), 25.

15. As Lembede put it, "Africans are naturally socialistic as illustrated in their social practices and customs. The achievement of national liberation will therefore herald or usher in a new era of African socialism. Our immediate task, however, is not socialism but national liberation." Anton Lembede, "Policy of the Congress Youth League," *Inkundla ya Bantu*, May 1946.

16. Nelson Mandela, *No Easy Walk to Freedom* (London, 1973), 147.

17. Ezekiel Mphahlele, *Down Second Avenue* (London, 1980), 188–89, 192, 15.

18. Ibid., 196. Mphahlele quotes this passage from his MA dissertation, "The Non-European Character in South English Fiction," University of South Africa, 1956.

19. Ibid., 183. Also, Lewis Nkosi, *Home and Exile* (London, 1965); Bloke Modisane, *Blame me on History* (London, 1963).

20. For example see Don Mattera, *Memory is the Weapon* (Johannesburg, 1987); Can Themba, *The Will to Die* (Cape Town, 1982); Essop Patel, ed., *The World of Nat Nakasa* (Johannesburg, 1985); Miriam Tlali, *Muriel at Metropolitan* (Johannesburg, 1975).

21. Albert Luthuli, *Let My People Go* (London, 1963), 26, 27, 31, 20, 29. For other personal memoirs of the 1950s by Congress activists see: Helen Joseph, *Side by Side* (New York, 1986); Frances Baard, *My Spirit is not Banned* (Harare, 1986); Raymond Suttner and Jeremy Cronin, *Thirty Years of the Freedom Charter* (Johannesburg, 1986).

22. *Inkundla* was a fortnightly newspaper which under Ngubane's Editor-proprietorship became a forum for Africanist/Youth League discussion.

23. Page references from Jordan Kush Ngubane, *Ushaba: A Zulu Umlando*

(Washington, 1976), 1, 7, 93. Other works by Ngubane: "African Political Movements," *African South* 1:1 (1956); *An African Explains Apartheid* (New York, 1963).

24. For example: Moses Kotane, *South Africa's Way Forward* (Cape Town, 1954); Kotane, *The Great Crisis Ahead: A Call to Unity* (Woodstock, 1957).

25. See especially: Nelson Mandela, "Freedom in Our Lifetime," *Liberation*, June 1956.

26. Ruth First, "Preface" in Govan Mbeki, *South Africa: The Peasants' Revolt* (Harmondsworth, 1964), 12.

27. Mbeki, *Peasants' Revolt*, 63, 117, 132. For interwar resistance to taxes in the Transkei see: William Beinart and Colin Bundy, *Hidden Struggles in Rural South Africa* (Johannesburg, 1987).

28. Mbeki, *Peasants Revolt*, 47, 17. Not all communists at this time shared Mbeki's view that South Africa comprised a single common society. Advocate and *New Age* editor, Lionel Forman, was "convinced that the way to freedom lay through a recognition and glad acceptance of South Africa's multi-national composition. Only when each national community was free to develop its own special qualities, could all sections of the population make their full contribution to the cause of liberation." Ray Alexander, ed., *Black and White in South African History: Lionel Forman Anniversary Booklet* (Cape Town, n.d., 1960?), 2.

29. Programme of the South African Communist Party, *The Road to South African Freedom* (London, n.d.), 33, 27, 28, 35.

30. Harold Wolpe, "The Theory of Internal Colonialism: The South African Case" in I. Oxaal, T. Barnett, and D. Booth, eds., *Beyond the Sociology of a Development: Economy and Society in Latin America and Africa* (London, 1975), 234. See also: Wolpe, "Capitalism and Cheap Labour Power," *Economy and Society* 1:4 (1972).

31. See for example: Joe Slovo, "South Africa—No Middle Road" in Basil Davidson, Anthony Wilkinson, and Joe Slovo, eds., *Southern Africa: The New Politics of Revolution* (Harmondsworth, 1976); A. Lerumo, *Fifty Fighting Years: The South African Communist Party, 1921–1971* (London, 1971).

32. For ANC's strategic program, adopted in 1969: "Strategy and Tactics of the South African Revolution" reprinted in Alex La Guma, ed., *Apartheid* (London, 1972).

33. Simons and Simons, *Class and Colour in South Africa, 1850–1950* (Harmondsworth, 1969), 184, 440–41, 195, 492, 609, 576.

34. For example: Edward Roux, *Time Longer than Rope* (London, 1948), 264; Eddie and Win Roux, *Rebel Pity* (London, 1970), 60–64.

35. H. J. and R. J. Simons, *Class and Colour*, 406, 625.

36. Brian Bunting, *The Rise of the South African Reich* (Harmondsworth, 1964), 117, 294, 303, 297.

37. Naboth Mokgatle, *Autobiography of an Unknown South African* (Berkeley, 1975), 284.

38. Magubane, *Political Economy of Race and Class*, xiii, 16.

39. Magubane, "African Opposition in South Africa," *The African Review* 2:3 (1972).

40. Magubane, *Political Economy of Race and Class*, 56, 65, 275–76, 68, 96, 294, 443.

41. Ibid., 214, 189, 128.

42. Adelaide Tambo, *Preparing for Power: Oliver Tambo Speaks* (London, 1987).

43. The African Students' Association was formed in 1960 by African university students with ANC sympathies. It supplied early political experience for a significant proportion of the ANC's contemporary leadership, including Sechaba editor Frances Meli, International Department Director Thabo Mbeki, and Umkhonto we Sizwe Chief of Staff Chris Hani, all three Fort Hare classmates.

44. Frances Meli, *South Africa Belongs to Us: a History of the ANC* (Harare, 1988), viii, 48, 53, 73.

45. Ibid., 73, 107, 113, x, 140.

46. "L," "Liberal Misconceptions about our Revolution," *The African Communist* 85 (1981), 119.

47. Meli, *South Africa Belongs to Us*, vi, 129.

48. John Pampallis, *National Struggle, Class Struggle: South Africa since 1870* (London, 1988). For a dissenting view of the ANC in this period written by a disaffected member of the Congress of Democrats (Baruch Hirson), see Socialist League of Africa, "Ten Years of the Stay-at-Home," *International Socialist* 5 (Summer, 1961).

49. Mary Benson, *Nelson Mandela* (London, 1980), and *Nelson Mandela* (Harmondsworth, 1986).

50. Fatima Meer, *Higher than Hope: Rolihlahla We Love You* (Johannesburg, 1988), 61, 119, 3, 4, 18, 7.

51. Ibid., 85, 52.

52, Ibid., 25, 132, 121, 58, 28, 135, 74.

53. "The Charter on the Mines," *SASPU National*, Last Quarter, 1987, Supplement on the Freedom Charter, 5.

54. Benson, *Nelson Mandela* (1986), 21–23. Other Mandela biographies include Nancy Harnison, *Winnie Mandela, Mother of a Nation* (London, 1985); Jim Haskins, *Winnie Mandela: Life of Struggle* (New York, 1988); Sharon Goulds, *Winnie Mandela* (London, 1988); Milton Meltzer, *Winnie Mandela: The Soul of South Africa* (New York, 1988). See also Winnie Mandela, *Part of My Soul* (Harmondsworth, 1985).

Chapter 8

I would especially like to thank Patrick Manning and the RHR Editorial Collective, and Christopher Saunders, Shamil Jeppie and Stanley Trapido for giving me the benefit of their valuable criticisms and comment on an earlier draft of this article.

1. Interview with L. T., retired schoolteacher, April 1988.

2. "Mnguni," *Three Hundred Years* (Cumberwood, 1988; first published 1952); Nosipho Majeke, *The Role of the Missionaries in Conquest* (Cumberwood, 1986; first published 1952); W. P. van Schoor, "The Origin and Development of Segregation in South Africa," in Maurice Hommel, ed., *Contribution of Non-European Peoples to World Civilization* (Johannesburg, 1989), 132.

3. Jack London, *Martin Eden* (Harmondsworth, 1980), 95.

4. L. Callinicos, "Working Class Politics in South Africa," *International Socialism*, 31 (1985), 46.

5. E. P. Thompson, *The Poverty of Theory and other essays* (London, 1978), 66.

6. Gwyn A. Williams, *Proletarian Order: Antonio Gramsci, Factory Councils and the Origins of Italian Communism, 1911–1921* (London, 1975), 29.

7. Sarah Mokone, "Majority Rule: Some Notes," *The Educational Journal* (Sept. 1977).

8. Ian Goldin, *Making Race: The Politics and Economics of Coloured Identity in South Africa* (Cape Town, 1987), 58.

9. Gavin Lewis, *Between the Wire and the Wall: A History of South African "Coloured" Politics* (Cape Town, 1987), 241.

10. "Richard Rive" in *Writing against Apartheid: Interviews with South African Authors*, NELM Interviews, Series Two (Grahamstown, 1987), 5. Rive was stabbed to death in his home in Cape Town in June 1989. His last novel, *Emergency Continues*, was published in Cape Town in November 1990.

11. Neville Alexander, *Sow the Wind: Contemporary Speeches* (Johannesburg, 1984), 38.

12. C. Saunders, "'Mnguni' and *Three Hundred Years* Revisited," *Kronos* II (1986), 75.

13. Colin Bundy, "Land and Liberation: Popular Rural Protest and the National Liberation Movements in South Africa 1920–1960" in Shula Marks and Stanley Trapido, eds., *The Politics of Race, Class and Nationalism in Twentieth Century South Africa* (London, 1987), 255.

14. See, for example, Lewis, *Between the Wire*, 241–43; Goldin, *Making Race*, 57–59; Callinicos, "Working Class Politics," 47; Alexander, "Aspects of Non-Collaboration," 12.

15. Bundy, "Land and Liberation," 255.

16. See, for example, the "Majority Rule" series by Sarah Mokone in the *Educational Journal*, 1977–78, reprinted as "Majority Rule: Some Notes," *Teachers' League of South Africa* (Cape Town, 1982).

17. Callinicos, "Working Class Politics," 47.

18. But it included scatterings of freethinking clergymen and artisans in rural areas. Hosea Jaffe, *A History of Africa* (London, 1985), 129.

19. Interview, C. K., March 1988. My thanks to Catherine Higgs for permitting me to quote from this interview.

20. Richard Rive, *Emergency* (Cape Town, 1988), 119.

21. Mpumelelo Temba, "Boycott as a Weapon of Struggle," in Hommel, *Non-European Peoples*, 193. See also Jonathan Hyslop, "Teacher Resistance in African Education from the 1940s to the 1980s," in Mokubung Nkomo, ed., *Pedagogy of Domination* (Trenton, 1990), 100–101.

22. Van Schoor, "Development of Segregation," 136, 139.

23. Neville Alexander, "Aspects of Non-Collaboration in the Western Cape 1943–1963," *Social Dynamics* 12:1 (1986), 2–3.

24. Gareth Stedman Jones, *Languages of Class: Studies in English Working Class History, 1832–1982* (Cambridge, 1983), 107; see also Robert Gray, "The Deconstructing of the English Working Class," *Social History* 11:3(1986), 368, 373; Gregory Claeys, "Language, Class and Historical Consciousness in Nineteenth Century Britain," *Economy and Society* 14:2 (1985), 259–60.

25. Gwyn A. Williams, "18 Brumaire: Karl Marx and Defeat," in Betty Matthews, ed., *Marx: 100 Years On* (London, 1983), 12.

26. B. M. Kies, "The Contribution of Non-European Peoples to World Civilisation," A. J. Abrahamse Memorial Lecture, Teachers League of South Africa, Cape Town, 1953, 16, 39–40.

27. Angelique Titus, "From Brown to Bakke," *The Educational Journal* (July-August 1978), 4–5.

28. J. Camp, "The World and South Africa," *The Educational Journal* (June 1988).

29. John Lonsdale, "From Colony to Industrial State: South African Historiography as Seen from England," *Social Dynamics* 9:1 (1983), 68.

30. Christopher Saunders, "Historians and Apartheid," in John Lonsdale, ed., *South Africa in Question* (Cambridge, 1988).

31. Alessandro Portelli, "Uchronic Dreams: Working Class Memory and Possible Worlds," paper presented at the Sixth International Oral History Conference, St John's College, Oxford, Sept. 1987.

32. R. O. Dudley, Foreword, in "Mnguni," *Three Hundred Years* (Cumberwood, 1988). "Bush College" is a long-standing term of contempt for black "ethnic" universities.

33. Perry Anderson "Communist Party History," in Raphael Samuel, ed., *People's History and Socialist Theory* (London, 1981), 154–55.

34. Bill Schwarz, "'The People' in History: The Communist Party Historians' Group, 1946–56," in Richard Johnson, Gregor McLennan, Bill Schwarz and David Sutton, eds., *Making Histories* (London, 1982), 95.

35. *Introduction to "Race" and Racism*, Cape Action League Workbook I (Cape Town, 1987).

36. Ibid.

37. Particularly, Frederick A. Johnstone, *Class, Race and Gold* (London, 1976); Luli Callinicos, *Gold and Workers, 1886–1923* (Johannesburg, 1980); and *Working Life: Factories, Townships and Popular Culture on the Rand, 1886–1940* (Johannesburg, 1987).

38. "Mnguni," *Three Hundred Years*, 132.

39. *Introduction to "Race" and Racism.* "Azania" is a Greek term in prehistory for an ancient and powerful African civilization in part of Eastern and Central Africa. As a historical symbol of black cultural pride and identity, it has been widely appropriated since the late 1970s by black consciousness groupings within the liberation movement, such as the Azanian People's Organisation and the Azanian Students' Organisation. See Basil Davidson, *Old Africa Rediscovered* (London, 1959), 191–96; Tom Lodge, *Black Politics in South Africa since 1945* (Johannesburg, 1983), 310.

40. Saunders, "Historians and Apartheid"; "Mnguni," *Three Hundred Years*, 77.

41. Bill Nasson, "Western Cape Politics: Aspects of Popular Political and Ideological Struggle," in Ingrid Obery and Glen Moss, eds., *South African Review* 5 (Johannesburg, 1989), 105.

42. Dudley, Foreword, *Three Hundred Years*.

43. Julian Cobbing, "Jettisoning the Mfecane (with Perestroika)," Centre for African Studies Seminar Paper, University of Cape Town, April 1989. I am grateful to the author for permission to quote from this unpublished work.

44. Christopher Saunders, "Historians and Apartheid"; "Mnguni," *Three Hundred Years*, 74–81; and *The Making of the South African Past: Major Historians on Race and Class* (Cape Town, 1988), 135–38; Ken Smith, *The Changing Past: Trends in South African Historical Writing* (Johannesburg, 1988), 157–59, 177–78.

45. L. Callinicos, "The People's Past: Towards Transforming the Present," *Critical Arts* 4:2 (1986), 22.

46. Nosipho Majeke, Introduction, *The Role of the Missionaries in Conquest* (Cumberwood, 1986).

47. Goldin, *Making Race*, 118.

48. Van Schoor, "Origin and Development of Segregation," 132.

49. *The Festival in Pictures: Van Riebeeck Festival*, 1952.

50. Interview with G. H., retired nurse, July 1988.

51. "Mnguni," *Three Hundred Years*, 175–76.

52. Majeke, Introduction, *Role of Missionaries*.

53. Baruch Hirson, "A Question of Class: The Writings of Kenneth A. Jordaan," *Searchlight South Africa* 2 (1989), 22.

54. Saunders, *Making of the South African Past*, 137.

55. Majeke, *Role of the Missionaries*, 18–19, 70.

56. "Mnguni," *Three Hundred Years*, 132–33.

57. Hosea Jaffe, "Fascism in South Africa," reprinted in his *The Pyramid of Nations* (Milan, 1980), 90–91.

58. Ibid., 83, 85, 91.

59. Jaffe, *History of Africa*, 89.

60. Lonsdale, "Colony to Industrial State," 69.

61. K. A. Jordaan, "Jan van Riebeeck: His Place in South African History," in Hommel, ed., *Non-European Peoples*, 139.

62. Cobbing, "Mfecane."
63. Ciraj Rassool, 'History and the Independent left in the 1950s: Towards uncovering a Marxist intellectual tradition', Popular history workshop paper, University of the Witwatersand History Workshop conference, February 1990.

Chapter 9

I would like to express thanks to Eddie Webster and Phil Bonner for their helpful comments.

1. This does not claim to be a comprehensive review of the literature on South African labor history. I have considered only a selection of work, and that largely to illustrate my own general argument in the article.
2. Labor history is more likely to find a home among sociologists. In the 1980s, at a time when issues of labor organization became increasingly marginal to the concerns of the History Workshop, labor history was well received and well represented in papers to the annual conference of the Association of Sociologists of Southern Africa.
3. See, addressing the broader international field, E. J. Hobsbawm, "Labor History and Ideology," *Journal of Social History* 7 (1974), 371–73.
4. E. P. Thompson, *The Making of the English Working Class* (London, 1980), 4.
5. See, for example, editions of the journal *Social History* in recent years.
6. G. Eley and K. Nield, "Why Does Social History Ignore Politics?" *Social History* 5:2 (1980).
7. M. J. Murray, "The Triumph of Marxist Approaches in South African Social and Labour History," *Journal of Asian and African Studies* 23 (1988), 98.
8. J. Zeitlin, "From Labour History to the History of Industrial Relations," *Economic History Review* 2nd series (1987).
9. E. Roux, *Time Longer than Rope: A History of the Black Man's Struggle for Freedom in South Africa* (Wisconsin, 1972); B. du Toit, *Ukubamba Amadolo: Workers Struggles in the South African Textile Industry* (London, 1978); H. J. and R. E. Simons, *Class and Colour in South Africa 1850–1950* (Harmondsworth, 1969); E. S. Sachs, *Garment Workers in Action: History of the Garment Workers of South Africa to 1952* (Johannesburg, 1957). There have of course been other more conservative offerings to come from within the trade union movement, for example: I. L. Walker and B. Weinbren, *2000 Casualties: a History of the Trade Unions and the Labour Movement in the Union of South Africa* (Johannesburg, 1961); J. A. Adams, *Wheels Within Wheels: Trade Unionism on the South African Railways and Harbours* (Johannesburg, 1952).
10. E. J. Hobsbawm, "Foreword," in J. Foster, *Class Struggle and the Industrial Revolution: Early Industrial Capitalism in Three English Towns* (London, 1974).

11. M. Horrell, *South African Trade Unionism: A Study of a Divided Working Class* (Johannesburg, 1961), 25–25, 124; M. Horrell, *South Africa's Workers: their Organisations and the Patterns of Employment* (Johannesburg, 1969), 88–89, 129–33.

12. S. T. van der Horst, *Native Labour in South Africa*, 2nd edn., (London, 1971), 157–58, 163–64.

13. C. W. de Kiewiet, *A History of South Africa, Social and Economic* (Oxford, 1957), 167.

14. S. Trapido, "South Africa in a Comparative Analysis of Industrialisation," *Journal of Development Studies* 7 (1970–71); H. Wolpe, "Capitalism and Cheap Labour Power in South Africa: from Segregation to Apartheid," *Economy and Society* 1 (1972); M. Legassick, "South Africa: Capital Accumulation and Violence," *Economy and Society* 3 (1974); F. A. Johnstone, *Class, Race and Gold: a Study of Class Relations and Discrimination in South Africa* (London, 1976).

15. Compare R. Lambert, "Political Unionism in South Africa: A Review of Feit's *Workers Without Weapons*," *South African Labour Bulletin* 6 (1980), with his "Trade Unions, Nationalism and the Socialist Project in South Africa," *South African Review 4* (Johannesburg, 1987).

16. My own first work on South African labor history was prompted by union requests for educational materials.

17. Among the ideological influences, Richard Turner's work should be mentioned. Turner himself was influenced by debates in Europe after 1968 about more libertarian forms of socialism. See his *Eye of the Needle: An Essay on Participatory Democracy* (Johannesburg, 1972). Turner was banned by the South African government in 1973 and assassinated in 1978.

18. For a summary of black trade unions and federations in the 1970s see J. Maree, "The Emergence, Struggles and Achievements of Black Trade Unions in South Africa 1973 to 1984," *Labour, Capital and Society* 18:2 (1985).

19. It should be mentioned that FOSATU'S alternative class-based approach, which informed the writing of labor history in the 1970s, was at odds with the South African Communist Party's "internal colonialism" thesis, as well as with the popular democratic strategies of the wider Congress alliance. Such differences were to become more critical after 1980 when the pendulum swung again in favor of mass popular struggles.

20. J. Lewis, "The New Unionism: Industrialisation and Industrial Unions in South Africa, 1925–1930"; and P. Bonner, "The Decline and Fall of the ICU: A Case of Self-Destruction?" in Eddie Webster, ed., *Essays in Southern African Labour History* (Johannesburg, 1978).

21. H. Bradford, *A Taste of Freedom: the ICU in Rural South Africa, 1924–1930* (New Haven, 1987).

22. J. Rex, "The Compound, Reserve and Urban Location—Essential Institutions of Southern African Labour Exploitation," *South African Labour Bul-*

letin 1:4 (1974); C. van Onselen, *Chibaro: African Mine Labour in Southern Rhodesia 1900–1933* (London, 1976); I. R. Phimister, "Origins and Aspects of African Worker Consciousness in Rhodesia," in Webster, *Essays in Southern African Labour History.*

23. Webster, *Essays in Southern African Labour History,* 2; Hobsbawm, *Worlds of Labour,* preface.

24. P. Warwick, *Black People and the South African War* (Cambridge, 1983); P. Richardson, *Chinese Mine Labour in the Transvaal* (London, 1982); P. Bonner, "The 1920 Black Mineworkers Strike: A Preliminary Account," in B. Bozzoli, ed., *Labour, Townships and Protest* (Johannesburg, 1979); S. Moroney, "The Development of the Compound as a Mechanism of Worker Control, 1900–1912," *South African Labour Bulletin* 4:3 (1978).

25. In the case of the mines, T. Dunbar Moodie's work marks a beginning. See, for example, "The Moral Economy of the Black Miners Strike of 1946," *Journal of Southern African Studies* 13:1 (1986). C. van Onselen's subsequent work on the social and economic history of the Witwatersrand to the First World War, while touching on the issues, is primarily concerned with ruling-class strategies to secure a docile working class and the strategies of those groups that sought to avoid wage labor altogether. See van Onselen, *New Ninevah, New Bablyon; Studies in the Social and Economic History of the Witwatersrand, 1886–1914,* 2 vols. (London, 1982).

26. R. H. Davies, *Capital, State and White Labour in South Africa 1900–1960: an Historical Materialist Analysis of Class Formation and Class Relations* (Brighton, 1979); D. O'Meara, *Volkskapitalisme: Class, Capital and Ideology in the Development of Afrikaner Nationalism 1934–48* (Cambridge, 1983); M. L. Morris, "The Development of Capitalism in South African Agriculture," *Economy and Society* 5:3 (1976); D. Kaplan, "The Politics of Industrial Protection in South Africa 1910–1939," *Journal of Southern African Studies* 3 (1976).

27. D. Innes and M. Plaut, "Class Struggle and Economic Development in South Africa: the Inter-War Years," Institute of Commonwealth Studies seminar paper, 1977.

28. D. O'Meara, "Analysing Afrikaner Nationalism: the Christian-National Assault on White Trade Unionism in South Africa, 1934–1948," *African Affairs* 77 (1978); R. H. Davies, "The Class Character of South Africa's Industrial Conciliation Legislation," *South African Labour Bulletin* 2:6 (1976); D. Lewis, "The South African State and African Trade Unions 1947–1953," unpublished, 1976.

29. For a summary of the registration debate, see J. Maree, ed., *The Independent Trade Unions 1974–1984: Ten Years of the South African Labour Bulletin* (Johannesburg, 1987), part four.

30. See, for example, E. Webster, "Workers Divided: Five Faces of the Hidden Abode," in B. Bozzoli, ed., *Class, Community and Conflict* (Johannesburg, 1987).

31. P. Bonner and R. Lambert, "Batons and Bare Heads: the Strike at Amato

Textiles, 1958"; and W. Beinart, "Worker Consciousness, Ethnic Particularism and Nationalism: the Experience of a South African Migrant, 1930–1960," in S. Marks and S. Trapido, eds., *The Politics of Race, Class and Nationalism in Twentieth Century South Africa* (London, 1987); A. Sitas, "African Worker Responses on the East Rand to Changes in South Africa's Metal Industry, 1960–1980," Ph.D. thesis, University of the Witwatersrand, 1983.

32. E. A. Mantzaris, "Radical Community: the Yiddish-Speaking Branch of the International Socialist League, 1918–1920," and E. Brink, "Maar 'n Klomp Factory Meide: Afrikaner Family and Community on the Witwatersrand During the 1920s," in Bozzoli, *Class, Community and Conflict*; E. Koch, "Without Visible Means of Subsistence: Slumyard Culture in Johannesburg 1918–1940"; and D. Moodie, "Mine Culture and Miners' Identity on the South African Gold Mines," in B. Bozzoli, ed., *Town and Countryside in the Transvaal* (Johannesburg, 1983).

33. S. Friedman, *Building Tomorrow Today: African Workers in Trade Unions 1970–1984* (Johannesburg, 1987). See the review in *South African Labour Bulletin* 12:3 (1987). D. Nchube, *The Influence of Capitalism and Apartheid on the Development of Black Trade Unions in South Africa* (Johannesburg, 1985), is another conspiratorial view of white communist dominance.

34. D. MacShane, M. Plaut, D. Ward, *Power! Black Workers, their Unions and the Struggle for Freedom in South Africa* (Nottingham, 1984). See the review in *South African Labour Bulletin* 10:4 (1985).

35. K. Luckhardt and B. Wall, *Organise or Starve: the History of the South African Congress of Trade Unions* (London, 1980). The rise of labor history in the 1970s has also left its mark on more general historical accounts. See T. Lodge, *Black Politics in South Africa since 1945* (Johannesburg, 1983); C. Walker, *Women and Resistance in South Africa* (London, 1982); D. Yudelman, *The Emergence of Modern South Africa: State, Capital and the Incorporation of Organised Labour on the South African Gold Fields 1902–1939* (Cape Town, 1984); B. Hirson, "The Making of an African Working Class on the Witwatersrand: Class and Community Struggles in an Urban Setting, 1932–1947," Ph.D. thesis, University of London, 1986. Similar labor history is woven in radical nationalist works, such as R. Suttner and J. Cronin, *Thirty Years of the Freedom Charter* (Johannesburg, 1986); F. Meli, *South Africa Belongs to Us: a History of the ANC* (Harare, 1988).

36. L. Callinicos, *A Peoples' History of South Africa. Volume I: Gold and Workers 1886–1924* (Johannesburg, 1981); *Volume II: Working Life 1886–1940: Factories, Townships and Popular Culture on the Rand* (Johannesburg, 1987); see also National Education Crisis Committee, *What is History? A New Approach to History for Students, Workers and Communities* (Johannesburg, 1987); Labour and Community Project/South African Council for Higher Education (LACOM/SACHED), *Freedom from Below: the Struggle for Trade Unions*

in South Africa (Durban, 1987); and also publications by the International Labour Research and Information Group and the Labour History Group.

37. L. Callinicos, "The Peoples' Past: Towards Transforming the Present," in Bozzoli, *Class, Community and Conflict*, 61.

38. See A. von Kotze, *Organise and Act: The Natal Workers Theatre Movement 1983–1987* (Durban, 1988).

39. In labor history, for example, M. Nicol's "A History of Garment and Tailoring Workers in Cape Town, 1900–1939," Ph.D. thesis, University of Cape Town, 1984, demonstrated the impact of industrial relations machinery on the operation of a union. For a summary of the major areas of concern in labor studies until 1984, see J. Maree, ed., *The Independent Trade Unions 1974–1984: Ten Years of the South African Labour Bulletin*, (Johannesburg, 1987).

40. J. Maree, "Democracy and Oligarchy in Trade Unions: the Independent Trade Unions in the Transvaal and the Western Province General Workers Union in the 1970s," *Social Dynamics* 8:1 (1982).

41. In round terms, African trade union membership grew from 70,000 in 1979 to approximately 1,500,000 in 1988.

42. See P. Bonner, "Family, Crime and Political Consciousness on the East Rand, 1939–1955," *Journal of Southern African Studies* 14:3 (1988); E. Brink, "The Afrikaner Women of the Garment Workers Union, 1918–1939," M.A. thesis, University of the Witwatersrand, 1987.

43. A. Sitas, "Moral Formations and Struggles Amongst Migrant Workers on the East Rand," *Labour, Capital, and Society* 18:2 (1985).

44. Bradford, *A Taste of Freedom*.

45. Bradford's discussion parallels Lambert's analysis of the South African Congress of Trade Union's political unionism. See below.

46. J. Lewis, *Industrialisation and Trade Union Organisation*. See also Webster, *Cast in a Racial Mold; Labor Process and Trade Unionism in the Foundries* (Johannesburg, 1985); O. Crankshaw, "Trade Union Strategy and the Labour Process: TUCSA Trade Unions in the Transport and Building Industries, 1955–1977," M.A. thesis, University of the Witwatersrand, 1987; J. W. Ewart, "Changing Labour Processes and Worker Response in the South African Newspaper and Printing Industry," Ph.D. thesis, University of Stellenbosch, 1988; D. Lincoln, "The Culture of the South African Sugar Mill: the Impress of the Sugarocracy," Ph.D. thesis, University of Cape Town, 1986; A. Kraak, "Restructuring Skills: Capital's Initiatives in the Black Education and Industrial Training Arenas since 1976," M.A. thesis, University of Cape Town, 1988.

47. M. Swilling, "The Politics of Working Class Struggles in Germiston, 1979–1983," paper presented at History Workshop Conference, University of the Witwatersrand, 1984; Labour Monitoring Group, "The November Stay-Away," *South African Labour Bulletin* 10:6 (1985). For continuing debate on

trade unions and politics see Maree, *The Independent Trade Unions, 1974–1984*, part five; and Lambert, "Trade Unions, Nationalism and the Socialist Project in South Africa."

48. R. Lambert, "Political Unionism in South Africa: The South African Congress of Trade Unions, 1955–1965," Ph.D thesis, University of the Witwatersrand, 1988. For a right-wing version of the argument—which argues that unions should stick to bread and butter issues—see E. Feit, *Workers Without Weapons: the South African Congress of Trade Unions and the Organisation of the African Workers* (Hamden, Conn., 1975).

49. R. Lambert, "Political Unionism and Working Class Hegemony: Perspectives on the South African Congress of Trade Unions, 1955–1965," *Labour, Capital and Society* 18:2 (1985); ILRIG also adopts a comparative approach: in a recent project they have looked into the development of political unionism in Europe during the "red years" following World War One.

50. See R. Cohen, "The 'New' International Labour Studies: a Definition," Working Paper Series No. 7, Centre for Developing-Area Studies, McGill University, n.d.; E. Webster, "The Rise of the New Labour Studies in South Africa: a Brief Report on Current Labour Research Activities," unpublished, 1985. Although debates within the labor movement and opposition politics clearly influenced labor historians' interpretation of political unionism, their interest also represents a response to certain intellectual influences. The work of Ernesto Laclau should be mentioned—*Politics and Ideologies in Marxist Theory* (London, 1977)—which demonstrated that class and nationalist politics are not necessarily antagonistic. These ideas are present in Philip Bonner's account of the radicalization of sections of the petty bourgeois leadership of the Transvaal Native Congress in response to the rising tide of black working-class militancy during 1870–1930. See "The Transvaal Native Congress: the Radicalization of the Black Petty Bourgeoisie on the Rand," in S. Marks and R. Rathbone, eds., *Industrialization and Social Change in South Africa: African Class Formation, Culture and Consciousness, 1870–1930* (London, 1983).

51. Current debates revolve around whether such alliances should be based upon a broad anti-apartheid alliance, or restricted to largely working-class constituencies. Also see the "errors of workerism" debate in *South African Labour Bulletin* 12:3 (1987) and 12:5 (1987).

52. As far as TUCSA is concerned, considerable research has already been done by Jeff Lever—although this work remains unpublished.

Chapter 10

1. On the theoretical importance of this distinction in the case of popular protest in the United States, see Frances Piven and Richard Cloward, *Poor People's Movements: Why They Succeed, How They Fail* (New York, 1979).

2. William Cobbett and Robin Cohen, eds., *Popular Struggle in South Africa* (Trenton, 1988).

3. Martin Murray, *South Africa, Time of Agony, Time of Destiny: The Upsurge of Popular Protest* (London, 1987).
4. Stephen M. Davis, *Apartheid's Rebels: Inside South Africa's Hidden War* (New Haven, 1987).

Chapter 11

1. See Nicholas Haysom, *Apartheid's Private Army: The Rise of Right-wing Vigilantes in South Africa* (London: Catholic Institute of International Relations, 1986), and Jeremy Keenan, "Counter-Revolution as Reform: Struggle in the Bantustans," in William Cobbett and Robin Cohen, *Popular Struggles in South Africa* (Trenton, 1988).

The *Weekly Mail* of 21 April 1989 reported that over 1300 people had been killed in the violence by that date. By August 1990 police figures had risen to well over 2000, while the ANC was citing a figure of over 4000 (*New York Times*, 3 October, 1990). There have been more UDF/COSATU aligned victims than Inkatha supporters killed, but anti-Inkatha violence has also been extensive. Moreover, these identifications can be tenuous. See, for example, the illuminating reports in *Weekly Mail*, 5 May 1989; and reports in *Indicator: South Africa* since 1986.

The discrepency between official and ANC figures may in part reflect a difference over whether to include deaths due to rural "faction-fights," which the police characterize as "tribal" rather than political. Although "faction-fights" have long existed, often tied to resource shortages, it is not clear how the emergence of UDF/Inkatha conflict may have affected them. Among other things, these conflicts between different Zulu "tribes" point up the vacuity of the concept of "tribe," often applied to the category "Zulu" as a whole by the U.S. media.

2. Gerhard Maré and Georgina Hamilton, *An Appetite for Power: Buthelezi, Inkatha and the Politics of Loyal Resistance* (Bloomington, 1988).
3. Buthelezi uses the term "black" as the state does, to include only those conventionally referred to as Africans. The usage of "black" to refer to all racially oppressed people classified by the state as "Black," "Asian," or "Coloured" is conventional among progressives.
4. See *An Appetite for Power*, 64–73, and the sources cited there, as well as John Brewer, "The membership of Inkatha in KwaMashu," *African Affairs* 84 (1985), and "From Ancient Rome to KwaZulu: Inkatha in South African Politics," in Philip Frankel et al. eds., *State, Resistance and change in South Africa* (New York, 1988); and Roger Southall, "Buthelezi, Inkatha, and the Politics of Compromise," *African Affairs* 80 (1981).
5. Inkatha's membership claims have consistently risen to keep them ahead of those of the UDF and COSATU. Of the three, COSATU's figures are most trustworthy. Much of the conflict in Natal in 1988 and 1989 arose around Inkatha membership drives, which often began with mass meetings called in pro-UDF areas and attended by large numbers of armed men

bused in from elsewhere. Locals condemned such meetings as intimidation, while Inkatha criticized efforts to prevent them as attempts to create "no-go areas" itself restricting political freedom. Vigilante attacks often followed such meetings, which frequently featured strong anti-UDF rhetoric, but Inkatha denied any organizational involvement or responsibility in the attacks.

6. Both the new Democratic Party and the National Party should be regarded as conservative. Although the DP encompasses the individuals holding positions from social democratic to Thatcherite, its official positions seem comparable to those of the Bush administration, reflecting the influence of its corporate sponsors.

7. See reports on the visit to South Africa by Democratic Senators Sam Nunn and David Boren, *Johannesburg Star*, 22 December 1988; and Michael Clough, "U.S. Policy in the Post-Crocker Era," *Weekly Mail*, 17 March 1989. Clough was an African adviser to Michael Dukakis.

8. Shula Marks, *The Ambiguities of Dependence: Race, Class and Nationalism in Twentieth Century South Africa* (Baltimore, 1986).

9. See, for example, Shula Marks, "Patriotism, Patriarchy and Purity: Natal and the Politics of Zulu Ethnic Consciousness," in Leroy Vail ed., *The Creation of Tribalism in Southern Africa* (Berkeley and Los Angeles, 1989), 215–240. This collection is an important contribution to the understanding of the dynamics of ethnicity in southern Africa.

10. Helen Bradford, *A Taste of Freedom: The ICU in Rural South Africa, 1924–1930* (New Haven, 1988), 96. Bradford says that in many places people would not join the ICU unless chiefs approved it, and that the ICU sought to recruit chiefs.(95–100) She also suggests that some people turned to independent African churches as an alternative to both the ICU and traditionalism.

11. See Josette Cole, *Crossroads: The Politics of Reform and Repression 1976–1986* (Johannesburg, 1987).

12. Marks cites Benedict Anderson, *Imagined Communities: Reflections on the Origin and Spread of Nationalism* (London, 1983). Recent southern African studies of ethnicity have laid much stress on the fact that ethnicity is socially and culturally constructed, the product of imagination, often with the implication that it is therefore not real, or not genuine, or less real than other social ties (See Vail, *Creation of Tribalism*, for examples). Such a reaction by historians is perhaps inevitable, given the propensity of ethnic ideology to claim authenticity for ethnic sentiment through spurious history. But imagined ethnic communities are analogous to consciousness of other social relations. For instance, class consciousness, particularly in forms which allow political mobilization across societies, is clearly a matter of imagined community, making ideological links between concrete local experiences of relations of production and property.

13. Thandeka Gqubule, "Chiefs to Salute Impis' Blood River Sacrifice," *Weekly Mail*, 15 December 1988, 6.

14. On the ANC's historical rural weakness, see Nelson Mandela, "Address to the South African Youth Congress, April 13, 1990," in *Speeches 1990* (New York, 1990) 46; Colin Bundy, "Land and Liberation: Popular Rural Protest and the National Liberation Movements in South Africa, 1920–1960," in Shula Marks and Stanley Trapido eds., *The Politics of Race, Class and Nationalism in Twentieth Century South Africa* (New York, 1987) 276–281; and Tom Lodge, "Resistance in the Countryside" in *Black Politics in South Africa Since 1945* (New York, 1983), 290.

The MDM organizes rural authorities through the Congress of Traditional Leaders of South Africa (Contralesa). Contralesa emerged out of opposition to plans for "independence" by chiefs in Kwandebele bantustan in 1986. "Traditional leaders" appear to include bantustan bureaucrats whose positions are structurally similar to Buthelezi's, but who take the right political line. Although SAYCO at first had close ties to Contralesa (partly through Enos Mabuza of Kangwane and his Inyanza Youth League), a split appears to be emerging. It is said that chiefs don't like to be organized by youth. See Thando Zuma, "The role of the Chiefs in the Liberation Struggle," *The African Communist* (1st quarter, 1990) 65–76; and "Mabuza Wants to 'Close Down' His Homeland," *Southern Africa Report* (Johannesburg) 23 March, 1990, 3 (especially the quotations from Patrick Lekota of the UDF).

Chapter 12

1. The Workshop's budget was limited (at least by U.S. standards). For the first six years, the Workshop survived on voluntary labor and small *ad hoc* grants for particular projects. After its establishment as a research unit in the university structure, it received between R13,000 and R18,000 a year. Most Open Days have been run on a budget of between R3,000 and R5,000.

2. See, for example, the four edited collections of History Workshop papers: Belinda Bozzoli, ed., *Labour, Townships and Protest* (Johannesburg, 1979); *Town and Countryside in the Transvaal* (Johannesburg, 1981); *Class, Community and Conflict: South African Perspectives* (Johannesburg, 1987). See also P. Bonner, I. Hofmeyr, D. James, and T. Lodge, eds., *Holding Their Ground* (Johannesburg, 1989).

3. See, for example, the popular histories written by Luli Callinicos: *Gold and Workers* (Johannesburg, 1981); *Working Life* (Johannesburg, 1987); *Workers Under Apartheid* (Johannesburg, forthcoming). See also the History Workshop "topic" series, which includes the two booklets by Paul la Hausse and Robert Edgar and the book of articles *New Nation, New History* (Johannesburg, 1989).

4. See L. Witz, *Write Your Own History* (Johannesburg, 1988), and his article on such projects in this volume.

5. Some of these arguments are pursued in more detail in Bozzoli, "Preface," in Bozzoli, *Class, Community and Conflict* and *Town and Countryside.*

6. Some of the reasons for this are given in Bozzoli, "Class, Community and Ideology in the Making of South African Society," in Bozzoli, *Class, Community and Conflict.* In summary, these are: the consistent use of racial ideology as a means to capitalist development; the failure of "class"-based communities to evolve because of ethnic factors as well as constant community removal and destruction; the absence of a class conscious artisanal stratum able to connect with black unskilled workers; and the role played by the state (as opposed to capital) in promoting proletarianization and impoverishment. The parallels between and differences from the U.S. case are instructive here; it would be interesting to pursue the "Why is there no socialism in the United States" argument for South Africa.

7. By "motherist" I mean ideologies which appeal to women's interests in broad social justice, and may thus appear to be akin to feminism, but which rely for their appeal on references to such symbols as motherhood, family, loyalty, and kinship.

8. See the chapter by Tom Lodge in this volume for a discussion of this factor.

9. For one view of the history of the white left, see H. J. and R. E. Simons, *Class and Colour in South Africa, 1850–1950* (London, 1970).

10. In contrast to the earlier times documented by Simons and Simons, *Class and Colour.*

11. Not least among their motivations has been a concern to ensure that post-apartheid South Africa continues to have an independent intelligentsia; complete subordination to political movements now could mean annihilation later. Some have even expressed concern that the selective cultural boycott—when administered by political groupings—represents an attempt to harness intransigent left-wing intellectuals to the goals of particular social movements.

12. Quoted in Paul Baran, "The Commitment of the Intellectual," in *Review of African Political Economy* 32 (April, 1985).

13. It should not be assumed that just because black culture contains its own versions of history (in opposition to those promulgated by the state) that these versions are necessarily valid. Often popular versions of the black past consist of myths about classless precapitalist societies, and the exploits of numerous heroic great men.

14. Over the years, the composition of the Workshop committee has changed. Some of the founder members remain involved; other members have included: Tom Lodge, Isabel Hofmeyr, Deborah James, the recently assassinated anthropologist David Webster, Andy Manson, Ahmed Essop, Sue Krige, Jon Hyslop, Peter Delius, Leslie Witz, Georgina Jaffee, Paul la Hausse, Debby Posel, Cynthia Kros, and Linda Chisolm.

15. A selection of photographs from this exhibition was later published; see

P. Kallaway and P. Pearson, *Johannesburg: Images and Continuities* (Johannesburg, 1987).

16. Interview in the *Rand Daily Mail*, 2 February 1981.

17. The "Open Day" format has been imitated by a variety of cultural and political groupings in the years since our first proper one in 1981. These include FOSATU, COSATU, the Johannesburg Democratic Action Committee, the UDF, and many others.

18. The derivation of these metaphors and symbols is something that needs to be explored, along lines suggested by George Rudé, in his exploration of the means whereby popular consciousness is transformed from "resistance" to "revolution"; see his *Ideology and Popular Protest* (London, 1981), chapter 3. Some may indeed have had their roots in the types of symbolic patterns being developed by researchers. Most, it is likely, emerged from a black township culture with its own momentum, although it very likely drew on written materials produced by white intellectuals for some of its historical and cultural rationale. The "new history" cannot be discounted as a cultural force in the changed consciousness of the eighties, whether "workerist" or "populist."

19. COSATU, perhaps influenced by the Black Consciousness background of some of its leaders, expressed criticisms of the role of white intellectuals (university-based sympathizers, rather than actual organizers) in the movement, and indeed has excluded them from the influential educational positions they held in FOSATU in the past. This seems to herald an era in which Black Consciousness critiques of white intellectuals find an unprecedented institutional base in a variety of places—including the apartheid-initiated black universities, where a number of black intellectuals now hold jobs, and seek a constituency, in competition with the existing and relatively influential left-wing whites.

20. We asked ourselves whether the History Workshop would ever expand its interest in the white working-class beyond those, such as Garment Workers, who adopt a less than hard-line racist ideology, to include an examination of those workers who have allied themselves explicitly with racism. Such an expanded view would undoubtedly involve confronting our sometimes romantic audiences with the more unpalatable side of worker ideology.

21. Using popular imagery and songs, portraying the history of black proletarianization through the eyes of a single woman, "Fight Where We Stand" attempted to cut across the established lines of discourse, falling neither into the "populist" nor the "workerist" camp, focusing on none of the formats of other open day presentations, many of which were designed to "fit" specific audience interests.

22. *Weekly Mail*, 17 February 1987.

23. See Mike Morris, "Social History and the Transition to Capitalism in the

South African Countryside," *Review of African Political Economy* 41 (Sept. 1988).

Chapter 15

1. Reader's Digest, *Illustrated History of South Africa: The Real Story* (Pleasantville, 1988).
2. Luli Callinicos, *Gold and Workers* (Johannesburg, 1981). The Labour History Group has produced six booklets published by Cape Town's Esquire Press: *The ICU*; *The 1922 White Mineworkers' Strike*; *Workers at War: CNETU and the 1946 African Mineworkers' Strike*; *Garment Workers Unite!*; *Organizing at the Cape Town Docks*; and *Asinamali! Organizing in the 1950s*.
3. Shamim Marie, *Divide and Profit* (Durban, 1986).
4. National Union of Mineworkers, *Five Brave Days: The Strike of 1946* (Johannesburg, 1986).
5. Ari Sitas, ed., *Black Mamba Rising* (Durban, 1988). Worker theater also has emerged as a form of popular history. See Bhekizizwe Peterson's chapter in this volume, and Astrid von Kotze, *Organize and Act* (Durban, 1988).
6. Glenda Kruss, *People's Education: An Examination of the Concept* (Cape Town, 1988), 21.
7. *Resolutions of the National Consultative Conference on the Crisis in Education* (Johannesburg, 1985).
8. Kruss, *People's Education*, 22.
9. See Melanie Walker's chapter in this volume.
10. An evaluation is being conducted by Wits University's Educational Policy Unit, which is partially funded by community organizations.
11. See History Workshop member Tom Lodge's *Black Politics in South Africa since 1945* (Johannesburg, 1984), and archaeologist Revil Mason's *Origins of the African People of the Johannesburg Area* (Johannesburg, 1988).
12. Culture and Working Life Project, University of Natal, Durban; ILRIG, University of Cape Town; People's Education Research Project, University of the Western Cape. The University of the Witwatersrand's Sociology of Work Programme also produces accessible reports of its research on health and safety. See, for example, *A Thousand Ways to Die*, produced in collaboration with NUM and published by the literacy press *Learn and Teach* in 1986.
13. See Andre Odendaal's chapter in this volume.
14. Robert Edgar, *Because They Chose the Plan of God: The Story of the Bullhoek Massacre* (Johannesburg, 1988); Paul la Hausse, *Brewers, Beerhalls and Boycotts: A History of Liquor in South Africa* (Johannesburg, 1988). See the chapter by David Anthony.
15. Luli Callinicos, *Working Life: Factories, Townships and Popular Culture* (Johannesburg, 1987). The third volume of the *People's History* trilogy (forthcoming) deals with the relationship between Afrikaner and African nationalism and the working class in the 1940s and 1950s.

16. *Working Life* received the Noma Award for the best book published in Africa in 1988.
17. History Workshop, *New Nation, New History* (Johannesburg, 1989). See the chapter by David Anthony.
18. *Fight Where We Stand*, as well as other slide, video and film histories, is obtainable from the History Workshop's Media Center.
19. People's College Comics, *Down Second Avenue* and *Equiano: The Slave Who Fought To Be Free* (Johannesburg, 1988). See the chapter by Joshua Brown.
20. In every edition, literacy magazines like *Learn and Teach* (Box 11074, Johannesburg 2000) and *Upbeat* (Box 11350, Johannesburg 2000), feature illustrated history articles based on recent academic research. For example, *Learn and Teach* recently published an article on longtime activist Edwin Mofutsenyama, now in his eighties and in exile in Lesotho, based on interviews conducted by American historian Robert Edgar. *Upbeat* also uses historians' research, often focusing on the history of young people. Topics include the history of urban gangs and child slavery in the nineteenth century.
21. Peter Kallaway and Patrick Pearson's discussion of photographs of Chinese miners in early Johannesburg in *Johannesburg: Images and Continuities: A History of Working Class Life through Pictures, 1885–1935* (Johannesburg, 1986), suggests an appropriate approach to visual history for writers of popular history.
22. Examples of the work of Afrapix photographers can be seen in Alex Harris, ed., *Beyond the Barricades* (New York, 1989).
23. For example, Mandlenkosi, *The Sun Shall Rise for the Workers* (Johannesburg, 1983); Petrus Tom, *My Life's Struggle* (Johannesburg, 1984); Don Mattera, *Memory is the Weapon* (Johannesburg, 1987); Godfrey Moloi, *My Life: Volume One* (Johannesburg, 1987); Alfred Temba Qabula, *A Working Life, Cruel Beyond Belief* (Durban, 1989). See Andries Oliphant's chapter about popular history in *Staffrider* magazine in this volume.
24. Popular books on women include: Institute of Black Research, *Factories and Families* (Durban, 1984); Jane Barret, et al., *Vukani Makhosikazi: South African Women Speak* (London, 1985); Lesley Lawson, *Working Women* (Johannesburg, 1986); National Union of Metal and Allied Workers of South Africa, *NUMSA Women Organise!* (Excome, 1989).
25. Members of the Joint Distribution Group include Ravan Press, Skotaville Press, Learn and Teach, the *South African Labour Bulletin*, the South African Council for Higher Education (SACHED), ILRIG, and the *South African Review* series.

Chapter 16

Textbooks Discussed

N. Fleurs et al, *Discovering History* (Pietermaritzburg, 1983)
P. Kallaway, ed., *History Alive* 9 and 10 (Pietermartizburg, 1987)

H. A. Lamprechts et al, *History* 10 (Goodwood, 1987)

H.G.J. Lintvelt et al, *Timelines* 6 and 10 (Pinelands, 1985)

C. Oosthuizen et al, *History to the Point* Std. 3 and Std. 4 (Johannesburg, 1981)

Notes

The terms "African," "Coloured," "Indian," and "White" have been coined by the South African government to refer to bureaucratically designated "racial" groups in South Africa. These terms are unacceptable to the majority of the population and are used only where clarity on government policy is relevant. The preferred term is black, referring to Africans, "Coloureds" and Indians. Black is not used to refer to those previously designated as "Native" or "Bantu" by the South African government.

Many of the insights that inform this paper have been generated firstly, by several years spent teaching history in a "Coloured" high school and trying to develop alternative resource materials, and more recently, by collaborative work with "African" teachers in the Primary Education Project from 1987–1989.

1. Denis Hirson, *The House Next Door* (Claremont, 1986).
2. Cynthia Kros, "History for Democracy," *Lengwitch* (March 1987), 21. I am indebted to her article for drawing my attention to Denis Hirson's autobiography.
3. Congress of South African Students (COSAS) member quoted in P. Christie, *The Right to Learn* (Johannesburg, 1985), 14.
4. South African Institute of Race Relations, *Race Relations Survey 1987/88* (Johannesburg, 1988), 151–170.
5. The *Argus*, 11 May 1989.
6. South African Institute of Race Relations, *Race Relations,* 165–167. The pupil-teacher ratio is calculated on the basis of each teacher teaching every period in the week. In practice this seldom happens so that a ratio of 1:41 in real situations may mean up to 90 children in each class. In the relatively better off urban primary schools in which the Primary Education Project is based, classes still average 55.
7. Quoted in B. Rose and R. Tunmer, *Documents in South African Education* (Johannesburg, 1975), 266, 262.
8. Quoted in E. Harsh, *South Africa: White Rule, Black Revolt* (New York, 1980), 99.
9. Saki Macozoma, "Notes of a Native Son," *Monitor—Human Rights in South Africa* (Port Elizabeth, 1988), 54.
10. N. Gwala, "State Control, Student Politics and the Crisis in Black Universities," in W. Cobbett and R. Cohen, ed., *Popular Struggles in South Africa* (Johannesburg, 1988).
11. Cynthia Kros, "The Making of a Class: Beyond Model Curricula—A Preliminary Critique of the Presentation of History in South African Schools," *Perspectives in Education* (June, 1988), 99.
12. Interview with teacher from Guguletu, Cape Town, 17 May 1988.

13. Oosthuizen, *History to the Point* Std. 3.

14. *WECTU News*, February 1988, 1. WECTU was established in September 1985 in the wake of widespread unrest in schools and in the Western Cape. The union has as its major objective a non-racial, non-sexist democratic education system in a democratic South Africa. Membership of this and other "progressive" teacher unions remains small but moves are underway to form a single non-racial teachers' union.

15. Quoted in G. Kruss, *People's Education: an examination of the concept* (Cape Town, 1988), 30.

16. Quoted in M. Cornevin, *Apartheid: Power and Historical Falsification* (Paris, 1980), 129.

17. Hirson, *The House*, 48.

18. Discussion with teachers at Primary Education Project Workshop, University of Cape Town, 13 October 1988.

19. P. Kallaway "History Textbooks for Schools: EPU Project 1984–1986," Africa Seminar, University of Cape Town, 1986, 2.

20. P. Kallaway, et al, "General Introduction," *History Alive* 10 (Pietermaritzburg, 1987).

21. S. N. Williams, "The Schools Council History Project: History 13–16: The First Ten Years of the Examination," *Teaching History* (1986) cited in Barbara Johanneson, "The Use of *History Alive 9* in Some Cape Town Schools: Problems and Practical Implications" (Cape Town, 1988), 16–19.

22. Rob Sieborger, "School History and the Historian in Contemporary South Africa," paper delivered to the conference of the South African Historical Society, January 1987, 7.

23. Institute of Christian National Education, 1948, Article 6, quoted in Johanneson, "The Use of *History Alive*," 11.

24. Carolyn Steedman, "Battlegrounds: History in Primary Schools," *History Workshop Journal* (1984), 110.

25. Elaine Unterhalter and Harold Wolpe, "The Politics of South African Education," paper delivered at the Research in Education in South Africa Conference, Grantham, March 1989, 19.

26. S. Maister, "The Teacher Today," *The Educational Journal* (October, 1985), 9.

Chapter 17

1. *New Nation, New History*, Vol. 1 (Johannesburg, 1989).

2. See the use of the term in Colin Bundy and Christopher Saunders, *Reader's Digest Illustrated History of South Africa: The Real Story* (Pleasantville, New York, and Montreal, 1988).

3. Robert Edgar, *Because They Chose the Plan of God: The Story of the Bulhoek Massacre* (Johannesburg and Athens, Ohio, 1988).

4. Robert Russell Edgar, "The Fifth Seal: Enoch Mgijima, the Israelites and the Bulhoek Massacre, 1921," Ph.D. dissertation, UCLA, 1977; Robert

Edgar, "The Prophet Motive: Enich Mgijima, the Israelites and the Background to the Bulhoek Massacre," *International Journal of African Historical Studies* 15:3 (1982), 401–422; Robert Edgar, *Prophets with Honour, a Documentary History of Lekhotla la Bafo* (Johannesburg, 1987).

5. Paul la Hausse, *Brewers, Beerhalls and Boycotts: A History of Liquor in South Africa* (Johannesburg and Athens, Ohio, 1988).

6. Paul la Hausse, "The Struggle for the City: Alcohol, the Ematsheni and Popular Culture in Durban, 1902–1936," M.A. thesis, University of Cape Town, 1984; Paul la Hausse, "'Mayihlome'!: Towards an Understanding of Amalaita Gangs in Durban, c. 1900–1930," African Studies Seminar Paper, University of the Witwatersrand, 27 April 1987.

Chapter 18

This paper has benefited from a period of collaborative work with Willie Currie and John Wright, sensitive readings by David William Cohen and Shula Marks, and the comments of my fellow students in the African History Seminar at The Johns Hopkins University in 1988.

1. The concept of "the production of history" used here is drawn from the enormously suggestive work of David William Cohen. See, in particular, his position paper on "The Production of History," prepared for the Fifth International Roundtable in Anthropology and History, Paris, 1986.

2. Cohen, "The Production of History," 64.

3. Ibid., 25.

4. The phrase is drawn from Mazizi Kunene's comments on writings about Shaka, in M. Kunene, *Emperor Shaka the Great* (London, 1979), xiii.

5. For a classic example see R. Plant, *The Zulu in Three Tenses, being a forecast of the Zulu's future in the light of his past and present* (Pietermaritzburg, 1905).

6. *Summary of the Report of the Commission for the Socio-Economic Development of the Bantu areas within the Union of South Africa* (Pretoria, 1955), chapters 1 and 2. Also see S. Marks, "South Africa: The Myth of the Empty Land," *History Today* (January, 1980), 8–12; and R. Cope's review, "The History of Land Occupation in South Africa—Myth and Reality" in *Some Basic Issues* (Johannesburg, 1981), 9–23.

7. For a comprehensive list of these ethnographic studies see C. A. Hamilton, "Ideology, Oral Traditions and the Struggle for Power in the Early Zulu Kingdom," M.A. dissertation, University of the Witwatersrand, 1985, 36, fn 5. Of all the South African "ethnic groups," the Zulu are the most popular subject on film. The ethnographic films include at least ten short Encyclopaedia Cinematographica films on various aspects of Zulu culture and way of life (songs, ritual, medical treatments, hairdressing practices) made between 1968 and 1971; and two films by Hugh Tracey in 1968–9 on Zulu dances. A number of propaganda films focusing on the "ethnic" complexity of South Africa were made by the government's Department of Information

to promote the policy of Separate Development. See K. Tomaselli et al, *Myth, Race and Power: South Africans Imaged on Film and TV* (Cape Town, 1986), 2.

8. E. A. Ritter, *Shaka Zulu* (London, 1956). P. Becker, *Path of Blood* (London, 1962); see also his *Rule of Fear* (London, 1964). See also E. Watt, *Febana* (London, 1962); C. Cowley, *Kwa-Zulu: Queen Mkabi's Story* (Capetown, 1966); and D. Morris' more sophisticated and less biased work, *The Washing of the Spears* (London, 1966).

9. See, for example, J. D. Omer-Cooper, *The Zulu Aftermath, A Nineteenth Center Revolution in Bantu Africa* (London, 1966); L. Thompson, ed., *African Societies in Southern Africa* (London, 1969); M. G. Gluckman, "The Individual in a Social Framework: The Rise of King Shaka of Zululand," *Journal of African Studies* 1 (1974), 113–44.

10. See Steve Biko, cited in D. A. Kotze, *African Politics in South Africa, 1964– 1974: Parties and Issues* (Pretoria, 1975); M.B.G. Mothlabi, "The Theory and Practice of Black Resistance to Apartheid: A Socio-Ethical Analysis of the Internal Struggle for Political and Social Change," Ph.D. thesis, Boston University, 1980, 203–4.

11. S. Badian, *La Mort de Chaka* (Paris, 1961); L. S. Senghor, *Selected Poems* (London, 1964); see also the detailed review of Shaka as a symbol of African achievement in the introduction to D. Burness, ed., *Shaka, King of the Zulus in African Literature* (Washington, 1976).

12. M. Kunene, *Anthem of the Decades* (London, 1981); speech delivered by M. G. Buthelezi, 16 December 1983, Imbali, Pietermaritzburg, on the occasion of "King Dingane's Day," speech delivered by M. G. Buthelezi, 23 September 1984, Glebelands Stadium, Durban, on the occasion of "King Shaka Day;" J. Ngubane, "Shaka's social, political and military ideas," in Burness, *Shaka*, 127–64.

13. D. W. Hedges, "Trade and Politics in Southern Mozambique and Zululand in the Eighteenth and Nineteenth Centuries," Ph.D. thesis, University of London, 1978. Also see H. Slater, "Transitions in the Political Economy of South-East Africa," Ph.D. theses, University of Sussex, 1976; J. B. Wright, "Pre-Shakan Age-Group Formation Among the Northern Nguni," *Natalia* 8 (1978), 23–9; J. Guy, *The Destruction of the Zulu Kingdom* (London, 1979); P. Bonner, *Kings, Commoners and Concessionaires: The Evolution and Dissolution of the Nineteenth-Century Swazi State* (Cambridge, 1983).

14. For a review of the efflorescence of popular history in this period see L. Calinicos, "The People's Past: Towards Transforming the Present," in B. Bozzoli, ed., *Class, Community and Conflict* (Johannesburg, 1987), 44–64.

15. S. Davis, *Apartheid's Rebels* (New Haven and London, 1987), 92.

16. *Weekly Mail*, 13–19 November 1987.

17. *Weekly Mail*, 20–26 February 1987.

18. *Shaka Zulu Souvenir Brochure* (Johannesburg, 1983), 3.

19. See for example, *Weekly Mail*, 31 October-6 November 1986; *The Sunday Star*, 12 October 1986; *Style*, February 1987; *The Star*, 10 October 1986.

20. *Souvenir Brochure*, 3.

21. *New York Times*, 2 November 1987, *Cape Times*, 16 July 1986; *The Star*, 4 October 1986; *The Sunday Star*, 12 October 1986; *The Star*, 10 October 1986.

22. *The Hartford Courant*, 28 February 1987; *Star-Telegram*, 22 February 1987; *The Houston Chronicle*, 8–14 March 1987; *San Francisco Chronicle, Datebook Television*, undated clipping, Harmony Gold publicity package; *New York City Tribute*, 2 March 1987.

23. *Drum*, January 1987.

24. *Weekly Mail*, 9–16 October 1986.

25. *The Star*, 9 October 1986.

26. H. F. Fynn, *The Diary of Henry Francis Fynn*, eds. J. Stuart and D. Mck. Malcolm (Pietermaritzburg, 1950); N. Isaacs, *Travels and Adventures in Eastern Africa*, eds. L. Herman and P. Kirby (Cape Town, 1970), xvi-xvii; J. Bird, ed., *The Annals of Natal 1495–1845*, vol. 1 (Pietermaritzburg, 1888); B. Roberts, *The Zulu Kings* (New York, 1974); L. du Buisson, *The White Man Cometh* (Johannesburg, 1987), 3–5, 35, 36–39.

27. *The Star*, 4 October 1986; *Houston Chronicle*, 8–14 March 1987; Harmony Gold publicity flyer, n.d.; *South African Today*, 3, 2 (1987); for a discussion of the authenticity of the weaponry used, see *The Historical Firearms Society of South African Newsletter*, 34 (1985).

28. *Houston Chronicle*, 8–14 March 1987; *United States Anti-Apartheid Newsletter*, 3, 1 (1988). On the making of local films and attempts to hide their origins, see the article by John Hookham in *Weekly Mail*, 13–19 May 1988, and the reply by filmmaker Chris Davies in *Weekly Mail*, 27 May-2 June 1988.

29. *The Beacon Journal*, 8 October 1987.

30. See note 4 above.

31. My discussion with Faure at his home in Florida, South Africa, 1980; telephone interview with Faure, 2 April 1988.

32. Sinclair was fired when he revised to follow editing instructions from the American distributors, Harmony Gold (*Style*, November 1986). These conclusions are based on an article in the *Cape Times*, 16 July 1986; a telephone interview with Faure, 2 April 1988; and a reading of Sinclair's publication in German of *Shaka Zulu* (Munich, 1986) based on his script. I am grateful to Anja Baumhof for assistance with the translation of key passages from Sinclair's German text into English.

33. Telephone interview with Faure, 2 April 1988.

34. K. Tomaselli, et al, *Myth, Race and Power* (Bellville, 1986), 43.

35. Telephone interview with Faure, 2 April 1988.

36. Isaacs, *Travels and Adventures*; also see the discussion of Isaacs above. Ritter, *Shaka Zulu*.

37. *Drum*, January 1987; *Weekly Mail*, 21–27 November 1986.

38. Isaacs, *Travels and Adventures*, ix-xii; for background on Fynn and Isaacs see Roberts, *The Zulu Kings*.
39. Fynn Papers, Natal Provincial Archives, Pietermaritzburg.
40. Ritter, *Shaka Zulu*, 3–14.
41. C. de B. Webb and J. B. Wright, eds., *The James Stuart Archive of Recorded Oral Evidence Relating to the History of the Zulu and Neighboring Peoples*, vols. 1–4 (Pietermaritzburg and Durban, 1976).
42. *Souvenir Brochure*, 2–14.
43. Ibid., 15.
44. K. Tomaselli, "Camera, Colour and Racism in Shaka Zulu," *History News*, 30 (November 1987), 9–11.
45. *Style*, November 1986.
46. Ibid.
47. *The Star*, 29 September 1986. *Souvenir Brochure*, 6.
48. *Style*, November 1986. *The Star*, 29 September 1986; *Style*, November 1986.
49. Harmony Gold publicity flyer, n.d.; ibid. On the riskiness of the venture also see *Electronic Media*, 22 September 1986.
50. *Style*, November 1986.
51. J. Saul and S. Gelb, *The Crisis in South Africa* (New York, 1986), 214; *The Star*, 23 December 1985.
52. Saul and Gelb, *The Crisis in South Africa*, 222.
53. *The Beacon Journal*, 8 October 1987.
54. *Race Relations Survey, 1985* (Johannesburg, 1985), 460.
55. See I. Wilkins and H. Strydom, *The Super-Afrikaners: Inside the Afrikaner Broederbond* (Johannesburg, 1978); P. Crankshaw, A. Williams, and G. Hayman, "To Educate, Entertain and Inform: The Meyer Commission Into TV," *The SAFTTA Journal*, 3 (1983), 20–27; G. Hayman and R. Tomaselli, "Technology in the Service of Ideology: The First 50 Years of Broadcasting in South Africa," in K. Tomaselli et al, eds., *Addressing the Nation: Studies in South African Media*, vol. 1 (Durban, 1986).
56. *Weekly Mail*, 21–27 November 1986; *The Star*, 1 October 1986. For Faure on the role of television in influencing racial attitudes see the interview with Faure, *New York Daily News*, 6 October 1987; and the interview with Faure and actor Henry Cele, *Houston Chronicle*, 8–14 March 1987.
57. *The Star*, 29 September 1986. In eighteen US cities *Shaka Zulu* delivered higher ratings than the local stations' 8 p.m. films. In Baltimore, *Shaka Zulu* gave WBFF-TV the highest rating and share in the M-F 8 p.m. movies, with an average increase of over 300%. Harmony Gold publication "Shaka-Zulu vs. M-F 8 O'clock Movies," n.d. These figures are based on Nielsen and Arbitron ratings.
58. Interview with Faure and Cele, *Daily News*, 6 October 1987.
59. Ibid.
60. *Washington Post TV Week*, 1–7 November 1987. *The Beacon Journal*, 8 Oc-

tober 1987; *Daily News*, 6 October 1987. The series has also been promoted as educational material in the United States. *Harmony Gold News*, n.d.; *New York City Tribute*, 2 March 1987; *The Sunday Republican*, 1 March 1987.

61. The phrase is Shula Marks', coined to express the tensions at the heart of politics in South Africa, and to describe the political activity of leadership figures in South Africa who negotiate a precarious course between traditionalism and modernism, action and restraint, the imperatives of the South African state and the expectations of black South Africans. S. Marks, *The Ambiguities of Dependence in South Africa* (Johannesburg, 1986), 6.

62. G. Maré and G. Hamilton, *An Appetite for Power* (Johannesburg, 1987), 1, 173; see also *The Guardian*, 6 July 1987; *The Star*, 30 September 1986; *The Star*, 4 October 1987.

63. Interview with Faure, *The Hartford Courant*, 28 February 1987.

64. Maré and Hamilton, *An Appetite for Power*, 6.

65. J. Wright and G. Maré, "The Splice of Coincidence," *The Sunday Tribune*, 7 December 1986.

66. Maré and Hamilton, *An Appetite for Power*, 3, 164.

67. Interview with Faure, *Daily News*, 6 October 1987.

68. *Drum*, January 1987. Also see *The Sunday Tribune*, 21 December 1986.

69. *The Star*, 4 October 1986; *The Sunday Star*, 12 October 1986; *Souvenir Brochure*, 12; interview with Faure, *The Houston Chronicle*, 8–14 1987; *The Guardian*, 6 July 1987.

70. *Drum*, January 1987.

71. G. Buthelezi, *Power is Ours* (New York, 1984).

72. Marks, *Ambiguities of Dependence*, conclusion.

73. Ibid., 123

74. Tomaselli, "Camera, Colour and Racism," 9–11.

Chapter 19

1. P. R. Kirby, *The Musical Instruments of the Native Races of South Africa* (Oxford, 1934).

2. See, for example, H. Tracey, *Chopi Musicians: Their Music, Poetry and Instruments* (London, 1948); "The Mbira class of instruments in Rhodesia," and "Measuring African Scales," both in *African Music* 4:3 (1948); "Behind the Lyrics," *African Music* 3:2 (1963).

3. Y. Husskisson, "The Social and Ceremonial Music of the Pedi," Ph.D. dissertation, Witwatersrand University, 1958.

4. D. Rycroft, "Nguni vocal polyphony," *Journal of the International Folk Music Council* 19 (1967); D. Hansen, "The Music of the Xhosa-speaking People," Ph.D. dissertation, Witwatersrand University, 1981.

5. See, for example, A. Tracey, *How to Play the Mbira dza Vadzimu*, International Library of African Music (Roodepoort, 1970); "Matepe Mbira Music," *African Music* 4:4 (1970); "The Nyanga Panpipe Dance," *African Music* 5:1 (1971).

6. J. Blacking, *The Role of Music Among the Venda of the Northern Transvaal* (Roodeport, 1956); "The Cultural Foundations of the Music of the Venda," Ph.D. dissertation, Witwatersrand University, 1964; *How Musical is Man?* (Washington, 1973); *Venda Children's Songs* (Johannesburg, 1967); "Songs, Dances, Mimes and Symbolism of Venda Girls' Initiation Schools," *African Studies* 28 (1969); "Initiation and the Balance of Power—the Tshikanda Girls; Initiation School of the Venda of the Northern Transvaal," *Ethnographic and Linguistic Studies in honour of N. J. van Warmelo* (Pretoria, 1969); "Musical Expeditions of the Venda," *African Music* 3:1 (1962).

7. T. Johnston, "The Music of the Shangana-Tsonga," Ph.D. dissertation, Witwatersrand University, 1971; "Tsonga Music in Cultural Perspective," *Anthropos* 70 (1975); "Possession music of the Shangana-Tsonga," *African Music* 5 (1973); "Power and Prestige through Music in Tsongaland," *Human Relations* 27:3 (1974).

8. A. Merriman, *The Anthropology of Music* (Evanston, 1964).

9. Exceptions were P. R. Kirby, "The Uses of European Musical Techniques by the Non-European Peoples of South Africa," *Journal of the International Folk Music Council* (1959); D. Rycroft, "The New 'Town' Music of Southern Africa," *Recorded Folk Music* 1 (1958); and "Evidence of Stylistic Continuity in Zulu 'Town' Music," in K. P. Wachsmann, *Essays for a Humanist* (New York, 1977).

10. D. Coplan, *In Township Tonight* (Johannesburg, 1985), 3; see also "The African Performer and the Johannesburg Entertainment Industry: The Struggle for African Culture on the Witwatersrand," in B. Bozzoli, ed., *Labour, Townships and Protest* (Johannesburg, 1979).

11. *Shebeens* are places (usually the home of the brewer) where home-brewed liquor is bought and consumed. The origins of the word *marabi* are unclear: "a possible source is *ho raba raba* (Sotho: to fly around). . . . Some Africans identify the word with Marabastad, the . . . Pretoria location where African domestic workers lived as early as 1880," Coplan, *In Township Tonight*, 94.

12. D. Coplan, "The Emergence of an African Working-Class Culture" in S. Marks and R. Rathbone, eds., *Industrialisation and Social change in South Africa* (London, 1982).

13. E. Koch, "'Without Visible Means of Subsistence': Slumyard Culture in Johannesburg 1918–1940," in B. Bozzoli, ed., *Town and Countryside in the Transvaal* (Johannesburg, 1983).

14. C. Ballantine, "Music and Emancipation: the social role of black jazz and vuadeville in South Africa between the 20s and the early 40s," *Journal of Southern African Studies* (forthcoming); "'Concert and Dance': the foundations of black Jazz in South Africa between the 20s and the early 40s," *Popular Music* (forthcoming)

15. Bozzoli, *Labour, Township and Protest*.

16. Coplan, *In Township Tonight* gives the Zulu meaning as "a stalking approach"; Veit Erlmann, "Migration and performance: Zulu migrant work-

ers' *isicathamiya* performance in South Africa, 1890–1950," *Ethnomusicology* 34,2 (1990).

17. M. Andersson, *Music in the Mix* (Johannesburg, 1981).

18. D. Coplan, "The Power of Oral Poetry: Narrative Songs of the Basotho Migrants," *Research in African Literatures* 18:1 (1987); Coplan, "Eloquent Knowledge: Lesotho Migrants' Songs and the Anthropology of Experience," *American Ethnologist* 14:3 (1987). Coplan's researches into this genre have resulted in a film, *The Songs of the Adventurers*, made in collaboration with Gei Zantzinger.

19. For further insight on this use of "ethnic" see Barth's introduction to *Ethnic Groups and Boundaries* (London, 1969).

20. J. Clegg, "The Music of Zulu immigrant workers in Johannesburg—a Focus on Concertina and Guitar," *Papers presented at the first symposium on ethnomusicology*, ILAM, (Grahamstown, 1980); "Towards an Understanding of African Dance: the Zulu *Isishameni* Dance Style," *Papers presented at the second symposium on ethnomusicology*, ILAM (Grahamstown, 1981); see also "Dance and Society in Africa South of the Sahara," unpublished Honours dissertation, Witwatersrand University, 1977; "An Examination of the Umzansi Dance Style," *Papers presented at the third and fourth symposia on ethnomusicology*, ILAM (Grahamstown, 1984).

21. Veit Erlmann, "Migration and Performance"; "A feeling of prejudice: Orpheus McAdoo and the Virginia Jubilee Singers in South Africa, 1880–1898" in *Journal of Southern African Sudies* 14, 3 (1988).

22. Erlmann, "Black Political Song in South Africa: Some Research Perspectives, "*Journal of Musicology* (forthcoming); "Apartheid, African Nationalism and Culture: the Case of Traditional African Music in Black Education in South Africa," *Perspectives in Education* 7:3 (1983).

23. P. Harries, "'A Forgotten Corner of the Transvaal': Reconstructing the History of a Relocated Community through Oral Testimony and Song," in B. Bozzoli, ed., *Class, Community and Conflict: South African Perspectives* (Johannesburg, 1987).

24. There have been some recent studies which examine urban music as a whole, although even these tend to concentrate on particular substyles and subcultures within the broader field. See for example H. Lunn, "Antecedents of the Music and Popular Culture of the African Post-1976 Generation," M.A. dissertation, Witwatersrand University, 1986; I. Jeffrey, "The Sharpetown Swingsters: Their Will to Survive," Honours dissertation, Witwatersrand University, 1985.

Chapter 20

1. For a detailed treatment of black theater see my article, "Apartheid and the Political Imagination in Black South African Theatre," *Journal of Southern African Studies* 16:2 (1990).

2. Egoli, "City of Gold," was the name given to Johannesburg.

3. Matsemela Manaka, *Egoli City of Gold* (Johannesburg, n.d.), 15–16.

4. The translation of the song is from Mandlenkosi Makhoba, *The Sun Shall Rise For The Workers* (Johannesburg, 1984).

5. See Labour Monitoring Group (Natal), "Monitoring the Sarmcol Struggle," *South African Labour Bulletin* 11:2 (1985), 89–113.

Chapter 21

1. *Weekly Mail*, 2–8 December 1988, 11.

2. *Fuse* (November/December 1982), 190–193.

3. W. A. Hachten and C. A. Giffard, *Total Onslaught, the South African Press under Attack* (Madison, 1984).

4. H. Gavshon, "Levels of Intervention in Films Made for Black South African Audiences," *Critical Arts* 2 (1983); Keyan Tomaselli, *The Cinema of Apartheid* (London, 1989).

5. Although Cannon International claims it has severed its production links with South Africa, it would appear that they have continued their South African connection through the company Nu Metro. See *Weekly Mail*, 4–10 February 1989.

6. Despite the threat of being placed on the United Nations blacklist, foreign actors continue to work in South Africa. In 1988 Bruce Willis, Cathy Moriarty, Rupert Everett, John Savage, Kiel Martin, and Oliver Reed, to name a few, passed through South Africa, most under shrouds of secrecy. See *Weekly Mail* 4–10 February 1989.

7. *Shot Down*, a film dealing with white alienation or "lazy white bull-shit," was directed by Andrew Worsdale and produced by Jeremy Nathan. *Mapantsula* was directed by Oliver Schmitz and Thomas Mogatlane and produced by Pierre Montocchio. *Mapantsula* has been passed for general distribution by the censorship board on condition that six minutes be cut from it. *Shot Down* has been able to acquire provisional exemption on occasion, also with cuts.

8. See T. Gutsche, *The History and Social Significance of Motion Pictures in South Africa 1895–1940* (Cape Town, 1972); Keyan Tomaselli, "The South African Film Industry," Johannesburg, African Studies Institute, University of the Witwatersrand, 1979.

9. R. Low, *The History of the British Film 1986–1906* (London, 1948); E. Strebel, "Primitive Propaganda: The Boer War Films," *Sight and Sound* 46 (1977); W. K. L. Dickson, *The Biograph in Battle* (London, 1901).

10. J. A. F. Van Zyl, "'No God, No Morality, No History': South African Ethnographic Film," *Critical Arts* 1 (1980).

11. Ibid., 32.

12. *Freedom Square and Back of the Moon* was directed by Angus Gibson and William Kentridge.

13. *This We Can Do for Justice and For Peace* was directed by Kevin Harris for the South African Council of Churches. *And Now We Have No Land*, a film

about forced population removals, was directed by Hennie Serfontein for the South African Catholic Bishop's Conference.

14. See B. Winston, "The Tradition of the Victim in Griersonian Documentary," in A. Rosenthal, ed., *New Challenges for Documentary* (Berkeley. 1988). To "read-back" is a journalists' term for reading back an interview or article to the subject before publication.
15. T. Cripps, *Slow Fade to Black* (London, 1977).
16. The first director of the Cape Video Resource Association (CVRA), Zimbabwean born Mark Kaplan, was detained as a result of his video work in 1982 for some months and finally deported from South Africa. He now works in video in Zimbabwe.
17. S. Worth, "Pictures Can't Say Ain't," *Versus* 12 (1975).

Chapter 22

1. J. Vansina, *Oral Tradition: A Study in Historical Methodology* (Chicago, 1965) remains the classic study of oral tradition as history. Over the last twenty-five years, Africanists employing oral tradition have been compelled to defend and refine their methodology. For a more recent discussion of issues relating to oral tradition and history see Joseph Miller, ed., *The African Past Speaks* (Folkstone, 1980).
2. David Cohen, *The Historical Tradition of Busoga* (Oxford, 1972); Stephen Feierman, *The Shambaa Kingdom* (Madison, 1974); and Joseph Miller, *Kings and Kinsmen: Early Mbundu States in Angola* (Oxford, 1976).
3. Philip Bonner, *Kings, Commoners and Concessionaires: The Evolution of and Dissolution of the Nineteenth-Century Swazi State* (Cambridge, 1983).
4. J. B. Peires, *The House of Phalo: A History of the Xhosa People in the Days of their Independence* (Johannesburg, 1981); William Beinart, *The Political Economy of Pondoland* (Cambridge, 1982); and Peter Delius, *The Land Belongs To Us: The Pedi Polity, the Boers and the British in the Nineteenth-Century Transvaal* (Johannesburg, 1983).
5. Significantly, Jeff Guy's pioneering *The Destruction of the Zulu Kingdom: The Civil War in Zululand, 1879–1884* (London, 1979), relies largely on written sources.
6. The case of the Swazi is perhaps most impressive in this regard. The Swaziland Oral History Project coordinated by Philip Bonner of the University of the Witwatersrand is currently engaged in gathering an extensive body of precolonial Swazi oral tradition.
7. Peter Delius, "Report on Research on the Nineteenth Century History of the Pedi," unpublished seminar paper, African History Seminar, University of London, 1977.
8. See Colin Bundy's chapter in this volume.
9. See T. Karis and G. M. Carter, eds., *From Protest to Challenge: A Documentary History of African Politics in South Africa 1882–1964, Volumes 1–4* (Stanford, 1972–77).

10. Tim Couzens, *The New African. A Study of the Life and Work of H. I. E. Dhlomo* (Johannesburg, 1985); B. Willan, *Sol Plaatje: A Biography* (Johannesburg, 1984). Couzens began his oral fieldwork in 1973.

11. See, for example, Raphael Samuel, "Local History and Oral History," in *History Workshop* 1 (Spring 1976); and Paul Thompson, *The Voice of the Past—Oral History* (Oxford, 1978).

12. See Belinda Bozzoli's chapter in this volume.

13. See Tim Keegan, *Rural Transformations in Industrialising South Africa* (Johannesburg, 1986); and also his *Facing the Storm: Portraits of Black Lives in Rural South Africa* (Cape Town, 1988).

14. Charles van Onselen, "Race and Class in the South African Countryside: Cultural Osmosis and Social Relations in the Sharecropping Economy of the South-Western Transvaal, 1900–1950," *American Historical Review* 95:1 (Feb., 1990).

15. See P. Harries, "' A Forgotten Corner of the Transvaal': Reconstructing the History of a Relocated Community through Oral Testimony and Song"; and J. B. Peires, "The Legend of Fenner-Solomon," in Belinda Bozzoli, ed., *Class, Community and Conflict* (Johannesburg, 1987).

16. Helen Bradford, *A Taste of Freedom: The I.C.U. in Rural South Africa, 1924–1930* (New Haven, 1987).

17. For an extended discussion, see William Beinart and Colin Bundy, *Hidden Struggles in Rural South Africa: Politics and Popular Movements in the Transkei and Eastern Cape, 1890–1930* (Johannesburg, 1987), 1–45.

18. See Peter Delius, "Sebatakgomo: Migrant Organisation, the A.N.C. and the Sekhukuneland Revolt," *Journal of Southern African Studies* 15 (October, 1989); and William Beinart, "The Rise of the Indlavini" unpublished paper presented to Conference on South Africa in the Fifties, Oxford University, 1987.

19. T. Dunbar Moodie, "The Moral Economy of the Black Miners' Strike of 1946," *Journal of Southern African Studies* (October 1988). For Moodie's discussion of other forms of migrant association on the mines, see "Migrancy and Male Sexuality on the South African Gold Mines," *Journal of Southern African Studies* 14 (January 1988).

20. J. Guy and M. Thabane, "Technology, Ethnicity and Ideology: Basotho Miners and Shaft-Sinking on the South African Gold Mines," *Journal of Southern African Studies* 14 (January 1988).

21. Ari Sitas, "From Grassroots Control to Democracy: A Case Study of Trade Unionism on Migrant Workers' Cultural Formations on the East Rand," *Social Dynamics* 11 (1985).

22. See J. Cock, "'Let me make history please': The Story of Johanna Masilela, Childminder," in Bozzoli, *Class, Community and Conflict*; and E. Webster, *Cast in a Racial Mould: Labour Process and Trade Unionism in the Foundries* (Johannesburg, 1985).

23. Philip Bonner, "Family, Crime and Political Consciousness on the East

Rand, 1939–1955," *Journal of Southern African Studies* 14 (April 1988); and "'Desirable or Undesirable Sotho Women?' Liquor, Prostitution and the Migration of Sotho Women to the Rand, 1920–1945," unpublished paper presented to the African Studies Institute seminar, 1988.

24. Paul la Hausse, "'The Cows of Nongoloza': Youth, Crime and Amalaita Gangs, 1900–1936", *Journal of Southern African Studies*, 16, 1 (March 1990).

25. I. Edwards, "Swing the Assegai peacefully? New Africa, Mkhumbane, the co-operative movement and attempts to transform Durban society in the late 1940s"; and B. Nasson, "'She preferred living in the cave with Harry the snake-catcher': Towards an Oral History of Popular Leisure and Class Expression in District Six, Cape Town, c. 1920–1950," in Philip Bonner, et al. eds., *Holding their Ground: Class, Locality and Conflict in 19th and 20th Century South Africa* (Johannesburg, 1989).

26. See *Oral History Project relating to the Zulu People: Catalogue of Interviews* (Durban, Killie Campbell Africana Library, 1983).

27. A. Manson, *The Troubles of Chief Abram Moilwa: The Hurutshe Resistance of 1954–58* (Johannesburg, 1983); T. Sideris, ed., *Sifuna Imali Yethu: The Life and Struggles of Durban Dock Workers, 1940–1980* (Johannesburg, 1983); and C. Cachalia, ed., *From Survival to Defiance: Indian Hawkers in Johannesburg, 1940–1980* (Johannesburg, 1983).

28. Guy and Thabane, "Technology, Ethnicity and Ideology," 258.

29. Bill Nasson, "The Oral Historian and Historical Formation in Cape Town," in C. Saunders, et al., eds., *Studies in the History of Cape Town* (Cape Town, 1988), 21. For a discussion of this project also see S. Jeppie, "Briefing: Western Cape Oral History Project," unpublished paper, University of Cape Town, 1988.

30. For example, in a recent interview I conducted in a Natal township, a burned-out bus stood in front of the informant's house while army troop-carriers trundled past the window at regular intervals.

31. For a particularly acute discussion of this last issue, see J. Guy and M. Thabane, "The Ma-Rashea: A Participant's Perspective," in Bozzoli, *Class, Community and Conflict*, 436–56. For some more general comments, see A. Manson, D. Cachalia, and C. Sideris, "Oral History Speaks Out," *Social Dynamics* 11 (December 1985); and Belinda Bozzoli, "Migrant women and South African social change: biographical approaches to social analysis," *African Studies* 44 (1985).

32. For discussion of a few of these issues see Paul Thompson's revised edition of *The Voice of the Past* (Oxford, 1988); R. Renaldo, "Doing Oral History," *Social Analysis* 4 (September 1980); E. Tonkin, "Steps to the redefinition of 'oral history': examples from Africa," *Social History* 7 (October 1983); and K. Figlio, "Oral History and the Unconscious," *History Workshop* 26 (1988).

33. See I. Hofmeyr, "The Narrative Logic of Oral History," unpublished paper presented to the African Studies Institute Seminar, University of the Wit-

watersrand, 1988; and Stephen Clingman, "Biography and Representation: Some analogies from Fiction," unpublished paper presented to the History Workshop Conference, University of the Witwatersrand, 1987.

Chapter 23

1. "Soweto Speaking to Miriam Tlali," *Staffrider* 1 (1978), 1; Mike Kirkwood, "Remembering Staffrider," in A. W. Oliphant and I. Vladislavic, eds., *Ten Years of Staffrider* (Johannesburg, 1988), 6.
2. Sol Plaatje, *Native Life in South Africa* (Johannesburg, 1982).
3. See Luli Callinicos, "The People's Past: Towards Transforming the Present," in Belinda Bozzoli, ed., *Class, Community and Conflict* (Johannesburg, 1987), 44–45.
4. For an overview of these books see Richard Rive, "Books by Black Writers," in *Staffrider* 5:1 (1982), 12.
5. See Tom Lodge, *Black Politics in South Africa Since 1945* (Johannesburg, 1983), chap. 13.
6. Mike Kirkwood, "*Staffrider:* an Informal Discussion," an interview with Nick Visser, *English in Africa* 7:1 (1980).
7. "About *Staffrider*," *Staffrider* (1987), 1.
8. Members of the editorial board include writers Njabulo Ndebele, Nadine Gordimer, Chris van Wyk, Gcipna Mhlope, Kelwyn Sole, photographers Paul Weinberg, David Koloane, Gary Rathbone, and popular historian Luli Calinicos. COSATU were requested to elect a representative; until this area is finalized Mi Hlathswayo,the National Cultural Co-ordinator for COSATU acts as an advisor. He and Frank Meintjies, a former publicity officer of this labor federation, served as guest editors for a special edition on "Worker Culture;" *Staffrider* 8:3&4 (1989).
9. For reasons of space, the fourth category of testimonies will not be discussed in this overview.
10. Studs Terkel, *Working* (New York, 1974).
11. Miriam Tlali, "Mr. X. Unlicensed Fresh Produce and Poultry Vendor," based on interview conducted 11 Feb. 1978, in *Staffrider* 1:1 (1978), 3.
12. Miriam Tlali, "Mrs. Leah Koane, Dressmaker," based on an interview conducted on 21 Jan. 1978, in *Staffrider* 1:1 (1978), 5.
13. Miriam Tlali, "Mrs. Sebenzile Lokoto: Market Researcher," based on an interview conducted in two parts in Jan. and Feb. 1978, in *Staffrider* 1:1 (1978), 6.
14. Miriam Tlali, "Soweto Hijack: A Story of our Times," in *Staffrider* 1:1 (1978), 15.
15. Letter printed in *Staffrider*, 1:2 (1978), 2.
16. See Robert Fuller, "Art and Revolution in South Africa: An Assessment of *Staffrider* Cultural Magazine," *The African Communist* 93 (1983), 75–84.
17. Simon Kumalo, "A Factory Worker's Story," in *Staffrider* 4:1 (1981), 2–3.

18. These are Zulu words which have become colloquialisms. "Indunas" are management appointed supervisors and "impimpis" are paid spies.
19. Lawrence Mshengu, "Forward with the Worker Struggle," *Staffrider* 6:1 (1984), 26.
20. This essay was presented as "The first story in the *Staffrider* Popular History series . . . based on an interview with Mrs. S. by Mnantho Nkotsoe for the Oral History Project funded by the HSRC and directed by the African Studies Institute, University of the Witwatersrand," in *Staffrider* 6:1 (1984).

Chapter 24

I am grateful to Nicky Roussouw, Miki Vlokkeman, Shamiel Jeppe, Linda Cooper, Cathy Kall, Eliza Kentridge, and Naseegh Jaffer for providing information and/or suggestions for this article.

1. C. C. Saunders, "F.Z.S. Peregrino and the South African Spectator," *Quarterly Bulletin of the South African Public Library* 22 (1978).
2. See, for example, "A Black Man's History of South Africa," *Umsebenzi*, 18 August 1934 and succeeding issues. My thanks to Bob Edgar for this reference.
3. See L. Forman, *Chapters in the History of the March to Freedom* (Cape Town, 1959), and Forman, *Black and White in South African History* (Cape Town, 1960).
4. Letter from L. Cooper, 7 June 1988.
5. Report for the funders of the Labour History Group, July 1986.
6. ILRIG information brochure and ILRIG project report, July 1985–June 1987.
7. L. Callinicos, "The People's Past: Towards Transforming the Present," *Critical Arts* 4 (1986).
8. Ibid.
9. *What is History? A New Approach to History for Students, Workers and Communities* (Skotaville, 1987).
10. C. Bundy, *Re-making the past: New Perspectives in South African History* (Cape Town, 1986), 69. In C. J. Joubert's *History for Standard 10*, only three black politicians—Mahatma Ghandi and the government collaborators Tom Swartz and Kaiser Matanzima—are mentioned in a fifty-page chapter on the "Political, Social and Economic Development of the Non-Whites."
11. The youth and community groups included the South African National Students Congress (SANSCO) for black students, its white counterpart, the National Union of South African Students (NUSAS), the school-based Western Cape Students Congress (WECSCO) and ERIC. The three teachers' organizations were the Democratic Teachers Union (DETU), operating in the African schools; the Western Cape Teachers Union (WECTU), in the "Coloured" schools; and Education for an Aware South Africa (EDASA), based in the white schools. Though working together and sharing common non-racial goals, these teachers' bodies were organized sepa-

rately in order to deal effectively with the particular conditions encountered in each of the apartheid education departments. Similar examples can be found in other sectors of the anti-apartheid struggle as well.

12. Community Education Resources memorandum, n.d.
13. UWC People's History Project reading package, 1987.
14. S. Jeppe, "The Other History," *South*, 29 September 1988.
15. Confidential interview.

Chapter 25

Thanks to Carolyn Hamilton for her constant support and encouragement of the project and for the many fruitful discussions we held on its implications. While our debates and discussions have informed aspects of this briefing, final responsibility for any errors of commission and omission is mine.

1. Jeremy Brecher, "A Report on Doing History from Below: The Brass Workers History Project," and L. Shopes, "Oral History and Community Involvement: The Baltimore Neighborhood Heritage Project," in Susan Porter Benson et al, eds., *Presenting the Past* (Philadelphia, 1986); K. Worpole, "A Ghostly Pavement: The Political Implications of Local Working-Class History," in Raphael Samuel, ed., *People's History and Socialist Theory* (London, 1981).
2. Graeme Bloch, "Popularising History: Some Reflections and Experiences," paper presented at History Workshop conference, University of the Witwatersrand, February 1987.
3. Luli Callinicos, "The People's History Workshop," *Perspectives in Education* 10:1 (1988), 84.
4. Quoted in Leslie Witz, *Write Your Own History* (Johannesburg, 1988).
5. Ibid., 17.
6. Ibid., 11.
7. Ibid., 105.
8. Grahamstown Oral History Project, "Worker Struggles in Grahamstown," paper presented at History Workshop conference, University of the Witwatersrand, 1987, 2.
9. C. Hamilton, "Swaziland Oral History Project," *History in Africa* 14 (1987), 383.
10. Witz, *Write Your Own History*, 108.
11. Ibid., 116.
12. Ibid., 119.
13. Ibid., 17.

Chapter 26

My thanks to Steve Brier, Cal Holder, Pat Manning, Karin Shapiro, and Jon Wiener for forcing me to be explicit when I hid behind implication.

1. Gus Silber, "Alternative, yeah. So where's da porn?" *Weekly Mail*, 19–25 June 1987, 23.

2. I am not saying there was no dichotomy between underground sensibilities and those of the New Left in the United States. Very few of the undergrounds addressed politics directly (and, in the light of later feminist and gay comix, some of the continuing work of the now-graying pioneers of the *Zap* generation has taken on a distinctly unsavory quality where their unregenerate libertarianism confuses iconoclastic expression with racist and sexist stereotypes). Conversely, I suspect (based on my experiences and on a very informal sampling of grizzled activists) that very few of the hard politicos were aficionados of "head comix." Certainly the coalition politics of the antiwar movement tended to muffle visual imagery to the extent that it had to adhere to the least offensive, most "ideologically-approved" icons. Nevertheless, like other aspects of the counterculture, the whacked-out iconoclasm of the undergrounds permeated the era, contributing to the consciousness of a movement, both for many of those active in it as well as for those who stood outside.

3. The authorities not only banned Zapiro's message, they briefly detained the messenger as well. Zapiro's cartoons, which have appeared in a range of anti-apartheid publications (from the liberal *South* to more militant End Conscription Campaign literature), are more traditionally political in their direct and pungent visual commentary. Another prominent political cartoonist is the *Weekly Mail's* Derek Bauer, although his masterly rendering (owing a lot to Ralph Steadman) carries a more ambivalent and detached message. In some sense, in quintessentially liberal fashion, his artwork operates as a refuge from a resistance movement with which he can identify so much and no further (see his comments in "His Political Medium is Black and White," *Newsday*, 29 December 1988, 57).

4. A number of other alternative comicstrips have appeared recently, including Stacy Stent's "Who's Left" and BP's "Comrade Joe" in the *Weekly Mail*.

5. Leonard Rifas, "Educational Comics: A Message in a Bubble," *Print* (November/December, 1988), 145–57, 203–4; "Comic Books and History: A Symposium," *Radical History Review* 28–30 (September, 1984), 229–52. It has been suggested that *Watchmen*, the popular reworking of the superhero story, may be the best example of an effective educational/political comic book. However, if *Watchmen* is considered in the company of other recent reinterpretations of costumed crusaders, such as the embittered, reactionary vigilante Batman portrayed in the popular *Dark Knight* series, it is fair to wonder if readers are not merely consuming a commercialized iconoclasm, failing to discern whether the comic books advocate right or left politics.

6. *Vusi Goes Back* was first published as part of a self-help *People's Workbook*, which interwove history with practical information on agricultural improvement, building construction, health care, and the legal rights of migrant workers. It was published as a separate comic book in 1984. For further background and comments on EDA's assessment of the effectiveness of the comic-book form, see Luli Callinicos, "The 'People's Past': Towards

Transforming the Present" in Belinda Bozzoli, ed., *Class, Community and Conflict: South African Perspectives* (Johannesburg, 1987), 48–49.

7. The SACHED Trust, *Equiano: The Slave Who Fought to be Free* (Johannesburg, 1988); The SACHED Trust, *Down Second Avenue* (Johannesburg, 1988).

8. Joshua Brown, "Of Mice and Memory," *Oral History Review* 16 (Spring 1988), 91–109.

9. I suppose this is the best place to bring up a related issue: the visual modernization of the characters. Equiano as an adult looks like Bobby Seale (if I might indulge in a little cultural imperialism here). He in no way resembles Equiano as portrayed in the frontispiece lithograph in the original book. Throughout the comic book, while whites appear in colonial dress and coiffures, blacks look very contemporary, as if donning costumes in an old Hollywood film. I suppose this is an effort to aid the reader in identifying with Equiano and other black characters, but I wonder if the effect is to pull blacks out of their historical moment.

10. The seemingly built-in accessibility of *Down Second Avenue*'s story, set in the recent South African past, is in fact deceptive. Teachers in the SACHED report noted that black students' knowledge is often extremely localized, both temporally and geographically: "if evictions . . . aren't happening in their area, they probably know nothing about them; similarly something that happened only a few years ago may be quite unknown to them. . . ." My thanks to Peter Delius for sending me the draft of the SACHED Comics Advisory Committee report.

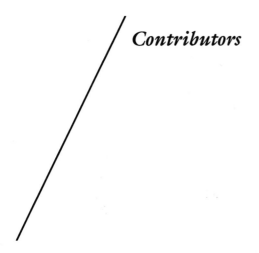

Contributors

David Anthony is Assistant Professor on the Board of Studies in History at Oakes College, University of California, Santa Cruz. He is currently working on a biography of Max Yergan, an African-American YMCA missionary to South Africa from 1921 to 1936.

Philip L. Bonner teaches history at the University of the Witwatersrand. He is author of *Kings, Commoners and Concessionaires* (1982) and various articles on black politics, social history, and trade unionism in South Africa. He is currently writing a book on black urbanization and politics on the Witwatersrand, 1930–1960.

Belinda Bozzoli is Professor of Sociology at the University of the Witwatersrand. She is author of *The Political Nature of a Ruling Class* and *Women of Phokeng*, and editor of three History Workshop collections.

Helen Bradford, in the preface to her new book, *A Taste of Freedom*, describes herself as a misanthrope ex-mathematician turned social historian. She is not sure which of these attributes led to her present appointment at the Department of Economic History at the University of Cape Town.

Joshua Brown is art director of the American Social History Project at Hunter College and a member of the *Radical History Review* editorial collective.

Colin Bundy has taught in England, the United States and currently holds chairs in the Universities of the Western Cape and of Cape Town. His research has been largely concerned with aspects of South Africa's rural history, which may be a product of a childhood in exaggeratedly small-town circumstances.

Luli Callinicos is a Senior Research Officer at the History Workshop and Chairperson of the Workers' Library Steering Committee. She is currently working on the third volume of *A People's History of South Africa*. The second volume, *Working Life: Factories, Township and Popular Culture on the Rand, 1886–1940*, won the Noma Award for Publishing in South Africa for 1983.

Stephen Clingman is the author of *The Novels of Nadine Gordimer: History from the Inside* (1986) and editor of Gordimer's *The Essential Gesture: Writing, Politics* *and Places* (1988). He is an Assistant Professor in the Department of English, University of Massachusetts, Amherst.

Peter Delius is Associate Professor of History at the University of the Witwatersrand. He is the author of *The Land Which Belongs to Us* and *The Conversion*, and co-editor of *Putting a Plough to the Ground.*

Harriet Gavshon is a lecturer in Cinema Studies at the School of Dramatic Art at the University of the Witwatersrand. She is a graduate of New York University and the University of the Witwatersrand and also produces and directs films.

C.R.D. Halisi teaches political science at Indiana University and is working on a book entitled *Dividing Lines: Black Political Thought and the Liberation Process in South Africa.*

Carolyn A. Hamilton recently completed her doctoral dissertation on the Shaka period in South Africa at Johns Hopkins University. She teaches in the social anthropology department at the University of Witwatersrand.

Paul la Hausse is a Research Officer in the African Studies Institute at the University of the Witwatersrand, and author of *Brewers, Beerhalls and Boycotts: A History of Liquor in South Africa* (1988). He is now researching his doctorate on aspects of African nationalism in Natal.

Deborah James teaches Social Anthropology at the University of the Witwatersrand. She has published work on removals and resistance, family and household, and inheritance in a village in the Pedi "Homeland" of Lebowa. She is currently researching Pedi migrant music and women's singing groups.

Jon Lewis was previously managing editor of the *South African Labour Bulletin* and lectured in the History Department of the University of Bophuthatswana, in one of South Africa's "independent" homelands. He is currently working for the Union of Democratic University Staff Associations.

Tom Lodge is directing the African Program at the Social Science Research Council in New York. Between 1978 and 1988 he worked at the University of the Witwatersrand as a member of the History Workshop.

Chris Lowe is a Ph.D. candidate at Yale University. He will complete his dissertation on "Land, Patriarchy and Politics in Colonial Swaziland, 1914–1950" in 1991. His research interests include Natal and Zulu history.

Patrick Manning is Professor of History and African-American Studies at Northeastern University. He is the author of a 1982 book on the economic history of Dahomey, and of *Francophone Sub-Saharan Africa, 1880–1985* (1987), and *Slavery and African Life* (1990). He is also a member of the *Radical History Review* editorial collective.

Santu Mofokeng has worked as a photographer for Afrapix and *New Nation*, and is now a documentary photographer for the African Studies Institute at the University of the Witwatersrand.

Gideon Mendel is a free-lance photographer based in Johannesburg. He is associated with the international photo agency Magnum.

Bill Nasson teaches Economic History at the University of Cape Town and has written on social history, oral history and education in South Africa. He first encountered Unity Movement teaching in the 1960s; a revelation all the more extreme in that it coincided with the onset of puberty. He is co-editor of *Education: From Poverty to Liberty* (1990), and author of *Abram Esau's War: a Black South African War in the Cape, 1899–1902* (1991).

Andre Odendaal is a Senior Lecturer at the University of the Western Cape and author of *Vukani Bantu! The Beginning of Black Protest Politics in South Africa to 1912.*

Andries Walter Oliphant is a poet, story writer, and editor of *Staffrider* magazine.

J. B. Peires is Professor of History at the University of Transkei. He is author of *The House of Phalo* (1981) and *The Dead Will Arise: Nongqawuse and the Great Xhosa Cattle-Killing Movement of 1856–57* (1989).

Bhekizizwe Peterson is a founder-member of the Afrika Cultural Centre and its Centre for Research and Training in African Theatre. He is also attached to the African Literature Department, University of the Witwatersrand.

Karin Shapiro, a history graduate student at Yale University, does both American and South African history. She will complete her dissertation, "The Tennessee Coal Miners' Revolt, 1891–92; Convict Labor, Political Culture, and Southern Rural Industrialization" in 1991. She is also a member of the *Radical History Review* editorial collective.

Melanie Walker used to teach history in "Coloured" high schools, has lectured at the University of Cape Town and University of the Western Cape, and is now Research Officer for the Primary Education Project at the University of Cape Town.

Jon Wiener teaches history at the University of California, Irvine. He is a member of the *Radical History Review* editorial collective, and a contributing editor to *The Nation.*

Leslie Witz is lecturing in the history department at the University of the Western Cape, and author of *Write Your Own History.*